SHADOW MAKER

The Life of
Gwendolyn MacEwen

ROSEMARY SULLIVAN

Harper*Perennial*Canada
HarperCollins*Publishers*Ltd

Shadow Maker: The Life of Gwendolyn MacEwen
Copyright © 1995 by Rosemary Sullivan.
All rights reserved. No part of this book may be
used or reproduced in any manner whatsoever
without prior written permission except in the
case of brief quotations embodied in reviews.
For information address
HarperCollins Publishers Ltd,
55 Avenue Road, Suite 2900,
Toronto, Ontario, Canada M5R 3L2

www.harpercanada.com

HarperCollins books may be purchased for educational, business, or sales promotional use.
For information please write:
Special Markets Department,
HarperCollins Canada,
55 Avenue Road, Suite 2900,
Toronto, Ontario, Canada M5R 3L2.

Extracts from *Mermaids and Ikons* and *Earthlight* reprinted by permission of Stoddart Publishing Co. Ltd. Extracts from *Afterworlds* reprinted by permission of McClelland & Stewart Inc. Extracts from *Noman* reprinted by permission of Oberon Press. Extracts from *The T.E. Lawrence Poems* reprinted by permission of Mosaic Press. Extracts from *Noman's Land* reprinted by permission of Coach House Press. Extracts from "Isis in Darkness" from *Wilderness Tips* by Margaret Atwood reprinted by permission of McClelland & Stewart.

Permission to quote from letters of Milton Acorn granted by the estate of Milton Acorn
(Mrs Mary Hooper).

Medical health files provided by Queen Street Mental Health Centre; The Toronto Hospital: Toronto Western Division; Clarke Institute of Psychiatry; Addiction Research Foundation. (Files were given to the estate of Gwendolyn MacEwen, which gave permission to quote.)

First HarperPerennialCanada edition

Canadian Cataloguing in Publication Data

Sullivan, Rosemary
Shadow maker : the life of Gwendolyn MacEwen

Includes bibliographical references and index.
ISBN 0-00-639141-9

1. MacEwen, Gwendolyn, 1941–1987 –
   Biography.
2. Authors, Canadian (English) –
   20th century – Biography.
I. Title

PS8525.E84Z86 2001   C811'.54
C2001-902341-3
PR9199.3.M313Z86 2001

RRD 9 8 7 6 5 4 3 2 1

Printed and bound in the United States

To Juan
and to my sisters, Patricia, Sharon, and Colleen

CONTENTS

Introduction ix
1: Thirty-eight Keele Street 1
2: The Third Floor 20
3: A Room in Winnipeg 34
4: Space Lady 50
5: Adam's Alphabet 71
6: Magicians Without Quick Wrists 87
7: The Bohemian Embassy 102
8: Mr. & Mrs. Acorn 123
9: The Beach of Jaffa 136
10: Breakup/Breakdown 149
11: Leo and Leo Revised 159
12: Saturnalia 167
13: Falling in Love with Arabic 184
14: To Cairo 199
15: Letter to an Old Lover 210

16: The Shadow Maker 231
17: Sign of the Fish 242
18: Memoirs of a Mad Cook 260
19: The Trojan Horse 278
20: Desolate Landscape 295
21: The Gwenness Gone 309
22: Reaching for Life 327
23: The Chosen Twin 336
24: Searching for Elsie 354
25: The Black Tunnel Wall 361
26: Back Alley Blues 375
27: Afterworlds 393
Afterword 411
Acknowledgements 413
Endnotes 416
Bibliography: Gwendolyn MacEwen 434
Index 436

INTRODUCTION

Gwendolyn MacEwen walked onto the stage of the Music Hall Theatre on the evening of September 8, 1982. Standing under its proscenium, she looked up at the oval ceiling with its low-relief, plaster decorations and out at the capacity audience of 1,600 shuffling uncomfortably in seats that probably hadn't been repaired since the theatre was built in 1919. A slight figure holding a book in her hands, she seemed exotic and almost unplaceable, as if she had stepped from an Egyptian frieze.

My first thought was that she created this effect with her dress—a long, purple, velvet affair traced with gold braiding. But then I saw her eyes, outlined in black kohl, preternaturally large, not so much blue as layered in blues and backlit, alert to life. The book she held was a prop; she did not read her poems—she recited them by heart.

She was reading from a new sequence she had just completed called *The T.E. Lawrence Poems*. The way she spoke, in a low, sensuous, hypnotic voice, suggested that poetry was always meant to be magic. "Poets are magicians without quick wrists," she had once said; there was a time when the poet was the bard who carried the stories of the tribe, speaking of love, human violence, the longings of the spirit, the mysteries of the race. Could this happen in 1982 on Danforth Avenue in the east end of Toronto? I asked myself. As she read, she became her words; her image merged with the strange twin she had chosen for herself—T.E. Lawrence, a lonely exile in an Arabian desert searching for a god among strangers. The end of the performance left me almost disoriented, hardly knowing where I had been.

That evening friends surrounded Gwendolyn MacEwen. The benefit concert had been organized to raise money for airfare for Marcelo Puente, a musician returning to Chile after nine years of exile. The new amnesty law passed by Chilean president General Augusto Pinochet, granting immunity to the military organizers of the 1973 coup d'état, also meant that most of the country's one million political exiles scattered across the globe were free to go home. Because she was one of the few writers whose work could speak to such a tragic history, Gwendolyn had inevitably been invited to read.

I had been asked to co-host the evening with a Chilean actor, and before the concert, I had seen a very pale Gwendolyn pacing nervously backstage. For her, performing was always traumatic, and she had been sick in the washroom. As she walked out under that proscenium, her transformation into a figure of courage and authority became a magic act. Even then I wondered, as I have many times since—what was the relationship between those two women, the one backstage and the one inventing herself out under the lights?

Gwendolyn was tiny, about five feet four, and slight until her last years. With that round alabaster face, almond-shaped blue eyes, and straight brown hair, some men said they found her mousy; she was not sexy; there was something of the hermaphrodite about her. But most women found her beautiful, unique, with a curious self-containedness that imposed itself on any atmosphere.

She was a mystery. Because of her poetry, when one thought of Gwendolyn, one thought of Egypt, cats, magicians, cryptograms, demon lovers. One also thought of bicycles and a strange apocalyptic Toronto full of music, madmen, amnesiacs. She had a pragmatic intelligence when she spoke, so lucidly, of history and world politics, and an outrageous humour when the subject turned to human beings. She rarely spoke of herself, though one sensed life had not matched her expectations nor lived up to her appetite.

Our odd connection was that her ex-husband Nikos Tsingos and the man I lived with worked in the same musical group, Compañeros. After that concert at the Music Hall, we sometimes went to listen to music on the Danforth at The Trojan Horse, the café that she and Tsingos had opened in 1973 and later lost. She often helped me with my poetry. I thought I knew her, but I had no idea, then, of the pain that life exacted as the price of being Gwendolyn.

The last time I saw her was in the late spring of 1987 at a cocktail party at the University of Toronto, where she was just finishing her term as writer-in-residence. The faculty club with its nineteenth-century Paisley gentility had imposed its decorum on the gathering. Gwendolyn sat beside the open fireplace with an air of bemusement, drinking little, too tired, it seemed, to make the effort to penetrate the room's careful camouflage. As we left, she remarked how strange it was that each tribe has its strategy for keeping life at a safe distance.

Crossing Harbord Street in the cold spring drizzle, we talked of a poet friend who had just married a man in prison. The wedding had been a lead item on the national news and we joked about the longevity of the demon lover, still alive in 1987. "Poets need the dark," she said, but her eyes laughed. I had thought it a light moment. As I watched her head towards Robert Street, a lonely figure hunched down in a brown wool coat, I had wanted to follow her, but the moment passed. She seemed so autonomous—I hadn't wanted to invade that privacy.

And then the story surfaced of her last appearance in public at a November poetry reading at The Bamboo Club on Queen Street in the middle of a Toronto blizzard. I hadn't gone. Gwendolyn had collapsed onstage, too drunk to read. When a friend leaned over to help her up, she had screamed: "Don't touch me." She was assisted from the room crying: "Don't touch me."[1] Gwendolyn, who had been so dignified, even decorous. It seemed inconceivable.

On Monday morning, November 30, 1987, Gwendolyn's friend the sculptor Ruben Zellermeyer let himself into her apartment with the key she had given him. He had not heard from her all weekend, and was worried. Making his way through the dim light of her dishevelled flat, he found her slumped across her bed. She was dead.

Obituaries the next day listed the cause of her death as undetermined. In a special to *The Globe and Mail* on December 2nd, a friend, M.T. Kelly, spoke of ominous hints in her last book of poems, *Afterworlds*, recalling her phrase: "a dark wound in the mind which nothing will ever heal." Rumours began to circulate of suicide. Gwendolyn had been drinking heavily in the last months; she seemed to have been watching the world close down around her. On January 20th a Tribute was held at the St. Lawrence Centre, where her reputation had been secured fifteen years earlier when she had launched *Armies of the Moon* and the capacity audience had called her back to the stage for encores. The writing and theatre community that had known her mourned the loss of an original. She had stood heads above most writers.

Like many people whose lives she touched, I was haunted by the mystery of Gwendolyn. She was so elusive. When I began this biography, I knew almost nothing of the details of her personal life. We had never talked of her family or childhood, nor, other than elliptically, of her lovers. We had talked about writing or music or romantic obsession. She had seemed to me secure in her literary career. I always saw her as the young bohemian who, at the age of twenty-one, had been launched at the head of the pack when her first book was published in New York along with the American Beats, Kerouac, Ginsberg, and Gregory Corso, and who had managed to stay there—publishing twenty books in twenty-six years. Her work only got better. What had there been in her life that had undermined her?

In search of answers, I headed, as a biographer does, to the archive of her papers at the University of Toronto Library, but the papers themselves seemed like a coded cryptogram. The manuscripts were there, with their endless revisions. There was correspondence in Greek, Arabic, Hebrew, and French, all the languages she had taught herself to speak, but the archive seemed to have been culled of private details. There were no journals or intimate letters. Had she wanted to remain hidden? And yet, I found her book of dreams in which the private Gwen I imagined surfaced—dreams of fantastic mythological proportions, of fears and obsessions, of longings that made her suddenly immediate. She had also saved several early travel diaries in which I could hear her intimate voice, the double voice of a young woman writer plagued by doubts and confusions, and yet full of a wonderfully ambitious presumption. In her will she had given instructions to her sister to send back all personal letters to their owners, but she had added the directive to keep whatever would be relevant to her biographer. Had she wanted to be found after all? I discovered a letter from a Syrian friend, Samar Attar, written to Gwendolyn's sister to express her shock at Gwen's death, "so young, so beautiful":

> I wrote to your sister for almost 19 years.... I wrote to her about my fears and worries, but she never wrote about hers. She seemed to me, through her letters at least, content with her life.... She sent me an eerie card about the Holocaust on Sept 14, 1987. That was the last time I heard from her. Did she commit suicide? And why? I don't know if you yourself know.[2]

Locked in her own intense privacy, Gwendolyn had lived her life in separate rooms; people were invited into the room that suited them. I realized that her papers in the archive could, as always, only be a beginning. And for a life like Gwen's, where the personal was held close and the public image carefully constructed, the clue to Gwendolyn would be in the grey area in between.

Biography is a form of revenge against life, a rebellion against the impossible fact that a life can disappear so easily—all that energy, passion, humour that constitutes an individual can one day simply stop. But how to write about Gwendolyn, who kept herself so hidden, and how to discover why that hiding was necessary? I decided to follow the clues as they came, recording the voices that surrounded her, all those versions of her life she left behind. It would mean that I would not be able to pretend, as biographers sometimes do, that one can turn a childhood into a seamless narrative when one is following forty years after the fact and constructing a childhood from the multiple versions of the survivors who are left behind. I would have to track down lost lovers, from whom there would be no letters and whom friends remembered only as a shadow or a name. Even then who was to say that the man I would meet and the man Gwendolyn had loved bore even the slightest resemblance to each other? What debris had gathered in the pockets of memory? To be faithful to the mystery that was Gwendolyn, I would have to lay bare the bones of my search for her, with little of the biographer's illusions of omniscience or objectivity.

More than ever, in writing about Gwendolyn, I had to confront the presumption that is involved in writing another's life. What is one hoping for? Perhaps simply that a single life, certainly one lived as intensely and eloquently as Gwendolyn's, is emblematic. In that life we see the threads of our own human lives crossing, and struggle to make intelligible meaning, since only insight gets us through. A life is a puzzle to be decoded, but it is not a solution to the puzzle that one is after; it is an unlayering of the depths of the puzzle so that its mystery can be revealed. I think of the Spanish verb *recordar*: to remember, to pass back through the heart.

Biography, it seems to me, should try to match what we do to our own lives. We live our lives as narratives, examining them, interrogating ourselves, attempting to make our stories cohere. Like the novel of a good writer, we do not will our own plot. The plot evolves moment by moment out of accident, contingency, intuitive leaps. Yet we believe there's something that's consistently us—call it our personality, our character—that strings the narrative together. We believe this identity we call ourselves is shaped by deep structures in our minds laid down in childhood, by the intrigues of our culture shaping our thinking, and by our own desire. We are willing to accept that the self is infinitely complex, but we are not quite willing to give it up. To write a biography, then, is to write a metaphysical detective work: looking for the clues to a life. I want to write this life of Gwendolyn admitting its hypothetical nature: what can and cannot be known about Gwendolyn MacEwen. I want this to be a book with its skeleton exposed.

In writing about another life, of course, there has to be something essential at stake. In Gwendolyn's life there are numerous narratives: the portrait of a tragic childhood and the remarkable invention a woman was able to make out of that foundation, though perhaps its legacy undermined her in the end; the portrait of a woman writer and the camouflages that seemed necessary to negotiate her way through the world and to solve the problem of loneliness, given the difficulty of finding a partner with whom to share her life; the portrait of a Canadian artist who was one of the most significant poets of her generation just at that time when Canadian writing was emerging from the frostbite of cultural colonialism; the portrait of an intellect—as the critic George Woodcock insisted, few poets had "a grasp as broad as MacEwen's of the poetic dimensions of history."[3] And perhaps Gwendolyn's narrative also provides a portrait of modern culture. There is in modern culture a nostalgic fascination with the artist, and yet no true grasp of how costly the practice of art is, not only because of the demands it makes on the psyche, but because little place is made for art in the contemporary world. Gwendolyn was ambitious. She believed that her art mattered, only to discover that poetry was dying in the collective imagination.

My obsession with Gwendolyn ties into a deeper one, my fascination with women's lives, how we as women construct ourselves. As a writer, publishing her first poem at the age of sixteen, Gwendolyn had been madly productive throughout her life. She always complained that her mind teemed with ideas. She had set everything aside—security, lovers, children—for the writing. And yet she had ended in premature silence, dead at the age of forty-six. When Gwen started out, did the writing life still exact an inordinate cost from a woman writer? Why did camouflage and loneliness seem an inevitable part of the story?

There were many secrets Gwendolyn hoarded. Her life, it seems to me, was sacrificed to secrets. From childhood she had been taught to hide. Keeping her secrets, constructing her life as an act of will and courage out of that confusion, Gwen became more and more alone. If I am to connect the woman I met backstage and the woman out under the lights, it must not simply be a betrayal of her secrets, of her fiercely won pride; I must show how, as I have come to believe, Gwendolyn's life *was* emblematic. This woman, who had cared for so many, had been deeply loved but almost never taken care of. Yet she had turned her life into an affirmative statement, reinventing herself, revealing how the private and the public connect. Writing begins, she had always said, "in the bleak lunar landscapes of our mirrors," but it shows us how to look at the stars. She called herself a shadow maker, a phrase she borrowed from Leonardo da Vinci's theory of chiaroscuro. Da Vinci had insisted that the human eye sees not by means of light but by means of shadow. The shadow, the darkness, is necessary to locate the outline of the light. Gwendolyn believed that most of us avoid confronting the dark side of the human enterprise and thereby also miss its beauty. She was a realist, never able to edit out of her experience how truly brutal human beings can be. How she evolved that understanding makes hers a crucial narrative, the story of a woman of courage who, with those luminous eyes, faced down her life at the end of the twentieth century.

1
THIRTY-EIGHT KEELE STREET

We spend the first decade of our lives in a state of suspended consciousness, endlessly receptive to the floods of sensation that overwhelm us, as though we were sieves through which being flows almost unimpeded. That decade shapes us for a lifetime. Looked back at, there are only a few memories that cohere to anchor us, but these will be repeated again and again in the depths of our unconscious throughout our lives.

In a dream journal she began to keep in her late twenties, Gwendolyn wrote a single isolated entry on the first page:

> 1945-50: Recurring d.[ream] of a giant key floating through dark skies like a space ship; silent, heavy, v.[ery] slow—fearful, reminiscent of army blimps."[1]

In 1945 Gwendolyn would have been four years old. This was the image, as she remembered it in retrospect, that occupied her dreaming mind until she was nine. The childhood world she lived in was threatening, a locked secret; it required a key to open it, but the key was inaccessible. Was it the adult Gwendolyn who coloured the image in military metaphors? And yet as children our minds are porous, coloured by things we do not understand. The image began to haunt her childhood in 1945, when all the world's metaphors would have focused on war. What was the dread secret that threatened the skies of her childhood? Even as a child, she knew there had to be a key; but lacking the key to the terror, she could only experience it. The dream would stop when she discovered what the key was.

Searching for that key that surfaced like a weapon colours my perception of Gwendolyn's childhood. But as a biographer, I must begin to tell her story from the outside. I sit before a photograph of Gwendolyn's childhood home.

Gwendolyn Margaret MacEwen was born on September 1, 1941, at 38 Keele Street in the west end of Toronto. In those days Toronto was known as Hogtown—ostensibly from the slaughterhouses that dotted its periphery, but in fact because it was still a rather small-minded puritanical little city of 681,802 inhabitants. Keele Street was then a working-class district, though behind and to the south stretched the wealthy neighbourhood of High Park. Thirty-eight Keele Street stood in odd isolation from the rest of the street; it was a large, three-storied, red brick structure up to which one had to climb by three staggered flights of forty-two steps from the street. Because of its elevation, the local children used to make up stories about seeing bats circling it at night and claimed that it was haunted.

On both sides of the house were open fields: on the south a small field that the city had divided up into Victory Gardens for local residents to cultivate their own vegetables against the war rationing; on the north a huge expanse where the kids gathered to sleigh and toboggan, and, in the summer, build castles in the sandpits. West, along Bloor Street, behind the old Roma Apartments between Quebec and Gothic avenues, were the Mineral Baths. Originally built as a spa fed by mineral springs, the "Minies," as the kids called them, had been converted into two pools, where, as a child, Gwen swam in the summer. Floating on her back, she could just see the old Victorian house on the hill. Thirty-eight Keele Street belonged to Aunt Margaret. Gwendolyn's father, Alick McEwen, had moved his family to the house of his sister-in-law Margaret and her husband, Charles Martin, in 1941, the year that Gwendolyn was born.

The houses we are born into are always more than domestic architecture. They are mental spaces that define the power dynamic of the world we enter unwittingly; those houses will surface repeatedly in our dreams and we will reconstruct them throughout a lifetime. Thirty-eight Keele Street was the first universe fate offered Gwendolyn. It was complex and full of secrets.

The structure of the three-storey house defined its dynamic, one might say a dynamic of disenfranchisement. The first floor was the domain of Margaret and Charlie, immigrants from working-class London before the First World War. On the second floor Elsie and Alick McEwen lived with their two daughters, Carol and Gwendolyn, in an apartment that was independent except for the communal bathroom and toilet, used by the eight or nine residents in the house, since these were the only facilities. On the third floor were the bedrooms of foster children, orphans from displaced families, sent there by the Protestant Children's Home—without the support of the PCH, the Martins could never have afforded 38 Keele Street. Aunt Margaret only accepted girls, and there were usually two or three in residence at one time. Most came and went over the years, though Dora and Marion Lyons stayed until they were married. Aunt Margaret, with her code of Victorian Protestantism, kept this organism functioning. She always claimed that it was she who brought up the McEwen daughters.

The mystery of our lives, of course, is that they start long before we do, determined by people whose private history we rarely know. Gwendolyn's began in Poplar, an impoverished working-class district in the notorious East End of London, where her mother, Elsie Mitchell, and Elsie's sister Margaret were born. The East End was the *Cockney* district, an Old English word that originally had a vicious, classist resonance. It derives from "Cock's Egg," a reference to the fabulous Land of Cockaigne, whose inhabitants were spoiled and shiftless children.

Aunt Margaret Mitchell was born in 1887 at 26 Byron Street, the same year that Jack the Ripper stalked the alleys of nearby Whitechapel. In the tracts and novels of the 1890s of Margaret's childhood, the boroughs of Stepney, Bethnal, Whitechapel, Hackney, Shadwell surface as ghettos of grime and poverty filled with brothels, lodging houses, grogshops and cellar dives, opium dens, factories, and warehouses. Here Sherlock Holmes would find many of his petty larcenists in Conan Doyle's stories that began to thrill London in the 1890s. Through this area, like a worm, ran the Thames estuary, and the docks brought the sailors and with them the cholera epidemics and the richest trade. In 1890 there were more than a thousand brothels in Ratcliff Highway, Shadwell. Likely "marks," female children of ten or twelve were sold into prostitution. A network of agents kept lists of prostitutes whose female children were marked as soon as they were born.

But this was only one aspect of the East End. There were also those whom sociologists used to call the respectable (or clean) poor. They lived in Poplar on streets like Byron, where for about one hundred and fifty yards, dingy little brick houses twenty-feet high lined up on the sidewalk in a row—there could be as many as thirty on each side of the narrow street. With one front wall in common, and three holes for windows and a door demarking each house, the effect was of a stables.

According to the nineteenth-century novelist Arthur Morrison, who was the first chronicler of the lives of the clean poor of Poplar, the sordid uniformity of their lives, together with the unrelieved poverty, was shocking. The layout of such neighbourhoods was fixed in a code of decreasing respectability. Round the corner there would be the baker's, then the chandler's (candle-maker), the mangler's (where sheets were pressed), and the brewer's shop as the streets became less rigidly respectable—"many grades of decency had to be passed to reach the slums."[2] The inhabitants often worked in the docks, the gasworks, or the shipyards; at half-past five in the morning, a night-watchman or local policeman rapped at the door to summon the sleepers to work, a service that cost four pence a week. The men emerged, followed by the children, who set off for the grim Board Schools. Only Sunday brought relief from this rigid schedule, where, after church and a sermon of fire and brimstone, the men could be found lounging at the beer-shop and the children playing in the street, though for the mothers it was the day to wash the house—and these grim little houses were clean. The code among these women was to be fiercely independent—it would be Aunt Margaret Mitchell's code: "Don't be a sheep."

The Mitchells were a typical family. Margaret was the eldest of nine girls (two brothers had died in infancy). Her father, a sailor, was usually absent from the family, until, at the age of forty-five, he returned to 26 Byron Street, vowing he would never work again. It was the mother who raised the nine children, often working as a charwoman and taking in local laundry. They lived in one of the "two up/two downs" as they were called, with two small dark rooms on the first floor—a living/dining room and a kitchen—and two bedrooms upstairs. The toilet would have been in the backyard. The house emptied quickly as each daughter left school at thirteen and was put out to work as a maid. Margaret was the first to go into service. The Mitchell daughters were raised to be "honest, hard-working, patriotic, God-fearing subjects of Her Majesty."[3]

Charlie Martin, or Uncle Charlie, came from what sociologists called the rough (or dirty) poor. He was one of thirteen children, only six of whom survived infancy. His father, he said, was a drunkard who beat his children; the mother drank as well. Charlie left school at nine to go to work as a labourer. When he was able to buy his first suit, his mother pawned it every Monday; Saturday afternoons when he got his pay, he would redeem it and wear it on his Sunday outings with Margaret.

Charlie's last job before immigrating to Canada was at the East India Docks. Wanting to explain the difference between Canada and England, in the stories he told his nieces he would always recount his "docks" anecdote. One morning he was loading a ship. Bent over double, with a 300-pound trunk on his back, he climbed the narrow gangplank. Just as he was reaching the top, he peered up to see a high black silk hat—Lord So and So, the owner of the ship, was descending. He backed all the way down the gangplank, trunk on his back, and stepped humbly aside. Amazed that he had once done that, he always shook his head: "That wouldn't happen in Canada." His docks experience left a particular legacy. To the end he remained violently prejudiced against people of Indian and Chinese origin, his fellow workers at the dock.

Charlie immigrated to Canada in the early 1910s, telling Margaret that when he earned enough money, he would send for her. It was not easy to find a job. At many of the construction sites, he was confronted by a sign: No Bronchos Need Apply—a racist term for "Limeys" or Englishmen. But he found a job at the Laidlaw Lumber Company at the corner of Dundas and Bloor streets (not before offering to work for two days without pay to show what he could do), and became known as Cheerful Charlie. He made friends among the Scottish immigrants, and soon brought Margaret to Canada. She stayed with his married friends until a modest wedding could be arranged.

The couple rented a flat on Keele Street, where they lived for almost a decade, but across the road, isolated on its hill, stood number thirty-eight. In 1925, Margaret suddenly discovered it was for sale. The city's plans to build on either side of it had fallen through and the price was cheap. The Martins bought it for seven thousand dollars, with a down payment of three hundred dollars, and stayed there until the late 1950s, by which time they had managed to pay off the mortgage by renting out the second floor and taking in foster children from the Protestant Children's Home. From the secure base of 38 Keele Street, Aunt Margaret began her relentless climb into the middle class, abruptly cutting off the history of her origins, which remained hidden even from her nieces. At the age of forty, when Gwendolyn returned to London in search of her mother's roots, she was appalled by the poverty she discovered in Poplar. She had never imagined it could have been so extreme.

Almost a decade and a half after she had immigrated, Margaret Mitchell was suddenly joined by her younger sister Elsie, who came to live at number thirty-eight. The circumstances that precipitated her hasty departure from London were not the happiest, and it's not likely Margaret was entirely welcoming. In May 1929, at the age of twenty-three, Elsie was packed off to live with her older sister in Canada when she suffered her second mental breakdown. Her family wanted to believe that it was nothing serious, nothing that couldn't be solved by changing countries. All she needed was a new world.

I am moving among these strangers, crafting their lives from anecdotes I collect from the survivors who remembered them. But with Gwendolyn's mother, Elsie Mitchell McEwen, it is different. Ironically, I can know the woman who was foundational to Gwen's life in ways her family didn't, from documents they wouldn't have seen—there are records of her history kept during the years of her periodic incarcerations as a mental patient in a variety of hospitals, records that wouldn't have been available to her daughters until after she was dead. The woman whose madness made her a kind of phantom at 38 Keele Street is more real to me than the others. I was able to find her story in four large manila files preserved at the Queen Street Mental Health Centre.

We are terrified by madness, perhaps because we feel it nascent in ourselves, ready to spring. Perhaps it is a biological fear—our genes are coded for madness. Yet I must attempt to know this woman. As I head to the records room of the hospital in search of Elsie McEwen, I watch her confraternity. A man paces the huge reception hall where patients gather for a coffee and a smoke. Tracing perfect squares, one foot placed carefully in front of the other, he makes a periodic diagonal dash across the room that feels like freedom, singing "My Mammy" at the top of his lungs in a rather good imitation of Al Jolson.

Another man, built like a football player, is wearing a winter parka and red leather shorts. Bare-legged, he totters in a pair of pink stiletto heels. Outside it is ten degrees below zero; his legs are still lobster red from the cold. A woman speeds past a young blond girl leaning desolately on the coffee machine. "I know someone who's got a crush on you," she says. "Who?" the girl brightens. "Attila the Hun." "Who's that?" she asks eagerly. "Darling, he's no one." In a far corner a man facing the wall is shouting: "But reincarnation was my fucking idea." This was where Elsie McEwen came regularly for safety when life became unbearable. In recording her story, this is the closest I will come to knowing what she experienced.

Elsie Mitchell was born on November 14, 1906, nineteen years younger than her sister Margaret, and the last of nine daughters. In her reports to her psychiatrists, repeated over the years, she explains that her father, after fighting in the Boer War, joined the navy, returning to Poplar, it seems, only to impregnate his wife. They despised him at home and there was constant friction. Elsie describes her mother, who kept the family together, as a conscientious, hard-working, domineering, fussy woman. She was fifty-two when she gave birth to Elsie in a difficult labour that confined her to bed for six months. In one report Elsie explains that before she was old enough to understand things, she felt she was just a mistake, tagging on at the end of a large family. Her mother could never have wanted her and was sorry she was born. At least she should have been a boy.

"Elsie was born without instruments," the doctors report.[4] "She was a normal healthy child at delivery, was breast fed for nine months, walked and talked and teethed at the usual ages." It seems she was gifted, entering school at four and a half, and passing her standard exams at age twelve, two years under the age limit, which meant spending the next two years sitting about in school until she was old enough to graduate at age fourteen.

She won three scholarships, but her family decided on the Trade Scholarship because it offered the most money. At Technical School, she studied interior decorating, and, at sixteen, began working for a department store specializing in drapes and the decoration of windows, loving the trade and the entrée it gave her into some of the better homes in London. If the files are to be trusted, things seem to have gone well for the next five years.

In 1927, when she was twenty-one, Elsie became engaged to a young man who remains nameless. After indulging in what she called "love play" that she felt was wrong, she began to have fits of hysterical laughter and crying spells. One day she didn't appear at the store because she felt she was doing her work inadequately. She moved to a second job, but it only lasted two weeks. Convinced she had folded a curtain the wrong way, that she could never do anything right again, she refused to return to work and her sister was sent to collect her pay. When her fiancé terminated the engagement, Elsie was devastated. Unable to cope with her crying spells, her family took her to London's Maudsley Psychiatric Hospital, where she was diagnosed as a hysteric.

In the Maudsley reports she is described as a shy, retiring, very self-conscious girl, completely dominated by her older sisters. Deeply ashamed of coming from the East End of London, she felt herself ignorant and always attached herself to someone more brilliant than she. Convinced that she was different from other people, she became obsessed by the idea that she was alone even in a crowd. Her incarceration at Maudsley Hospital lasted eight months.

On her release, Elsie was advised to take a job with less responsibility and to get married and have children. She began work as a shop assistant in a department store, but within three weeks, the manager decided she had more ability than the rest of his sales staff and promoted her to supervisor. With the added responsibility and what she perceived to be the jealousy of the other girls, she lost her self-confidence and asked to go back to shop assistant. Six months after her first release, Elsie returned to the Out-Patient Department of Maudsley Hospital. When her mother found out she wanted to be admitted again as a full-time patient, she put her foot down. Instead, Elsie was packed off to live with her older sister in Canada.

In one of the four large manila folders at the Queen Street Mental Health Centre, where they were attempting to make sense of this young woman, I read a doctor's summary of Elsie McEwen's mental status:

> Elsie has been the youngest in a large family who allowed her to remain dependent on others so that she never attained an emotional maturity and always requires a great deal of reassurance. Her exaggerated ambitiousness with her inability to stand her failures and her inner insecurity make her situation intolerable ... She evades her responsibilities and when taken from them she reacts in a healthy way. She is just a typical neurotic person who has lost her courage, inner security and self-confidence.[5]

I find an effort of sympathy for Elsie among the pages of these files, but little help or, indeed, understanding. Who was Elsie McEwen? A youngest child, lost at the back of a family, indulged and dismissed. A woman of "consistently superior intelligence" (at the Queen Street Mental Health Centre she passed most of her endless hospital tests at the Superior Adult Level I) who was terrified of the dark and had nightmares in which she sank into a terrible abyss until one of her sisters pulled her back. A woman who wondered if she would ever be normal. Elsie reported to her doctors that when she was ten years old, she was told by her mother to tell her dad she had nightmares if he questioned her. Was there something else in her childhood that profoundly undermined her? The remark passes. It is too elliptical. There is nothing to suggest its meaning.

When Elsie Mitchell arrived in Canada, among her sister Margaret's circle of Scottish friends were two young Glaswegians, Maud and Alick McEwen. The McEwens had grown up in the middle-class Maryhill district of Glasgow, where their father had worked for Kodak at the turn of the century. Of the two, Maud seemed the more assured. She had attended St. Mary's College and then worked for Thomas Machell & Sons, building organs for nine years before deciding to immigrate on her own to Canada. In a letter of reference Machell wrote: "Miss

McEwen has a very good knowledge of tools."[6] Maud was unusual: she had worked with the suffragist movement in Glasgow and trained herself as an elocutionist. On the ship, the RMS *Montclare*, which she took to North America in September 1927, she appears on the playbill reciting her favourite poems: "The Bachelor's Soliloquy to a Cigarette," and "The Shot. A Tale of the Indian Mutiny." In 1929, her brother, Alick, for whom she had always been a kind of model, decided to join his unmarried sister in Canada.

Alick McEwen, eight years younger than Maud, was born in 1904. He matriculated at North Kelvinside School in 1920 and then, at sixteen, found a job on the technical staff at the Central Municipal Laboratories in Glasgow. At first glance he appears to have been a conventional and ambitious young man bent on educating himself. At night, he studied chemistry at the Royal Technical College of Glasgow, graduating in 1923. By 1929 he was in charge of the chemical laboratory at the Dalmuir Sewage Purification Works. When he decided to immigrate, the city analyst at the Municipal Laboratories wrote a letter of recommendation that follows the usual rhetoric: "reliable work, strict attention to duty, and the display of an untiring and keen interest in all he has undertaken ... a young man of the highest personal character."[7]

Yet at night school Alick also studied drawing, and developed a passion for photography. One of his early surviving photos is of three battered and abandoned pairs of shoes—a strangely eloquent study in that one can almost imagine the phantom feet of the people who wore them. I conceive of Alick McEwen as a man of peculiarly Scottish temperament: imagination and a fierce individualism underlay his rectitude and attention to duty. Yet perhaps I am reading backwards from the man I know he would become—a man at war within himself whose gifts would be wasted.

Alick settled in Toronto with Maud, immediately finding a job as a clerk at the Toronto General Hospital, and then in April 1931, at the University of Toronto in the Banting Institute of Physiological Hygiene as a laboratory technician. By this time he had already met Elsie Mitchell, a pretty sales clerk in the interior decorating department of the Robert Simpson Company. Like many young men in their mid-twenties, he seems to have been looking for a wife.

It is hard, growing up, to comprehend that our parents had full and intricate existences before we were born. By the time the stories begin to concern us, they are already lost, since time erases, vandalizes. No one is left to say whether Elsie's and Alick's was a romantic beginning: what it was like when they met, what attracted them, how they decided to marry. All that is recorded is that Elsie once said to her doctor that she admired this young man. She thought him superior and married him because she loved the way he spoke—he was not an East Ender.

But there was one secret that was withheld from Alick McEwen when he married Elsie Mitchell. He was not told of his young bride's mental history. Aunt Margaret always said she thought it unfair he wasn't told, though who was to tell him if not she is unclear. For her to have broken the secret would have been to violate family solidarity. How could one warn the fiancé against one's own sister? Besides, Elsie was meant to be cured now that she had changed countries.

After a two-year courtship, Elsie and Alick were married on December 30, 1932. They took an apartment in the west end of the city and within three months Elsie was pregnant, giving birth to Carol on December 30, 1933, at St. Mary's Hospital. Shortly after the birth, Elsie had a hysterical attack—her first, it seems, in five years. The bad dreams had returned and she was suddenly terrified of nursing her child. If the baby cried, she felt she had done something wrong with its care and was afraid to attend to the next feeding. Complaining that she was the youngest in her family and had never seen a baby brought up, she began to disappear from the apartment, phoning to say she couldn't return home.

On April 6th, she took all the sleeping pills her doctor had prescribed and wandered out on the street. Finding her lying on the side of the road, the police took her to the local station, from where she was admitted to the Toronto Psychiatric Hospital.

Alick was completely devastated. It was not just that his worst fears had been confirmed now that his young wife's eccentric behaviour of the last several months had culminated in attempted suicide, but he also discovered that she had a history of mental instability he had never suspected. To his anxiety at confronting her illness was added the feeling that he had been betrayed. He must also have wondered at his own delusion. In their two-year conventional courtship, had there been signs he had completely missed?

On April 28th, after a three-week admission, Elsie was released. The only advice the hospital seems to have been able to offer Alick was that he seek an agency to give his wife daily instructions in caring for her child and that he make some arrangement whereby she would spend less time at home alone.

The night of her release from hospital, insecure and miserable, Elsie paced from room to room. She complained that she couldn't care for her baby, was terrified of criticism, and worried over her sister Margaret's interfering with her. Out walking in High Park the next day, she behaved so oddly that she was picked up by a policeman and returned to the hospital, where she was recognized and sent home. She explained that she had been acting peculiarly "to fight the wrong in her." In despair, Alick broke down in tears and took her back to the Toronto Psychiatric Hospital, where she was diagnosed as a reactive-depressive and discharged within a week.

In the clinical records Alick is always described as "a well dressed, well kept, polite, cheerful, cooperative man who is willing to have us do anything to restore his wife's mental health."[8] But now he must have been desperate, since it was clear that his young wife was very ill. He also knew that when Elsie felt she was losing hold, her only solution was to run. Perhaps worried about the safety of his young daughter, he moved the family briefly into 38 Keele Street, but it was not satisfactory. By 1936 they moved again, this time to Gilmour Avenue, at a safe distance from Margaret, whom Elsie felt dominated her. When Elsie was visited by a social worker in October, she seemed to have adapted, reporting delightedly that she was taking night courses in public speaking at Western Technical School. "She seems perfectly happy and regards her illness as quite a thing of the past," the record states.[9]

For the next three years, there was relative peace, although doctors and medication became a permanent part of Elsie's life. Alick sought escape in his hobby, photography, joining a series of photographic clubs and evolving an original technique of water-colouring his photographs. From 1939, his photos were selected for exhibitions in Toronto, Vancouver, Montreal, and Hamilton, and in 1941, he became a member of the Royal Photographic Society. Overwhelmed by her husband's initiative, Elsie must have felt desperate to distinguish herself, thus those night courses in public speaking, effacing the Poplar accent. Had not Alick's sister, Maud, studied elocution?

The next crisis did not occur until September 1939. Elsie and Alick had a wonderful holiday at Woodland Beach on Georgian Bay, where they often went with Maud and her family. They returned to Toronto the day the Second World War was declared. Elsie seems to have become anxious about her family in London and fearful that Alick would have to go to war, though her psychiatrists believed that what secretly terrified her was the prospect of her husband leaving her with the responsibility of her home and child. One day she showed up at the Banting Institute at the University of Toronto, insisting she be taken to hospital before she "put her head in the oven." In hospital the problems that had been hidden surfaced.

Elsie complained that Alick was so self-sufficient he never admitted his need of her. When she craved his attention, he sought refuge in photography; she would never get used to his Scottish reserve. Yet she also felt that sexuality was somehow improper and impure, and she was afraid of pregnancy. She worried that she was failing her child. Alick described to Elsie's doctors how Carol, age five, would just sit and stare at her mother, baffled by her unpredictable behaviour. Elsie might spank Carol for having dirty hands; or Carol's childish scream might send her mother into hysterics. Elsie would complain that Alick never took Carol on his knee and kissed her, and he would retort: "How can you talk when you walk out on her all the time?" She would think: "What is the use of Carol growing up if she is just going to be like me."

Elsie was released on September 26th. There were new resolves: the couple would get out more to see other people and he would try to be more considerate if she would do her part and make him want to love her. The prognosis was not hopeful. The constant demonstrations of affection and reassurance Elsie needed seemed beyond anything one person might offer; the damage was far too deep. For a week, Alick abandoned photography, playing cards instead, and included Elsie in all his plans. She was happy and felt completely well. She delighted in her daughter. "When I saw my little girl, Carol, so overjoyed to see me," she reports, "I said to myself, I'll never leave her again, I love her, she is my daughter and I have a mother's love for her."[10] But the sentiment is abstract—one does not speak of one's mother love unless one cannot feel it—and the anxiety swiftly returned. Her husband and child had a cold, and it was her fault; she was not feeding them properly. Not knowing what to cook became a crisis. At night she was terrified of the dark. She thought of suicide. Within ten days, she was back in hospital. By February 1940 she had been through five admissions and discharges. In the hospital Elsie felt she could be "mothered." Only there was it safe.

Doctors determined that Elsie McEwen was manic-depressive. In the 1930s, clinically this meant that her treatment included shock therapy and drugs. Practically it meant that they were unable to tell her how to function in the world. Reading her history, it is possible to feel that her illness was compounded by being female. There were many women like Elsie in institutions in the 1920s and 1930s. Some message told Elsie she could never be good enough, and everything in society's ethical and social structure confirmed this. The most terrifying statement I read in her charts is: "This woman has apparently never been close to anyone in her life."[11] Lost in the enclosed circle of self, how could she risk contact with another? Anything that awakened her self-contempt and insecurity detonated a critical mass of suffering.

We feel more comfortable if we can find an explanation for madness in the personality of the individual, but what if madness is simply located on the extremes of the spectrum of normalcy, and therefore also tied in to our social structure? After her mother's death in 1982, Gwendolyn began work on a poem called "The Black Tunnel Wall." She remembered her mother telling her of her experiences as a child during the First World War. On nights of the full moon when the German Zeppelins were cruising the sky with death, the family had sought shelter from the bombs in a local tunnel. Elsie remembered that black tunnel with terror. There was a curious incident referred to in her file that is mentioned only once. It seems it may have been her first attack. When she was sixteen, she was accidentally locked in a dark room and was later found, weeping and hysterical. Perhaps she was trapped once again inside the black tunnel of those childhood years. But, of course, this is only speculation. Real lives are not like fiction; there can be no comfortable sense of closure, all the loose ends tied, solving the puzzle of a life.

Most of Elsie's records are medical descriptions of her condition and paraphrases of her explanations of her own history. But on one occasion, I hear her troubled voice. It is the record of a conversation at the Whitby Psychiatric Hospital on February 6, 1940. Elsie would have been thirty-four. The patient is presented in conference with five doctors:

Dr. A: What has been the trouble lately?
Patient: There wasn't any trouble, when I got here, because I have no responsibility, somebody is over me.
Dr. A: A lot of truth in that. What is the matter at home then?
Patient: Recently, the last months, I would say that part of the trouble is that I feel the need of somebody to make decisions for me and tell me what to do. I'm not ordinarily that way.

Dr. A: Have you always been dependent on somebody?
Patient: No, not always, at different times. I feel if there was somebody there to tell me, I would feel confident of doing anything they tell me....
Dr. A: Latterly has life got unbearable?
Patient: I felt definitely unbearable to other people.
Dr. A: Thought you would be better out of the way?
Patient: Yes. I don't know, there would not seem any alternative but a hospital of this kind.... then I realized I was getting to like it too much ...
Dr. A: Do you enjoy your work?
Patient: I do usually. Not lately. I think it is so foolish. The house doesn't get dirty, nobody is there. I wonder what I'm doing. What is the use. I think, well, I'm going to Whitby anyway ...
Dr. A: Are you and your husband happy?
Patient: Yes. We are different natures. I have talked about it so often, we don't want separation. I realize there is something—
Dr. A: If you get the house cleaned you would think the good man was coming home to enjoy it?
Patient: I never think that.
Dr. A: It is only the things one does to give happiness to others that they get satisfaction from. Self is a funny thing. We get fed up with it unless we use it to spread around what we are capable of. We don't get satisfaction out of self alone. It is the things that come from us to others that make up the virtues and attributes.
Patient: Yes, I know that. I have maintained for 6 or 7 months that something must have happened. If you people could fool me—put me to sleep, of course it is not sleep I want—but put me out of consciousness and did something and then when I found out I would be all right.

Dr. A: That would be lying....
Patient: If you decide for me to stay here, where will I stay?
Dr. A: Crossing bridges—
Patient: I know myself.
Dr. A: You should, better than anyone else. All these symptoms you have are quite familiar to us.
Patient: You must have lots of cases.
Dr. A: Your symptoms are mild compared to the woman coming next.
Patient: I know. There are lots outside like here. I'm trying to get out of staying inside. The longer I stay the longer and harder it will be to pull up financially when I get out.
Dr. A: Things will have a different colour.
Patient: Tell me what to do while I'm here.
Dr. A: We will get a program for you.
Dr. B: What is the longest period you have felt good?
Patient: Two or three years, not steadily, the feeling of elation two or three weeks.
Dr. B: Are you fond of your little girl?
Patient: Yes.
Dr. A: Get a kick out of bringing her up?
Patient: Yes.
Dr. B: Ever feel as if you were going insane?
Patient: No.
Dr. A: People never do who think of those things. You leave it to us. We will get you a program.
Patient: See that I get something to do—what is the word?
Dr. C: Constructive?
Patient: Yes.[12]

Underneath her surface calm hides a desperate woman in the grip of psychosis. Her illness was terrifying, both to herself and to those around her. Of what use were the doctor's platitudes to her?

Sometime in 1941 Alick McEwen moved his family back to 38 Keele Street. Why had he finally conceded to live with his in-laws? I speculate that it was because he now knew he would need Margaret's help. During January of 1941, Elsie had become pregnant with Gwendolyn.

Gwendolyn was born on September 1, 1941, eight days early. At home Elsie seemed happy, but the baby gained weight irregularly and the doctors advised she be weaned. Blaming herself, Elsie stopped eating. On the 24th, she became agitated and the idea crossed her mind of throwing her baby on the floor and jumping off the Danforth viaduct. Alarmed at the impulse, she called her doctor. She was readmitted to Whitby Psychiatric Hospital, where she remained for ten days before returning to 38 Keele Street.

Gwendolyn would be her last child. In 1944, when Elsie became pregnant again, she elected to have a therapeutic abortion and was sterilized.

2
THE THIRD FLOOR

There is only one intimate witness who can describe the life of those strangers in that second-floor flat of 38 Keele Street—Gwendolyn's sister, Carol. Yet no two children have the same record of their shared history. Each of us constructs our own childhood from the islands of memories that shaped us, and the privacy of that construct when we seek to share it with siblings is astonishing. Were this Carol's biography, the story would be as follows.

Carol came to believe she was her mother's second child. When she was sixteen, her friend Audrey had been invited to board briefly with the McEwen family. As she walked into the kitchen one morning, Carol overheard a conversation in which her mother was telling Audrey that when she had discovered herself pregnant shortly after her marriage, she had aborted herself—she did not want children. And she hadn't wanted her second child. It was an outrageous betrayal. The hurt of those words would frame Carol's view of her mother: "I guess I wasn't the happiest addition to the family, although I think it all worked out," she explained to me.[1]

Carol always understood that after her birth there had been a crisis. Alick returned from work one day to find the apartment empty, and Carol abandoned in her crib. Elsie had left a note in the crib saying no one was ever going to see her in the world again. When the police were called and a search begun, Elsie was found sitting on a park bench across the street. She had sat there all afternoon "enjoying the excitement she had created." Alick took his small family to live at 38 Keele Street under Margaret's supervision.

This was how the story was told to Carol in the family apocrypha. For the biographer it has the complexities of all such stories. It probably refers to the family's first unsuccessful return to 38 Keele Street briefly in 1935, for by their permanent return in 1941 when Gwendolyn was born, Carol would have been eight. What is telling is the painful bitterness Carol repeats in that angry word "enjoying."

At the centre of the McEwen household Elsie remains the ghost in the house. Her life was divided by the family into her good periods and her bad periods. Carol remembered that her bad periods appeared cyclically, at intervals of eighteen months. She would disappear, and the family would find she had checked herself into the hospital. Carol simply understood that periodically her mother abandoned them. She was not told why. In the early stages, the family had little idea of how to deal with Elsie's illness and dismissed it as indulgence: she was looking for attention. They made their commitment to normalcy and pretended that nothing was wrong. Such conspiracies of denial are a familiar strategy: if one denies the truth of something, one gains the illusion of control. And it was easy to parody normalcy. To outsiders, Elsie appeared the model young mother.

There are no photos that survive of Elsie and Alick alone together. (And Carol has no memory of a moment of intimacy between her parents.) The scenes are always family poses, black-and-white snaps that have a flat, orchestrated feeling about them. In one, taken in 1945, the family of four is framed against a backdrop of trees. Seated on a dining-room chair in the garden looking at a magazine, Elsie looks charming; a pretty woman, large bosomed and ample, in a tidy poplin dress with carefully coiffed hair loosely pinned in a 1940s wave on the top of her head. She reminds me of the mothers in *Good Housekeeping*. Her face is large, moon-shaped, with a prominent nose and close-set eyes as she squints from the sun. Her husband, dressed in a heavy wool suit and tie, leans over her shoulder. He too is looking at the magazine. His face is hardly visible beneath a wide forehead and receding sandy hair, but he looks drawn and tired, with a quizzical, worrisome expression that belongs on an older man. The children are beautifully dressed, their hair carefully done up in braids and bows. Gwendolyn is at her mother's knee, squinting at the page; Carol is at her shoulder, smiling to herself as if absorbed in her own world. What is most disturbing is the false intimacy of the portrait—Elsie dominates, obliviously turning the others into satellites, but her attention is elsewhere.

In Carol's portrait of her father, Alick McEwen was a man upon whom it would slowly dawn that he had lost his life. From a young husband with expectations, he found himself living in a communal house with in-laws, unwittingly controlled by the vagaries of his wife's illness. His profession may have been laboratory technician, but his daughter knew his deepest passion was photography. Everyone, with the possible exception of Elsie, who resented his dabbling, remembered his excitement when one of his photos of the Banting Institute appeared in *Life* magazine. He also loved to paint water-colours and sketch in pencil. Carol felt he had been betrayed; and his stoical solution was to cope. He was a kind, patient man, though a bit taciturn and strict, little given to outward displays of affection. He deferred control to his wife's sister Margaret, but he must often have asked himself what he was doing at 38 Keele Street, since there was so little space for him in his home.

Who was Aunt Margaret? When Gwen was born she would have been fifty-five. In photographs she has a grandmotherly look: she is portly, with glasses, and a rather thin, severe mouth. She often wears a satin dress with the scalloped high neck covered in pseudo-lace. But there is one photo that is different. Her hair is curled in a wave that lies tightly on her head, her eyes are laughing, and her mouth is drawn up in a bow. She wears pearl drops in her ears and one can almost imagine her in a music hall singing war songs and swilling beer. Her arm is warmly laced through Charlie's, who sits there in his double-breasted suit, tied and bespectacled, with a slightly mischievous smile on his face. They look rather shy—neither looks at the camera.

Margaret was not a simple woman, even if, in her fierce aspirations to middle-class propriety, she seemed to run the house like a major-domo. In the Old Country, it seems she had been jollier. When Margaret first met her husband, Charlie, her nieces understood that he had been part of a gymnast team that had toured England and there was a family story that once he appeared on the same stage as Charlie Chaplin, though this is probably apocryphal.

The Martins were poor but respectable, living in the Toronto of the Depression and the war. Shortly after starting at Laidlaw Lumber, Charlie began studying nights to get his third-class stationary engineer's papers and, much to his delight, soon qualified to drive the crane lifting the logs into piles. As a semi-skilled worker in a non-unionized plant, he worked long hours at an hourly wage, but like many during the Depression, he would often find himself home at 3:00 p.m. in that terrible period when there were not enough orders to fill a day's work. Charlie became a company man, loyally rejecting a job in another unionized yard at higher pay, and stayed at Laidlaw for forty years, for most of that time working five and a half days per week with no paid holiday. The job kept the family fed. When he turned sixty-five, Laidlaw Lumber gave Charlie a light job as a security guard at the gate; proud of his blue uniform and peaked cap, he used to write a newsletter for the staff, which he called "Here's Charlie." He always felt that in comparison to his English relatives, he had been a success. To him, 38 Keele Street was a palace, though he was realistic enough to say: "I don't own this house. The mortgage company does. Perhaps I own the sunroom."[2]

At home Charlie conceded the house to Margaret, devoting all his attention, spring and summer, to his garden, refusing to go away for summer holidays because he would have to abandon it. The garden was the sign of his ascendancy. He had grown up in the East End of London, without a blade of grass underfoot. Each spring, he and Margaret would pore diligently over the seed catalogues, choosing the year's annuals— they couldn't afford perennials.

Charlie kept his plants trellised, and in one corner had built a small triangular summer house, where the family could lunch in summers. In another corner was the hutch for the rabbits Alick saved from the Banting lab, where they were used in experiments to test serums. Everybody who came to visit was walked through Charlie's garden.

Margaret was very religious, and Charlie deemed himself an upright Christian as well (he went to church Sunday evenings, not as often as Margaret, but then he would say, "God's in my garden"). Though Alick was a declared agnostic, his daughters went to St. Martin's Anglican Church, where Sunday school was taught by local nuns. Sunday was always a severe day; yet Margaret and Charlie persisted in amateur theatricals, involving themselves in church theatre, both acting and working backstage. At Christmas Charlie played Santa at the Carmelite House Orphanage for girls on College Street and then continued the ritual at home. For years, the children were puzzled that Uncle Charlie always missed Santa's visit.

Sometimes of an evening the extended family would gather in the small living room in front of the gas-grated fireplace and Alick too became involved, playing the mandolin and singing. Charlie would do his comedy routine, as Margaret looked on a little bored but indulgent (she had heard it many times before). Behind her severity, Margaret was kind, and was the source of many of the good memories in that house. She was a wonderful cook and Carol could remember a ritual she and Gwen developed. There was a flight of narrow steps connecting their flat to Margaret's kitchen and what was called the "breakfast room," where Margaret fed Charlie and whichever foster girls were in residence. Carol and Gwen would time the family dessert exactly and, when it was served, could be found sitting on the lower step outside the door; they would always be invited in. For Carol this was a good memory, and yet the image is poignant: in that house, there were always ledges, door frames, where Gwendolyn and her sister stood waiting to be invited to enter.

Margaret added to the family's meagre finances with the rent from the McEwens. She also cooked lunches for local school teachers. At lunch there could be about four teachers at table. Childless herself, she took in the foster children—they were like older sisters to Carol, though to Gwen, so much younger, they were always adults.

But in Carol's family memories, Elsie is always an absence, only remembered as the one who, every once in a while, would become completely unreasonable and turn on you, screaming. Sometimes you would know the bad times were coming when Elsie became erratic and began frantically phoning. Anyone would do, even casual strangers, who would hear her bitter stories about her husband or her domineering sister. Many who received those calls would be friends from the Banting lab, or from hospitals where Elsie had been a patient, who had some understanding. Others lost patience and simply hung up. At night, from their bedroom, Carol would hear fights in the rooms below among Margaret and Elsie and Alick. There would be a slap, Margaret hitting Elsie, and Alick trying to stop her. Or Alick would question Margaret heatedly and she would respond imperiously that she was right. She was always right.

Alick provided the only stability. Carol adored her father, perhaps because he was the reasonable one. If Elsie got angry, she would scream or pull your hair or push you, but Alick would sit you down and explain why you should or shouldn't do something. Things were explained in such a way that you didn't want to disappoint him. Carol could never remember him ever hitting either her or Gwendolyn. And the mysteries of the real world gathered around him: the trips to the Banting Institute, or visits to the red-filtered darkness of the darkroom he had constructed in the basement of 38 Keele Street.

To his children Alick was an artist; their love of books, of writers, of music came from him. It was he who encouraged Carol to take elocution lessons when she was eight (he may have been thinking of his sister, Maud, though it was common for children to take elocution in those days). He was very particular about the way his children spoke; there were proper words to express things, a proper grammar—one didn't use slang. When Gwendolyn was eight years old, he encouraged her to take up the violin in a public programme sponsored by the city that cost twenty-five cents a lesson. The violin was Gwen's first escape from the chaos of 38 Keele Street.

For Carol there was disaster in that house. She and Gwendolyn could sense it. It seemed to focus on their mother. But what was the matter? It was not the kind of thing a child could ask about. Their Aunt Margaret and their father served as huge shields, and the secret of Elsie's madness was kept from her children. When Carol asked what was wrong with her mother, why she disappeared, she would be told her mother was tired, or being silly. It was terrifying not to understand. Secrets are not inactive: they leave an empty gap in the child's imagination; the world becomes an inexplicable place with lost and missing pieces. Was this why, in the skies of Gwendolyn's childhood from the age of four, a key floated, huge and sinister, like an army blimp. She needed that key to unlock the mystery in the household, but she also had the child's prescience to know that were she ever to hold that key, it could fracture her childhood unbearably.

I am trying to reconstruct a family from a child's point of view. I remind myself that the child's view of pain is always starker than the adult's, perhaps because the child has none of those defences by which we automatically adjust and try to put unmanageable things in safe places. For some reason it is the red-filtered darkness of that darkroom in the basement of 38 Keele Street that insists on providing me with metaphors. The child's lens takes in more of reality—I think of a curved fish lens: what we accept as normal they see as grotesque; what we dismiss as trivial they know to be momentous. In the process does the child see more than we do? I feel I have a print beneath my fingers—it keeps changing shape as I bathe it in its different chemical solutions, but what I am driving at, the image Gwendolyn saw, directs my sense of the negative I wish to develop. I look to the next solution. There are still other witnesses to the life at 38 Keele Street—the children on the third floor.

Dora Lyons, age six, and her sister, Marion, age eight and a half, were sent by the Protestant Children's Home to live at 38 Keele Street in 1930 when their own family disintegrated. Elsie was already there, having recently arrived from England. Dora Lyons remembered her only as a beautiful young woman.[3] She recalled Elsie's wedding in 1932, when the house was done up with flowers from Charlie's garden and everything was festive. She also remembered her return with Alick in 1941, to live permanently in the second-floor flat with her husband and two children.

But 38 Keele Street was a refuge for Dora. She had fond memories of her strict foster mother, Aunt Margaret, or Auntie as they called her—even if, when one got into trouble, one always hoped Charlie returned home before the infraction was discovered since he was the kinder one. She remembered his Charlie Chaplin act with Margaret grimacing in the background, and Uncle Alick's rabbits in the hutch in the backyard. At the age of sixty-nine, Dora still treasures a playbill from Margaret's amateur theatre group called "St. Jude's Thespians," named for the church where they performed. The playbill reads: "THE STREET CALLED SHAM/A COMEDY IN THREE ACTS/DIRECTED BY MRS. CHARLES MARTIN/UNDER THE RUNNEYMEDE UNITED CHURCH WOMEN'S ASSOCIATION/TO BE HELD IN THE CHURCH MAY 12, 1935."[4] Aunt Maud (Alick McEwen's sister) had the part of Mrs. Ray's coloured maid and Uncle Charlie played Jaspar Free.

One day, Dora's sister, Marion, got the idea of composing a newspaper, and both children could be found hours on end in the little summer house in the garden, writing the stories of the neighbourhood. They would read their newspaper to Charlie and Margaret on the porch on Sundays. One begins: "Ladies and Gentlemen, and Niggers, Lend me your ears," not the formulation of a child. One assumes the phrasing was picked up from the quiet racism of those sentimental church plays.

Dora was vaguely aware of Aunt Elsie's illness. Sometimes Elsie just went off, abandoning her children to Aunt Margaret. She would check herself into hospital, where she said she felt safer. Dora was also aware that Margaret was not happy to have the burden of Elsie's children.

Dora Lyons was seventeen when Gwendolyn was born. She stayed at 38 Keele Street until 1950 and of those nine years of Gwendolyn's childhood she has only one vivid memory. At the bottom of the staircase that connected the third floor to the first-floor entrance to the dining room—the staircase had a wonderful banister you could slide down as a child—Margaret had hung beautiful blue velour curtains. She was very proud of her house; it had been such a struggle to keep it during the Depression. Those curtains were among her most treasured possessions. One day as Dora was descending the stairs, she saw Gwen, who must have been about five years old, swinging on those curtains. To Dora it was shocking. Gwen was a model child, neat, tidy, quiet, and this was so out of character. The quiet Gwendolyn swinging in ecstasy on Margaret's velour curtains. To Dora it seemed a spectacular rebellion, to be held in the memory for fifty years.

I met Marion Lyons after her sister and so I came to her story of childhood second, and it shifts the portrait through yet another permutation. As we sit on her living-room couch before a photograph album, she shows me a photograph of a beautiful young woman in her twenties, looking refined and delicate in an elegant dress. Beside it is another photo, of a child: eyes eager, expectant, and happy. "That is me," Marion says. "The other is my mother. Why are we so well dressed? What went wrong if we were so well dressed?"[5] She has a vague memory of grandparents and a farm when she was four. "Where are they?" One imagines them hiding their shame behind lace curtains in some distant farmhouse.

The childhood of Marion and Dora Lyons disintegrated when their mother suffered a mental breakdown in her early twenties and was sent to Whitby Psychiatric Hospital. (With life's ironic capacity to weave coincidences, Elsie McEwen and their mother would meet there in the early 1940s.)

Marion remembers Auntie Margaret as opinionated, articulate, and often in a rage. Margaret, she feels, was a feminist before the word was invented. She longed to be a somebody. Had she been born to a different class and been educated, she might have had a different life. She would say: "How I would love to get a job." Her dream was to run a small corner grocery with Charlie, but the Depression made that impossible. Instead she aspired to the heights of the middle class, soon weaning herself of her Cockney accent (complaining when Charlie dropped his "h's"). The sign of her ascendancy was to keep her living room spotless. The foster children were not allowed to enter this part of the house, except on special occasions, or to listen to the Sunday evening radio programmes—Jack Benny, Bob Hope, or Burns and Allen. If they had anything to say, they said it from the doorway to the living room. House rules were strict. Dora and Marion were admonished to respect the privacy of the "people" in the second-floor flat, and were allowed to have a bath only once a week. Daily washing and tooth brushing was done in the kitchen sink, or, as they grew older, in the basement washtubs. Amenities were few. The Martins had neither refrigerator nor ice-box. In summer perishables would go into the all-purpose basement with fresh vegetables under a dripping tap. Dora and Marion would often tell Auntie they would one day earn enough money to buy her a refrigerator.

Ambitious, Margaret turned to the church, beginning with the Salvation Army (no card playing on Sunday) and slowly moving upward from St. Jude's, the Low Anglican, to St. Martin's, the High Anglican church, becoming president of the Ladies Guild, which raised money for missionaries by producing plays. She learned to play bridge. When the other churchwomen came to her house, they always addressed each other as Mrs. Martin, Mrs. So-and-so. One didn't use first names.

Marion wanted to think of Margaret as a substitute mother, but she was always aware that Margaret thought of her and Dora and the other foster children who came and went as a means of earning money. When Margaret was annoyed with Marion she would say: "I'm going to tell Miss Hobden [the social worker] about this," or "I don't get enough money for you. They don't consider that you use soap." Marion was aware as a child that she was a contract: "I don't have to do this. This is not part of the agreement." Once, desperate for approval, she complained that Margaret cared more for Gwen and Carol than for her and Dora. Margaret replied coldly but honestly: "Blood is thicker than water." She would add: "I know I'm not loving. I'm very strict but I'm fair."

Margaret was not helpful to Marion in her childish efforts to hide her shameful secrets from her friends: that she was a foster child and that her mother was a mental patient. When she was fourteen, another secret, that of her illegitimacy, was added to her list. The man she had always thought of as her father came to claim her and Dora. Only then did Marion discover that, though he may have been Dora's father, he had no rights over her. "He is not your father," the social worker told her, "you do not have to go." Who her father was she never learned, but her half-sister, Dora, then twelve years old, disappeared from her life; she was not to see her again for the next six years.

Marion later learned that as soon as Dora turned sixteen, her father put her to work in a chocolate factory to help support his family. At eighteen, and old enough to make her own decisions, Dora returned to Margaret's house, preferring life there to the strain of living with her father.

Marion was luckier than Dora. By remaining at 38 Keele Street, she was allowed to go to university; the Toronto social services for orphaned children lent her the money for tuition. Life, after all, was not so terrible at 38 Keele Street. Though she did not get the love she craved, she did find stability; Margaret never threatened to turn her out. She had high hopes for Marion, who would always remember her for one enduring gift—Margaret taught her to believe in her own intellect.

And then there was Uncle Charlie. His kindness, cheerfulness, and gentleness went a long way to mitigating Margaret's harshness. In the early years he was a joy. On the night that he got his pay, he always brought her a copy of *The Girl's Own*, a weekly British magazine about girls in a private school out of whose exotic stories she constructed her own fantasy life. He insisted Margaret give her and Dora their twenty-five-cent allowance, even though, as Margaret often retorted, it was not required by the Protestant Children's Home—Margaret and Charlie often quarrelled about her strictness. The children loved his stories about his youth, about the pickpockets in Petticoat Lane, or the East India Docks. Charlie was proud to be working class.

By the summer of 1935, Margaret had saved enough money to visit England. Charlie stayed at home with his garden, and it was agreed Marion, aged thirteen, would look after him. A few weeks after Margaret's departure, Charlie began to enter Marion's attic bedroom at night on the pretext of shutting the window. He would then lie down on top of her. Though there was a sheet between them, Marion could hear his heavy breathing and feel his erection. Throughout the ordeal, he never spoke a word and his silence made his actions even more terrifying.

Marion could not understand what was happening. She had just started to menstruate, and her bleeding suddenly stopped. All she knew of pregnancy was that it came from some interaction between male and female sexual organs and that one stopped menstruating. The only person in that household to whom she could think to tell her dread secret was Elsie, but when Marion revealed Charlie's nocturnal visits, Elsie showed no outrage. She did not offer to confront her brother-in-law. She calmly reassured the young girl: "Don't worry. That couldn't possibly make you pregnant," and let the matter drop. Elsie was not good at offering anyone maternal protection.

Marion does not remember how often Charlie entered her room, though she does remember lying in fear, listening alertly to determine whether he was coming up the narrow attic stairs.

"The deepest pain," Marion explains to me, "is that in my mind the loved and the feared became indistinguishable." We talk of the violators, seemingly ordinary men whose acts are a brutal invasion of a child's privacy, and I ask Marion what makes it possible for them to cross the inviolable pure line of the child's vulnerability? Is it a cultural sickness? God was in his garden, Charlie always said. In his religion, sex was consigned to the dark and dirty world of guilt. When he entered Marion's room and closed the door, was it possible for him to pretend the room did not exist, that he could disappear into it and emerge, knowing that he need not admit to anyone, let alone to himself, that he had ever been there? Even as an adult, Marion never found a way to confront Uncle Charlie.

Perhaps for reasons of her own, Elsie kept Marion's secret. And I wonder, did it happen to any of the other children who came and went from 38 Keele Street? If so, they did not share the secret. Did it happen to Gwen? Carol had no idea of the dark side of her Uncle Charlie and believed her sister did not know of it either. When Margaret returned, Charlie never entered Marion's bedroom again.

The bitterest consequence for Marion was that the person she loved had failed her. She had adored Uncle Charlie. Though he had once been kind, she now discovered he was the inflexible and intolerant one. When she went to university, he was contemptuous: "You call that work; the only real work is the work you do with your hands—that requires strength." Clearly Marion's ambition damaged his self-esteem. Margaret, however cutting over other things, always defended Marion's "work."

Marion had no memories of Gwendolyn, who was nineteen years younger and just a child in the second-floor flat, but she did remember Alick, on whom she had a teenage crush. He was kind to her, lending her books. To this day she can remember two of them: Philip Wylie's *Generation of Vipers* and a biography of Clarence Darrow. She came to feel it was a defeat for Alick to live at 38 Keele Street under Charlie's roof. Alick, who wasn't a real "manly" worker in the lumber-yards like Charlie, must have had to deal with his scorn.

Elsie too she found warm. There was one hilarious incident when Elsie had been left to cook for all the children. She had decided to make stew in the new pressure cooker, but the pressure released too soon, the lid flew up, and the stew landed on the ceiling. Elsie scraped it off and the children sat down to table, eating through their laughter. Yet Elsie's extreme irresponsibility often shocked Marion. Once she remembered coming home to find the baby carriage, with Carol in it, abandoned in the snow. Elsie had disappeared without a word. Margaret sometimes talked to Marion of Elsie's illness, finding it almost impossible to accept that Elsie couldn't help herself. There was always the illusion that she could just shape up if she used a bit of will. But in fact Marion was little aware of the lives of the children in that apartment. "In some ways, perhaps, our lives were more stable than Carol's and Gwendolyn's," she suggests, "yet in other ways we were rejected too. It was a crazy life for all of us."

3
A ROOM IN WINNIPEG

This was the psychic architecture of Gwendolyn's childhood home—38 Keele Street and its secrets would recur in nightmares throughout her life. In her dream journal from 1967 to 1970, she records two dreams that look back to that time:

> Something terrible happening inside the house & I am forced to sit on a high window ledge, my only escape to fly down.
>
> Recurring d.[ream] from childhood of night sky, filled w.[ith] multicolored jigsaw of faces & forms—these crack and fall to earth.[1]

What did Gwendolyn think of her childhood? Among her papers is a brief unpublished essay that provides a strange clue. When she wrote it is not clear, but she describes attending an exhibition of the work of Canadian painter Louis de Niverville, in which all his portraits were of children.

> I find myself face to face with a great lumpy immobile child—a strangely sexless thing frozen between surprise and terror ... the child wears an expression I can only describe as a What-am-I-doing-here, I-didn't-ask-to-be-born kind of bewilderment, made infinitely more terrible by the rather luminous and unreal eyes.... The stony mother might know, but she's not talking.... In all these canvases there is a feeling that the figures have been *put* there, almost against their will. The children seem to have been *plunked* down in the middle of a peculiarly flat landscape, made hostile by its very lack of continuity with the figures themselves.... I'm struck by the fact that each figure and each thing occupies exclusively its own space, each unit having little or no vital continuity with any other.... Of all the various fears one can experience, the earliest and possibly the most devastating is the imponderable agony of just *being here*.[2]

Surely this is more than an eccentric description of de Niverville's work. Gwendolyn's words resonate with a shock of recognition, as if the paintings awakened a terrifying image of what childhood meant to her, as if she carried somewhere deep within herself that strange lumpy sexless child frozen between fear and surprise.

Gwendolyn was as orphaned emotionally as the children on the third floor since her mother was often absent from the family. In 1946, Alick insisted his wife either straighten up or get a job. Elsie was hired by St. Andrew's College north of Toronto to work in the cafeteria and, for six months, lived on campus; Alick brought the children for weekend visits. In 1947, when Gwen was five, her mother was committed for a stay of seven months to Whitby Psychiatric Hospital, seventy kilometres from Toronto. On such occasions, Aunt Margaret always stepped in and took over, but Gwendolyn had to watch her mother continually disappear from her life; and in her dreaming mind she saw faces in night skies shatter and fall to earth.

In 1947, Alick McEwen must have decided to take control of his life. In April, he left biochemistry and took a job that brought him closer to his passion: he was appointed an instructor of photography at the Ontario Visual Arts School. Specializing in the new technique of colour photography, he became expert in the use of colour correction in what was called the magenta masking method of colour reproduction. The following January he found a job with Kodak as a sales representative. Two years later, in the spring of 1950, Kodak transferred him to Winnipeg. It must have felt as if this might be a new start for his family, outside the orbit of 38 Keele Street.

At first things went well. Carol remembered the trip by train across Canada as a wonderful adventure. It was April and her father was already in Winnipeg. Since Kodak was paying for the family's relocation, Elsie and her daughters had a private compartment and a friendly porter took Elsie under his wing, offering hilarious demonstrations of how the toilet disappeared under the bed and taking the children's photograph on the platform in Thunder Bay.

In Winnipeg, Elsie seemed almost light-hearted: it was all so new, going down Portage Avenue in the streetcars, laughing at the policemen in their comical beaver hats. When Elsie was happy, she could be great fun. But that spring, Winnipeg experienced the worst flood in its history, the Red River Flood, when the entire city was inundated with water. Precipitously, Elsie headed back to Toronto with her daughters. She returned to Winnipeg in June, and the family settled into the upper floors of a little duplex at 509½ Dominion Street in the old West End.

Soon Alick was travelling on sales trips, and Elsie often found herself alone with her children. She was not a woman who could cope with loneliness, and her mental stability began to fracture. Carol instinctively took over Aunt Margaret's role of protecting her eight-and-a-half-year-old sister. If Gwen asked what was going on, what was wrong,

Carol would say: "It doesn't matter. You're too young to know." But Carol herself still didn't understand the true dimensions of the disaster they all lived with. One night that fall, now that the shield that was Aunt Margaret had disappeared, the full seriousness of Elsie's illness finally came home to her. She was sixteen.

As the two girls were sleeping in the upstairs bedroom, Carol awoke to hear screaming—her father was calling her name. She raced downstairs. His voice was coming from the bathroom, but the door was locked on the inside.

When her father finally managed to fling the door open, the scene that confronted Carol was devastating. The bathroom was covered in blood. Her mother held a razor in one hand—she had cut her throat and blood was pouring from the wound—and she was trying to slash her husband. His arms were already badly cut. Alick screamed to Carol to call the police.

Carol remembers Gwendolyn racing down the stairs. Her one thought was to stop her sister from getting into that bathroom. She remembers calling the police and forcing Gwendolyn back up the stairs. When the police arrived, Elsie was subdued and taken to hospital.

What did Gwendolyn see that night? Carol was fairly sure she did not get into that bathroom, but whatever she saw, she had come closer to the disaster than she had ever been before. By her own account, this was the year she stopped dreaming of the key floating in the sky like a menacing army blimp. She had unlocked the family secret. She now knew what the inaccessible key to the latent despair at 38 Keele Street had always been: it was her mother's madness. What Gwendolyn discovered in Winnipeg was enough to shatter her childhood world irrevocably. At nine years old, she had witnessed the violence of Elsie's illness, but the secret now had to be kept from the rest of the world—friends were to be told that Mother was sick.

And suddenly I hear the echo of Gwen's words: "Of all the various fears one can experience, the earliest and possibly the most devastating is the impossible agony of *just being here*." This is what it meant to Gwendolyn to be a child.

Elsie was released from hospital within two weeks, but her condition continued to deteriorate. Within days she disappeared and the family received a call that she'd been picked up in Grand Bend walking naked on the railway tracks. On another occasion she was found by police, claiming she had drunk half a bottle of lye. She had what were called hysterical symptoms—she completely lost the capacity to speak, and heard voices. All that fall she was in and out of hospital. Carol remembered that a housekeeper was hired to take care of the household in her absence.

It was in Winnipeg that Alick too began to lose hold and turned seriously to alcohol. For years he had been trying to make a name for himself in photography and nothing was happening. Lonely, a Kodak salesman travelling on the road, visiting small prairie towns many miles apart, staying in cheap hotels, eating bad food—that was not the career he had envisaged. And with a mad wife. Perhaps he had hoped for the life of a professional artist, with commissions and national exhibitions.

Alick McEwen was a very good photographer, sharing, it seems, his daughter's hypersensitivity to the natural world. His black-and-white photographs are usually of landscapes. One, which Gwendolyn would use for the cover to her last book of poems, *Afterworlds*, is of four little children sitting on the edge of Lake Simcoe, where the McEwens were visiting the cottage of a friend. The children are merely black silhouettes on a bench staring at a sunset, but the way the tiny feet dangle in mid-air and a lone tree anchors the portrait as they sit with their backs to the viewer, mesmerized by the galloping clouds and the light breaking on the lake, locates a loneliness and mystery that crash through the photograph.

I wonder how much it mattered to his life that he was a British immigrant. He had come from the heart of the empire in the second decade of this century to a country that was, in temperament at least, still colonial. To the end of his life he would speak with a slight Scottish accent, and affirm the virtues of good diction. Yet he came from working-class Glasgow, one of the sorriest experiments of British industrialism. In such a personal history, there would have to be lacunae: a divided and ambivalent loyalty to pasts and to countries. Did he immigrate to the New World thinking of it as a place where he would be free to invent himself? If so, he was deeply disappointed. Gwendolyn's vision of her father was of a man galloping in the desert of his dreams. It would be her responsibility to carry on his legacy.

With his few friends, younger men whom he met through Kodak, Alick would often go out for drinks after work rather than return to the sadness of 509½ Dominion Street. Elsie's anger at being left alone all day while the children were at school, only to have her husband return home late and drunk, would build to a frenzy. Her frantic telephone calls might resume, now to any casual acquaintance she might meet through Alick. One night she put a new lock on the door and refused to let him in. As she screamed at her daughters that their father was no good, Carol took her father's side and opened the door. The anger, verbal rather than physical, that was loosed in the house was unbearable.

In July 1952, Gwen and Carol travelled to Toronto to visit Margaret. Elsie was ill and did not accompany them. Carol, now eighteen, had not told her family, but she had secretly decided she would never return to Winnipeg, and remained with Aunt Margaret. The ten-year-old Gwen made the train trip back to Winnipeg unaccompanied. Within two years Carol would move to Halifax and marry a man in the navy in a gesture to save herself. Gwendolyn was now on her own.

What happened in the next thirteen months before Gwen and her mother returned to live permanently in Toronto remains mainly dark. All that is clear is that Elsie spent nine and a half of those months in the Selkirk Mental Hospital and the Manitoba Psychiatric Hospital and that the family continued to deteriorate as Alick's drinking became a serious problem. With Carol gone there are no intimate witnesses to turn to and Gwendolyn becomes a small figure about whom I can only conjecture. She went to school, had girlfriends, played the violin in a school trio. But there is one revealing fact I do know. She had already begun to write. In a small sealed white envelope, she saved the pencil with which she wrote her first poem: on the back is written, in the large lettering of a child, 1951. That poem did not survive, but in an undated draft among her papers, she left jottings of memories of her childhood.

From her brief notes I imagine a brave, defiant little girl at Laura Secord Primary School, where she was top pupil, reciting Kipling's "If" and Carroll's "Jabberwocky" with her two friends Faye and Penny—the three made up the school's prime violin trio. I hear the child's vulnerability as she describes Faye's amazingly complex, ornamental lunches. She hated to be seen eating with her friend because her own lunches were so perfunctory. Her solution to shyness was to be a tomboy: she wanted to be where the action was. After school she remembered being the only girl in a boy's gang, imagining herself as Joan of Arc leading them in their ritualized war games. She loved comic books. Once the local druggist caught her stealing the latest issue of *Wonder Woman* from his magazine rack and chased her through the icy streets of Winnipeg, which she remembered with a mixture of humour and terror.[3]

Her father became her only anchor. She remembered, with love, the respect he accorded her: how even in a roomful of adults, he could stop the conversation to listen to her opinion. And how once, he had invited the magician Harry Blackstone home to 509½ Dominion Street and Blackstone had performed his magic just for her.

But the most telling anecdote is offered by Carol. At the age of twelve, Gwendolyn changed her name.

Naming is a curious ritual, and it fits a kind of logic that there would be confusion about Gwendolyn's naming. When she was born the family had wanted to call her Wendy—for her mother and father it was a magical name from J.M. Barrie's world of Peter Pan. But the Anglican minister resisted the family's wish, insisting that Wendy was a nickname, not a proper name to put on a birth certificate. The family acquiesced and she was officially called Gwendolyn Margaret, though within the family she was always called Wendy.

Now, age twelve, Gwendolyn insisted that her name henceforth would be Gwendolyn. The motive she offered her family was fascinating. She told them that she thought one day she might be somebody important, and Wendy was not the name of somebody important. Carol would always remember this as Gwen's explanation.

For creative children there often comes a moment when they insist on naming themselves, on shaping their own identity. Now Gwendolyn had determined she was going to be important and the new name signalled that departure. But there is also the possibility of a more tragic motive. In her own way, was Gwendolyn, like her sister, Carol, separating herself from her family, from that history, in order to save herself? Her mother would always refuse to call her anything but Wendy, though her father came to call her Gwen. In future letters that her mother would write to Wendy, Gwendolyn could always feel she was writing to someone else. Even a young child can withdraw from its family, in its deepest core, leave home.

My attempt to read Gwendolyn's narrative leads me to conclude that at an early age, from some deep recess of her imagination (psychologists might call it an unconscious compensation impulse, but I would insist it is much more active than this) Gwendolyn decided, out of the pain and despair of those childhood years, out of her isolation and vulnerability, that she would construct a myth of her own selection. If she was ostracized from normalcy by what seemed the unalterable tenets of existence, then she would turn her loneliness into a gift; she would be the unapproachable initiate into mysteries others barely understood. Perhaps that encounter with Harry Blackstone had given her her first, precocious access to magic and its metaphors—she too would become a magician.

At age twelve, she devised her own magic game of numbers: "One was The Bond; three was Divine Interception; five was Impending Doom; seven was Weakness."[4] This was her childhood code, as she later described it to a friend, which she used "to control reality" in her childhood. How frightening reality must have been if numbers had to carry such weight.

We reconstruct our childhood—we can never really know it—but how we do so must surely be a product of choice: which versions of those foundations we choose to build on. In a poignant anecdote, undated but probably written in her late twenties, Gwendolyn recalls the child she was. She does not write about pain—the eerie hospital corridors she must have walked to visit her sick mother or the meeting halls where she would find her alcoholic father. She concentrates on the magic, imagined world she created as a child. The dream of flying she records was too deeply engraved in Gwendolyn's imagination not to believe this anecdote took place as she recounts it:

> You can fly if you pretend your bedjacket is a cape. You're in Winnipeg and you're 11 years old and getting used to writing your age with two digits.... You've been through all the issues of the Marvel Family for the last three years at least and you know all the key words to utter to bring about the thundering transformation. Long red boots coming to the knees and yellow embroidery sewn in like lightning to your skirt.
>
> Now for you Shazam is elementary. Your knees are clean and efficient, and you have your own word to utter. You know you can fly, the way they do, straight out, with the arms forward and poised like upside-down divers....
>
> You are standing above the ravine and it's a long way down. There is no one to watch you. You will have no witnesses. You wanted it that way, didn't you.
>
> Maybe the Très-Haut wills it otherwise. Maybe he will kill you for your insolence. The Marvel Family has no quarrel with God, neither does Wonder Woman, but then she's a pagan and makes her peace with Greek statues. Later you learn that there is a distinction between Wonder Woman and Sappho, but not now. You don't like Wonder Woman because her uniform is American.

The Marvel Family's uniform is better; it's crass and corny, and starting from the last issue, they've lengthened Mary Marvel's skirt to a point below the knees and she looks awful and you're writing a letter to the editor demanding an explanation.

You're still murmuring the formulae; you realize you're coming to the end and you'll have to take off then over the ravine. You planned on doing it like a high diver ... a running space, then a leap and a spring.

You know you can do it.
Something else delays you.

Is the Marvel Family as religious as you? There's something blasphemous in the way they do it; they're so casual, so easy; are they aware of infinity? Are they?...

You say to yourself, now I know my soul is greater than Mary Marvel's soul ... Do they ever discuss things, for instance? Are they interested in HOW they can fly? No, they just fly, they just go casually flipping off ineffables ... What about ETERNITY and INFINITY? Can they even spell them?...

You realize how paltry is their flying, their lightning. You walk away in your satin bedjacket, knowing something greater has taken place than your flying, than your journey over the ravine.[5]

Beneath Gwendolyn's humour, one sees clearly the lonely child at the edge of that ravine, in her bedcape, her head full of Marvel comics and magic, wishing to fly; just as in her dream of childhood, her only escape from the window ledge and the "something terrible happening" inside 38 Keele Street had been to fly. Of course it is the adult who has crafted a vision of the knowing child as hierophant and initiate in this fantasy of escape. But as children, in our self-absorption, we do instinctively stray into that intensity of time we call eternity, communing with the "Très-Haut." Gwendolyn would always retain what the child knew: how to fill the present and be filled by it to the point where identity fades into nothing. The habit of loneliness can also be an ambiguous gift, a training ground for the creative child.

But there was still reality to contend with. As a mature woman, Gwendolyn rarely talked intimately about herself, but the few anecdotes she offered to friends in later years indicate that she had many painful memories of Winnipeg. She gave the distinct impression that she lived alone with her father and kept house for him; her mother was mostly absent. Moreover, her father's drinking had become a serious problem.

One wonders if there had been a history of drinking, since Alick's deterioration was so rapid. Dora Lyons remembered Uncle Alick drinking too much and Aunt Margaret complaining there were always so many wine bottles out in front of 38 Keele Street that she was embarrassed before the trashmen. But Carol does not remember her father drinking. Perhaps Marion Lyons's explanation is the more accurate. She remembered going out on the town in the early forties on a double-date with Elsie and Alick. It was New Year's Eve and they had gone to a fancy nightclub, sharing a mickey of whisky among the four of them. Alick had begun the evening completely sober and could not have had much more than a quarter of the mickey himself, but he later staggered and fell in the streetcar, for her the signs of a man who had no tolerance for alcohol.

Yet one has to consider the possibility that he might have been a secret drinker. This would be his daughter's fate, and that of his sister, Maud. Maud's son can still recover his vexation, now tinged with amusement, at his mother's habit of watering the Scotch or putting empty beer bottles with their caps carefully replaced back into the new carton that the delivery boy brought every Saturday.[6]

In Winnipeg Gwendolyn had memories of going with her father to meetings of Alcoholics Anonymous. AA was then a new organization; it had only been founded in 1935, though by 1950 it already had 100,000 members. The image of Gwen, age twelve, at AA meetings is moving. With his wife in hospital, Alick would have been responsible for Gwen and would not have thought it odd to take her. The meetings were like folksy revival gatherings. In those days, it was mostly men who went to AA, though their wives might well accompany them. The strategy of the cure was the same then as now: a man serving as witness would explain how his life had been healed. But he would also recount his failures: how hard it had been in the past to get through the day without hurting someone or letting someone down, which must have been deeply distressing for the impressionable Gwen. Carol found it hard to believe that her father attended such meetings—in Winnipeg she could not think that he was that far gone into alcoholism—but Gwen recounted the experience vividly to several friends. Perhaps a pact had already been engineered between Gwen and her father that, together, they could save him from alcoholism. The imperative in her mind would always be to save her father.

On the eve of her twelfth birthday, Gwendolyn watched her parents separate. Released from the Selkirk Mental Hospital on August 19th, Elsie decided to leave her husband and return to Toronto. I read in the hospital report from that time the cool diagnosis: "The patient was depressed over her husband's alcoholism, and was given a course of E.C.T. and advised to separate from her husband."[7] In those months, Gwen must have overheard scenes of anger and bitter recrimination between her parents. She always remembered her response when she heard her mother say that her father would certainly be fired if he continued his drinking. She went into hysterics—"horror, screams, miseries," as she later described it with a mixture of humour and despair.[8] She thought it meant that her father would be burned up.

There is a strange anecdote connected with Elsie's abrupt departure for Toronto, a story Gwendolyn would recount to several friends. Carol was absolutely sure that her mother and Gwendolyn returned to Toronto together, but Gwendolyn remembered it otherwise. At the end she was alone with her father; her mother had left her behind. One day a social worker from the Winnipeg Children's Aid Society showed up at 509½ Dominion Street to invite Gwendolyn to take a lovely ride through the city. Trustingly she went. Soon they were at the train station and, struggling frantically, she was hustled aboard by the aid worker. Through her tears, as she looked out the train window, she could see her father rushing into the station, shouting her name as the train pulled out. He was shouting: "Don't let them make you forget me." The trip on that train, in the company of a stranger, would have been the loneliest trip of her life. "The impossible agony of just being here," she would write.

Did it happen? The Winnipeg Children's Aid Society has no record of a Gwendolyn (or Wendy) McEwen, age twelve, being taken to Toronto in August 1953 to join her mother, but then, a record of a single occasion such as this would not have been saved. It was almost in character that Elsie would just disappear from Winnipeg, leaving Gwen behind. Her father would write to her that November assuring her it was not his idea she be *sent* to Toronto. The image of herself on that train receding from her desperate father would be buried in her heart for a lifetime. When she arrived in Toronto crying so unremittingly that Aunt Margaret called a doctor, Gwen was told she must stop. She mustn't disturb her mother.

How do children emerge from such a childhood? Both Carol and Marion shucked off their pasts like dead skins, burying the hurt in some lost place and building constructive lives; both became mothers with independent careers. They refused to look back (only at sixty-five did Marion begin to search for her mother, and Carol at sixty actively participates in the archaeology of her family), knowing that the cost of doing so earlier would have been too high. Both have that directness and candour one finds in women who have constructed themselves by their own wills out of broken pasts.

But Gwendolyn was different. From an early age, Gwendolyn decided that she would never accept a version of the world that did not take her parents' fates into account. If they had gone over a dark edge, she too would know that edge and that darkness. It was extraordinarily brave, but it was not a survivor's strategy. When she was just eighteen, barely detached from that childhood, Gwen wrote a story called "The Day of Twelve Princes."

The narrator is a little boy called Samuel, whose private retreat is the attic (I think of the space assigned to those foster children on the third floor of 38 Keele Street). Below is the extended family: mother, aunt, and uncle; the spirit-father, as the child calls him, was killed in the European war and is riding forever "through the deserts of his dreams." In the attic, stuffy like a tomb yet private, Samuel feels he is above them all, "standing on their heads, rising like the Holy Ghost above their shoulders." "If he stamped his heels," Gwendolyn asks, "would he crack their skulls and gain entry into their heads?... He stamped sharply." Samuel has invented magic codes and secret rituals for self-protection because the house is dangerous: "The whole house was pregnant like Sarah, waiting to let loose something dark, unspeakable." Sarah, who assumes the role of the aunt in the story and not the mother, is mad: "Of course," Sarah said, "I'm not sick, you know, I'm merely living on a higher plane than the rest of you. Occasionally my spirit gains control of my body and forces it to do strange things, but is that so bad?"

> [Sarah's] tyranny wasn't the tyranny of the sick, the weak. She was neither of these. She was merely mad, and her madness was fourteen years old, as old as Samuel. It involved little more than having hallucinations in the house ... red bats and yellow vermin, for instance, were always assailing her. It was a flagrant, uncomplicated sort of madness, beneath which there was an aura of dreadful sanity.... She was capable of sheer confusion and terrible clarity, wild hallucinations and poignant, cutting perceptions of reality. She had few actual fears, except the fear of open spaces—so the garden was fenced off from the acres of land around. She claimed the fences had a reverse purpose; they were the world-limits, not the limits

of her garden; they made prisoners of everyone in the world except those who lived within them....

Her power was the echo of a distant matriarchy ... Sometimes her madness was almost graphic, her face an acute map that seemed to have been drawn by all the explorers that ever were.[9]

When the boy hands Sarah a red flower, a wild one he'd found growing alone in the garden, at first she seems pleased, but then she lets out a moan that "climbs the scale to a whine, the night sound of an animal." She drops the flower on the floor and weeps and weeps. And the child runs upstairs. If not this exact moment, Gwendolyn knew this despair of rejection directly.

Fiction is not autobiography, and cannot be used as a witness to testify against real life, but when we write we are transmuting or transforming the world as we *feel* it. In this story, the hated figure is the uncle and the most harrowing moment is the boy's discovery that the uncle, Aubrey, has seduced his mother, Hannah.

I do not hear the evil door closing behind Aubrey and Hannah ... No, I hear nothing. Father I hear nothing, he said ... there was a white man and a white lady inside and through the half-open door he caught a glimpse of the white man holding something squiggly and red in the air. He went down and filled a large bucket of water and carried it outside, and the bucket was suddenly heavy; he carried tears, water, bows and arrows, rocks and stones, flowers, years, everything. The sun painted a bright yellow arc across the sky; the trees were all burning, each one a Moses bush; rocks were like mirrors throwing off the light, and the birds were all albinos. There was no sound, no sound at all, and then everything lost its colour and became white, white. Slowly but surely the sun was changing its direction, turning and going backwards, becoming a pendulum. And he thought he was walking backwards into the house and taking the water bucket back to the sink where the water was sucked back into the faucet; then he was walking backwards upstairs and seeing the squiggly red thing again, and returning to his bed, and going back fourteen years until by a strange magnetism he was sucked back into the body of Hannah. And then there was darkness.[10]

It would be unwise to conclude that the seduction of the mother by the uncle that Gwen describes here is based on any literal incident she witnessed, and in any case, the seduction is not central. It is the reaction of the child, that backwards suction into the world of non-being that the child experiences, that makes the scene so devastating. Certainly, Gwendolyn, as a writer, would have had no difficulty re-creating the terror of sexuality for the lonely, unprotected child. But the moment has an explosiveness that is uncanny: one has to ask whether it finds its roots in another experience entirely, and is something that Gwendolyn has displaced from a more personal pain.

On the evidence, I can only conclude one thing for certain: Gwendolyn knew this sinking back into the womb, the black hole of non-being. Throughout her life, she could revisit this site. She had a well-developed sense of non-being and knew the self can be lost and that one can spend an existence in haunted, closed, tormented spaces trying to find it.

But the child has spunk. "I got fire," Samuel says in his desolate isolation. From the age of twelve, Gwendolyn was in rebellion. She would side with her mother's tottering version of reality, rather than the sham of normalcy and domesticity of Margaret and Charlie's world. She would seek every risk. From her secret place in the attic, she pounded with her feet, with all her might, on authority's head. "You can't have me," the child cries to the uncle, "I'm not *you*." Gwendolyn would find a weapon to defeat that world.

4
SPACE LADY

Back in Toronto in the fall of 1953, Gwendolyn and her mother found an apartment for several months at 89 Indian Grove and then returned to 38 Keele Street. Elsie took a job as a seamstress at Eaton's, work she had done when she first arrived in Canada, and Gwendolyn was enrolled at Keele Street Public School on the 8th of September under the name Wendy Margaret McEwen, but that was not her name. She was now Gwendolyn.

Her father wrote frantic letters from Winnipeg to Wendy. It would still take him a few months before he would remember to call her Gwen.

519 Beverley St, Winnipeg
[undated]

Dear Wendy,

I have been looking all week for a letter from you, and am very sorry that nothing arrived.... You are constantly in my thoughts, and I do hope that you will write regularly, and tell me how you are feeling, just what kind of place you are living in, how you are progressing with your studies and your music, and most important of all—do you want to remain in Toronto, or would you rather come back to Winnipeg? I simply *must* know this, so that I can go ahead and plan something....

I have not had a single word from Carol or your mother since you left, and think that they are both crazy, because how the dickens do they suppose that I am going to build another home, unless I know their wishes....

Life has been lonely without you, but do your best to carry on until I can arrange something better. Whatever you do, don't neglect your music, as you have a very definite talent, and I feel sure you will be a top player in the future. Write very soon.

Lots of love from Dad.[1]

Alick wrote again on November 15th. He was still trying to survive at Kodak, but he must have felt desperately cut off, worried as he was about Gwendolyn's well-being, and acutely aware of Elsie's instability and perhaps of his own failure.

> 519 Beverley St., Winnipeg
> Nov 15/53

Dear Wendy,

How are you getting along? I hope that you are well and happy, as you usually are. Please let me know just what kind of place you are living in, and what you do about meals and clothes etc. I guess you are a bit puzzled, the same as I am, about all the things which have taken place, and that is why it is so important for you to keep telling me just exactly how things are going and *what you want to do*. It is hard to expect a girl of your age to make decisions, but you have always been wise and sensible for your age, and I will plan to carry out whatever you would like me to do. Don't think of my feelings or worry about me, but tell me truly just what you feel is best for you, as you are the chief consideration in life for me, and I want to make you happy, comfortable and well educated, and make sure that your music studies are completed.

If you have any problems write to me *at once*, or talk to Aunty Maud [Alick's sister], who is willing and ready to help you at any time.... I miss you very much indeed, and in the meantime if we cannot see each other, the best thing to do is to keep in touch by letter....

PS. It is now late at night, but I have just thought of adding a little more to your letter. Do try to remember that I did not *send* you to Toronto. It was an idea of the doctors and Mrs. Wilks [the social worker?]. In the meantime, until I find a suitable home, you are better off down there, so just be patient and do your best to be happy and enjoy yourself until I can work something out.

I have never let you down yet, and don't intend to do so now. Don't be afraid to speak up and let people know what you want at any time, as Aunty Maud and I are keeping a close watch on your progress, and will make quite sure that you are looked after properly.

More love, Dad[2]

Gwendolyn was twelve years old. What must it have been like to receive these letters from her father two thousand kilometres away?

She was too young to understand the parental battle that was ensuing above her head. Her father needed to justify himself—he was puzzled by what happened, he had never let her down, he was keeping a close watch. I try to think of Gwen, a small schoolgirl in the seventh grade, receiving this letter. Surely twelve is the most vulnerable age for a young girl—one's body suddenly has its own imperatives, sprouting breasts, blood, needs. There are secret delights, shames, ceremonies to be dealt with. She must have felt terribly alone, so that these missives from Winnipeg, saved for decades, would have felt like a safety raft. What she probably heard most clearly in her father's words was that he still loved her and that he believed in her. He spoke to his twelve-year-old daughter as if she were an adult, expecting great things from her. She too would expect them from herself.

The next letter that survives is dated August 31, 1954, the day before Gwen's thirteenth birthday. Her father writes that he hopes his letter does not come too late, that he has been in touch with his sister, Maud, and arranged to get her a birthday present, so that she can open it soon. He would be speaking to Maud the next day, and would like to phone Gwen also, but just couldn't afford two calls. "I do hope that you have the happiest birthday of your life." "Happy, happy Birthday, old pal, Lots of love, Dad."[3] It is hard not to be astonished by this birthday letter, written to arrive too late, and explaining why a birthday phone call would never come. How subtly and inadvertently Gwendolyn was being habituated to settling for less than she deserved.

Trying desperately to understand her father, Gwendolyn had begun, at the young age of thirteen, to write stories about him. In a curious little parable called "Eternally Lost," she describes a man climbing a path to a goal he had sworn to achieve, but he is stopped, wondering where he faltered: "he had plucked his life-giving fruit from the tree of self-denial. He laughed mirthlessly and a look of ugliness crept over his face as he remembered his life had never been his own ... He begged forgiveness of a Power he had forgotten could exist in any world, least of all his own."[4] The story has the poignant high-mindedness and the moral earnestness of the child. If only she could make her father see, she might save him. Gwen was right about her father's weakness—the cynicism masking a failure of nerve. When he looked for an explanation of his failure, he always found it outside himself, but for Gwen the explanation lay in his own self-denial. Even at a young age, the child of an alcoholic father can recognize self-deception, but her father's love was all she had.

In 1955 Gwen graduated to Western Technical-Commercial School. A monstrous pseudo-Gothic brick structure in Toronto's west end that looks like a cross between a prison and a barracks, it was built in 1928 to meet the increasing demand for technical education in high schools. Photos of the male alumni, sports trophies, and trophies to the war dead fill its winding corridors. In the entrance to the auditorium is a memorial plaque: of the one thousand ex-students who served in the Second World War, more than two hundred were killed in action. The school was decidedly working class.

Gwen had hated the thought of Western Tech, desperately wanting to go to the scholastic school Humberside Collegiate Institute, but her mother insisted on a vocational school. She herself had studied a trade when she was a girl. Marion Lyons remembered that Gwen wept for two days, and then she found a way to foil her mother. She took all the arts classes—her passion was of course English—and joined the student orchestra as first violin. Her marks were excellent in literature, composition, history, French, and geometry, but she had poor grades in sewing and physical education. She thought it absurd that she was supposed to study home economics—all that cooking, and sewing, and cleaning when she had already done all this for her father. When it came to the dreaded columns where the personality is assessed, she got an A in emotional maturity and a C in health and vitality.

Gwen was a mystery at Western Tech. Summing her up in the school magazine, the wits described her: "'Space Lady.' Fiddles in Orchestra and scribbles in spare time. What's up on the hill?"[5] Was the hill 38 Keele Street and what did the other students guess about life in that house? During Gwen's years at high school, Elsie was in the hospital several times after suicide attempts. Did the ambulances arriving and departing provoke gossip? Throughout her life Gwen would have an inordinate fear of gossip.

In the summer of 1957, when Gwen would have been almost sixteen, Margaret decided that Elsie could no longer live at 38 Keele

Street. She and Charlie had at last made plans to spend the summer in London together and they explained that they were afraid to leave Elsie alone in the house. It was of course an excuse; they had finally decided they could no longer cope with her. Terrified for her future, on July 8th Elsie took twenty aspirins and was rushed to Toronto General Hospital. When she recovered, with the aid of an Anglican nun, Sister Estelle, she found lodgings on Balmoral Avenue under the supervision of Social Services. The disintegration of the McEwen family was now complete. The second-floor flat at 38 Keele Street was rented out and a room was made for Gwendolyn in the basement.

Alick had returned from Winnipeg in 1955. With no family, and no one to lean upon, he had lost his job in Winnipeg and hit bottom very quickly. In Toronto he would find jobs and lose them: as a radiation surveyor at Atomic Energy of Canada in 1955; as a technician and photographer at the Crime Detection Laboratories in Toronto in 1956; at Toronto Western Hospital in 1957; and then as a runner at the Toronto Stock Exchange. The jobs disappeared almost as quickly as they came. Once Alick was on the downward spiral, he found that no matter how hard he tried to reestablish himself, he could not find a way back in.

As he moved through a series of cheap rooms, the anger he had stored for years occasionally surfaced. He was never physically violent, but his accumulated rage could be directed at anyone. When destitute, he would turn to Gwendolyn for money. Once he showed up at Kresge's, where Gwen worked after school and on weekends, and once he came to Keele Street. Margaret had no sympathy for him and turned him out, but Gwen was his child. He was asking for the only pocket money she had, but she gave it to him, insisting that if he wanted to drink that was his right. On his good days, he could still reclaim the wonderful father. Gwendolyn would go to one of his downtown rooms and read to him from the shelf of books he had still managed to save. Gwen always spoke with great warmth and sympathy of her father and of those reading days.

Western Tech was a tough school. Those were the days when Elvis Presley had taken over the world. The guys all took shop and wore ducktails laced with Brylcreem, and leather jackets. They stood in school hallways making lewd and suggestive remarks from the side of their mouth that wasn't holding the cigarette or cracking gum at the girls with crinolines under their skirts and white socks folded over their penny loafers or saddle shoes. Gwen was the outsider, the Space Lady, the girl who got 90 averages in English and published poems in the school magazine *Westward Ho!*, winning all the prizes.

In her version of those days, most of the kids wouldn't be caught dead walking down the hall with her—their social life would be shot to hell—but a few stuck like glue because they loved the "strange blue haze of poetry and other-worldliness which surrounded me at all times, as dense as the smoke from the Players and Export A secretly inhaled in the washrooms at lunch hour."[6] She claimed to be able to ride a motorcycle fearlessly. The friends she chose were the school clowns, who were exciting because they challenged her to "prove" that she too could be "spontaneous." Beneath her careful camouflage, she longed to abandon her self-consciousness and belong.

She used her violin and her writing to construct the world in her own terms, and in both arts she was original and rebellious. When she studied violin, she had a habit of taking the assigned pieces and distorting the measure and tempo until she arrived at a rhythm (or lack of rhythm) that pleased her. The tune would be unrecognizable, the teacher angry, and Gwen happy. She also took up painting, and some of her sketches and oils appeared in student exhibitions.

But something was beginning to happen to Gwen that happened to many intelligent young girls in the mid-fifties. She was learning to distance herself from other girls, or at least from the idea of the female that the culture offered her. She wrote to her father: "I have never found school quite so wonderful as I do this year. [She had just turned seventeen.] I am at last surrounded by students who want to learn just as I do, and who are not just biding their time as in other years—with the exception of the girls who, I feel, are quite hopeless. That is one reason why I hate the fact that I am also a female."[7] The world that was culturally assigned to girls in the 1950s was the world of self-decoration—they were trivial; they didn't have minds and all they thought of was boys. Surely the interesting things, the intellectual things had to be found in the world of men. A young girl learned to deny her femaleness—women weren't interesting—and to seek male allies. And if one had a mother like Elsie, whose life was a non-life, there would be a code—never to marry conventionally and become a WIFE. And perhaps, more desperately, a girl like Gwen, who had such a devastating relationship with her mother, may even have been afraid of women, afraid that she would never be accepted or loved. She could find safety among the boys.

Despite her remarks to her father, Gwen obviously had one or two female pals. Years later she would write about the pranks she and a girlfriend got up to when, after school, they would climb on the Dundas Street streetcar and head for the back seats, where they would whip out their violins and play Bach's "Concerto for Two Violins in D Minor" all the way to Yonge Street. "This was to startle people and make them notice us." Or they would speak loudly in a language made up on the spur of the moment, syllable by syllable, though that never worked, since one more unrecognizable language on a Toronto streetcar made little impression.[8] It was not one's female friendships that suffered from the misogyny of the fifties, but rather one's intellectual concept of being a woman.

A sympathetic teacher (for the young writer there is, often, that one teacher, but Gwen never named her and I have been unable to trace her) introduced her to anthologies of modern British and American poetry and in those pages she found "a world I never knew existed ... a world of breathless, intoxicating language."[9] She felt this teacher was an ally. She knew what Gwen knew: that a line of poetry could make one weep with its beauty. She told Gwen her poetry was so cryptic and deep she hadn't the foggiest idea what she was saying, but she had better get on with it.

In her history classes, Gwen was reading of ancient Egypt, whose myths and landscapes immediately became material for her writing. At fifteen she wrote "Nefertiti":

> ... poor, pampered child, weep not now,
> your subjects on the sunny morrow line the streets
> to see you pass, high, supreme, glorious in your satin chair,
> smelling of spice from the East,
> on the sunny morrow when the high priest
> steps soundlessly behind your chair,
> whispering incantations to the murmuring gods that created you,
> lovely willowy petal, their daughter,
> daughter of the gods, divinity incarnate,
> hush now, wipe your emerald eyes and plant your ruby lips
> on the paw of the sphinx there (allay his anger),
> lest he reap the harvests of betrayal,
> and tell your lord, Osiris, that this night on the midnight sands
> a sloe-eyed child sat at his feet,
> and Nefertiti cried.[10]

This is the poem of a young girl in love with words and the poetry of Keats, but Gwen has read enough to know the Egyptian myth accurately. Nefertiti is real for her, as is that imaginary place with its deserts and suns and the crying child.

Gwen was also writing poems laced with references to the Koran. Perhaps the catalyst for this interest was one of the first shadowy figures I encounter in her narrative—there will be many shadowy figures. Gwen's sister, Carol, remembers a young Arabic student who fell in love with Gwen in high school. He is never mentioned by her in letters and she did not keep diaries. The registry of Western Tech students offers me no clues to his identity, but it may have been he who interested her in the Koran and Egyptian mythology and first awakened her lifelong fascination with Mediterranean cultures.

The only anecdote that survives of this young Arab is that when Gwen needed to break off the relationship, he was devastated. He would appear outside her basement window at 38 Keele Street, threatening to commit suicide. And I think, Gwendolyn would always be drawn by needy men who would make inordinate claims on her out of their own despair. Are we so obviously imprinted? There seems always one parent to whom we feel most indebted and who looms like a shadow over those we will love in the world. Gwendolyn's definition of love came from the drama of her father's need and the responsibility she felt to save him. Perhaps only if a love relationship was traumatic could it then feel real.

Gwen's intellectual arrogance at this young age is amusing. Her sketches in *Westward Ho!* were usually fierce diatribes spoken by characters who pity people because "their ability to accept anything that shatters the glass barrier between themselves and the unknown, amounts to nothing." She invents magi, magicians, and archaeologists who find that their scientific pursuits have led them into mysteries they were not prepared for. Small wonder that her fellow students called her "Space Lady"; she was compelled by imperatives they knew nothing about. "I was a baby sorcerer," she writes in a poem written when she was fifteen. (She saved all her early poems, clipping them in small rectangles, like meditation cards.) She had what could be called a rage for life. The world of 38 Keele Street had been devoted to a pathetic respectability—those blue velour curtains she had swung on defiantly in childhood. She would not find the poems there. With no one to heed her comings and goings, she took to slipping out at night to the Wah Mai Café on Queen Street West, near the theatre where she had gone to see the magician Harry Blackstone make everything disappear. The prostitutes and pimps hung out at Wah Mai—when the police raided the place, they were puzzled by the kid in the brown corduroy jumper and white socks. She told them she was there because she WAS GOING TO BE A WRITER. In her mind she said: "Actually I'm just a page/But one day I'm going to be a book."[11]

Gwen published her first poem in *The Canadian Forum* in 1958 when she had just turned seventeen. By this time, Marion Lyons had married a professor, and when they had children, Gwen often babysat for pocket money. She showed her poems to Marion's husband and, recognizing her gifts, he insisted she submit some work to the *Forum*, where he was an editor. The poem, called "Mountain of Glory," is naïve and stylized; its subject is a solitary mountain caught between the "hate-hardened earth" and an enchanted sky, but it ends with a powerful triplet: "Hold fast/—and if shrink you must/Shrink last."[12]

Gwendolyn would hold fast. She was driven; she would be a poet. Having read that the Macs were the Scottish bards, she decided to change her name again, from McEwen to MacEwen. Poetry would provide a way of being in the impossible world. On her own she searched out the literary world. People remembered the young Gwendolyn MacEwen, age sixteen, in the audience of poetry readings at the YMHA on Spadina—she always came and left alone.

By this time, much of Gwendolyn's family life was carried on by correspondence and brief visits: to her mother in the hospital, or to her father at his various addresses. Poignantly, she always put her address on her father's letters, as if to remind him where she was. To her father she was sending news of prizes she was winning in school and copies of her poetry for his criticisms. She must have thought that her successes could be the spur for him to recover his own life.

> 38 Keele St.
>
> Toronto
> October 17 [1957]
>
> Dear Dad,
>
> Since it's rather hard to keep in touch with one another, I thought it a good idea to drop a line here and there.
>
> First of all I have some wonderful news I'm sure you'll be delighted to hear. I am going to receive a cheque for $100 at the Commencement service this year at school! It is, of course, to further my education, and also the percent I got last year was an important factor. I am really thrilled—it makes me feel that my

work and interest in school aren't in vain, now that I've accomplished something!...

[She included a poem called "Mirrored Gem" explaining that a poem is a mirror, reflecting its own words, since the only "force" that can understand it is "the very force which first placed the thought in the poet's mind."]

Sometimes I think you worry about me a little more than you should, Dad. I wish I could really explain to you exactly why this whole "business" doesn't affect me as it should any more. Maybe I can explain—I want to try and make you see that your own worries are sufficient without adding any of mine, which don't exist anyway!

Up to now there's been a strange sort of pattern to my life. In Winnipeg I was too young to let what happened, change my way of thinking. Yet, perhaps, without my knowing, it did. Now, at the time of my life when it should affect me, it doesn't. I remember once, a year or two ago, everything came upon me all at once. I said to myself, there's two ways out of this—first, I can let it get me down and be a darn fool because of it—second, I can pretend it never happened. I took the second way, because I was coming to a stage where I began to know that my ideas and thoughts were perhaps, a little deeper, a little different, than most people, and I knew that if I was to go on in life that way (which I must, as you know) I could let nothing, absolutely nothing "distract" me. Now you can see how I am now, and not have to wonder if things get me down at times. Things, let's say "material" things seldom do that to me, because somewhere along the line, I picked up, a more meaningful conception of how to live. Somehow, I believe I must take after you in that respect. We both seem to have somewhat different (to say the least) ideas, than most people. Oh well, there's two of us anyway. At least we can understand each other, even if no one else does!

It's getting late—I should be in bed. I'll drop a line once in a while, and most likely will see you soon.

Bye for now—Love Gwen.[13]

And her father was a friend. He wrote back to say: "Go right ahead and develop your own ideas, and never allow yourself to be distracted or diverged from your own chosen path, just so long as you are doing something which you believe to be quite sincere, and expresses your own honest thought." I keep thinking of the gifted photographer who did get distracted; who now stood writing in a "silly room" at a high dresser (there was no table) so that his back ached and the letter was short. His future was precarious, though he still believed something would happen to "finish the uncertainty."[14] Seeing his daughter had become the only bright occasion in his life.

Alcohol serves as an anaesthetic for those who can't bear reality, but the reality that can't be borne varies—fear, shame, self-contempt, even too much knowing. Like any drug, it gives one the momentary illusion of control, the illusion of distance, so that one seems to be outside everything. Alick had not found out how to stand his own suffering or cope with the storm he felt inside him. A part of him must have recognized he had failed his children, and hated himself for it. Perhaps worst of all, when he was drinking, he knew they ceased to be real for him. He annihilated them, the ones he most loved. He was slowly killing himself, alone at the bottom of something and he couldn't crawl out.

Only five letters are left from this time, but it is possible to trace the pattern of visits. In one letter, Gwen writes that they can meet on Sunday, and take up where they left off at the museum—"or else, if I have enough money we can go to a concert and stay downtown for supper."[15] In another he writes: "Dear Gwen: Sorry to have to tell you my hopes of employment are once again shattered.... I am not working now, so can meet you at 5 pm, 6:30 pm or any other suitable time in the evening, or at any time whatever during the week-end. Let me know what is the best."[16]

Gwen was also writing of her progress to her mother at her various group homes until February 1959, and then at the Queen Street Mental Health Centre, where Elsie was admitted in February 1959 and stayed for a year. Her mother would ask about her exams, or for details of the paintings she was exhibiting at school. In one undated letter, Elsie writes:

> I'm also wondering what you're using for money for canvases & oils. Are you still working at Eatons? I hope so. I was very interested in the Public Speaking contest. What was the subject? How did you rate? Please let me know in your next letter, wont you? What is the 'Near Eastern studies' course. What was the outcome of your interview at the University? All questions!!! but I know you'll find time to answer & you *do* have a typewriter. Did you hear about the essay you sent in? Could you enclose a copy of the school magazine (Westward HO)—I never saw the last copy you know & I didn't even see which poems you had in. [She asks that *Wendy* get her clothes and knitting from her boarding house and get them dropped by at the door of the hospital if anyone is driving past.][17]

It must have been frustrating and painful to receive such letters. Elsie has kept up with everything Gwen is doing—she has a mother's interest in the details of her life, but the knife is always there—that she, Elsie, is being neglected—no one need see her; her things can be dropped at the door. Among Gwen's papers is also a terrifying Easter card, written obviously when Elsie was very ill, possibly under the effects of her medications: "Dear Wendy, I a was was very sorry to sorry you didndnt & maybe you be you be able to write & or come. I would love you come come, Love Love to come come."[18]

Ill and out of control, Elsie could also be extraordinarily cruel and vindictive in her desperate need. And both Gwendolyn and her father were helpless in that net. In one letter Alick comforts his daughter, though he never identifies the incident that had hurt her, nor can he bring himself to call Elsie by her name. She had become "the party concerned." Gwendolyn so rarely complained that whatever Elsie did to her must have been deeply hurtful:

> Dear Gwen:
> When I returned here after our meeting yesterday my thoughts were in something of a turmoil over the account of the events of the past week or so, which had befallen you. In the first place I felt desperately sorry that you had to suffer such a trying emotional experience with no one to whom you could turn for understanding and affection. Then, on the other hand, I was fighting down a feeling of cold smouldering anger against the person who could be so cruel and callous as to treat you in such a horrible manner. When I think of your continued loyalty and devotion through the years, with their times of unhappiness for you, I stand appalled and shocked.
> However, Gwen, in one way it was better for you to find this out for yourself, and to form your own conclusions, knowing that in doing so it was not because of influence or pressure from me. By now I hope that you have regained your customary equilibrium and suggest strongly that you simply consider the whole affair as in the past. There is nothing to be gained by dwelling on the subject or trying to re-open your argument in the hope of proving yourself in the right. I believe in you completely and so would the others who are aware of past unreasonable and vindictive behaviour of a similar nature, emanating from the party concerned. At the moment she is to some extent

in the driver's seat, and is capable of any vicious action if unduly annoyed. This—and the kind of thing you went through, I know too well from experience, and you must see clearly now the constant struggle I had to maintain an even keel during many years of unhappiness. In my present position, not contributing financially to your upkeep, I feel I have no right to voice any criticism, but inwardly it has left me seething mad and I would gladly tell her a few things, which she would not care to hear....

It is my constant burning wish that I will be able to play my rightful part in helping to ensure your future happiness, and surely, when I am dedicated to such a cause, something will happen to change my circumstances and give me the opportunity to work and fight and think for you. When I am doing these things again, I too, will be happy.

Some day soon I hope you will be free to devote *most of a day* to meeting me, so that we can just meander around somewhere and discuss at our ease, our particular problems and perhaps succeed in formulating a plan of sorts for both your future and mine. Such a task would be worthwhile and might provide us with a goal to set our efforts towards. I would be glad to meet you at any time suitable to you.

In the meantime let me know when I can see you this week. Carry on with the good work, and find all the enjoyment you can in your spare time, and always remember that there is one person whose thoughts are with you and for you at all times.

Your loving Dad[19]

This is an eloquent, intelligent, and movingly self-controlled letter written by a father to his daughter to comfort her in pain. What did

Gwen feel it said—did she treasure it as a demonstration of her father's unquestioning support of her gifts? Yet it is such a human letter. One feels that both mother and father, trapped in their non-lives, have turned to their daughter to live vicariously through her. To an outsider, Gwen's father's evasions are apparent; Elsie's doctors would have called him too a dependent personality. He wants a day devoted to meeting him; there must be a plan for both their futures—as if she were the last life-raft he could cling to. But this desperation was much harder for his daughter to penetrate. Elsie and Alick were fighting for Gwen's loyalty in gestures of self-justification, and a terrible imbalance was being established for Gwendolyn. Though an outsider might step back and point out Alick's profound failings to his daughter, Gwendolyn's loyalty had swung irrevocably to her father. While her father failed, there was always one thing she could count on—his uncritical love. To be angry at him would feel like forgoing the one source of love she knew, since her mother was someone who could not be trusted emotionally.

In September of 1959, Gwendolyn suddenly decided she had had enough of school. The problem was to explain this to her father, who spoke so often of goals and objectives that she must have been terrified of disappointing him. She wrote to him:

> Dear Dad,
>
> I seem to have a devil of a problem all of a sudden, and I thought if I wrote and told you about it, then by the time I see you this Sunday, we could talk it over.
>
> This is the first time in my life that I have ever even remotely thought of this, and this fact alone makes it even more frightening to me, and yet, I am beginning to realize that it has more or less been sleeping within me for quite a while now, and has just recently come to the surface.
>
> The fact is I have lost all interest in school entirely. Now I'll try and explain.... the point is that there is something in me which is struggling to come to the surface, but

it is cramped and hemmed in simply because I must devote my energy into channels which seem to completely contradict my beliefs and convictions.... I find myself getting more and more frustrated and irritable, because I see so much that I can achieve—I MUST ACHIEVE, and yet I am forced to over look this and devote my time to studies which have become nothing more than worthless.

I must write. I must express myself, or I can't stand it.... I simply cannot bear the thought of spending the next five years of my life LISTENING—believing what I must read in a book, associating with people my own age who haven't the slightest inkling of what the words art, and humanity, mean. It's simply driving me up a wall.

... Why should the study of life, of art, of religion and philosophy be carried out in the pages of a textbook? THESE THINGS ARE LIFE. Dad, you know even better than I that for a person such as myself, the only way to create, and to understand life and people is to live and experience.

... I do not agree with or believe half the things I am being taught. I am constantly questioning it, defying it— and this is no good. I cannot tolerate the children I am forced to associate with, and, worst of all—I am unable to do what I love ... To try and ignore this would be even worse than trying to keep it in the background until I am "authorized" to use what abilities I possess. I would rather be self-taught, self-educated, because then in the long run, I am sure I would be able to concentrate my efforts into the proper channels and be a better person for it....

When I am not doing these things, I am unhappy, desperately unhappy, because I feel that I am not using the ability I have—it is like a slow death to me....

    See you Sunday   Love, Gwen[20]

Her father replied with a letter written as if to himself, referring to Gwen in the third person, though including a list of questions directed to her.

> Sat. Oct 10/59
>
> This has been a week of perplexity and indecision. My own affairs, complicated as they are with the almost insoluble problem of just how to approach the task of re-establishing myself, assuming the financial future of Gwen, and meeting a thousand and one other obligations—and all this on a salary which any decent self-respecting office boy would refuse, in this day and age!
>
> Then, to completely overshadow this, there is the *story* followed by the *letter* from Gwen.
>
> After long periods of concentration and spells of the deepest pre-occupation, no answers seemed to be forthcoming, until, eventually the concrete idea entered my head, as it should have done much sooner, had my mental state been as calm and normal as it usually is; but this incessant driving urge for self-expression, with no immediate outlet available, must have played havoc on my analytical and fairly perceptive mind. Instead of struggling to resolve those two problems simultaneously they must be handled *separately*....
>
> At any rate, now I'm *thinking* again.... [The letter] affects me deeply, and leaves me with a feeling of great admiration, and even more love than I have borne for her before, to realize that Gwen, in many ways my "alter ego", finds herself driven by such an idealistic and humanitarian compulsion that she finds herself compelled to reach such a conclusion.
>
> But the answer to this problem is not easy. Too many factors are involved. Such down to earth things as

"how to live in this jungle" and at the same time, try to follow a definite plan of study and practice in order to reach a pre-conceived goal—while *existing* on *what?*—must be considered. The only way to tackle this is by the time worn method of considering the *pros* and *cons*. So lets do just that—

Before doing so, it is only fair for me to state, that my advice to Gwen, provided that she is sincere and satisfied that the thoughts mentioned in her letter are her true feelings (and they must be) then my advice is to *leave school* but *not* until we have found an *alternative* which I hope will prove possible to-morrow.
1. If you leave school, then what's the next move?
2. Are Aunty and Uncle aware of your intentions? After all, they have stated, that in spite of anything which happens, they will see you through U of T. Remind me to mention this *again*.
3. Suppose you miss matriculation. Is this going to debar you from entering your chosen career? It's difficult to find a job of *any kind* without this qualification.
4. If your driving desire is to write, the only answer is *to write, write, write*. Are you going to starve in the meantime?
5. What do you hope to BE?[21]

Alick had said what Gwendolyn had hoped to hear, and the first part of his letter is a considered response with her best interests at heart. He clearly loved her deeply. But there is something disturbing in the way, goaded by his daughter's evident energy, he attempts to mirror it, speaking of his need for self-expression and of her as his alter-ego. In truth, he had completely lost hold of his life. Quite shockingly, the latter part of the letter disintegrates into alcoholic gibberish. How confusing for Gwendolyn: these paternal claims on her sympathy would prove costly, though, for now, Alick's faith in her was enough.

That winter she and her father seemed to be exchanging manuscripts of stories. In the margins of two of her own, she has written: "from an idea by Alick McEwen." Only two of his sketches have survived, both portraits of men down on their luck in Cabbagetown. The stories have flair, yet they are incomplete, as if, here too, he could not find the will to go on. In one letter, Alick responds to a story Gwen has sent him; the story has not survived, but his critique is revealing.

> An important character is missing—the one who can explain Shelley's behaviour—unless of course this happens later in the book. But, half way through, Shelley does not belong to any particular class. His actions only suggest that he is taking the easy way out of everything. He appears to be quite spineless & completely without courage, and this is not what you intended to imply. As he stands he will invite neither admiration, love, or pity. He is only despicable.[22]

Was Gwendolyn writing in code, inventing characters that might provoke her father into action? Did Alick find the explanation for his defeat in the issue of class? There is too little here to go on. But I ask myself about the emotional demands fathers make, unwittingly, unconsciously, manipulatively, on their children.

In the face of warnings from Aunt Margaret about her folly and her smashed future, Gwendolyn got up in the middle of a chemistry lab that October and walked out of Western Tech. She was just a few months short of her spring matriculation, but she couldn't wait it out. She was convinced, as she would always be throughout her life, that she could do better on her own.

5
ADAM'S ALPHABET

Gwendolyn had just turned eighteen and there were now no props to her life. She would have been visiting her father as he deteriorated in his makeshift rooms, and her mother at the Queen Street Mental Health Centre. Carol had returned from Nova Scotia to Toronto in 1957, but her marriage was fraught with problems and she now had three children to attend to. She remembers Gwen dropping by—often she came with Alick—but her own life was too chaotic to have any sense of what her sister was up to. No one was watching Gwen.

Gwen now lived in the basement where her father had once had his darkroom, in a spartan room with a bed and a desk where she worked on becoming a writer. Suddenly it is as if she has disappeared and I can only thread her story from the odd anecdote I gather or from her abandoned manuscripts. She has not yet met those people who will pick up her narrative for me.

She once told an editor that by eighteen she had written three novels, two of them "execrable"—she destroyed the manuscripts—and a third that she later condensed into the short story "The Day of Twelve

Princes."[1] She worked part-time at Eaton's Annex, behind the old Eaton's on Queen Street, in the discount store where there were no frills and the money travelled efficiently in metal tubes along steel pipes to the upstairs office. At night she would have emerged from her basement room to slip down to the Wah Mai Café, or to Queen Street to catch a performance of the magician Harry Blackstone. There was a little store on Yonge Street run by a Russian, where she went to buy the comic books she still loved: *Batman, Wonder Woman, Justice League, Plastic Man*. A few years later when the poet George Bowering would visit, she would say she discovered the ideal rapport between poets: they sat, beer in hand, the comic books spread on the floor, reading silently.[2]

On her desk there would have been books borrowed from the local library—the novels of Virginia Woolf, and the poetry of Hart Crane and Kenneth Patchen, her favourite writers of the moment. She even wrote a fan letter to Patchen and received a thank-you note from his wife.[3] But there would also have been other, stranger, books—the Zohar, various Gnostic texts, the Cabala, the Book of Tokens, the Book of the Law—and perhaps a deck of Tarot cards.[4]

Emerging from such a childhood, Gwen must have stored a great deal of rage, but where was she to vent it? Not easily against her mother, who was so emotionally untrustworthy. Anger would have been a terrifying emotion; she had lived too close to it. A part of Gwendolyn must have felt guilty for having failed her mother, failed in pity or in love, since, terrified of finding her mother's madness nascent in herself, she had to keep her distance. There is a stray reference in Elsie's files to one occasion when the nurses discovered her weeping in her bed; she explained that she was upset because her daughter "found it funny when she put her arms around her in an affectionate manner."[5]

To rail against her father as she watched him slowly destroying himself would have been not only pointless, but also dangerous. To do so would have been to jeopardize her own survival, for she was entirely dependent on his love. And yet I think, how curious it is that as children we serve as defence attorneys for our parents. Gwen could never tell her father of her feelings of hurt, anger, and betrayal, but the cost of hiding would be high—throughout her life she would accept behaviour from others, particularly from men, that was distressful and exploitive.

Instead, this young eighteen-year-old turned her rage upon reality itself. Something had to be wrong with reality if it led to these half-lives. As a fifteen-year-old schoolgirl, she had despaired of people: "their ability to accept anything that shatters the glass barrier between themselves and the unknown, amounts to nothing." She still believed this, but now, with fierceness and self-discipline, she would train herself to contradict the collective perception of reality.

She had discovered esoteric philosophy—she was reading the Zohar, the Pistis Sophia, and the Cabala. While other young girls of her age were finishing high school, or working at menial jobs and thinking of marriage and children, Gwen's head was filled with Gnostic theories of the Pleroma, the Archons, the pneumatic self, the demiurge. She had found a philosophy that suggested we live in this world as alienated beings, sleep-walkers, and that waking to consciousness is a difficult process requiring discipline. Such ideas would have made compelling sense to her.

She spent that fall, when she was not working at Eaton's, walking the streets of the west end of Toronto, alone and planning her future. Aunt Margaret would have been scathing—she should have gone to university; her mother imagined a trade; only her father would have approved. She must have felt terribly isolated. Where were the other young poets to be found? In other cultures there was always a bookstore one could go to, a club, a meeting place. But Gwen was one year early. There were writers in Toronto, but the city was still Hogtown and the counter-cultural scene was only just beginning to percolate beneath its staid surface.

Years later she told her friend the poet Margaret Avison that on her rambling walks to keep out of Aunt Margaret's hair, she used to pass a *cheder* or Hebrew school; she would stop each afternoon to watch the Jewish students pouring out from their classes.[6] One day she screwed up her courage and walked in, asking if they would teach her Hebrew.

On Maria Street, not far from her old high school, stood the synagogue, Congregation Knesseth Israel. In those days, down the street at 129 was a makeshift *cheder* put together in a run-down two-storey house. There were two *melameds* (or teachers), one on each floor, and under them the students learned to read and write Hebrew and, in the advanced classes, studied the Bible and biblical exegesis. Students paid what they could, sometimes as little as two dollars a week. All school records disappeared when the *cheder* was closed, but it seems likely that this was where Gwen was welcomed.

In one of her letters to her father she again explained why she left high school: "When the day comes that I am ready to go to the East and find my true purpose—fulfil what I was meant to do, it will mean nothing that I was at a desk in Canada for five years learning about the people, the countries—better that I have the strength and courage to rely upon my own convictions, my own interpretations."[7] Used to being bewildered by his extraordinary child, he was still taken aback by her assertion that she must go to the East: "How can you know this? What experience or knowledge have you acquired to make you feel this compulsion? What is to be learned in those far off lands?" he asked.[8]

By East Gwen meant the Mediterranean and the Middle East; by her purpose she meant she intended to train herself to be a visionary. She was learning Hebrew so that she could study, firsthand, the Jewish mystical tradition. Gwendolyn would always be seduced by an intellectual architecture that seemed a magnificent autonomous game. She was young; it was thrilling. In her esoteric studies she had found a home for the mind, one of the first intellectual interests that made her truly happy.

Twenty-eight books that were once Gwen's were given to me by one of her last lovers.[9] They constitute the library she carted around with her through the many places she lived, those books she felt it vital to save. Several, dating from 1960 and earlier, are Hebrew grammar books. She also saved a little book called *List of Words: Occurring Frequently in The Hebrew Bible*; the Book of Genesis and the Book of Psalms in

Hebrew; and two volumes of *The History and Practice of Magic*. Words, magic, mysticism had become her obsession. She learned quickly to write the exotic Hebrew alphabet: her favourite words repeated in exercise books were desert, nakedness, rock, Adversary, One, Whole, tongue. She began a long poem called *Adam's Alphabet*.

Adam's Alphabet was an incredibly abstruse game in which she wrote twenty-two acrostic poems based on the twenty-two letters of the Hebrew alphabet, in the process reconceiving Psalm 119. She had stepped so quickly from the child who had written "Nefertiti" to this new sophistication. She believed, as it is possible for a young poet to do, in the mystical power of Naming: "Names like those antique Hebrew names with levels of interpretation a hundredfold. Names enclosing names; names with the twists of vowels to give them souls; names with the turn of consonants to give them bones," she wrote. Words were codes that hid all secrets. She explained in the introduction to *Adam's Alphabet*:

> It is, however, in the books of the Cabala, the mystical writings of the Jews, that we find a sense of alphabet, a sense of letter which is a more significant one. The 22 letters of the Hebrew alphabet are given definite interpretation and function—the intriguing concept, for example, that the world was created by these 22 letters. The eternal Tetragrammaton, the creative Word, the ineffable name of God—YHVH—are four sacred letters which can correspond to the four elements of creation:
>
> Y—yod—life, fire
> H—heh—mind, water
> V—vau—truth, air
> H—heh—love, earth
>
> These in turn were given high pictorial symbolism also in the vision of Ezekiel, where the letters were represented by four animals—lion, eagle, man, ox.

"Modern poets can still write psalms," she wrote aggressively; can still be prophets, is what she meant:

> We can celebrate or swim in negations; we can cry out against Greece or Rome, our own oppressive societies, or ourselves. Israel in the clutch of foreign oppressors can be the heart, the intellect, or the will in the clutches of anything which is foreign to it which shackles its forward flow; it is all the same thing.[10]

She thought of the poems as a "letting off of steam" from her own soul. They are prayers; sophisticated to be sure, but still prayers to the "Très Haut" of her childhood, filled with spiritual longing:

> For I wish width, the door of self
> mouthed open. Let broaden
> let the heart groan its scarlet
> hinge-s
> and split the red air wide.[11]

Three years later, when she was still trying to get *Adam's Alphabet* published, she wrote to Margaret Atwood, who by then had become a friend:

> It's a chronic sort of work, if you know what I mean, refuses to complete itself, insists on being infinite; hence I revise regularly, like taking regular pills for a chronic stomach or something. At present it's more or less static and Abelard-Schumann might be biting; heard they've sent it to New York office for O.K. I've also had some growing ideas for illustrations—except I keep seeing spindly line-drawings of oxen, fish-hooks etc. all the definite lines of which end up in curly-cues ... I don't know.

> The poems are tight as drums/some vibrate on their own, some can't ... so the ALPHABET is singular in the most plural sense. Poses still a chewing sort of problem.[12]

The dated manuscripts make it clear that the revisions she speaks of were slight. *Adam's Alphabet* was essentially the work of an extraordinarily precocious eighteen-year-old. As it turned out, the U.S. office didn't approve and it was never published.

But there was another side to the esoteric Gwendolyn; there was the pragmatist who wandered the streets of Toronto, knowing intimately the power dynamic of the world she felt had sabotaged her mother and father. The modern Jewish narrative of persecution, which she must have been learning at the *cheder*, was as compelling as Israel's ancient history.

With a mind like a sponge, completely absorptive, she began a novel called *Gabriela*. It was to be a *political* novel, set in Palestine in the 1940s. Its main character would be Gabriela, a young musical prodigy growing up on a kibbutz during the years when Israel became a nation. Gwen had never been to Israel. She had never known war. Yet, she would create a convincing portrait of that historical moment.

She was a brilliant autodidact. Her notes show that she outlined her plot and characters, made a thorough study of modern Jewish history in Palestine/Israel: maps and geography, crops and farming, chronologies of historical and political events, the kibbutz settlements and their habits, lists of appropriate idioms and vocabulary (*ain davar*—it doesn't matter; *lo ton lo*—never again), the movements of DPs and refugees to Palestine after the war, Jewish religious and mystical traditions, Arab revolts. At the *cheder* she would have been wracking the brains of her fellow students for the words and details she needed.

Gwen understood the political situation she was writing about with remarkable sophistication. Given the characteristic disregard of Arab aspirations in the 1950s, she was astonishingly ahead of her time. In her novel, she records the dramatic early settlement of the kibbutz by Jewish immigrants (Gabriela's family is from Poland): the draining of the marshes, the irrigation and cultivation of a hostile desert, the construction and organization of the kibbutz, the eternity of labour. Yet, in the backdrop are the Arab families, exploited by their Arab landlords who have sold the land to the new settlers, watching in bitterness as the desert is made fertile. Gabriela's childhood friend is a young Arab urchin called Joseph, who is forced to watch as the British execute his father and mother in front of his eyes as Arab revolutionaries; he then disappears into a DP camp. Gwen was already aware of the legacy of injustice towards the displaced Palestinians that would poison the Middle East for decades. When Palestine becomes Israel in 1948, and the British politicians withdraw, the inevitable war between Arab and Israeli begins. An armageddon of violence takes over. There is no way out.

Gwen has not fudged the political complexities. She records the arrival of Jewish survivors from Nazi concentration camps at the end of the war and the horrific moment when 4,500 refugees are summarily deported back to Germany by the British. She affirms the Jewish desire for a homeland, but she also knows that it conflicts with Palestinian aspirations.

She makes the crisis of her novel take place in an underground shelter at Beersheba. As the bombardment begins, the children are left in the shelter as the settlers, militants and pacifists, take up their inadequate arms and emerge to fight. Gabriela, aged nine, cannot identify with the other youngsters, who cower in the corner; she seeks the comfort of the aged rabbi, who had stood for the voice of reason and peace. She writes: "Of all the people there, in that stifling hole, she could sense that he alone stood for something other than violence—something above and beyond that fearful quality in man that makes him become an animal, arms, backs laden down with weapons of death and destruction. Her own people had been reduced to this state...."[13] And the child watches the beauty of violence, its corrupt seductive grace, transform those around her. When even the rabbi rises, his face wild with pain, to chant the songs of war, she tries to stop him. When he too dies, the only escape the child can find is to hide under the skirts of the corpse, where she is found, hours later, when the bombardment is over and the Arabs have moved on, having totally destroyed the settlement.

But what does Gwen mean with this gesture of the child crawling in under the skirts of the corpse? For a young novelist, it is a powerful moment.

> She huddled up as close to him as she could, so that when she breathed, the movement would lose itself against the other's flesh, working like a cushion for the expansion and contraction of her stomach. It was dark and warm there—the horrible sounds around were somewhat muffled. She thought of a half-remembered crib—a safe, soft place of security where there was only Gabriela and God ... she even vaguely sensed something she had known before the crib—some moist, warm cavernous thing, long, long before the crib ... before anything ...[14]

I think of another novel, *The Tin Drum*, where a child refuses to grow up in a world addicted to war. Here, Gwen's character reneges on birth itself. Where could Gwen, born in pacifistic Toronto, have found this disgust at human violence? What, I ask myself, was the source of that image of the underground shelter in the mind of an eighteen-year-old Canadian girl? And why does it repeat a fantasy in her earlier story, the unravelling backwards to a purity, what she called the death-beg, the temptation of non-being?

I have found a poem to her mother that Gwen was drafting around this time. The poem is placed in London's Poplar district, where an old woman selling cockles runs through the streets slurring "Alive, Alive-O" in the charred ruins of war. It would have been the First World War, her mother's war. A child, bomb echoes in her ears, forever screams up the long hallway of the house. "All I know of war," Gwen writes, "are the children I have seen come out of its loins ... children growing and everyone wondering why they spend their time in mental homes. A catatonic child with her great statement of silence."[15]

The character she creates in the bomb shelter in Beersheba is the age her mother would have been when the people of Poplar were forced to flee to the black tunnel. "Guts. Like two hundred people waiting in a hall for the bombs to fall and at the peak of the silence a cockney voice crying 'Anyone want to buy a gold watch?'" In the brief two-page draft for the poem, Gwen manages to locate a house where a child is motherless, a social hierarchy personified by the "Pearly King and Pearly Queen," the beggar's royalty, a world where human worth is fixed and maintained by the "fire-dogs of war." "So you still believe these children are individually insane?" she asks. Alive, alive-o. The bomb shelter at the heart of human civilization. Why? Where does this sickness come from? She could not understand.

A friend of Gwen's said that "most people manage to remain adolescents throughout their lives. They never make it to adulthood. Gwen was adult when she was eighteen."[16] She had already seen more than most children. I recognize in her character Gabriela much that I identify as Gwen herself. "She's got to be made to face the world now or she'll never face it later," the adults say as the deaths accumulate around her. Gwen writes in the margins: "Emphasize this." What would it mean to be Gwen? Her mother inhabiting a terrifying madness that had its own logic, her father disintegrating in despair in transient rooms. As she grows up and away from the war, Gabriela becomes a closed figure, hermetically sealed in her own pain. Once she says to the young man in love with her and trying to break through her solipsism: "How do you know I want to come out of myself? I'm getting used to it down here." Has Gwen invested in her character that part of herself terrified by life? Is the book an exorcism? She knew the paradoxical double-edge of the tomb/womb image she had created for the climax of her novel. Like all of us, she would have to crawl out of the cave of her own fears if she was ever to emerge released from her past. She said to Gabriela: "Let the sad part die."

Gwendolyn never sought to publish her first novel, though in 1960 she did send one chapter to Robert Weaver, then editor of *The Tamarack Review*. He wrote back: "Was it a mistake, I wonder, to place a novel in so far away a locale as Israel at this stage of your career?"[17] Gwen realized her novel was too raw and the writing not up to her standards. She wrote furiously to herself in the margins: "Fix this up!"; "Guts!"; "Are you kidding?"; "What are you talking about?" and then abandoned it. But the legacy she leaves her character at the end when Gabriela chooses to accept life is telling: to survive, she would need "a staunchness of the heart." Gwen also added the warning: "Artists make every situation as dramatic as they can to derive inspiration from it." There would always be a part of Gwendolyn that would deliberately court the darker territories of the psyche, knowing that was where her material lay.

Writing biography, one discovers there is always someone who will be able to trace our footsteps, if not give the full texture of our narrative. With the serendipitous connections that always occur, I was able to find a man who, I was told, had been Gwen's boyfriend in that year of 1960.

Joe Blumenthal was a nineteen-year-old high-school dropout who was working in a government income tax department, though he was passionate about theatre. He used to gather with his friends at the Honey Dew on the northeast corner of Yonge and Carlton streets to sit and watch the passing parade. In early December a striking young woman, somehow exotic even in her long tweed coat, entered the restaurant to talk to his friend. She piqued his interest. "Who was she?" he asked. "I call her the mouse," his friend said. "She wants to be a writer."

Blumenthal was a garrulous young man and by January had managed to strike up a conversation with her. He remembers the bitterly cold night when he first walked Gwen to the Bloor Street subway. They met again. Within a month they could always be found together.[18]

Gwen was now living at the Winola Court Apartments at 1709 Bloor Street West across from High Park. Her aunt and uncle had finally sold 38 Keele Street and had taken her with them. Joe remembers sitting with Gwen in the apartment stairwell leading up to the roof, talking for hours until the superintendent chased them away. He recalls her room because it was so tiny, just large enough to contain a bed under a window that looked out on the back of the building, a desk, and a bookcase on which she kept her small bust of Nefertiti (the kind to be found in any variety store); behind the bust she had propped her violin. There was always sheet music scattered about the room.

They hung out together. One of their favourite neighbourhoods was the south side of Queen Street between Yonge and University before the area was torn down for the new city hall that would be built on the north side. Shea's Theatre around the corner on Bay, which Joe remembered as the place where teenage girls had torn down the doors to see their idol Elvis Presley, had already been demolished, but on the south side the Casino Theatre and the Broadway Theatre east of it were still standing, and there were several pawnshops, a few old-fashioned beverage rooms, and the hotel where Gwen would go to meet her transvestite friend whom she called Shelley, though his real name was Gordon. Joe did not know Shelley, but felt that Gwen was oddly fascinated by homosexual culture, suggesting there was probably a side of her life Joe knew nothing about.

Their talk always began with politics. Gwen was militantly CCF. She was working class and so was he, which he felt was the basis for their getting on so well. It also helped that he was Jewish. They talked of the Middle East, and once she mentioned going to service at the Hebrew Men of England Synagogue on Baldwin Street, though she never talked of studying at the *cheder*. He remembered meeting Elsie a half-dozen times. She was now an out-patient at the Queen Street Mental Health Centre, but he had no idea where she was living, though he knew Gwen visited her at least once a week. Alick was living at the West End Y. Joe would meet him with Gwen at the Honey Dew lunch counter. He seemed an exceedingly nice man to whom Gwen was devoted, and so it came as a shock when Gwen told him her father was a chronic alcoholic.

Joe, who lived at home with his parents, remembered the phone ringing in the middle of the night of July 24th. It was Gwen, crying hysterically. She said her father had just died. When he tried to calm her, offering to come immediately, she only replied: "Don't worry. Don't come. I'll see you later."

Alick McEwen had collapsed that morning on Yonge Street and been rushed to St. Michael's Hospital suffering from a heart attack. Only Carol was immediately called. At the hospital that afternoon, she remembered a long, good conversation with her father in which he had assured her: "Everything's going to be all right, old girl." The nurses sent her home saying there was nothing she could do. That evening, she was called back to the hospital and told that Alick had died. At fifty-six, his heart had been irreparably damaged by alcohol.

From the hospital, for the first time, Carol phoned Gwen and asked her to come. She also phoned Elsie, who said it didn't matter to her; she wanted nothing to do with the man. When Gwen arrived at the hospital she learned that her father was dead. Carol told her she felt their father was finally happy to be released from it all, but Gwendolyn was devastated. She wanted to see his body, but her sister insisted there was no point. When Carol later learned that Gwen had left the hospital and gone to her father's room, where she had found only empty bottles, she was furious. Unwittingly, they were fighting for some kind of ownership of their father's affection, some acknowledgement of a special relationship with him that the other wouldn't have had. There was so little outward demonstration of love in their family, they had to battle desperately for what they could find.

Gwen was alone, since her aunt and uncle had left at the beginning of the summer for a holiday in Northern Ontario. Because they didn't want to leave her on her own in the apartment (Joe felt they were afraid he would seduce her; they didn't approve of him), Gwen had had to find a room on Ossington Avenue with a girl she knew. Joe went to her room the next morning at 11:00. He holds in his memory an image of her bedclothes soaked with tears.

Carol planned the funeral. To her relief, whatever company her father had been working for at the time offered to pay the expenses, and she kept them to a minimum. Margaret and Charlie felt it was pointless to return south, but Alick's sister Maud and her son Lawrence came, as well as Alick's old friend Redge Leavens, from the Banting Institute days, and Joe Blumenthal came with his parents. Elsie made her entrance in the middle of the service. When it was over, the family gathered at Maud's for a Scottish wake. Alick was cremated; there would be no grave to visit.

Watching Gwen in tears as the hearse disappeared, Joe's mother insisted that, after the family wake, she come to stay with them. She protested weakly, and then accepted. By the third or fourth day of her visit, she had become one of the family and acted as if nothing had happened. It was as if she had put her father's death out of her mind; in conversations the family never referred to it. She stayed with the Blumenthals for two weeks, and then left the city to attend a summer camp of Jews for Jesus. She said she had found an ad in the newspaper about the camp; it was cheap and might help her Hebrew.

Joe remembered that he and Gwen spoke once of marriage, though theirs was never a sexual relationship. They continued to meet at the coffee shop on Carlton Street and, in late August, he attended her first public reading at the First Floor Club on 33 Asquith Avenue, a jazz club where a poet called Michael John Nimchuk had started a reading series. By mid-November, they drifted apart; Gwen had begun another phase in her life.

Looking back, Joe Blumenthal remarks that those nine months changed the course of his life. He had never met anyone as brilliant as Gwen, nor someone so young who knew succinctly what she was about. But while he felt that he and Gwen were deeply intimate, it was always difficult to get her to talk about things that bothered her. He did not know what she was holding back. He remembered several occasions when she would suddenly burst into tears, and then explain she was terrified by dreams. The tears would stop and, ten minutes later, it was as if nothing had happened. After a while he became accustomed to it. She had, he felt, a remarkable ability to take even the most traumatic things and, "relatively speaking," put them out of her mind almost immediately, as she had done with her father's death. She seemed to have more resilience than most people; she didn't want to burden anyone with her pain. Or perhaps, I think to myself, there was always a battle within Gwen: her need to remain hidden was always at war with her desire to be found.

But if Gwen buried her thoughts in secret rooms, this did little to mitigate her pain. She had been preparing for her father's death for a long time. Uncannily, in *Gabriela*, she had already written her reaction to Alick's death before it occurred.

There is an eerie scene in the novel when the young Gabriela returns to the kibbutz to discover that the night sentry has been killed. She knows her father has been on sentry duty that night, but as she runs to the tower, she sees him coming towards her. "By that insane casualness of life's luck—the sort of thing one can't dwell on for fear of going mad," she discovers that another man, who had taken her father's place at the last minute, is dead. But that night Gabriela dreams:

> She slept fitfully through the long hot night, with wild visions bouncing through her half-slumber—visions of things long imagined, dreams lived countless times, images of a thousand angels, devils, gods—Deberorah [sic] and Barak, the swift madness of fingers on piano keys, and lastly, a grey water tower against the sky, and the plummeting downward of a familiar figure. She strained her senses to see its face, and when the image became clear in her mind's eye, cold beads of perspiration crept over her brow. Try as she would, it would not go away—and she lived eternities of terror as her father gasped and fell, gasped and fell, over and over and over, tumbling, shrieking, coughing as the slow ooze of blood stained his dear face. Dawn could not come quickly enough for Gabriela Levi.[19]

For years, Gwendolyn's father's death surfaced in her nightmares. The dream would always be a version of the same horror:

> We the family are burying Dad again—this time we know he is alive—the funeral is a rehearsal—I interrupt saying "O my God what are we doing?" The attendants are angry we didn't tell them before that he was alive.[20]

Gwendolyn believed her father had been deprived of his life; he had been imprisoned within his own hell and the family had been part of the metal bars that had kept him there. But while the dream is desperately sad, it is also aggressive. Each part of a dream is a projection of the dreamer. There was an angry part of Gwen that wanted to bury her father, an unacceptable part that had to be displaced onto her mother and sister, while she alone could see what they were doing. It would be years, if ever, before she would be able to keep her father peacefully in his grave.

6
MAGICIANS WITHOUT QUICK WRISTS

Two young girls who lived at 38 Keele Street somehow received the message that they could save themselves with their minds. Marion Lyons entered the University of Toronto in 1940, supported by a loan arranged by her social worker. Given her personal history, she was astonishingly brave and determined. Gwen went further. Her sense of the strength of her own mind convinced her that she could carve out her own intellectual path without the props of an educational institution. She would be an autodidact.

Now I confront something that will be a dilemma for me as a biographer throughout my narrative of Gwen's life. I cannot imagine another life, except perhaps that of another youngster, Arthur Rimbaud, also a scavenger among the Gnostic visionaries, where the life of the mind and the daily life seem to move on separate parallel planes. While Gwen's life was painful and desolate, her mind was busy creating alternate realities. She was so sure of her direction that she bashed on regardless, which often made her seem a misfit, an alien, a mind that had implanted itself from elsewhere. Those who would look at Gwendolyn with pity would be vastly underestimating how exciting it can be to live in the mind.

A child watches a magician. Gold coins disappear under his knuckles like water; birds fly from his fingers. All this comes from the magic stick he holds in his hand. What matters is that the child believes in the stick. A scarf can become a flower. That's not the hard part. The transformations are not remarkable. It is the stick that the child wants—the thing that does this. As a ten-year-old child watching her first magician in Winnipeg, Gwendolyn learned to believe in the power of illusion, the suspension of disbelief, and the enormous joy it brought. If she was to understand how human beings have so distorted reality, there had to be a clue there.

For Gwendolyn, the magician continued to live beyond her childhood. She became fascinated by escape artists, seeking out real ones down in the theatres on Queen Street: Harry Blackstone, Sid Lorraine, and Mario Manzini, and writing them letters and poems to learn about their art. She once confessed to renting a rabbit from a Mr. Melrose in North Toronto, who bred rabbits especially for magicians. She even managed a professional friendship with Manzini, who wrote to her from Brooklyn about his performances:

> Dear Gwendolyn,
> ... For myself, I've been playing the Ringling Bros. & Barnum & Baily Circus at Madison Square Garden in N.Y.C ... [and] the RKO Theatres lately with my full stage show which runs about $1^1/_2$ hours consisting of all Escapes such as different rope ties, challenge rope ties, Escape from 100 feet of rope, Escape from roped & tied chair, Escape from Iron Water Boiler filled with water & locked on top (Death Trap) nailed into Wooden Packing Case & roped & chained up, strapped into a regulation strait-jacket as used to confine the murderous

insane, and also the Original Chain & Water Torture Cell that Houdini performed in the climax of his career.[1]

Gwendolyn took these death-traps seriously. Why would the escape artist perform, night after night, year after year, this obsessive courting of the illusion of death and escape? Gwendolyn felt she was a fellow adept in the trade of magic, and that her art was no less pragmatic than theirs. What was important was that it existed on the same knife-edge between reality and illusion, and depended on the same principle, the spectacular suspension of logic. Because, of course, logic was the straitjacket that she did not believe in. As with Manzini, for her what the world called illusion was the more real. She wanted "to push through reality and come at it from the other side," she once told a friend.[2] Poets were "magicians without quick wrists," their tools of magic the same.[3] If the magician was working in visual parables, the poet worked in verbal parables—Manzini's chains, as she identified them in the poem she wrote for him, were the chains of flesh: "fighting time and the drenched/muscular ropes, as though his tendons were worn/on the outside—/as though his own guts were the ropes/encircling him; it was beautiful; it was thursday; listen—/there was this boy, Manzini."[4] At sixteen she had written in one of her stories: "'People are fools, Jack,' was Morgan's slow reply. 'With their pitifully limited insight.'"[5] She still felt people were fools.

At the age of eighteen in the spring of 1960, Gwendolyn wrote her first novel of magic, called *Julian the Magician*. (She would only turn nineteen that September.) It is a palimpsest of her mind, layered with her obsessions. She was reading carefully, cumulatively, and yet, like any young artist, she followed her own whim. She read Thorndike's *A History of Magic and Experimental Science*; Schure's *Jesus, The Last Great Initiate*; Frazer's *The Golden Bough*; and the whole of the Old and New Testaments. Her magician was not to be a modern magician, but someone trained in the esoteric science of alchemy.

In her fervent youthful belief that the life of the mind is more real than what we call material reality, Gwen had turned to the Cabala and to the Gnostics. Following her reading pattern, I feel as though I am entering a labyrinth of the archaic human imagination as it has dreamed through history. I can see why Gwendolyn loved this material—you cannot read these books like a scholar, a sceptical collector of intellectual systems. It touches a deeper longing. With her precociously vivid imagination, the Gnostics became living historical antecedents whose imaginations simply paralleled her own. Somehow she had picked up the notion that human time is so brief in the scale of things that there was little difference between her and the Nefertiti she had imagined when she was fifteen gazing at the Sphinx over the wastes of desert. "We *are* our ancestry," she would say. Now she was looking to find fellow travellers, adepts in the labyrinths of myth.

What, then, was this esoteric philosophy that attracted her? "Gnosticism" serves as a collective heading for a variety of sectarian doctrines appearing within and around Christianity during its critical first centuries. Palestine was seething with eschatological (i.e. salvational) movements and the emergence of the Christian sect was anything but an isolated incident. The name "Gnosticism" derives from *gnosis*, the Greek word for knowledge. It is impossible to summarize the ancient Gnostic religion except to say that it was essentially a dualistic metaphysics: God is transmundane, unknowable. The deity did not actively create the world; it was created by a lapse of divine consciousness—and to the divine realm of light, our cosmos is opposed as a world of darkness under the control of lower, actively demonic powers. We live as somnambulists, as alienated beings, and awakening to consciousness is an unnatural process. But we are sparks of the divine. The soul's way out of the world, often comprising sacramental and magical preparations for its future ascent as it moves through the spheres, is through a rigorous discipline and inner illumination. The "gnosis" is a revelatory experience, the reception of truth on an extra-rational basis. Sin has no place in the Gnostic concept of salvation; in its place is put ignorance.

Gwendolyn loved the idea of a historical era when prophets and pseudo-Messiahs were swarming through Phoenicia and Palestine: Simon Magus, Valentinus, Mani, the mystic Christ. She saw them as real people, identifying with their "golden hunger" for the god. And she had also found an explanation for what she thought of, even at eighteen, as our soul's amnesia and essential hunger. Most people live benumbed, asleep, ignorant. She would shock them awake.

The fictional world she was inventing in her novel *Julian* is a strange quasi-medieval landscape in which a magician travels the countryside in a horse-drawn wagon performing his tricks. Who is he? What sets him in motion? When she was looking for a publisher for the novel in 1961, Gwendolyn would tell a friend and fellow-writer, Tom Arnott, that *Julian* was her first experiment in describing a person seduced by the myths generated in his own unconscious. Her magician, Julian, eventually convinces himself that he is a Gnostic master, repeating the fate of the greatest magician-prophet, Jesus Christ. Gwen was asking a very sophisticated question: when the force of belief reaches a certain point does a myth become true?

I can imagine Gwendolyn at her desk as Julian grew day by day more real. Writing is a strange alchemy because for long moments of attention a character becomes as real as oneself, since all one's emotional intelligence and experience is poured into its making until the character seems to have its own disembodied, if illusory, life. This is the mystery of the writer's life, the paradox if you will. When Gwendolyn began this novel in 1960, her father was dying of alcoholism, her mother was continuously institutionalized. Yet juxtaposed to the real world was the parallel world of her fierce intelligence and the esoteric order she could create there. No matter how painful her life, there was the deep pleasure that came with writing, a pleasure as real as the real pain.

The Julian she invents is middle-European, the illegitimate son of a Gypsy father and Aryan mother (it is fantastic, of course; she was after all still a kid). She offers brief glimpses of his childhood recorded in his diary:

> So I can leave the farm and mother staring out at the moon at night, the moon at noon, the moon in the morning and seeing her lover's face drift drift black and happy there, and my vague cousins folding and unfolding the land like paper, and the licewide cows and the steady puppet bulls and the whole rotten mystical mess where I am called a joyous juggler and a magic madman, where my books gather haysmell and mildew and an elementary drunken bible is pressed into my face like God's right hand where there is no hand, where in the wrong sort of hands, the Book is an ugly sandwich fit for no eating.[6]

Julian decides to study alchemy under a master called Kardin, but he is sceptical: "Kardin will spoon me alchemy until my ears bleed sulphur and my spit turns to mercury and my excretion is pure salt." Wanting to know mysteries surpassing alchemy, he trains himself to be a magician, modelling his greatest trick on an anecdote he has read about the young Jesus, described in the Apocrypha of the Pseudo-Matthew as making sparrows of clay and commanding them to fly—"Fly through all the earth and live!" As a magician, Julian learns to "to suspend logic like a whale on a thread." His audiences idolize him: they feel close to a mystery, not knowing what they have seen, but feeling a sacred delight in having seen it. But Julian too is transformed by his art. He begins to feel the audience's slow seductive power and to long for and fear their collective force of belief, their post-performance hysteria.

In the background of Gwen's text there is always the recurring image of a river. At first it is choked by winter—not "allowed to flow under the collar of ice blocking its throat-pulse." It is quite clearly an image for the unconscious that will gradually be unlocked from its ice until it rages as a sweeping torrent. Submitting to the forces of his own unconscious, Julian begins to imitate the historical life of Christ.

The logic of Julian's fate is inexorable. After the first euphoria of belief in his miracles—curing a madman, changing water to wine (Gwen always describes these "miracles" in such a way that they might easily be the product of the people's credulity)—the masses' adoration of Julian turns to hatred. "All necessary phantoms are housed in the mind," Julian tells them. (Reading this, I wondered, was Gwen also talking to her mother?) The audience demands his death in return for the death of their own belief, and the repetition of the crucifixion is inevitable. But Julian, dead, simply looks like a magician tied to a cross and propped against a tree. There is no drama to it. The river slides by, bored and placid.

With the "objective" story ended, Gwendolyn does something quite remarkable. She hypothesizes the discovery of Julian's diary by his assistant Peter. We now enter the story from the inside, with footnotes from the editor-commentator on the dead text.

We find a young man driven by the "golden" hunger for the unknown. When he decides to become a magician, he reports his mother's complaints:

> Mother again. Back to her who shoves the bible in my face perpetually and informs me, as though I were sprouting devilwings, that what I do is God's left hand working. His *left hand!* Dear mother mine—if God has hands, I'm not interested. Dear mother mine—what I do is a celebration of God, strewn out like seed, spun-about, giranduled God in the green world.[7]

This is where Gwendolyn can become lyrical as she slips her own identity and becomes Julian:

> Enough of raging. I am a quiet man. While I write I endeavour to squash too much into too little. The page is thin, too thin—like the transparency of a fly-wing and the ink too thick, made, it seems, from frog's blood and tree-sap. The quill has a mind of its own; it digs into the leaf without mercy while my mind, O my mind, is a

> restrained thing; would not under any conditions, involve itself in aggression.
>
> Save quiet aggression. Erratum. Of course the mind of the magician must impress, indent, find its own doors into other minds, and if not finding them, it must make them anew. But the saws for those doors are velvet. O remember they are velvet, and the friction is almost nil. Velvet aggression against the soft silk of the brain.[8]

Gwendolyn herself would always practise this velvet aggression; and yet how gay this eighteen-year-old can be, weighted with her own wisdom. We discover what a day could be for Julian/Gwendolyn:

> Each day, like the pigs and the apple blossoms, opens a new part of me, and with each new opening, another is in sight. The file runs down like mirrors facing each other creating through their union their infinity of children, each resembling the parents, each farther away in space and time, each in its separate removal, each demanding the milk of more mind ... on and on until all things unite in large grace and the rain seeps for the last time into the leaf and the stone falls into rock and the ice moves into the sun ... without any loss of individual character, shape or substance, but with each piece of matter giving up its identity to a collective whole; a perfume-box that houses a million separate scents and allows none to lose distinction.[9]

At one point Gwendolyn has Julian say: "My mind is decidedly bisexual; thus I can navigate in both female and male territory as freely as grass, and anticipate both female and male qualities in all things—with neither one blocked off in a singular blinker by an over-abundance of one or the other."

And I suddenly remember that once Gwendolyn and I had a conversation about childhood dreams in which I had remarked that I often flew in my dreams but, oddly, when flying I was always male. To me, looking back, it was simply an indication that as a young girl I had wanted male power and freedom. Gwen had replied: "I know what you mean. My mind is bisexual." I had thought, then, I had understood her—we are all bisexual in our dreams—but now I wonder if she may have been saying that her mind was not only androgynous, but autonomous. She didn't need the world; she could cross-fertilize herself. How dangerous, I think now, to be so precocious, so self-sufficient, so self-enclosed.

"You have a screaming imagination," Julian says to himself in a kind of despair. "Your imagination is a mad she-wolf giving suck to anything that approaches it." At the end of the novel, Gwendolyn acknowledges that, Julian gone, we cannot know whether he has come to "gnosis," to any encompassing vision of the transcendent. The central human tragedy, she understood, is that we cannot know the point of being human.

A writer's book is a psychic defence against the pressures pushing inwardly on the mind. In this so esoteric book, Gwen was writing about what it was like to have a mind like Gwendolyn's. One can hear Gwendolyn crying that she needed a thread of reality to hang on to. Her kind of writing was dangerous, spun on the intersecting cross of time and the timeless. It is dangerous to attempt to be master of the soul's metaphors. I keep thinking of her pragmatic character, Peter, in the midst of Julian's brilliant esoteric rants, holding on to a pig's nose to try to squeeze some reality out of it. Gwendolyn's mind housed both voices: the voice filled with the "golden hunger" for the god and the sceptical voice of disillusion.

A few years later in January 1963 (she would have been all of twenty-one), Gwen wrote to the poet Irving Layton with her peculiar mixture of humour, high-seriousness, and self-parody. She writes with easy self-confidence to the man who was by then Canada's pre-eminent poet, explaining what writing meant to her (and I think of her Julian seduced by his own metaphors):

How is it ever ever reconciled ... the two big fighting Russian bears—the inward vision and the outward world? NO, you say, it need not be just reconciled; poetry is the capturing of that dualism— ... refusing to compromise any element of either because consciousness of one's own reality has proven there are no limits to reality; the last is the poetry, but it is also the madness....

At present, midnight, Thursday, I want to know how you personally have survived; I am angling desperately for a workable philosophy, no, not precisely—it is a future concern. I don't want to know 'how one does it,' because I know too well, and I don't want to know how the fire is retained ... ironically enough I want to know the exact opposite of these ... how to guard oneself against the intensity of one's own vision.

It's that other end of the creative scale which is the most formidable. Not these: the questions you probably have piled on you constantly: How does one make it, how does one reinforce one's voice, etc etc ... but I fear my own poetry. Fear the actual strength of the voice. How does one *minimize*, the mind protected from itself.

More terrible when we permit ourselves to realize we haven't even got one reference point; there is no one reality; I am not assured by the existence of the hard wooden table underneath me because it is in motion; we do not even understand the nature of that motion! Mein Gott, until science can give us one, just one proven scheme of realities, we are writing on water—

I am not totally off my nut yet. Won't be probably since there are still some reins on the wild horses. The present letter is pitiful as I read it over; I am reassured by the fact that I am not the first poet to be overwhelmed by such matters, nor the last.

Again and again I ask—and I can't work beyond this wall—is it correct to assume the reality of the transcending man (take Nietzsche because he's handy)—and if so, in what terms? Because we have perceived his seeds in ourselves, yes; because he exists as a future reality, yes ... but once stated, that existence becomes itself a danger—like an animal laughter.

There are poems we should, for our own safety, never permit ourselves to perceive the meaning of. Perhaps this.

There are those who move, or try to move, bodily into the metaphors they have made for themselves—some classic Nietzschean dissociation, or whatever—because their real image can no longer support itself; the overconsciousness of the potential; the movement into the sad giant, the ridiculous genius whose only function is self-destruction because he, in turn, cannot be reconciled with his environment.

nietzsche should have been aborted at three months.

In this light even the use of a metaphor itself becomes a fiendish thing. The last thing we want to see is one of our metaphors overtaking its subject.... Yet how stubbornly and urgently we poets insist on extending 'reality.'

In the light of this I don't know what poetry is. Except that few listen when you scream: Mysticism? Mysticism is ultimately LIFE!...

Anyway, also sprach Gwen, and am finished. You won't have time to answer this, and it wasn't written with that end in mind. Mail it back to me 5 years from now and I'll eat it with my porridge.

Sinceres,

g. macewen

in more solid mental state will be in montreal sometime.[10]

Gwen was being cocky, of course, but she was also serious. It is possible to get trapped in one's own metaphors. She did not have any fantasies about the romantic extremism of the self-destructive genius—that was a "pathetic" idea. But her own imagination was so alive. I think of the dreams she was recording in her journal at this time:

> Civilization of "python people" who slide instead of walk, but like cobras which slide down grey mud-flats, a superior civilization. N.B. resembles Lovecraft's ... subterranean civ. of tubular creatures.
>
> A flying contest between myself in white and a magician in black—we "climb" an invisible rope to heavens, each struggling to gain altitude over the other.[11]

"How stubbornly we poets insist on extending reality," Gwendolyn complained to Layton. She knew the dangers of the poetic territory that her imagination drew her to. But she was young, and she believed fervently that there would be strategies to harness the wild horses.

After a number of tries, Gwendolyn finally found a publisher for *Julian the Magician* in October 1963. Someone must have suggested she send it to Eli Wilentz of the Eighth Street Book Shop in New York. Wilentz had founded his press, Corinth Books, with his brother Ted in 1959 to publish the writers who hung out at their Greenwich Village shop. They brought out *The Beat Scene* in 1960 and, long before they became culture heroes of the avant-garde, published Allen Ginsberg's *Empty Mirror*, Jack Kerouac's *The Scripture of the Golden Eternity*, and the first three books of Charles Olson's *The Maximus Poems*.[12] When Gwendolyn's *Julian* came in over the transom, Wilentz accepted it immediately; it was a major undertaking since it was one of the largest books he had yet published.

Gwendolyn must have been thrilled to find herself launched internationally, and by Corinth, which was becoming a "cult" press; she must have felt she was on the edge of fame. *Julian* was handsomely done with dustjacket copy that read: "This compelling first novel by 22 year old Gwendolyn MacEwen is a brilliant tour de force."

Gwendolyn didn't have the money to go to New York when the book came out, and Corinth certainly didn't have the money to invite her, but its publication must have confirmed her confidence in herself as a writer. When she had quit school three years earlier, she had explained to her father that she could not wait to be "authorized" to use the abilities she possessed; she had too much to achieve. Now she had proven herself, though it was too late for her father to enjoy her success. Once *Julian* had found an American publisher, it was also accepted by Macmillan of Canada, who had earlier turned it down.

In a symposium in 1969 at the University of California at Berkeley, the American poet Robert Duncan defined the category in which he believed *Julian* belonged. Gwen treasured the recognition, saving the article among her papers.

> There is much ... that I have enjoyed or have recognized as admirable in contemporary writing, even that has a glint of something I suspect deeper—the ground of my pleasure in reading is larger but these are works over the past ten years that have particularly struck me and drawn me to reread: in prose, Tolkien's saga of the Ring; Ernest Juenger's The Glass Bees; Harry Mathews' The Conversations; the writings of Borges, Gwendolyn MacEwen's Julian the Magician.[13]

But in the early sixties, Gwen felt she was still a writer in training. "I am embryonic," she told friends. In a letter to Peter Miller, an editor at the small publishing house Contact Press, who was interested in her work, she wrote that what she had wanted in *Julian* was "a sort of powerful poetic mad half-abandoned prose somewhere between Patchen and Virginia Woolf, though the standards changed for me about once a week regularly."[14] She was always fond of *Julian*, but she would come to feel it was "too passive" a novel. (She turned it into a play in three acts for children in 1967, and reworked it as a television script a few years later, though it was never produced.) She wrote to the poet Phyllis Webb in 1963 that many of its ideas already seemed remote to her: "I wrote the book about three years ago and have now departed from many of its ideas ... I feel less mystical about things now than I previously did."

Webb had found *Julian the Magician* by chance in the Eighth Street Book Shop when she was visiting New York, and, immediately fascinated, had asked for directions in reading about mysticism. Gwen wrote playfully:

> I'm caught on magicians. To me they represent the final symbol of man's control over himself and environment—and those lovely black wands, like fingers or phalli get to the point where they can command everything ...
>
> Re your mystical searchings—I found that after going through all the standard occultists (Waite, Cabala, Gnostics, etc etc)—that the REAL things started to happen when I veered from them over to the writings which are on that weird borderline between mysticism and science ... and all those people that are in effect, treating science itself as the ultimate magic—you know what I mean....
>
> You asked me for clues to books. What about Frazer's Golden Bough, or the Hebraic Zohar, or good old Alistair Crowley who was a nut, or the Tarot cards, or (and this is really fun when you get into alchemy)—Paracelsus, Albertus Magnus, Nostradamus, etc. etc. There again you depart from mysticism and get into science. Apparently there was a Julian the Apostate, and a couple of other Julians too—oh, and Jung's Psychology and Alchemy, which is a real thing....

Now I'm getting carried away. Then there are the medieval Christian mystics who weren't really mystics at all—Duns Scotus, but I'm off the track a bit.

What about Montague Summers' studies of witchcraft history. Then there's Blavatsky and all those people, but they're too ponderous. My main contention with the strictly occult writers is that in their psychological wanderings, they forget that the source of their "voices" and "ghosts" is their own interior memory-experience bank. I mean that they try to give their own writings an exterior reference, and in this way deny the potential genius of man, and credit his brilliance to astral beings. It's like the poet saying (that old absurd cry)—oh, I just write what I hear, as though someone else is dictating. I used to say that too until I realized that I and I alone was the dictator.

But you know all this, and I just feel chatty in this letter....[15]

Gwen was reading as a poet would. She was not interested in dogma and was sceptical of the overdetermination of systems; she was not a convert, always rejecting the label "mystic." "In Canada," she complained to a friend, "there seems so little of the surreal, the bizarre, the dream."[16] She loved the play of ideas and was madly searching for something experiential and immediate, something that would help her to cull the endless volatility of her own teeming imagination.

7
THE BOHEMIAN EMBASSY

In the 1950s, Toronto was still a Presbyterian construct, devoted to order and cleanliness, but that veneer had begun to crack as the city grew up and away from its colonial roots. Toronto's cultural escapees could be found downtown in the jazz clubs that opened towards the end of the decade. The first was the Melody Mill on Jarvis Street, east of Yonge, where the jazz sessions began at 1:00 a.m. and the music lasted until four in the morning. Then came the House of Hambourg. The early careers of musicians like Moe Koffman, Guido Basso, and Teddy Roderman began in Clem Hambourg's place on Bay Street one block south of Bloor. Clem had a small sound studio and American musicians playing at the Colonial Tavern would drop by; eventually his wife began to charge for her coffee and the House of Hambourg was born like a jazz improvisation.

The next club to open was the First Floor Club, an old coach house a few blocks north on Asquith, owned by Salome Bey's husband, Howard Matthews, and soon folk music crept in and, with it, a new idea called the Vocal Magazine, where actors and writers read plays and poetry. The actor-musician Don Francks started there with his young back-up guitarist Ian Tyson. Then came the Village Corner, entirely devoted to folk music, and the short-lived Clef Club. Finally The Bohemian Embassy opened on June 1, 1960, in a warehouse off Yonge and Wellesley at the end of what was then a cobbled lane, St. Nicholas Street.

The location was no surprise, since this was the Gerrard Street Village, Toronto's only bohemia, the place where you went to find relief in Hogtown. The Village dated back before the war, when it had been full of cocktail bars like Malloneys flanked by painters' studios in the back alley; artists like Fred Varley could often be found at Malloneys. But the Village had become a scene in the early fifties after the painter Albert Franck and his wife moved to a ratty little house at number 94 Gerrard Street, which also served as Franck's shop. Dutch by birth, Franck restored paintings to make money, for which he was affectionately called "Old Dutch Cleanser." From Gerrard Street, he made his treks into the backyards and alleys of Toronto hunting for subjects to paint.

Across the street from the Francks' house was Mary Johns, where the tables were squeezed together like tiles and you could get a meal for sixty cents, as you sat under the multi-varnished travel posters. In a loving memoir of Franck and the area, Harold Town remembered how people tried to open the bow of the Cunard liner on the wall, thinking it was the washroom. If you were flush, you went to Old Angelo's, at Chestnut and Edward streets, dominated by the waitress Rosina-with-the-profile-of-a-Roman-coin, who directed you haughtily to your table. And there were a handful of other places: Larry's, The Rumanian Grill, Little Denmark on Bay Street, and 11A in adjacent Chinatown. 11A, down a flight of narrow steps from the street, was always dark and sinister, and the line-ups to get in were legendary. In those days, rumours still circulated that beneath Chinatown was an underground world of gambling and weird goings-on late into the night after the city closed down. That part of Dundas Street felt like a Charlie Chan movie set, and every once in a while a club would be busted for gambling, confirming Chinatown's exotic flavour.

All the young painters came to Gerrard Village like filings to a magnet to see Franck—Town, Walter Yarwood, Kazuo Nakamura. In 1956 the painter Barry Kerneman opened the Gallery of Contemporary Art on Gerrard and its style set the art boom that was to follow: it featured a black egg-crate ceiling, displays of pre-Columbian art, Hokusai drawings, and champagne openings. The area had its characters who were characters because, as Town said, they were "totally unaware of eccentricity as a commodity"[1]—Willie Fedio, the lamp-maker; Madam Alice, who read tea leaves; Nancy Pocock, famous for her pet skunk and for her painting of a naked lady who ran past her door one day and later explained to the judge that she was invisible. There was always something going on in the Village.

When The Bohemian Embassy opened, it was a modest affair. In his late twenties, Don Cullen was working as a copy clerk at CBC TV, rewriting stories for the Sunday-night newscasts, though he also did stints as an actor and comedian, working as a back-up for Wayne and Shuster on their comedy series. Cullen knew people were looking for an alternative to the Celebrity Club on Jarvis Street, where the CBC types gathered for three-hour lunches and to drink and play darts. His idea—he was still enough involved in his fundamentalist past to think it would work—was a liquorless night club. A group of five from the news office put down a hundred dollars each and The Bohemian Embassy was born. To inaugurate the club, Cullen bought two fourteen-cup aluminum percolators and a hot plate from Eaton's basement and churned out advertising flyers on a Gestetner. He would go up to the football games at Varsity Stadium to hand out his flyers, saying: "Would you like some subversive literature?"[2]

The building that housed The Embassy dated from the days of horses, with a pulley outside to haul up the goods through a hole in the wall. Up two flights of narrow banisterless steps on the second floor, the club was a barn of a room, with its walls painted black. There were tables, all with dripping candles, and chairs for about 120 people, with a stage at the back and a sound system of sorts. The washroom was a cubicle that opened directly on the main room. It had no lock, and wary patrons had to learn how to urinate with one hand on the door if they weren't to find themselves, pants down, staring into the audience under the spotlight of the naked bulb swinging above their heads.

The Embassy was run as a private club; membership was $2.25 a year, with an additional one-dollar cover charge at the door. Suspicious of the after-hours part, the police often tried to close the club down. If there was a drug bust at a coffee-house in New York City, not to be outdone, Toronto's finest would come calling. The Embassy was threatened with closure so often that a judge advised Cullen to counter-charge with police persecution. The plainclothesmen were readily identifiable in the audience, but there was not much for them to do, since The Embassy never served alcohol and frowned on drugs. Cullen was adamant about this. He felt that certain kinds of talent, unleashed too early on the rough and tumble of the local bar scene, could be destroyed. The Embassy nurtured the new. It was anti-bourgeois—Cullen was hugely amused to get the occasional letter from people who, thinking it a real embassy, inquired about visas. There was an ingenuousness about The Embassy. Looking back, Cullen thinks of it as curiously "sincere and kind of dear."

The week had a set schedule. It opened at 10:00 p.m., when most of the city rolled up its sidewalks, and could last until 6:00 a.m. Monday was an open evening. For a while there was an acting teacher who gave lessons; occasionally there might be fencing lessons. Thursday was the literary evening, Friday was folk music, Saturday jazz. The Embassy also featured social and satirical revues and comedy improvs. Its strength was that it would do anything. The North American premiere of Jean Genet's *The Maids* was produced at The Embassy and the first plays of David French and David Freeman opened there.

Soon most of the counter-cultural set found their way to the club. Sylvia Fricker (Tyson) sang her first paid performance there. Sharon and Bram from Sharon, Lois, and Bram, Denny Doherty from the Mamas and the Papas, Zal Yanovsky from The Lovin' Spoonful, and Bob Dylan played there. And a young black comic up from the U.S. called Bill

Cosby treated the place like home. Those who dropped into town, from Leonard Cohen to Harry Belafonte, wound up at The Embassy.

John Robert Colombo, a student at the University of Toronto and only beginning his protean literary career as a pack-rat of Canadian culture and history, was responsible for the Thursday-night poetry readings. Everyone came, but in those days English Canadian poetry was still so young that only a few reputations were already set. Modern poetry was something that happened in the cultural capital of Montreal, not Toronto, starting with the McGill University poets of the twenties and erupting in the internecine wars between the formalist and the socialist poets in the forties. But many of the books that would become Canadian classics had just been published, and most of the poets had had to reach their forties before they could make the leap from mimeographed books and small presses to the bigger publishing houses.

Irving Layton, who would drop into The Embassy when he came down from Montreal, was considered the pre-eminent figure. His career had begun to take off in 1953, but he'd reached national stature with the publication of his Governor General's Award–winning *A Red Carpet for the Sun* in 1959. Margaret Avison, then forty-two, had just issued *Winter Sun* in 1960, and won the GGA. Jay Macpherson had published *The Boatman* in 1957, at the young age of twenty-nine, and also won the GGA. Phyllis Webb, who would initiate the CBC programme "Ideas" in 1966, was a new figure on the scene. But everyone had read Leonard Cohen's *Let Us Compare Mythologies*, published in 1956, aware that he had broken the pattern and rocketed to fame at the green age of twenty-two. Among the younger unpublished poets in their early twenties were Joe Rosenblatt, Victor Coleman, David Donnell, Dennis Lee, and Margaret Atwood. No one knew who would last. Everything seemed on the edge and about to explode.

Raymond Souster, who, while carrying on a day-time career in the securities department of the Canadian Bank of Commerce, had been publishing his delicate, understated poems and launching small poetry magazines since the 1940s, ran poetry workshops at The Embassy. One of his students, Bryan Finn, used to show up in an outfit made of drapes, with his head shaved, and liked to read his poem: "Society is a son-of-a-bitch/Society is a cock sucker/Society sucks me off."[3] Everyone would be convulsed with laughter. But they also knew The Embassy was important; it provided the first venue that made a kind of collegiality possible among creative people in Toronto in the early sixties. The scene was small and there was a sense of being together on the fringe.

Most people wrote poetry—you could count on one hand the novels published in Canada in 1960 and 1961—because poetry was cheap to publish and you could do it yourself. Just about everybody did. The Embassy published its own mimeographed magazine called *The Sheet*, edited by Larry Stone, a young lawyer with artistic leanings.

As if by radar, Gwen found her way to The Embassy. After she and Joe Blumenthal had drifted apart in mid-November, she became one of the regulars. She now had a part-time job as a clerical assistant at Boys and Girls House, the children's division of the Toronto Public Library on St. George Street. Somehow she managed to slip Aunt Margaret's leash to spend late evenings at the club; perhaps she explained she was staying at Carol's, who was living close by at 159 Edna Avenue with her husband and four children. Finally, she had discovered her own world.

To Don Cullen she seemed a shy, doe-like creature who came faithfully every Thursday—and hung around. She assumed the rituals, showing up at a particular time, sitting in a particular seat, wearing a particular style of clothes. She had taken to painting her eyes with kohl, so that she often looked like a figure from an Egyptian frieze. Sometimes she looked quite wonderful and accessible. At other times, he remembered, she looked "like a cartoon of a Tasmanian devil who wanted to be left alone." As he sits across from me at Dooney's Café on Bloor Street, looking back thirty years, Cullen becomes reflective: "Gwendolyn was so vulnerable," he says. "It's only much later in life that you realize such vulnerability is a gift."

When Gwendolyn finally read, Cullen was shocked. "You get to expect a certain kind of thing from somebody. You know, this loner who scuttles in, sits there, etc.," and then she read superbly. "It cleared everybody's sinuses, and we suddenly realized she was someone to reckon with." Gwendolyn was invited into The Bohemian's family of nine to fifteen intimates who closed the place down and walked to Chinatown to eat at Henry's on Dundas Street. The poets had adopted Henry's because it played country-and-western tunes like "Red River Valley" in Chinese on the jukebox. Cullen remembered that "if someone got a bee in his or her bonnet about something," discussions could last well into the dawn.

When Gwen marched into The Embassy, she found for the first time women as intelligent and ambitious as herself. Jay Macpherson and Margaret Avison were older, but there was Margaret Atwood, then twenty-one. They were isolated, two young mavericks starting out together. Atwood still remembers the initial impact Gwen had on her: "'Oh my god,' I thought, 'where did this come from? How come she's so young? And what is this unearthly being?'"[4] Years later, she would recreate Gwen at The Embassy as a character called Selina in her story "Isis in Darkness." "The story," she explains, "was written as a thinly disguised tribute":

> It was a warm, rich voice, darkly spiced, like cinnamon, and too huge to be coming from such a small person. It was a seductive voice, but not in any blunt way. What it offered was an entrée to amazement, to a shared and tingling secret, to splendours. But there was an undercurrent of amusement too, as if you were a fool for being taken in by its voluptuousness; as if there were a cosmic joke in the offing, a simple, mysterious joke, like the jokes of children.
>
> What she read was a series of short connected lyrics. "Isis in Darkness." The Egyptian Queen of Heaven and Earth was wandering in the Underworld, gathering up the pieces of the murdered and dismembered body of her lover Osiris. At the same time, it was her own body she

was putting back together; and it was also the physical universe. She was creating the universe by an act of love.

All of it was taking place, not in the ancient Middle Kingdom of the Egyptians, but in flat, dingy Toronto, on Spadina Avenue, at night, among the darkened garment factories and delicatessens and bars and pawnshops. It was a lament, and a celebration.[5]

Margaret Atwood is on her knees scrounging among boxes of Christmas decorations in her hall closet, looking through her trunks of papers for Gwen's letters. Eureka! and she pulls out seventy letters, offering me a dialogue carried on between two young women writers thirty-three years ago. "It's been hard for me to know what to do with these," she tells me, and so she's carted them, along with hundreds of other writers' letters, from one house to the next. Is it a betrayal to offer a friend's letters when they were written under a code of trust? she wonders. But she concludes that Gwendolyn no longer needs privacy. There is a point where our private stories turn into strangely impersonal narratives that simply record what it is to be human. Gwendolyn, having crafted herself into such an original, teases even her friend Margaret Atwood with the desire to know, to understand.

As she sorts Gwen's letters, Atwood tells me about the cultural moment in which their writing lives began: "You found yourself at the centre very fast in those days. The writing community was so small, beleaguered, and desirous of reinforcement, that it was welcoming to any newcomer with talent, including women."[6] If you were good, you were accorded the kind of fame a colonial outback offered. But, she explains, for a woman it was important to locate friends among other women writers because the attitude towards women was still paradoxically, if not intentionally, hypocritical. "All the propaganda had it that creativity was male."

"One expected it at the university," she tells me. She remembers her student adviser asking her why she didn't just get married instead of going to graduate school, and the chairman of English announced publicly and frequently that he would not lower his standards so much as to hire women. "But not even the artistic community offered you a viable choice as a woman," she adds. Irving Layton informed everyone that women were "genetically incapable of being writers and anyway it was an invasion of men's territory."

She believes the hardest thing for her and Gwendolyn was to find a space for female creativity in what was essentially a male world. "It was the early sixties, the years in which *Playboy* was very big among men. That women's liberation thing started with men spitting on women. If you go back and read *The Ginger Man*, it's all there; or *On the Road*. The perfect woman in *On the Road* is a woman who lets her man come and go as he pleases and smiles all the time. Now *that's* a woman! What woman could actually *be* that? Or who *wanted* to be that?"

She and Gwen shared one axiom: the vision from hell was middle-class marriage. She remembers a couple of early stories she wrote in high school that curl her hair now. In one of them, a high-school girl bumps into the mother of a school friend who had gotten knocked up and married. That was the most horrible thing that could happen to you—you could get married and end up with a washing machine in the suburbs. "So, of course, you had great contempt for all those who allowed it to happen to them and they were no friends of yours. They wanted to pull the legs off you because you did not want to stand in the corner with them and talk about nappies. You wanted to be where the action was, which was creating the word. Doing the writing."

It didn't take her long, of course, to understand that this was simply another way women were alienated from one another and from their own desire for maternity—all subjects she would deal with in her poetry and fiction as she would learn to use her satirical scalpel to scrape away at the myths invented for women. Even though she would have to wait until her late thirties, she was eventually able to find the support system that made maternity possible. But Gwen, she remarks, would never find a life practical enough that it could include children.

For now, the question she and Gwendolyn puzzled over was: What was creativity for a woman? That long, exhausting dialogue of the sixties: Why weren't there great women painters? Why weren't there great women writers? Was creativity different for a man and a woman? Could women create? had only just begun.

"Creativity in those days was seen as ejaculatory," she tells me, laughing. "It goes with action painting. Jackson Pollock—what is that stuff on the canvas? *We* know! It was supposed to be a kind of spasm, instant painting, a kind of spasm of creation. And the poets adopted that as what a poem should be. It was essentially wanking off, whereas earlier poets, such as John Milton, were giving surrogate birth. 'O Muse, descend, impregnate me. I will bear this book within me; then I'll give birth to it.' The earlier metaphor was very much an appropriation of female birth giving, and they then used that as the reason women couldn't write: because they could have the real thing. Whereas in the fifties ejaculatory school, women couldn't write because they couldn't jerk off and cause dribbles on the page." We laugh hilariously, but Atwood adds: "It's true."

All this may seem esoteric, if not simply mad, but it had its impact. Firstly in how you thought of yourself as a woman poet, and secondly in the relationships male poets offered you. The confusions involved not just one's work but also the sexual self. Like many young women of intelligence in those days, Gwen had internalized the paradoxical male contempt for the female.

Beautiful women were trivial and they destroyed men. She was afraid to be seen as a seductress. In an earlier story she had written of a female poet afraid to "place herself in a position to prove attractive to the male, because in so doing, she is duplicating the spider-like, 'black widow' type of female who destroys men." It was inhibiting. What was one to do with one's sexuality? The dynamic worked so unfairly—it was the men who were vulnerable. Women, who were accorded so little power, had the power to destroy men through their sexuality. The male poet said he longed for a so-called free woman, but when he encountered her, the reality was threatening. How difficult it was to be female in those days.

Meanwhile Margaret and Gwendolyn pursued their interest in mythology. It was a topic of endless discussion at The Embassy, having filtered down from Robert Graves and from Northrop Frye's lectures at the University of Toronto; everyone had read Leonard Cohen's *Let Us Compare Mythologies* and Jay Macpherson's *The Boatman*.

Atwood explains that the BIG TEXT on the subject in those years was Graves's *The White Goddess*, a brilliant book that at first seemed to offer something new for women poets like herself and Gwendolyn. Graves insisted that the language of poetic myth came from the ancient Moon Goddess, and had been distorted by patriarchal culture. But even here it was obvious that this was an eccentric elaboration of an old misogyny. Graves writes:

> The Goddess is a lovely, slender woman with a hooked nose, deathly pale face, lips as red as rowan-berries, startlingly blue eyes and long fair hair; she will suddenly transform herself into sow, mare, bitch, vixen, she-ass, weasel, serpent, owl, she-wolf, tigress, mermaid or loathsome hag. Her names and titles are innumerable.... The test of a poet's vision, one might say, is the accuracy of his portrayal of the White Goddess and the island over which she rules. The reason why the hairs stand on end, the eyes water, the throat is constricted, the skin crawls and a shiver runs down the spine when one writes or reads a true poem is that a true poem is necessarily an invocation of the White Goddess, or Muse, or Mother of All Living, the ancient power of fright and lust—the female spider or the queen-bee whose embrace is death.[7]

As Atwood says to me wryly: "Ah, yes, the Moon Goddess: Man does/woman is." Poets were still, by definition, male. She explains: "Not only did a woman poet have to be a goddess, she had to be a man-destroying goddess. Because what the White Goddess did was to bite off your head. Every spring and fall, I forget when—this head biting took place twice a year. Do away with one and you have another."

By 1960 Atwood had begun work on a sequence called *Double Persephone*, reconstructing the ancient myth. When she sent the poems to Gwen, Gwen wrote back excitedly:

> With the onslaught of Persephone, both of them, I at last struck that very subtle and rather vicious vein of authenticity under the sometimes innocent skeleton caging it ... like it very much is what I mean—partly because I like to strip away rose petals and find insects underneath—not insects for their own sake, but put there to emphasize the flower by their contrast to it. Forget the metaphors, but I did see in 'persephone' a kind of half-sister to Marie-Claire Blais (if you've read her in trans. or otherwise) who also sees the other, less pleasant, side of the mirror. This must be essential ... possibly the female poet has to emphasize the anti-primrose and candyfloss business more than the male ... hair ribbons and all that—can be hampering, I think. To achieve that clean-cut, uncompromising slant on things is an achievement. (what a sentence that was) ... —Gwen[8]

There was a lot of humour in the friendship between these two young women poets. Gwendolyn loved the intersection of the banal and the numinous. She could come up with the idea that the universe was shaped like a doughnut and then she would name the brand.[9] But they were also deeply involved in an important dialogue: sorting out the nature of the muse for the female writer. The muse is a metaphor for the flash of connection, that conduit to the other world that Gwen was so preoccupied with. She would say, quoting Nietzsche: "All our so-called consciousness is a more or less fantastic commentary upon an unknown text, one that is perhaps unknowable, but still felt."[10] Her assumption was that the muse, the one who inspired her poetry, which came from that unknowable place, was male, and that is difficult. Atwood explains:

> I myself always thought the muse was female, but Gwen's way of handling it was to say, okay, my inspiration is this and I have this sort of male person who is a muse, not to be confused very much with real people, or at least not for a very long time. Because her lovers/muse did come and go. But what she got from them was inspiration. In other words it was a mirror reversal. If the muse is a woman for the woman poet, unless the poet is a lesbian, the sexual connection gets removed, and it's more like a second self, a twin, a mother, or a wise old woman. It can be any of these things. I did a survey of people and their muses, which was very revealing, and most muses, for both men and women, are women. So it turns out. Probably if you want to be psychological, it is the voice, and the voice is the mother's voice. That's how we learn to speak, usually from our mothers.[11]

I keep thinking that for Gwendolyn it was the father's voice she heard; the mother's was too deeply suspect. Because her muse was male, there was always the potential to confuse the muse in her head with persons in the real world. Men would be complicated figures onto which to project one's muse. They wouldn't suffer the projection gladly. They would be willing to be mentor, as long as Gwendolyn was the supplicant; few would allow her to be equal, or indeed better. Gwen would find herself caught in the gendered territory of sexual politics. One of the first "muses" Gwendolyn encountered was the Maritime poet Milton Acorn.

Almost as soon as The Bohemian Embassy opened, Milton Acorn marched in and took it over, as if it had been created especially for him.

Acorn was bizarre even for the early sixties. He was, as one would have said then, completely off the wall. Born in Prince Edward Island, he claimed to have been a carpenter until the day he pawned his tools in Montreal and declared he would live by poetry. "I got my political education in the streets of Charlottetown," he would say. "The middle class terrorized me as a kid and as an adult I've done my best to terrorize them. I like to stand in for the devil on his day off." "There are men on earth who usually tell the truth," he'd add. "I know. I'm one of them."[12] Acorn's trademark was the smelly Cuban cigar screwed into the corner of his mouth, a lumberjack shirt, and running shoes well aerated by holes. But he had a fine talent and nothing mattered as much as poetry.

Acorn was born into a United Empire Loyalist family of farmers, and the family tradition of conservative stock—his father was a federal civil servant with Customs and Excise—hadn't prepared them for the arrival of a poet. Acorn preferred to trace his ancestry back through his sea-captain grandfather and claimed he had Native Indian roots, though the rest of the family considered this addition Milton's own private mythology. When he would talk about his Indian ancestor, his mother would say: "Oh, Milton, you're not doing that again."

Acorn had been a sickly child until the age of fourteen, doted on by his mother. Wanting to be a man and with a romantic idea of war, he dropped out of school at sixteen, lied about his age, and enlisted. On the trip across the Atlantic, his ship came under torpedo attack, and though it wasn't hit, Milton claimed he was injured, his hearing and equilibrium permanently damaged. He spent the rest of the trip in sick bay and then eight months in hospital in England before being shipped home to spend his war in Canada. In 1943, he was awarded a disability pension by Veterans Affairs, which he turned down, but in the midfifties after he suffered his first mental breakdown in Montreal, his mother had come to visit and said: "Let's get you that pension." His family always traced his periodic breakdowns back to that war accident. Like many whose sons returned traumatized by the war's violence, they said Milton suffered from a case of nerves.[13]

After the war Milton supported himself with a variety of jobs, including as a civil servant and then as a warehouse stock-keeper in Moncton. He did actually work intermittently as a carpenter with his uncle, though when he could, he preferred to stay home and write poetry.

In the mid-fifties, Acorn moved to Montreal, where he began to achieve a small reputation as a poet. Unlike Toronto, Montreal was a mecca for poets in the fifties, where literary battles were waged in the small presses and magazines and self-proclaimed geniuses spawned like fish. Acorn, as a declared Trotskyite, had "liberated" a mimeograph machine from the offices of the Communist Party, and he and his friend the poet Al Purdy had turned out a little magazine called *Moment* on the floor of Purdy's Maplewood Avenue apartment. With a writer called Joe Sage, Milton founded the first English coffee-house in Montreal, called The Place. Soon he sold his tools in a dramatic gesture in 1956, although Purdy tried to convince him to wait until he'd made some money from writing.

When he moved to Toronto, Acorn became a fixture at The Embassy. At first glance, he seemed like a caricature: the workingman's poet, the butt of the stogie always between his red-necked fingers. His face was a craggy rock, made asymmetrical by a nervous tic, and seemingly anchored only by heavy ridged eyebrows. It was said that he had suffered Bell's paralysis, which had left him with little control over the muscles on one side of his face.

Acorn was a maverick who drank hard and played hard, but it was also evident that he was driven, and exuded energy and commitment. His insistence that one must stand up and speak, in loud and vulgar noises, was exciting. Despite the bravura persona of the primal man, antediluvian and durable, he could quote from memory what seemed to be the collected poems of Shelley and Yeats, and would argue, with an almost academic bent, theories on Marxist politics and Russian steel-production figures, Peking man, and the Bible as mythic literature. An evening with Acorn deep in drink could be hilarious. Friends could remember watching Milton dance a competent jig to a Bach partita at an Embassy party. He cultivated the edge, and could write a poem to Al Purdy, who had been talking into his beer of suicide, saying that with Al dead, it would be exciting to write his obituary, though living he was a problem, but say it with such affection that he could carry it off.[14]

Many saw Milton as a man who lacked a protective coating on his nerves. His friend the actor Cedric Smith said, "He was the kind of man capable of really weeping and grieving over the death of Louis Riel or Inuit women forcibly sterilized in the North."[15] But there was also an aggressive side to Milton. He was astonishingly intolerant. An Embassy friend, Tom Arnott, remarked: "Milt wouldn't accept an idea from anyone without kicking the hell out of it first."[16] This surfaced particularly in his radical left politics. Only he, Milton, spoke for the working people. Everyone else was "lice and vermin." Don Cullen would say: "I adored the guy, but there was an obsessive-compulsive side to Milton that was really hard to take." Even Al Purdy found Milton intolerant in his ideas. "It was hell on a friendship. You could not disagree with Milt; there was a part of him that loved to tear strips off other people."[17] Years later he complained to Gwen: "Acorn is the only person I could ever say what I liked with, I think. And his goddamn sheer thoughtlessness in someone who is undoubtedly genuinely concerned with what he says and does ... sometimes just staggers me with irritation."[18]

Mostly, it is men who remember Milton with fondness. Margaret Atwood, while respectful of the talent, is more ambivalent about the man's aggressive arrogance: "He was from the kind of red-blooded truck driver school. 'If you want to be a poet, you can't go to college. You have to be a truck driver.' And I would think, 'What gender does he think he's talking to?' And the message seemed, *you* can't be a poet, which is what it probably was. Well, I'd been a waitress. 'Will a waitress do?' I used to think. There was quite a lot of inverse snobbery going on."[19]

In 1960, when Gwen met him, Acorn would have been thirty-eight. He had published a self-financed chapbook in 1956 called *In*

Love and Anger and a second book, *The Brain's the Target*, would appear in 1960. His real fame wouldn't come until *I've Tasted My Blood* in 1969, but there was no question of Milton's brilliance as a poet. In Toronto, claiming he was the only "unassailable" poet around, he stepped into his role as the prophet of Canadian socialism and the saviour of poetry.

When Milton saw Gwendolyn, he must have been overwhelmed. She was beautiful—small, delicate, and yet there were those kohl-limned sapphire eyes and the dangling cigarette, so that her exotic performance had an element of self-amusement. She also had the richest poetic temperament, erudite and sensual. She was vulnerable, and desperate to learn. And she was so defensive that perhaps only Milton would have had the arrogance to shatter her shell. The Embassy had opened in June. By December, Milton proposed marriage. His letter has not survived, though it seems clear he spoke of needing her to complete his life. But Gwendolyn's response exists. Its tenderness and honesty are moving. At nineteen, she had a clear perception of herself:

> Dec. 28/60
>
> Dear Milt -
> Probably the most beautiful and honest thing that I've ever received was your little letter. I can't match it
>
> Sincerity like this staggers me; I've seen too little and too much of it one way and another; I've valued it so highly that when someone hands it to me as directly as you have, I'm not quite sure whether I should jump for joy or burst into tears. (In a way I'm much more a child than you'd like to believe)
>
> I'm going to say many things here—not to be long-winded, not to give the impression of point where there isn't any—But because I want to tell you things somehow. I think if I could paint one long *me* through all the

different tones and shades and intensities it'd truly be an achievement ...

Milt, don't ever write a novel—or two—or three ... after a while you become unable to condense thoughts, feelings. I'm so over-conscious of words now that I can't (as you so beautifully can) imply and mean so very much in so very little.

Sincerity. This is what my dear father named the Number One Virtue in life. (Why couldn't you be just a little insincere and make it easy for me?) But then I think that's what drew me to you really—one enormous plus sign—

And insincerity to oneself—probably the most deadly thing that can happen to a person—I've seen that in action too ... and its outcome.

So much for the background of those words—all I've done (and not too well I'm afraid) is given you a glimpse of the reason honesty has such an impact on me

Love. Again I've had too little and too much of it. Probably too much (if that is possible). So much, in fact, that I'm convinced I'll eventually be swallowed up in it, completely. Horrible fact!

I believe everything I do, think, or feel is touched off by love. And I have such a capacity for it I don't know how to focus it in any one direction. I might go out tomorrow morning and kiss a dozen butterflies! (This is not a piece of imagery from a poem—this is a fact)

A love for people. (I'm still young enough not to have this facet of love shattered. If it will be then I'm determined not to grow any older. Not the least little bit.)

This idea, Milt, is what I call my blissful ignorance, and will remain so until life forces me to alter it—if ever.

Although I believe in some ways that what I've experienced thus far—would make some people absolute cynics, or failing that, prompt them to take a long neat dive from a tall bridge.

No, no—I'm not bemoaning it all. Somewhere along the line I developed one terrific resistance—which I'm grateful for. But what is more important I retained a whole big chunk of that initial love, trust, and joy of life that we are born with. And along with it, an immense and overwhelming delight and sensitivity in, yes—almost anything. This has made me something of a poet (am I permitted to be so presumptuous?)

I didn't mean to ramble on so, really I didn't. So much for SONG OF MYSELF.

Of course I love you! But I am neither capable nor ready for the kind of love you offer me. I don't even have a half-decent letter to give you, let alone myself!

Milt, my love is not the same as yours ... you're a mature man, and I'm (and I'll defend this to my dying day) still in a sense a little girl poking my head out the window at the world. Existence? I'm still establishing it to myself. At this point I need no proof for it—I feel no need to *find* myself physically, sensually, emotionally in another person—I'm still laying the foundations! I'm still getting acquainted with life, with myself ...

I don't want that song of myself to end, to be completed; to me there is no expectancy, no conception of fulfilment. There is today and tomorrow and tomorrow and tomorrow and me listening to you and you listening to me (though I don't say much) and gaining what I can from you (you've taught me so much already, you know) and feeling myself wonderfully diminished with you (because sometimes I get O so big)

But beyond this rather endless list—nothing more. Your "completeness" can't find a place in all this for me, I know it ... as I see our relationship, this is not a natural outcome at all. I feel this way, Milt—because as I said before—your feelings are those of a mature man, while mine ... well you know the rest.

Because you fit another sort of niche in my life altogether, one which I know and understand—one of the few things I do understand—you'll never quite realize just what you've *already* given me

Completion, fulfilment in themselves—I'm aware of the need for it as I possibly can be at this stage. When I eventually find this particular need in myself, however, I'll try not to worry.

Milt—I can't possibly give you back a fraction of what you've given me—I mean this. So when you're suddenly loaded down with droves of little fluffy animals and things, please take pity on me, because it's the best I can do—

I want, I wish so much for you—because your life, your happiness, your desires truly matter to me. I want to see a hundred more little miltons going out and damning us with their honesty

but most of all I want you just now to understand what I've said, what I've tried to say in this insane little letter (when I read it over I'm tempted to throw my career in writing out the window entirely and become a missionary instead)

because my father's "Number One Virtue" is the most difficult thing for me to use—only because I value it so highly. Each word, each phrase must be just as I mean it, or it won't do at all ...

But believe it or not, I can't remember when I've been able to open up like this for anyone. It's confused,

it's contrary, yes, but it's also me. Please accept it; please
don't be hurt or angry—I wouldn't have been able to tell
you even this much if your feelings hadn't meant enough
to me to warrant my giving you the best, the most truth-
ful answer to what you've asked that I am capable of
   Gwen[20]

Gwendolyn was exquisitely feminine and that came with a gutsi-
ness—she was going to take the world on, with no special pleading. She
might believe she was a misfit, a foreigner, an orphan, but it would still
be her terms for her life. She knew, instinctively, that she did not want
to be moulded by another, and Milton was nineteen years older. He was
dictatorial and detested having anyone disagree with him. She did not
want to play Galatea to his Pygmalion. Yet, I think, how self-apologetic
women have to be in their tenderness. The friendship continued.

8
MR. & MRS. ACORN

In the spring of 1961, Gwendolyn's professional career began; she was nineteen. She had been submitting poems with little success to Milton Wilson at *The Canadian Forum*, to Robert Weaver at *The Tamarack Review*, and to Raymond Souster at Contact Press. Their replies were always generous, but Souster warned her that she could expect little from "this business of being a serious poet ... [it is] a heart-breaking and lonely affair."[1] Gwen was undaunted. Calling herself Aleph Press (after the first letter of the Hebrew alphabet), she brought out a little pamphlet, *Selah*, printed in a run of one hundred copies on the Gestetner at the Boys and Girls House library.[2] Then Aleph Press issued a printed monograph called *The Drunken Clock*, which contained twelve poems and sold for fifty cents. Most poets began this way. Such self-publications were even accorded review space in journals like *The University of Toronto Quarterly*, so small was the total number of Canadian books published each year. In fact, *The Drunken Clock* received eight reviews by writers as diverse as Frank Davey and Eli Mandel. Perhaps the person most delighted with Gwen's foray into publishing was Elsie. She wrote to her doctor at the Queen Street Mental Health Centre: "As you see Wendy (my daughter) had this book published at her own expense. She has made the cost plus profit.... I am proud of her."[3]

The Drunken Clock was broadcast on CFMO radio, Ottawa, and Gwen was invited to read at a little coffee-house called Le Hibou, with an offer of travel expenses and fifty dollars. She invited Elsie to accompany her. Elsie must have fancied that she was now participating in the literary set, for she sent a card to Milton Acorn: "I tried to get a funny? card for you with a hammer!!! No could do. We (Wendy (Gwen)) have received a warm welcome in Ottawa. Cheerio."[4] The hammer, had she found it, would presumably have been a gesture to Milton's politics. Instead she chose an illustration of a bird singing in a cage with a door ajar. Most telling in her note were the double brackets. She still had trouble knowing what to call Gwendolyn.

In an article she wrote for a mimeographed magazine called *Tean dadóir*, Gwendolyn attempted to explain her motivations for poetry:

> My poetry is largely founded on archaic subjects or suggestions from such; or—and this is more correct—has such a thick vein of *time* flowing through it that it appears I'm trying to navigate in a fourth dimension. This is true....
>
> Yesterday (or today, or tomorrow as the case may be) a small boy stands on the corner of a street, gathers energy, and gives one great leap into the air for no reason at all. He comes down, of course, but that doesn't concern us yet. The duration of the jump might be equivalent to the time taken in the swift inhalation of a breath. The poem is caught in that space of time between his feet leaving the ground and regaining it. The essence of the poetry lies in the unaccountable, the almost ritualistic motivation of the jump.[5]

All her efforts went into creating the poem as an experience, a kind of bardic chant that would ring the senses awake, reaching behind the mind to another kind of thinking. To read Gwen's poems one has to let oneself *be* in her imaginary landscape; in a garden, for instance:

Certain Flowers

some unthinking god
threw me cold violets last morning
when the rain was a prince in the garden

said: here, define a certain fear in flowers,
chalk out quickly the peril of beauty,

said softly this, as I worried private light
among the blooms
and stretched a half-winged bird of verse
to band the prince, the bloodless blossoms.

some unthinking god
is made of towering flowers; his eye
in the tall blue tulip sky
a profound petal there; I arrest its blooming.

! I want the flowers beheaded,
the garden sink,
the rain deny its claim to princedom there

> and stand in a garden of void
> applauding, tracing the biographies
> of brief past flowers, capturing the moment of bloom
> in a cage of my own sunlight[6]

 The poem is exquisite, but elusive and mysterious. Who is the unthinking god who sets her the task to define a certain "fear in flowers"? I try to think of Gwen standing in a real garden in the rain, where the beauty is so powerful that it is threatening and she fears she might lose herself. She wants the flowers beheaded, the world narrowed to the cage of sunlight she has created with her poem, even as she recognizes that she will then stand in a "garden of void." How extraordinary to be able to write like this at nineteen.

Only Gwen knew the vulnerability, the void, that lay within. The persona she crafted for herself was one of enormous poetic assurance. To those on the outside she appeared self-confident, controlled, and resilient. That spring she began to date one of the young poets who hung out at The Embassy, David Donnell, but the relationship lasted only three months before he ended it; they would always remain friends. In early summer she joined Milton in the Laurentian Mountains outside Montreal, where he had been offered a small cabin on the property of his friends, the Goldbergs, and they became lovers. There she helped him edit his mimeographed magazine *Moment*.

 Milton seems to have begun a poetry tour, probably to promote his new book, *The Brain's the Target*, and Gwen returned alone to Toronto. In July, she was invited back to Montreal to read from her chapbooks. She was flying, just as she had always imagined she would. She wrote to Milton:

> Hello Dear—Magnificent reading all round—best reception ever—sold 50 books!! Am being treated like a national celebrity by these people—am stunned by their

enthusiasm and interest—after 50 minutes of reading you could hear a pin drop ... Whoopee! Maybe I'm God. —Love you. Gwen.[7]

When she returned alone to Toronto after her reading, she wrote again to recount a disturbing incident:

> July, 61
>
> Dearest Milt—
> You know the tall skyscraper on Stanley Street or thereabouts? When I went for the train, there was the strangest rumble and tremulous metallic sound—ridiculous—I swore to high heaven the thing was about to fall down! I believed it! I ran like hell, baggage and all into the station, thought it was the Last Day for me. Never realized what a terrific impression such a thing could make—never believed anything so firmly as I believed the building was collapsing.
> Rubbish. I'm back in Toronto, of course and missing you—have moved into somewhat cramped quarters with my sister and family and trying to re-orientate myself....
> Have an enormous amount of work mapped out for next few months. My nephew stands by the typewriter and tries to read this letter—impossible.
> Do write soon. There are no elephants here, none at all—miss you.
> Gwen.[8]

The sight of Gwendolyn with all her baggage, fleeing into the station to escape the falling skyscraper, is almost comic were it not so real. Gwendolyn was full of physical fears. It was the one area where all the tension of her psychic life found exit. She would always be prone to physical terrors. Milton, who characterized himself as a lumbering elephant, must have felt like a source of strength against those fears. She missed her elephant.

That winter of 1961, Milton returned to Prince Edward Island, as he did every winter, and wrote Gwen about his trip. He was like a character in a comedy—disaster always courted him. He recounted stepping off the train in Cornwall to buy smokes, and then the train went off without him. He had to wire to secure his luggage, and continued on by bus, arriving in Montreal at the Goldbergs' house at 4 a.m. While in Montreal, he decided to track down his story "The Winged Dingus" and discovered that *Exchange*, to which he had submitted it, had folded and didn't have the money for stamps to return it. Irving Layton had somehow lost his other story, "Red and Green Pony."

Milton always returned to P.E.I. like an exile, having ceased to believe in it while he was away. He described it to Gwen: "Dear Gwen ... After the desolation of new brunswick [sic] with its barnless farms, machinery rusting in the open, tar-paper shacks where people lived, I spent as much time as the cold would allow me on the back platform of the car, reeling thru Christmas post-card countryside.... and the train hooted and rattled on an incredible up and down round and about track, sweeping around curve after curve.... The pevular [sic] pastoral beauty of the Island is indescribable. It's not like a part of Canada at all, but a sort of fairyland." The prodigal return made him reflective:

> As for me there is a vein of ice running thru me somewhere. I understand what it is makes human beings tick and wish I could be like them, but a malignant ego, combined with a continued rage against injustice, eats up all my emotions. Somewhere back I learned to accept love when it offers, and it always offers ... even to fight for it when the offer is hesitant and bound with doubts and conditions. I thought this was a great discovery, but now I wonder if there isn't something more ... something I've lacked.
> Thinking of you   Milton[9]

Alone in Toronto with Milton gone, Gwendolyn suddenly felt anchorless. She may have panicked, believing she might never see him again. Her childhood had taught her that the ones she loved disappeared. She knew what it was to be loved *and* abandoned. When Milton returned, she was ready to marry him.

They were married at city hall on February 8, 1962, with only her mother and Al Purdy, as best man, in attendance. But there was a reception at Carol's with all Gwen's family: Elsie, Carol's children, Aunt Margaret, Aunt Maud, and her son Lawrence. Everyone remembered that the married couple looked like two waifs: Milton in his lumberjack shirt, blue blazer, and army boots, with the inevitable stogie ("he was foul smelling," said Lawrence, "and had bad breath") and the delicate Gwendolyn in black on his arm. "Here we are, Mr. & Mrs. Acorn," she said. "Just a couple of nuts." The occasion was remembered as memorable because it was the first time Elsie and Margaret both smoked cigars in public.[10]

Everyone was disturbed by the wedding. To Carol it signalled Gwen's father-complex. Purdy was cynical about the May/December love affair. He thought Gwen was with Milton because Milton was "getting attention." Margaret Avison thought pathos hung round it—"He needed love and security; she needed a nest—he was a big papa, a big cushiony papa. He needed, she needed, and their needs dovetailed for a little and that was all."[11] Gwen's friend the pianist Aasta Levene saw it as a mother-complex: she was getting back to the mother: "If your mother has been in institutions since your childhood, you yourself are not whole and you will look for someone never completely whole."[12] When Margaret Atwood, away at graduate school at Radcliffe, heard of the marriage, she was shocked. It was the archetypal story of Beauty and the Beast. (One wonders, had she been in Toronto, could she have succeeded in dissuading Gwen from what seems a precipitous act?) Perhaps only Elsie was pleased. She thought of Milton as a famous poet.

The marriage was a puzzle, one that would haunt Gwen throughout her life, but there is one clue I have come across in a rather odd way. Gwendolyn had so little money that she had developed the habit of recycling paper. She would type her poems on the backs of pages she had already used for other writing. On the reverse sides of a manuscript she was trying to put together in 1962 are the intermittent pages of a novel she had obviously played with but then abandoned.

It was to be about a young woman poet, Angela, and her husband, Eric, also a poet. Novels are not autobiography, yet often Gwendolyn's only way of keeping any control over her world was to write about it—otherwise she would be overwhelmed. In this abandoned novel she seems to be speaking about herself. She writes of Angela: "Not even Eric could pin her to the earth for long. Earth staggered Angela—better to try and rhyme the riddle of heaven than battle the strange sensual firmament." "Angela: Was there anything in your little empire like a hand on a forearm, like a someone who spoke?"[13] Perhaps Gwen's attachment to Milton was humanly simple. He was one of the few people who could touch her in her profound isolation—an arm, a voice. She had selected Milton, almost a parody of physical excess, to pin her to the earth.

Gwendolyn and Milton lived briefly in an apartment on Hazelton Avenue, but soon found a house on Ward's Island in Toronto Harbour. In the early sixties, the houses on the island were mostly summer homes, cheap and insubstantial clapboard, sided in insulbrick. Little money was spent on renovations since it was assumed the city would one day expropriate the properties for a public park. The island was reached by ferry; cars had to be left on the mainland. Narrow unpaved streets like bicycle paths meandered through the cottages past the woodpiles and patchy gardens. The island was a place for cultural refugees, many of them artists who came because it was cheap—the rent was usually fifty dollars a month. Islanders could look back across the water at the city skyline and feel they had stepped out of civilization into some kind of sylvan wilderness. But the price was that in winter, with the fierce winds sweeping in off the lake, one froze to death. The bedroom walls would be covered with ice and space had to be made for the mice driven in by the cold. People built their log fires up to dangerous levels and houses were often lost that way.

Gwen and Milton's house, number 10 on 2nd Street, was a one-storey four-room cottage. It had only the requisite furniture: a bed covered in Indian cotton that also served as a couch, a tiny sink, and stove. There was an old oak table with a tablecloth and candelabra on it, and on the wall above, giving the table the feeling of an altar, a large Kurelek-style painting depicting an albatross crucified on a large cross. Tiny people strolled past the apparition without seeming to notice it.

Those who visited the house remembered it as dingy and dirty. Beauty and order meant nothing to Milton in his living arrangements. Beauty was outside in nature. Gwendolyn, who loved order and neatness, must have found this extremely difficult. They would have had little money to live on. Milton could not have managed to make more than one thousand dollars a year on his poetry and Gwendolyn would have brought in much less.

Al Purdy remembers visiting Milton and Gwen on the island. He felt, then, the enormous contrast between them—he self-confident because he had begun to get public attention and because he had a girl as wonderful as Gwen, and she shy and rather, as Purdy perceived it, in awe of Milton.

Milton loved the island. In the heart of the megalopolis, it reminded him of his Prince Edward Island home. On one visit Purdy remembered him explaining how wonderful it was to be out in the GREEN, to be able to swim in the lake. It was early spring and the ice had barely thawed from the shoreline, but Milton decided he was going swimming. Acorn in bathing trunks was, Purdy said, a sight. He was "homely as a board, as a red fire hydrant—he had little bits of extra flesh like warts growing on his back."[14] He sat in a little hole in the ice, Gwen and Purdy circling him, encouraging him. As he turned blue, Purdy asked: "How long are you going to stay in there?" He looked up at them and, in a tortured voice, shouted: "Go away!" "I'll never forget—that man in a hole in the ice—that was Milton shouting *Go Away*." Purdy adds to the anecdote: "In later days, Milt took a bath once a year. Literally. You could smell him around two blocks. Quasimodo? Yes, I could imagine him climbing Notre Dame. Isn't that unkind? He was a very fine poet. Unlike anybody else. Gwen once said she tried bathing Milt. But when he got out of her mile-high soap suds he smelled exactly the same."

Almost as soon as she had married, Gwendolyn recognized that she had made a terrible mistake. The problems were multiple. Poignantly, she hadn't anticipated that Milton really wanted a wife. His revolutionary bent was actually deeply conservative and family values were important. He regretted not having a normal family life (as a young man he had fathered an illegitimate son who was given up for adoption) and Gwen seemed to be the closest he had ever come to that possibility. He thought they would be husband and wife and there would be supper on the table every night. In Gwen, fiercely independent, he got more than he'd bargained for. She certainly didn't know how to cook.

They had made a contract on marriage that each would be allowed other lovers, a rather unusual contract for the early sixties. Milton had a peculiar vanity: he thought he was very attractive to women. Purdy could remember walking on a beach in Vancouver and Milton turning to him as they passed a group of girls: "Look at them look at me. They think I'm fascinating." Purdy was amused, but he adds, with an odd myopia, "Women are attracted to geniuses. What else is there to attract them?" Milton had had a great deal of sexual experience, but Gwen was almost certainly a virgin. In the manner of the early sixties, before the contraceptive pill, Gwen had never "gone the whole way" in her previous relationships. And she was sexually insecure. Purdy remembers her having a phobia about being flat-chested and being embarrassed when, walking down Bloor Street, he and Milt had been amusing themselves, quite deliberately "talking dirty" in her presence.

The grapevine at The Embassy had it that the first occasion of infidelity arose with Milton. But despite their contract—indeed the contract might have been Gwen's idea—the thought of other lovers for Gwen, of course, sent Milton into a rage. Milton's possessiveness was extreme and Milton, jealous, would not have been pleasant.

There were political differences as well. Milton could excommunicate anyone for what he considered a political heresy, and he spoke as the final authority, the People's Poet. Gwendolyn did not trust ideological dogmatism. She believed that the notion of speaking for the common man was sentimentality and condescension. Who after all was defining the common man? When she had attended a poetry reading by Al Purdy in which a political audience seemed to have been questioning the purity of Purdy's socialist credentials, she was disgusted and wrote to him: "When you say you are a socialist, do you mean you are concerned with problems of immediate social significance? Of course, but these problems cannot be isolated from the psychological concerns of the individual psyche. You as a poet realize the terrible interdependencies of the external and the internal world, the moving dialectics of these." "Of course it is desirable to love one's fellow man," she continued. "But who is he? These people ask of you a love which is *unbased*, they ask an automatic, groundless love, a love not born out of respect for individual achievement, a love which must exist only because it is one's obligation.... I am not obligated to love my fellow man because he is theoretically deserving of it."[15] To Milton this would have been the deepest heresy. Yet so often his theoretical love *was* ego driven, a need to assert control. Like many revolutionary temperaments in the 1960s, Milton believed the revolution was out there, to be waged against the bourgeoisie; the test of his capacity to accord freedom to others had nothing to do with the woman he lived with.

The final problem was, of course, that the relationship was totally imbalanced. Most who remembered Milton and Gwendolyn always thought the logic of the marriage rested on her father-complex. Did Gwendolyn, in marrying Milton, have a father-complex? The answer is probably yes, if it is understood in a complex way. I would venture that she was not attaching herself parasitically to Milton's strength, but rather, paradoxically, to his weakness. The father-complex rested on his willingness to make claims on her that she found impossible to refuse. Milton *loved* her very much (if that's what is meant by love). He was alcoholic and needy. One pictures Milton in that hole in the ice, or as a man walking city streets wanting to talk, desperate to unburden himself if only in the obsessively disguised language of others' needs. Acorn was another orphan lumbering through his own deserts. It must have been hard to be loved by someone wanting so badly to be loved. And certainly, for Gwendolyn, impossible to turn away except as a last resort, to save herself. Gwendolyn made her first break when she decided that, alone, she would visit the country that had so long occupied her imagination, Israel. Somehow she had managed to save enough money for the trip.

Before she left in mid-July, however, The Bohemian Embassy erupted in one of its most famous controversies. Milton was always looking for a way to bring poetry into the streets, into the lives of real people. Tired of reading to the select group at The Embassy, he felt it was time to take poetry into the parks. Allan Gardens at Sherbourne and Carlton streets was selected for the first Sunday-afternoon reading. When the reading started under the statue of Robert Burns, however, the police arrived and ordered the poets to disband. They were in contravention of a city by-law that prohibited reading poetry without a public-speaking licence. Toronto in the early sixties had a baroque arrangement for its parks: of the city's 146 parks, you could hold a public meeting in only 3; however, 22 had been set aside for religious gatherings. In Allan Gardens you could preach a sermon but not read a poem.

The poets refused to disband and their names were recorded in little black books. By Tuesday a group of eight poets, spearheaded by Milton with Gwendolyn in attendance, met in the dingy warehouse behind The Embassy, where Don Cullen lived with several other writers, and created a group called Interpoet, committed to civil disobedience.

The next Sunday, under Burns's statue, Milton opened his Bible and began by reading the Song of Songs—the by-law after all allowed religious speakers—but then he read his poem "I Shout Love" and, turning to the police, shouted: "Listen, you money-plated bastards, when I shout love I mean your destruction."[16] The poets earned a cartoon in *The Toronto Star*—carted off by Gestapo-like police, one poet clutching a manuscript "I Shout Love Love Love," another his "Ode to an Id." Gwen, Milton, Tom Arnott, and Joe Rosenblatt found their faces on section two of the national newspapers.

The poets continued to read on Sundays and benefits were held at The Embassy for a defence fund to raise money for the fines of twenty-five dollars that each poet had to pay when he or she appeared in court to be remanded for trial. The next week the police department cracked eight poetry-reading cases. Milton himself ended up with three summonses.

The trial dates for the poets in magistrate's court set for late August were eventually deferred as city council decided to review the law. It would take a full year, until the summer of 1963, before city council voted to make reading poetry in the parks legal and dropped all charges against the poets. There was a proviso to the new by-law: speakers still had to apply for a permit and weren't allowed to bring any "furniture" to the parks—this presumably meant soapboxes.

Only a few editorials took the protest seriously, and for all its Keystone Kops tone, it was serious. One journalist, Ken Lefolii, put the issue succinctly: "In Canada we seem to be all too sure that a municipal police, backed by a municipal bylaw, not only can but should run in any wouldbe poet who reads his verse aloud in a park that has been ruled off limits by a city council.... A press and a people that is ready to respect law against reason is too fond of authority, or too lazy, for its own good."[17]

Gwen would have delighted in the whole episode. In one interview she told reporters: "Our object is to get the poets out of their isolated cells and expose the people to their work." While Milton was working to liberate the parks from the bastards, she was wondering who would come to listen to poetry when the parks were liberated. But in mid-July, she was able to leave the Interpoet committee in Milton's capable hands and head to Israel. More important to her than Interpoet was the compulsion to undertake her own private odyssey to the sacred city of Jerusalem.

9
THE BEACH OF JAFFA

On July 10th, after five months of marriage, Gwen set out for Israel. There was no question of Milton accompanying her, even if The Bohemian Embassy hadn't been in such an uproar. This was a trip she intended to take on her own. A writer moves instinctively. Gwen understood she needed to go to Jerusalem for her writing, but she could not have understood exactly why. Only the trip would tell her. She was almost twenty-one, though she looked sixteen; she had never been outside Canada before.

She must have been one of the few women travelling alone in what was then a somewhat dangerous country to visit. Jerusalem in 1962 was a divided city—sandbags and barbed wire divorced the Old from the New Jerusalem, East from West, with Arab and Israeli soldiers staring at one another across the no man's land at its heart. If one went too close to no man's land one could get one's head blown off by Jordanian snipers. The old Jerusalem—the Wailing Wall, the Mosque of the Dome—all the ancient past was inaccessible behind the Jordanian walls. Signs of warning were dug into a number of the ruins: THE ENEMY IS

WATCHING YOU and Gwen would wonder, which enemy? Arab? Israeli? Moloch? The one within? It would have been strange to find herself in the literal territory of the imaginative space she had been reading about for years. Unlike most tourists and even many Israelis, she would know the history layered beneath her feet as she walked. She thought of Jerusalem as an intersection of times, "a history-girandole," a fire wheel on which so much human meaning spun.

In her journal she wrote: "Day One—July 10: Easy to leave you [Milton], wanting, I remember, to hold a hand on my wrist & gold & red & goodbye & the fingers of your hands. Left Toronto."[1] Milton's gentle gesture is poignant. Did he intuit what Gwen had only begun to know?—this was one of those innocuous moments that carry their own inexorable momentum: she was leaving him.

Gwen landed in Tel Aviv. The flight had been "a gas," as she used to say in those days: running the sun, and time and the world shrinking into patchwork landscapes beneath the wing—37,000 feet, 530 MPH. She was thrilled that it took her six hours to reach noon in Paris and delighted with the Jewish Hasidim who prayed loudly when the plane took off and again when it landed. How young she was and, for the first time, free. "Dying for Jaffa, Jerusalem, Safed, Nazareth, All— & hoping I can live cheap & easy & walk lots.... Israel. I needn't believe you yet and in this sense you crowded out the poetry ... Israel impossible before me!" For a writer, most travel is a narrative with its own plot line. She would recognize this in retrospect: "I went to kill Jerusalem," she would say.[2] What she meant was: to destroy the interior city, the intellectual refuge, the idealized space she had constructed in her mind.

She went immediately to Jaffa, sister-city to modern Tel Aviv. As she walked its bread-coloured beaches, where Jonah was said to have been cast out of the whale, Jaffa was an assault of heat and colour: yellow and white and the blue, then leaf-green of the Mediterranean; of smells: leather and semi-sweet of baking bread; of frenetic activity: furniture-making in the streets, fruit-sellers, cobblers; and so many beggars sitting before their cache of threads, ribbons, needles with "the world scraped out at the eyes." Fresh from Toronto, exhilarated, she walked, took photos, jotted lines for poems. Her Hebrew, she discovered, was excellent.

She was brave to be there, alone, with so little money that she walked everywhere. Tiny, moon-faced, her hair in a braid down her back, and with those luminous blue eyes, she amused herself by thinking she looked like a twelve-year-old Canadian Indian. Early in the morning of the third day, on the beach of Jaffa as she poked among the rocks looking for fossils in the litter of shells and fish skulls, the sea pulsing like a gigantic clock at her back, she was approached by a young Arab. She had just picked up a gigantic fish-head skull, which she called "Jonah's Jaw," when he propositioned her. She used all her languages: French, English, and Hebrew to refuse him; when he kneed her in the groin she kneed him back. Minutes later they were in the sand, fighting. She watched the outline of his fine white teeth. There was no help. She could see only ruins—deserted, two-dimensional houses like studio backdrops. Suddenly kids, emerging from the ruins trailing their kites, surrounded them. And cheered. Finally the boy wandered off, cursing in Arabic.

In her diary she is astonishingly casual about the incident: "took many photos, not knowing exact age of things but judging by relative differences in wall texture & materials, discerned where old ended and new began. Propositioned and half-raped by Morocco Arab boy of 12 on beach. Took tile & jawbone of something. Fantastic. Building materials mainly sandstone & shells—one wall almost entirely of shells. Suspicions confirmed later in French by beach man who informed me these walls were Arab walls." She is so cool, folding the "half-rape" between the details of her archaeological excursions. Perhaps a young woman might expect such an assault as the hazards of travelling alone in the early sixties. She explained it to herself as a product of the political context.

A few sentences on in her diary she writes: "Possible this boy wanted me *because* I was white & he descendent of crushed Arabs in Jaffa." "The Arabs are proud. My stupid heart wells out to them." After all, she had walked into a territory of grotesque political scars and did not expect to find herself exempt from its violence. Still, there was bitterness. What had occasioned the attack, she felt, were her naked female Anglo-Saxon knees. A young male poet setting out to know the world would not have been offered this lesson quite so brutally. Mostly she was determined not to let it frighten her.

That night she noted: "As Hell has it, I've fallen in with writers again—going to club this evening with young Abraham [Ben-Shahar] who wants Canadian short story markets. Mediterranean very warm." Determined to be humorous, she added: "Knee hurts where I landed it in Arab boy's groin." While she was ambivalent about writers—they were so often careerists who wanted something from you—she was glad to have met someone. He was a writer of novels and a journalist. "Lonely, love hungry, gentle mother-need type," she wrote. He wanted her to stay with him with no sex; he would bring her fresh lemons in the morning. But she wanted to be alone: "Must get to Jerusalem *alone* without *fear* now I know what's there."

The fear she felt was complex. It wasn't just the Arab boy on the beach. It was the fear into which one is thrown by solitary travel—all one's props gone, and no visible connection to the world.

On July 15th, she wrote in the journal: "Dizzy spells again. The marked *counterpointal* thought which accumulates unconsciously, then is referred to somehow by a thing in conscious thought & blindly in a flash they try & fuse. The dizziness & nausea coming from terrible realization that that counterpoint thought is still with you." She complained that she was feeling paralysed, totally numb. The next night she wrote: "Good [day] save for bad stomach, diarrhoea & large bug in the hole in wall—sick at intervals today—because I had no project the mind keeps turning back to Toronto." Then, for fifteen lines, the diary has been scratched over with black ink and is illegible.

What was Gwendolyn talking about in such coded language? Perhaps the thoughts of Toronto refer to Milton; to leave him would have been costly. It was fear of her own loneliness that had led her to marry him, and she also knew the separation would be desperate—he would fight to hold on to her. It might have been a panic attack—where feelings have been churning in the unconscious, unacknowledged, and therefore surface with the aggressive shock of an attack. And yet, she had left Milton standing at the airport, without much regret. There was something else.

Isolated and at the whim of her own emotions in a way one rarely is outside of this kind of travel, she was thinking often in her journal about her father's death—he who had died so precipitously and with so much left unfinished, who had been her only anchor. Or was there yet more? She speaks of the present moment that initiated the panic. Was the present moment the Arab boy's assault on the beach? Did this waken in a flash an earlier, secret, "counterpoint" memory that brought only pain and nausea? What, once written, had to be effaced so carefully? It is impossible to know. Gwen may have kept the secret even from herself.

She travelled by bus to Jerusalem, past the ribs of burned-out jeeps lining the roads, decorated with wreaths to the dead. She was given the choice suite in a hotel on Yafo Street for six lira a night (must be a catch somewhere, she thought), where she found a departed tourist's copy of Engels's *Dialectics of Nature* left behind on the bookshelf. This book would become her casual tourist reading.

And again the loneliness assaulted her:

> A loneliness such as I've never known creeps over me—a moment ago I thought perhaps it was because I am sensing the agony & many deaths this Jerusalem has known—that may be imagination. A fantastic loneliness—and I confess to fear. Somehow the fear is connected with space-time—with my inability to reach out and touch what I know—for what that's worth & the infinity of days stretching ahead of me & Canada hopelessly far and my strangeness & my knowing all gone together—yet Jerusalem is *not* strange—its smell, its colour—I know it—do I sense death? Whose? All the deaths Jerusalem has known—this is bad—just as well I cannot see the Old city—it might be the end of me. One face—the face of Abraham would sustain me—not

someone to follow around but a tangible face I could touch if necessary and leave when I wanted to. Distance—space—the reality of these things only now hits home to me.... I turn to Engels for consolation.³

This was a spectacular loneliness, longing for just one face, even that of a stranger, to touch, to make the world real. Gwen, with her history, was so terribly alone.

Somehow Gwendolyn recovered her equilibrium. Her diary records that she was beginning to have a wonderful time learning the stretch of her own responsiveness to place—at the tomb of David, with the "sexy" guard who brought her coffee and took her through the tombs scribbled with ancient graffiti: "love notes from the past." Or playing with ideas for a poem, based on an inscription she had copied from the Koran in the archaeological museum: "The Eternal God; He begetteth not; neither is He begotten." "Work," she told herself, "on similarity between this & dialectical immutability of matter—can neither be created nor destroyed," this, of course, courtesy of her reading of Engels. Her fertile mind was at play, noting "one vulva orange-gold ring in a store for $1.10," or walking back to the hotel, inside "nets of sun, glowing faces eerie rose-brown & profile of blind Hasid boy with amazing blue eyes."

She "tackled" Israel, visiting Jerusalem, Beersheba, Tiberias, Safed, Haifa, all the sites that were accessible to her within the Israeli zone: the tomb of Herod, which had served as a good bomb shelter for the British; the Necropolis of the Sanhedra with its blue and pink rock houses; Mount Zion and the room of the Last Supper, so much smaller and dirtier than the room depicted in classical art; the excavated site of Mount Hazor scratching about for pot-shards; the Hebrew University to see the Dead Sea Scrolls, envying the students whose fluent language enabled them to read the lines effortlessly; Chagall's windows in Hadassah Synagogue, with their unbearably deep reds and blues and gold yellows with the twelve tribes dancing above her head; scouring the Bedouin markets. She was fascinated by the Negev desert: "How do you place yourself in the scheme of the cosmos when the desert is all around you," she asked herself in her notebook.

Walking in an Arab village called Lifta on Jerusalem's outskirts, she again ran into trouble. Five or six Arab boys spotted her and began gesticulating wildly. Remembering Jaffa beach, she turned heel. The boys, laughing, threw stones. One gashed her on the back of the head and she staggered, blood pouring from the wound. "Part of me looking on, amused, while the other part infuriated with this particular inconvenience." A middle-aged tourist couple took her to hospital, where a metal clamp was used to close the wound. But Gwen would not allow this to ruin the beauty of Lifta. "I still believed it beautiful." She knew the political context of this attack also, and felt pain for both Arabs and Israelis: every Arab village was still a tacit war zone in which enemies looked at each other across a no man's land. But how easily one becomes the enemy, she thought. The irony of being stoned on the road to Jerusalem did not escape her.

Men continued to be a problem, as they always are for a young woman travelling—one thinks, not without a certain envy, of Paul Theroux setting out for Africa with impunity on his apprentice trips. Everyone propositioned her, including an old artist, Ephraim, in Safed— he did it solemnly with blue grapes. The man who ran the roadside shack called the Holyland Buffet begged her to go to Haifa with him, trying to embrace her and assuring her they were made for each other: "as soon as he saw me walking up the road, weighted down with pounds of concealed potshards, soaked with sweat and scabs on my knees, he knew I was his release from the Holyland Buffet." She was laughing, of course. What is one supposed to do when even as a twelve-year-old Indian with battered knees one attracts the male. "Half-raped by jewelry store man with fantastic Yemenite filigree bracelet," she adds in another note. Sometimes it was amusing, sometimes threatening. Could there be any explanation for a woman being on her own other than that she was available, on the hunt? Only once did Gwen break down: "Oh Christ!—these men always following ... the disgusting persistence. Their dull insolent eyes on me always.... They will not let me go. I cannot even be alone with this ... Once again I must leave this scene to retrospect *due to fear* of *present* situation ... I *can't bear it*! Will they force me to be a frightened tourist? Can I not even do what I came to do because of them! O please—"

She did make the casual friends one does on a trip—a "fantastic" woman at the Yafo Street hotel in Jerusalem who was amazed at her youth and willpower. They talked for hours of Zion, Scotland, Hitler, Russia. In the hotel in Tiberias, the ancient owner invited her one night for tea and fruit and showed her sepia-toned photographs of his days in the desert. One photo she immediately recognized as being of Lawrence of Arabia. "I rode with him once a long time ago," her host told her. She already knew Lawrence. Twenty years later Lawrence's story would be the inspiration for her finest sequence of poems.

In Safed on the eleventh day of her trip she met Jonah Sokolowsky, a young writer working as a tourist guide. Though at first she was indifferent, he was struck with her and they became brief holiday lovers. It was rather sweet, but Jonah too became something of an intrusion, possessive, resentful when she wanted to be alone.

Curiously, it was a stranger who made more of an impression on her than almost anyone else she met. He was an Arab beggar in Jerusalem who sat outside the bus terminal on a little square of pavement—a beggar who did not beg. He was known to the locals: in his oversized torn suit, long haired and wild eyed, he came at the same time every day, collecting a few piastres to buy bread and grapes, cursing at those who dared to give him money after he had reached his quota. She learned from a shop woman he came of a good family, but had had a "shock"—he had watched his family burn in a village in Iraq and as Gwendolyn wrote: "they were still burning." She tried to give him cigarettes and was cursed roundly in Arabic: "God brand you!" She watched his struggle to find a piece of paper in which to wrap his bread—hesitating outside a store and then being frightened away. She wanted to communicate with him, and followed him. He "stole away my own loneliness in the presence of his own deeper subtler loneliness and confusion." In her mind she mythologized him: long, thin, with an intense dignity of face and feature, and lean hands that made strange caressive movements in the air, he was a modern John the Baptist, broken and without a mission and no expectations of the prophet to follow. He stood in her mind for the brutal human history of Jerusalem where you were always walking on somebody's grave. Gwendolyn would always be drawn to such figures to wrap her loneliness in their greater loneliness. Before leaving Jerusalem she wrote "John" a note in Hebrew: "Thank you, friend." Of course, he only cursed and brushed her aside. She later found the note opened but crumpled in the gutter.

She was thrust into reveries on her father's death. "Must tackle it," she said to herself. She had a nightmare: "Nightmare last night re me sleeping & voices outside room saying SH Gwen is there, we mustn't disturb her & me screaming Please! Please! wake me—first real sense of death I had." I think of those children who have had their childhood destroyed. They are forced to grow up immediately and they have two alternatives. Either they learn to hide, always defended as though in a chrysalis, or they choose to go out into the world. After the trauma of her childhood, Gwen's father had died and left her hanging. She kept going out into the world but it was costly. Yet she needed to do this if she was to be a writer.

During the two-week stretch she was in Jerusalem, she rented a typewriter and began to work on poems. In these few days she wrote "Absolute Dance," and "Universe And":

Universe And

something we know of mountains
and craters within craters—
big braille under a blind God's hands,

space; our timorous temples turn
inward, our introverted temples
turn as the flyer hoists our vision
higher.

38 Keele Street

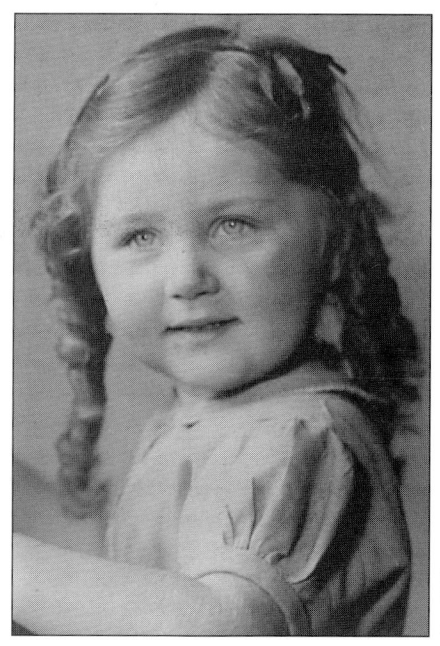

Gwendolyn MacEwen at age three.

Gwendolyn in the "Wishing Tree," High Park, Toronto.
Photo study by Alick McEwen.

Carol Wilson

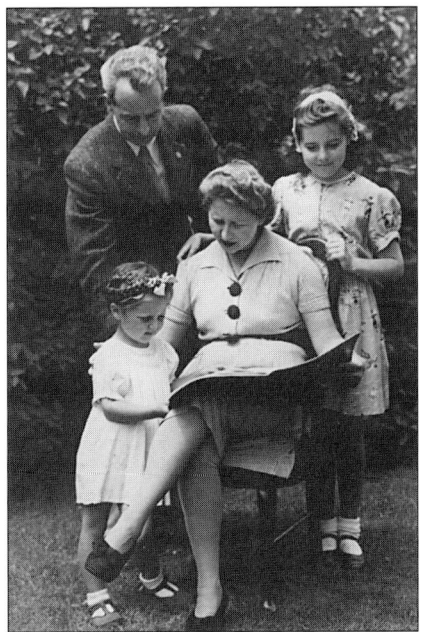

Family looking at book in garden of 38 Keele Street. Elsie McEwen, centre; from left to right: Gwendolyn, age three, Alick McEwen, and Carol, age ten.

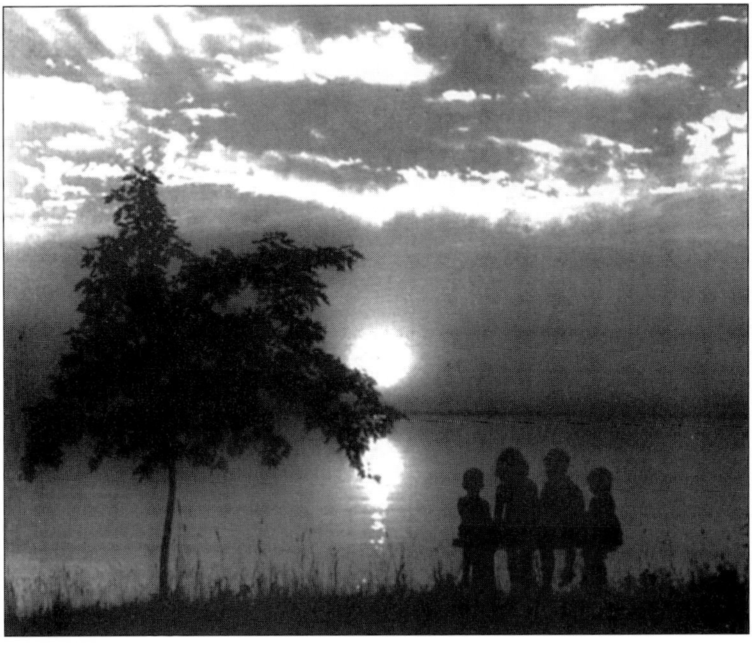

Carol Wilson

Photograph of children at Malibar Cottage, Lake Simcoe. Study by Alick McEwen. Carol is second from left, Gwendolyn on the far right.

Uncle Charlie and Aunt Margaret Martin in their apartment at Winola Court, Bloor Street, on their forty-fifth wedding anniversary.

Carol Wilson

Gwendolyn at right, with her friends Penny and Faye, who formed the violin trio at Laura Secord Primary School, Winnipeg, 1952.

Carol Wilson

From left to right: Elsie McEwen, Charles Martin, Gwendolyn, and Margaret Martin in the yard of 38 Keele Street, celebrating Gwendolyn's award of a scholarship at Western Technical-Commercial School, 1957.

Carol Wilson

Gwendolyn and her father in 1958 or 1959.

Carol Wilson

Lawrence Stone

The Bohemian Embassy, early 1960s. From left to right: Marie Kingston, Margaret Atwood, unidentified, Lawrence Stone. Sylvia Fricker (Tyson) performing.

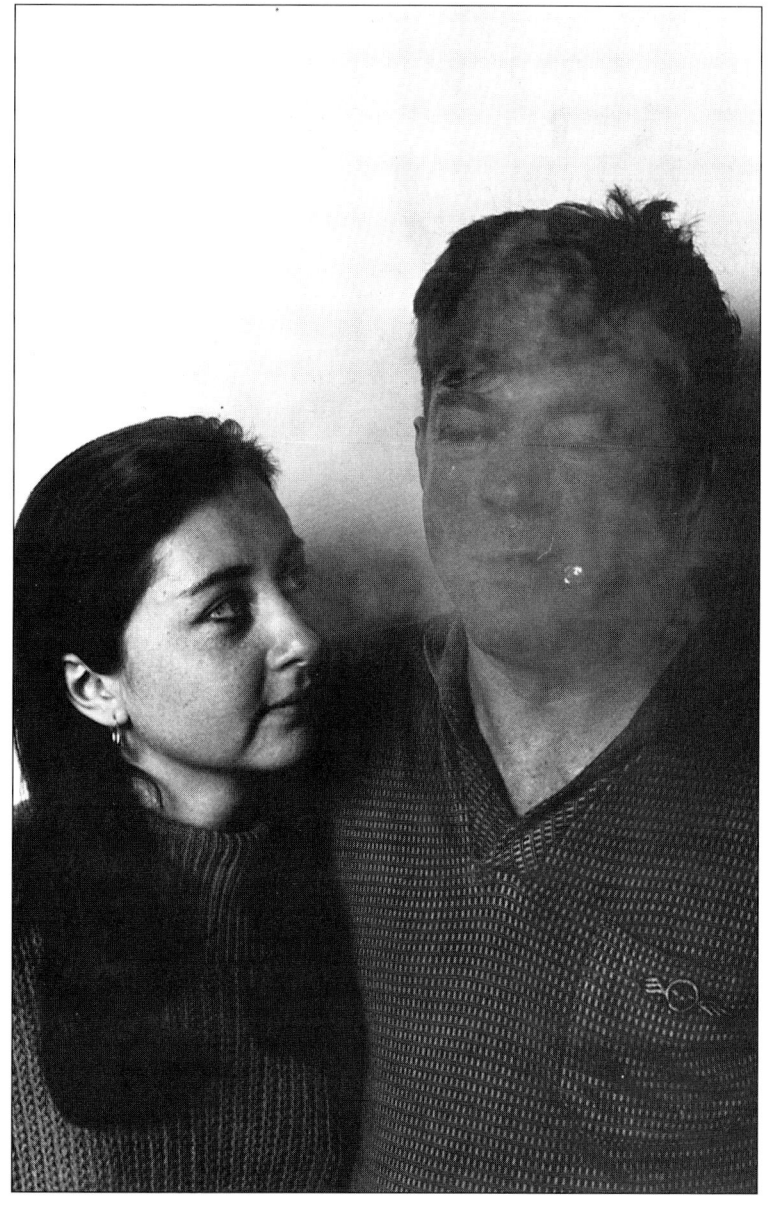

Susan Crean

Gwendolyn and Milton Acorn, around 1960.

Milton Acorn at "Interpoet" protest in Allan Gardens, 29 July 1962 or 1963

> on earth the machines of our myth
> grind down, grind slowly now, rusting
> the wheels of human sense;
>
>> we drink white milk while
>> high galactic fields open
>> the floodgates open
>
> and the terrible laughter of our children
> is heard in that pocket, that high
> white place above our thunder[4]

This was the reality of space and time that only now, as she said, hit her. She was reading the world like braille—she was one of those people who know you can easily reach a space where the pointlessness of life can assault with its vertigo. And how to crawl up then?

She visited Safed on August 10th, the home of medieval Jewish mysticism, in the high hills of Galilee. No place could have been more ideal for the creation of Cabala, the system of esoteric theosophy initiated by rabbis in the seventh century to interpret Scripture. Safed *is* Cabala, she wrote: "the doctrine of light is immediate, the character of light is clean and sharply defined, and nowhere are the *Shekinah*, emanations of primal suns more visibly exact than in the death throes of Safed's sun over the mammalian contours of the distant mountains."[5] How little emphasis is placed on environmental and social factors in the creation of religions, she complained. It was the isolation and inaccessibility of Safed, a place where "time and event have no meaning apart from sunrise and sunset," that nurtured Jewish mysticism.

But now the orthodox clung to the lower slopes of the city, while the upper part, like a Jewish Greenwich Village, was left to the tourist and the sacrilegious disbelievers, the artists smoking on the sabbath. She aligned herself with the sceptics on the crest and thought of the "ultimate backwash and irony of all revolutionary religions: the Holy Hasidim recreate what they set out to destroy in the old doctrines." Any orthodoxy becomes conservative and reactionary, she warned herself. But Safed itself was beautiful and she entertained the fantasy of returning to live there.

On August 15th she wrote: "I came to destroy Jerusalem—to separate dead stones from human meaning." She elaborated this jotting in the travelogue she began about her trip on her return (it was never published):

> Perhaps, ultimately, our reason for creating Ideals is in order to have the luscious sensual pleasure of watching them crumble. We desire this of those Ideals which we know are fabricated ones—constructed out of sterile symbols, and having their Genesis in abstract aspiration rather than extending mightily from what we know to be actual potential, immediate and intrinsic to our nature.
>
> And so in the summer of 1962 I set out singlehandedly to destroy Jerusalem. I desired its death as I would have desired the death of an internal cancer. I desired to transfer it from a subjective to an objective reality and so set straight the strange stunted perspective that internal City had caused me to labour with.... I could continue to desire the city, yes, but I had broken the hold of the symbol.[6]

At twenty-one, she looked back at the body of her work. As a "crazy teenager" she had written "Adam's Alphabet," each stanza bearing a plea for some ideal Zion. She thought of the Hasidim in Safed, old men still moaning for Zion as though it were an attainable place, and not as much theirs now as it would ever be. She now felt that Zion, if there is one, had to be "found within, in human blood and bone." She considered that the long preoccupation with biblical literature and myth and ancient histories that had permeated her poetry was misdirected: they were only jumping-off points. She wanted more of the human element, human concerns, in her poetry to carry it beyond the esoteric content. She would write, as she told herself in her journal, the "Zion of the interior anatomy."

She was reaching the last ten days of her six-week trip when, on August 15th, she met a young playwright, Josef Avisar. He invited her to his roof-house, on top of a cinema, saying it was the only place in Jerusalem to hear good jazz. It was an outpost of Jerusalem's artists where his musician friends collected to jam and drink wine. They talked music—Charlie Parker—and poetry—Charles Olson's breath-line. Ginsberg had stayed with him. Apart from Ginsberg, she was the only "American" artist to visit. Josef railed at the conservatism of Israeli art that he felt was politically censored, and asked about the latest developments in the Western scene. To him the West was an artistic utopia. She could see his naïvety and the difficulty of being progressive in Israel surrounded by enemies that would lead him to invent the West as utopia. Yet, much to her own surprise, Gwendolyn found herself speaking with pride of Canada. The realization suddenly struck her that she was one of the strong voices of her time. It thrilled her. "The necessity of knowing where your contemporaries are!" More sober minded the next morning, she was a little disgusted at her own pronouncements about the duty to bring about the artistic renaissance, and yet she had begun to feel that she was a part of her age, that she could speak for her generation.

Knowing she wanted to get closer to the Old City, Josef took her to a cemetery halfway down the Mount of Olives overlooking the Holy City. They sat on someone's gravestone watching the cats pass apolitically through the divided city, listening to the crackling static of radios from the sentry posts filling the night with stories of wars fought and still to be fought. Josef had shown her photos of his plays—of actors with mime-like faces all dying in different ways: some going mad, losing grip on reality, others just winding down like clocks. "In the West," Josef said, "you hunger for violence; you flirt with it. In the East we have it. That is the difference." She saw the meaning of war in Jerusalem. She would write later in a poem called "Letter to Josef": "Are the kids still screaming in the streets below you? Tell them to stop, tell them all to stop and watch your mime-white clowns dancing down the foolish night, playing live, playing dead, playing everything that is allowed in the theatres of war. The folly, Josef, the foolishness of it all.... Death stutters its idiot message in the throats of the guns."[7]

Gwendolyn left Jerusalem on August 28th. Though she thought she would return, she never did. She had killed Jerusalem, the sterile symbol in her mind. It had become real, a locus that collapsed her version of longing, aspiration, love, hatred, and violence, the paradoxical site of the human heart. In "One Arab Flute" she found the girl she had been when she arrived in Jerusalem amusing:

> I was innocent as a postcard
> among the dark robes and bazaars;
> my exiled smile shone under
> the stern judicial sun;
>   I drank Turkish coffee
>   in the divided city
> with a singular lack of irony
> over the sunken tomb of Herod's family
> with lovenotes scribbled on the wall ...[8]

Gwendolyn was going home, feeling she had sabotaged her own innocence. She had come to an old land, only to discover her own century. "I can hardly bear what fills me now," she wrote in her journal. "Work!"

10
BREAKUP/BREAKDOWN

Gwen returned from Israel with a sense of exhilaration that was almost "unbearable": she had discovered with a shock that she could belong "Here & Now."[1] She had written to Milton from Safed: "I am committed to life—to the chaos & ambiguity of my generation—I see it in the city [she was speaking of Toronto], the buildings, faces of people."[2] She was young and still naïve, but there was that new confidence. She wanted to do something wild, to be provocative, even obnoxious. She wanted to be perverse in going the other way, to write the things she knew about that nobody else could easily gain access to. She was at play, like a hot wind. What would you do if you had all this talent, in a damp culture? Why, shock it awake. She didn't want to play it safe. She felt aggressive, hortatory, apocalyptic. She had come home from one war zone to another, where people didn't even know there was a war—an unofficial war for their minds.

The Breakfast

under the knuckles of the warlord sun how long do we have
how long do we have, you ask, in the vast magenta wastes

of the morning world when the bone buckles under for war
when the bone intersects as tangents in the district of the sun
centipedes and infidels; snakes and the absence of doves?
a breakfast hysteria; perhaps you have felt it,
the weight of the food you eat, the end of the meal coming
before you lift the spoon; or eat only apples
to improvise an eden, or forget the end takes place
in each step of your function.

look, the spoon is lifted halfway through invisible tables
of dangerous logarithms in the abstract morning spaces;
come, come—eat leviathans in the breakfast wastelands
eat bestiaries and marine zoos and apples and aviaries.
by eating the world you may enclose it.

seek simplicities; the fingertips of the sun only
and the fingernail of the moon duplicating you in your body,
the cosmos fits your measure; has no ending;

place one hand before the sun and make it smaller,
hold the spoon in your hand up to the sky
and marvel at its relative size; comfort yourself
with the measures of a momentary breakfast table.

ah lord sun
ah terrible atomic breakfast
ah twilight of purple fallout
ah last deck of evening cards—

deal, infidel, the night is indeed difficult[3]

The world had taken up the myth of the Last Supper, of sacrifice, and distorted the meaning of love in codes of humility and self-effacement. She had found her first and perhaps favourite metaphor. She would celebrate appetite and the subversive Breakfast—breakfast is the most profound and sacramental meal; she thought of it as the pact you make with yourself to see the day through. For most people, the meal is over before they lift the spoon. Eat! she would say. "The cosmos fits!" It was the early sixties: a time of "snakes and the absence of doves" when the seeds for a huge cultural revamping were being sown.

It is amusing to think of the young risk takers Canada produced in the early sixties: Leonard Cohen hunting flowers for Hitler, David Cronenberg scouring the drains of Yorkville for homicidal plants, Margaret Atwood unravelling the culture's safe circle games, Michael Ondaatje in Kingston already looking for dainty monsters. They are all in Gwendolyn's line—a curious combination of voices: subversive, humorous, wry, intelligent, lyrical, ironic. It is Cohen and Gwendolyn who fit most easily together as romantic and lyrical subversives.

It was all very well to be clear and didactic in poems—in the poems Gwendolyn could create her own world, invent her own myths. But her life was now a complete mess. Leaving Milton would be one of the hardest things she would do.

Neither she nor her sister, Carol, had learned to expect anything of life except terrible confusion. At the end of August Carol broke from her husband and, leaving her children briefly in the care of a sister-in-law, ended up on Gwendolyn's island. Milton had fled and it was the only place Carol could go. Two women in a not unusual position—breaking from controlling husbands they had been too young to marry. Carol stayed only a couple of weeks, but it must have been chaotic in that tiny cottage, with no money to provide an escape route.

Milton could not have known the resolve that Gwen's trip to Israel had given her. He was counting on the intimacy of the bond of marriage. Like most people he probably believed that marital and sexual intimacy guarantees knowledge, but of course that is an illusion. Gwendolyn's trip had been the psychological upheaval she had been preparing for and she had travelled leagues in her mind without him. Had he been able to listen, he might have understood her needs. But Milton could not listen. He was about to be shocked awake.

Gwendolyn found a lover. His name was Bob Mallory, a painter living on the island. They met just after Gwen's return from Israel, just as she was turning twenty-one. Gwen probably didn't have the courage to confront Milton alone and finding someone else made the decision irrevocable. Milton became suspicious and insanely jealous. By November Gwendolyn moved into her own apartment on Hazelton Avenue in the city.

Milton was devastated. When he showed up at The Bohemian Embassy, Don Cullen thought him quite unhinged. There was a rifle they used as a prop in some of their revues; it was a real rifle, and Cullen took to removing the bolt, since he began to think Milton might use it on himself. Milton fled to Al Purdy's house in Ameliasburg. To keep him busy, Purdy suggested they could erect his new TV aerial. "We were lifting the 300- or 400-pound aerial above our heads on my slanted gabled roof, and Milt cried out: 'I love her, I love her.' He was shaking. 'For Christ's sake' I shouted: 'You're going to kill us.'"[4] It would have been comic, Milton looking like King Kong on the roof, swinging from the aerial, were it not so tragic. However, Purdy adds: "Milton got better very quickly. He had an affair with a girl he didn't respect to prove he was still potent."

Yet the breakup was very costly to Milton. He took the only route he knew how to take. He had a breakdown, not for the first time, and ended up in the mental ward of Sunnybrook Hospital in Toronto. One might see this, perhaps unfairly, as his last and most dramatic gesture to recover Gwen.

While he was in hospital, Gwen wrote to him:

> Milton, You remember the letter I wrote you from Safed this summer. There was no one else that letter could have been addressed to—no one who could have understood the commitment I was trying to express—the intensity of

it. I know wherein the commitment lies in my life and my art—and I am young/the struggles and the ambiguities are in the finding of a vehicle for it. Think of it—no one else the letter could have been addressed to, and no one else who could have prompted me as you have—brought out the meanings in myself I wouldn't have found for years.

You are a great artist, you are not smashed. The injustice I dealt you was not in leaving, but in marrying you right off—with an idea of time and permanence I actually believed I could deal with. Little I knew of myself, even after what you showed me. Because you were gone that winter—back to the east I was afraid, believed I would not see you again/believed nothing could bring you back—I married you then out of a certain need for *balance & permanence*—yet did not then understand what more I needed to experience and expand—more things contributing to the life and the art—understand it—I know you can. I feel I've dealt you a blow. I have—& I don't lack the guilt for it.

Your poems themselves enclose all this already—think of it! Write me & thrash out things—anything—I'll always answer—will come to see you wherever you wish—we both have yet to learn much of ourselves.... Write—Gwen[5]

Gwen was distraught and guilty. She wanted Milton to understand his importance to her, but was also appealing to him, whose poetry spoke for the people, to understand the needs of her art. His responses were vicious. He congratulated her for trickery, her villainy, for making a sucker out of him, and then fell into a ranting litany of expletives that only Milton could deliver. Gwendolyn knew this kind of letter. She had received similar ones from her mother, but it must have been horrifying: another voice from a mental hospital to be responsible for in her life.[6]

The man she had counted on turned venomous. But for Gwendolyn this was not as desperate a transformation as it would have been for most. She knew not to take this attack as the only story. She might even have smiled at one of his accusations: he called her "realistic." Anyway, she had had experience with madness. She would wait him out; she sent him poems.

But Milton was not to be placated. He wrote back furiously, rejecting her phoney concern, "her rancid heart." She had cheated, lied, and deserted him while he had been the innocent victim. She had tried to explain that her leaving wasn't "whim" or "wildness" but for Milton, it was only that: she had run off with another man. And then Milton inserted the knife: she'd better stop writing love poems. Any adolescent girl could write better poems than she. He told her to go to hell.

Gwen had obviously lied about her involvement with Mallory, anticipating his reaction. But Milton was also wrong. She had not left him for Mallory. She had left him because she knew he compromised her independence. He, who had been so nurturing of her talent, took the first opportunity to attack her work. Milton's vituperation is so off the mark that she may have been able to dismiss it. But then, it's also a familiar story: the mentor was not interested in her as a writer, but as *his* woman and his pride was hurt. He would continue to condescend to her writing in letters over the years, always suggesting she had failed her early promise. People remembered that he would occasionally show up at her readings at the back of the audience, raving about his lost "red-haired" son, that first illegitimate child he had probably never seen.

Gwendolyn spent months sorting things out in a variety of letters to Milton, who had moved in May to the Westminster Department of Veterans Affairs Hospital in London, Ontario, where he remained until at least September before he was released and fled to Vancouver. It was her year of what she called "extreme scab-picking."

We have a tendency to treat all relationships as if they are pathological. "Love is when the rocks in your head fit into the holes in another's head," as a friend, Arlene Lampert, puts it. From the outside everyone asked why this beautiful, delicate young woman would marry a "Quasimodo" figure like Milton whom many found almost physically repulsive. But it is hardly a new story. Young women often choose men for their minds. There is a litany of young creative women who preceded Gwen: I think of Frida Kahlo and Diego Rivera (Kahlo's friends said it was like an elephant marrying a dove). Gwen thought she knew why she had married Milton—it was simple: he was an artist and she loved the strength and honesty of his voice and indeed his anarchy. She had married her idea of him. Much more intriguing, however, was the fact that she could discount the warnings of his mental instability that were obvious to those around her.

As always Gwendolyn was being asked to be the guilty one, the nurse, the one who takes responsibility. In one letter she does refer to her own "naive florence nightingale attitudes," her tendency to take in the strays. In fact, she probably had felt an impulse to protect, to set herself as a buffer between Milton and the world, that romantic mothering impulse often found in young women who attach themselves to chaotic males before they have fully established their own talent. But she dismissed this and wrote to Milton:

> Dear Milton,
>
> I moved my things over today, am finally settled.
>
> No, I don't believe my actions indicate any need to care for someone ... anymore than I married to care for you ... if the cards look that way on the surface, it is because circumstance has flung them in one direction; I don't, for instance, want to 'care for' Mallory ... only two men have been *strong* enough to draw out the depths of *me*—you and he. You may not understand the last, but it is so.
>
> Please remember that for you ... many experiences were *behind* you, trials and errors, that you had had your time of discoveries in love, and wanted most to be settled with one. I thought I too wanted that ... but realized

quickly that I hadn't had *my* time ... it was not a whim or wildness which made me go, but a sudden clear realization that tho you were the first man of importance, you could not be the last....

Yes, I did break the promise of marriage; only because I made it not knowing many things of myself, made it for all the wrong reasons.

Now I am out of it. I would not have it any other way. My wish is that you will begin things again for yourself ... yet you say you can't ... surely it was more than me that has emptied you like this ... somehow it is terrible and frightening for me to think that I could hold that size of life-meaning for another human being; it is heavy; it does not make me proud. Yet for you it was a settling, a surety, after you had had experience, whereas for me it was a beginning, a growth in myself. In spite of our bonds, which were rare and beautiful, we cannot pull these two ends together. Gwen.[7]

Gwendolyn was refusing the guilt that would make her responsible for Milton's life. No one is accountable for another's life-meaning, she asserted. She would not be bullied by Milton into believing she was destroying him. And perhaps she was also thinking of her mother and father. In the recurring nightmare she had had of her father after his death, she, Carol, and her mother repeatedly buried him alive. Was she beginning to free herself of the irrational but potent idea that she had destroyed her father, had not managed to save him? Leaving Milton was a courageous gesture of self-assertion—she felt she was strong enough to protect and nurture herself.

But Gwen still felt she had to examine the ruthlessness that allowed her, in a sense, to use Milton—he had been a mentor—and then to leave him so precipitously, with so little warning. She knew she hadn't had the courage of her own honesty. She should have confronted him directly about her new lover. "Lately, she wrote to Milton, "in myself I've discovered so much which is not beauty.... I knew so little somehow. In my attempts to be rational I've found myself doing more harm than good." There was in fact no point in being "rational" with Milton, but she kept trying.

It did become clearer to her what the whirlwind had been about:

> Dear Milton,
>
> I want to say in a dozen different ways, but can never say it exactly: yes, I left you; yes, I pulled the solid ground out from under my own feet, BUT, and it's that 'but' which I want you to grasp, a 'but' which is not an apologia, but something else.... Most recently, the reality of your present situation has hit home to me. Hard. I want to shout to the world; look, it was not *this* way, more was involved, but I can not shout it. I consider it, among other things, an honour to have been with you. And the memory is further honour ... [but] I had no alternative to anything I have done....
>
> I end on that eternal remark again, one which we both know and knew; you knew it more poignantly than I—and more difficult for you to know it—that had I had all my loves, as you had yours,—had I had them all, all the experiences as you had had it before me—all the trials and the mistakes and the learning from them, as you had—then you would have been the last. It is the terrible irony of age, and circumstance. And you understood it better than I, yet could believe us anyway ... while I believed us and understood it not, and made no allowances for it.[8]

She was, of course, being too careful. Milton understood nothing of the sort. If she had been naïve, he, so much older, had been self-deceived.

Beneath the carefulness of her language there is a great deal of repressed anger at the older man who raids the life of a young woman, believing he will be sufficient. She would not be anchored like "a passive verb." She would be her own motive for action. How could she, so ambitious in her art, have settled within the protective preserve of Milton's chaotic devotion? She had urgent journeys to make.

Breaking with Milton, she now understood, was as much a literary struggle as a personal one. She wrote to him that she had been hiding, clinging in her work to a Julian, a magician or superman, to whom all is possible. Ironically, Milton had, for a moment, provided safety of a kind, but then she had felt cut off from the experiences she would need to write. She wrote to him: "The next few years, writing-wise, are going to mean me picking my bones apart constantly and putting them together again; I'm just now learning how that feels." And she advised him: "I pray you write like mad, because you've given out with the thunder, but I believe the real storm is still to come." She was right. Milton's best poems were ahead of him, as were hers. She would look back on Milton and on love with a recognition of its poignant fragility:

> ... our skulls like drums,
> like tonal caves
> echo, enclose.

> while the ribs of our bodies are great hulls
> and the separate ships of our senses
> for a minute

> anchor.

> for a minute in the same harbour

> anchor.[9]

11
LEO AND LEO REVISED

In January Gwendolyn moved back to the cottage on 2nd Street, Ward's Island; Milton was still in hospital and there was no reason not to. With her she took Bob Mallory, only the second man, as she had told Milton, who was "*strong* enough to draw out the depths of *me*." I try to construct her life in those days with the help of old friends and acquaintances, whose voices feel to me like echoes swirling around shadows.

Who was Mallory? I ask. He was, it turns out, as chaotic as Milton, though in a quite different way. A lifelong friend of Gwendolyn's, the sculptor Mac Reynolds, conjures him for me: "Mallory was like a character in a cartoon. He often wore a turban, and even a black cape. In my mind I see him slinking from tree to tree, stealthily. He looked like a magician with fiery, burning eyes."[1] Gwen had not given up her magician, but now he was a human magician, a lot messier and a lot more modern. He was almost the same age as she; they moved on a level playing field.

Ward's Island had its own particular politics. There were three classes of people. There were the island families who had lived there winter and summer for several generations, and who thought of it as their island. There were those who came just for the summer, often renting their cottages out in the winter. Among these were the literary people like the young Robert Fulford and Peter Gzowski. Gzowski arrived in 1964, living next door to Gwen at number 8. He'd heard about Gwen the poet and her companion Mallory, but he saw nothing of them. "Who were those shadows?" he wonders now.

The third group of islanders were the hippies and island beatniks who began to arrive in the early sixties, the people in beards who smoked dope. There was tension between the islanders and the new people. Mallory was classified among the latter. "People were afraid of him," Gzowski tells me, "and would have nothing to do with him."[2] One of the exceptions was David Mason, an antiquarian book dealer who lived on the island with his wife for five or six years. "Bob," he says, "was the neighbourhood weirdo or crazy, and people shied away from him. But I liked him."[3]

Mallory was a painter. He edited a magazine called *The Revised Catalogue of the Sorcerers*—the title came from his idea that people were willing to let themselves be censored like books, but he would give them an alternative reading. He also edited something called *The Caligula Times*, and could often be found in the Gerrard Street Village selling his magazine at the Village Book Store, owned by Marty Ahvenus. He would set up at a wooden table with his bust of Buddha, painted in different colours depending on his mood; sales went better with the Buddha near. His conversation was laced with arcane and occult references. Mason assumed he had had a scientific education because he spoke cogently about mathematics and Einsteinian theories of relativity and his drawings and paintings were full of mathematical equations. He had also developed a mathematical system for betting on the horses.

To many, Mallory's conversation was incomprehensible: he talked with the assumption that people shared certain beliefs about synchronisity, precognition, hypnagogic images, convergences, multiple dimensions. Mallory's paranoia was also legendary. He avoided telephones and preferred to talk in open spaces. He knew there existed what he called

"They," "the Controllers" who want to control your life. Mason remembers that Mallory might take the slightest glance in the wrong way, which would be the basis for breaking off all contact. "But there was a gentleness and shyness to Bob even then, despite the bravura of his persona. I always thought of him as a wild animal, taking to his heels."

Mason's affection for Mallory is palpable. He has one compelling image of him from the mid-sixties that he can neither get rid of nor adequately explain. One day, when he was at home on the island, Mallory arrived with his paintings, which Mason found stunning. They were all portraits, but over each face, Mallory had painted another image.

> When I was in Tangier I saw an exhibition of schizophrenic art that was touring from a French mental hospital. It was *that* kind of art. Have you ever seen the picture of a cat looking out at you and it scares the hell out of you? I'll never get rid of the image. There's this guy you know casually, yet whom you can't understand and who looks weird and who talks even more weirdly. Then, finally, you get to see his work and you recognize an enormous talent there, if not genius. But the craziness is right there for you to see because he's painted over the earlier sketch, but not enough to cover what was underneath; just enough to turn it all insane.

One of the people on Ward's Island in those days was the poet Victor Coleman, whose family had lived there for generations. Eighteen, and desperate to get out of his mother's hair, he moved into a communal cottage and found himself living with Bob Mallory. Mallory, he thought, was completely crazy. "We used to do seances with candles and organ music and had a timer on the record player to wake us to the boom of a pipe organ each morning. Mallory would claim that he was not from this planet, that he just got stuck here, which was quite believable."[4] Coleman thought Mallory a brilliant technician as a painter, but his subjects were weird—

such as a parade of children who had Bibles stuck to their faces. He was fascinating about anything to do with science, which he seemed to know well, but then he believed in UFOs. Coleman remembered the time he covered the whole of the outside of the cottage in silver tinfoil, probably to make it a conductor. From time to time he would change his name. Once he insisted on being called Leo, and later, after another rebirth, Leo Revised. By the end of 1962, Coleman was living on Scollard Avenue in the city and when Gwen and Mallory visited him for supper one evening—he in his turban and ratty beard and she in black with her kohl eyes—they looked so odd that his horrified landlady gave him notice the next day.

I have met Mallory. I had asked Mason to look out for him, and he phoned one day to say that Mallory would be willing to meet me in one hour in the restaurant of *The Toronto Sun* on King Street. Mallory had told him: "If she can't see me today, then I'll be free again next spring." I was told I would recognize Mallory as the man in the turban.

Mallory was sitting at the very back of the restaurant when I arrived, leaning over a few sheaves of paper on which he was sketching. I was taken aback. He didn't look like the ethereal magician I had expected, but rather like a congenial genie, with a large, putty-coloured, empathic face. His striped colourful turban was flat and expansive on his head and I thought, if I look under the table he will have matching slippers with pointy toes. I reminded myself that this man was thirty years older than the magician Gwendolyn knew.

We began carefully by talking about artists, about Gustave Doré, the child prodigy in optical art and his illustrations of Rabelais, about Albrecht Dürer, also a prodigy, and the Catalan surrealist Remedios Varo. We moved carefully to Gwen. He spoke of her elliptically but with a kind of reverence. "Anything one says about Gwen will be a compliment: her looks, her work, her abstract ability."[5] They had been together two and a half years. He remembered it as a sweet time; they rarely quarrelled. She never talked of Milton or her father, though he had met her mother and sister, Carol, many times. (Carol's strongest memory of Mallory had been the occasion when she had visited Gwen's cottage with her children to find Mallory stretched across the floor painting a door. Too poor to buy canvas, he had ripped a door from its hinges to paint on it. Handing brushes to the children, he invited them to join him.)

"We both loved magic, of course," Mallory told me, and conjured up names of people they had met: Janus, alias Joe Nickell, who demonstrated magic at the Houdini museum in Niagara Falls, Leon Mandrake, and Jack Bateman, the magician-billionaire. There are degrees to magic, Mallory explained, and Bateman was the best. "With him it was never cheap conjuring. Gwen would have been a competent magician," he added, "though no one knows what kind. Her gifts were innate. She had that capacity for flash-understanding. If you are going to write about Gwen," he warned, "you must get her moods, how she dressed. Her moods were so strong." She tended to be quiet, and then she would explode with enthusiasm. Her style of clothing was austere, the designs always simple, though she loved exotic colours—royal purple or dark green; she avoided the bright ones: white, yellow, and red. Mallory described their days: they played chess, listened to music—his favourites were Sibelius and Camille Saint-Saëns. He remembered a Bob Dylan song from the sixties about a lover who wore an Egyptian ring that sparkled before she spoke. "I used to think—Gwen has a clone somewhere." He recalled her saying to him: "Till I met you I didn't know there was such a thing as food. I always ate perfunctorily," reminding me of the child in Winnipeg, with her perfunctory lunches, who kept house for her dad—no one had ever taken care of Gwendolyn before.

I had been warned that Mallory was a character, almost a bag man now haunting Queen Street in his turban, though occasionally he substituted a panama; that he wore multiple layers of clothing, the shared insignia of those who are medicated and out of hospitals. How and where he lived was not clear and he didn't take well to being asked. Did I invent the kindly, intelligent man I met? There were odd flashes to our conversations—once he checked to see if I was wearing black, wondering if I might be the satanic woman he had encountered in poems he was just then reading. One time he complained that Thursday had disappeared and the police were following him. They had formed a conspiracy to eliminate his Thursday. Though I met Mallory on a number of occasions, he did not allow me to penetrate any of his veils. Mallory was someone I would never know, nor could I recover Gwen's mad magician.

When Mallory began to live with Gwen in the spring of 1963, *Julian the Magician* had just been published in New York. For the cover, Gwen had selected a self-portrait by Albrecht Dürer—the young artist stands in a wild, Gothic, castellated landscape staring from the corner of the canvas with a look that is both aggressive and defensive. On the back is Mallory's portrait of Gwen. It is a curious portrait, more child than woman, with a cherubic face and sleepy eyes. Perhaps this was how he saw her. Gwen dedicated the book to him and was delighted with it.

Her reputation had begun to build. Peter Miller, an editor at Contact Press, had approached her the previous year to ask if she had enough poems for a first collection. Founded in 1952 by Raymond Souster, Irving Layton, and Louis Dudek, Contact was by 1962 the most influential literary press in the country. Peter Miller's problem, it turned out, was to select from the mountain of poems Gwen had given him. Her first printed book of poems, *The Rising Fire*, came out just after *Julian the Magician* and Gwen was booked for a poetry tour that included Montreal, Toronto, and Vancouver. She felt she was on the lip of fame: good things were about to happen.

A number of the poems in *The Rising Fire* are to Mallory. He is her lovely madman, wearing "the whole cosmos like a conical hat/with the raw brain set under it,"[6] "the hair on fire from the brain burning beneath it." The poem called "To Mallory" begins:

> the geography is doubtful of the world
> which turns you, and the graphic outlines
> of things can break down anytime

>from the sweet anatomies of animals
>to the smashing of the cores of gardens,
>the slow split in the bowels of mountains
>—earthquake or the earth grins widely
>cracking its face for the sake of us— ...[7]

She wrote to Irving Layton: "Oh, lord, I type these copies and am in half-tears with the power of some images; can we ever have the strength our poetry has, ever? the two for Mallory break my brain in half, and this Mallory, though you must tell no one, is now in psychiatric observation because he has dared to think powerful thoughts and broken under the pressure of them ... this was the reason I ran off so quickly over the weekend ... anyway, I don't know why I elaborate like this except to try and equate the poetry with the reality."[8]

Like so many, Gwendolyn was dedicated to the alternative, and wanted the death of the stencilled kind of sameness of the lower-middle-class world she had been educated in. The Bohemian Embassy or Marty Ahvenus's Village Book Store were places where that world could not get at her. There all were welcome if they had their own style; odd behaviour, even mental illness, was not taken as an aberration but rather as a sign of selection. One thinks of Leonard Cohen's song "Suzanne" or Bob Dylan's "Mr. Tambourine Man" and the myth of the holy fool, the beautiful loser, the ones who had stepped outside of reality. But Gwen chose to live with Mallory. Perhaps she was drawn yet again by the romantic impulse to place herself between Mallory and the world. With such raw sensitivity, she had a reflexive empathy that had its tragic dimension; she could not protect herself from suffering. And yet, she also clearly thought Mallory's version of the world was more convincing than the world's version of itself.

Gwendolyn had decided she would take all risks for her writing. In this she had found what she thought was an ally in Irving Layton: she would complain, conspiratorially, that Toronto bred only metaphysicians.

> There is an overt distinction here between what a poet writes and what he lives (I've got to exclude myself, of course, for I have experienced drunken clocks and magicians) ... I find it impossible to visualize a Macpherson or whoever actually sleeping with a snake ... Toronto poets don't go properly berserk—they write of their bacchanals, their wild Nietzschean dances, their rage, their ecstasies—yet whether these things are done, carried out in the flesh is another matter. The art of directly experiencing one's poems is unknown in this city—the art of verifying what one has had the gall to write. Introspection itself should be a passionate thing, being sponsored from outside.[9]

She thought she would hire Antaeus to undermine Toronto Island and release it, floating the entire land mass down the St. Lawrence River to Montreal like Cleopatra's barge manned by twelve hundred Amazons. She would disembark to a welcome of flutes and flowers. She was for appetite; she would test her life. She could not imagine safety. She would also, of course, find herself crashing head-on into other lives, only to have to extricate herself.

12
SATURNALIA

In Bob Mallory, Gwendolyn found her mad magician roaming the streets of Toronto, theatrical, insolently outrageous, an unexpected dancing presence. He was Julian in a second incarnation, not esoteric and medieval, but here, now. He was tragic, of course, because the world had no interest in his fascination with our cosmic predicament—that our senses tie us to a physical world, while our minds intuit endless, imaginal realities. But then, Gwen was a poet and poets are stranger creatures than other writers. Poets seemed doomed to search for someone in life who receives the projection of the muse, if only momentarily.

Gwen even knew what she was up to. She had said Mallory was only the second man to draw out her depths. She was using him as an archetype, a person who reflected a fantasy within herself. Having read her Jung, she called it the twin, the male self within her. She wrote to her friend Al Purdy: "People can be embodiments of the archetype, manifold so that each person can choose whichever personality within another he likes."[1] It is cavalier, of course, but Gwendolyn was young when she wrote that and believed in playing with fire. And certainly, we are all chameleons (which has both a joyous and tragic potential), mostly doomed, at least when young, to transform the other into our own inventions. If Mallory was helpful as a catalyst to her ideas, he was also a support. He had the sense to leave her alone to write. He believed profoundly in what she was up to.

During those two and a half years on Ward's Island, with the city and its skyscape of construction cranes at her back, Gwendolyn worked on her magician in a new novel she called *Saturnalia*. He was a metaphor for the artist shifting the mind's hard shadows. She had declared that the exciting territory was *inside*, that we starve our imaginations; our rationalist world did not give the mind enough oxygen. It was hard work, but she was exceedingly disciplined. Her friends, like Tom Arnott, knew that Gwendolyn at work was not to be disturbed before late afternoon.

As she was writing *Saturnalia*, she was thrilled with it. It was to be a wonderfully complex game. She wrote to Al Purdy that it would be in six books—about six characters who were really one character—were, in fact, "the absolutely corny archetypal hilarious divisions of one personality." She picked outlandish mythological names: Jubelas, Absalom, Tantalus, Kali, Omphale, Isis—three male, three female in one person. "My mind is bisexual," she had said. The magician (Absalom who incorporated them all) would end by copulating with his author, "which means, I hope, that the old classic author-subject dialectic is resolved." "Best thing I've done yet."[2]

All her self-doubts and vulnerabilities disappeared when she was writing. Her magician was to be the archetypal Canadian. She and Mallory had visited Prime Minister Mackenzie King's estate at Kingsmere outside Ottawa and had been astonished by the grotesque naïvety of his menagerie of pseudo-classical arches filched from British banks and churches and set against the backdrop of raw wilderness. It expressed such a misguided longing for an appropriated cultural identity, while distorting the beauty of the wilderness itself. Her magician would start his odyssey there. But the book proved endlessly difficult to write and wouldn't be published until 1972 under the title *Noman*.

Gwen was trying desperately to find a popular formulation for her ideas, to speak to "her generation." She hated being called a metaphysician, someone whose work was abstract, cool. "I am so much concerned with reality, I have to work my way around it to get to it," she complained. She turned to automatic writing, to dreams, to myths, to force the mind into other language codes. Curiously she did not try drugs to "expand" her consciousness as many did in the sixties. And for now, alcohol was out. Gwen had a fear of alcoholism as the disease that killed her father. Mallory corroborated this, as did Victor Coleman, who never associated alcohol with the two magicians on the island.

Gwendolyn, of course, believed the mind had capacities for other than rational thought. She was searching for other ways of thinking. She loved to play with Tarot cards, not because she believed that the future could be predicted by a deck of cards, but rather the archaic symbols resonated, waking the mind to insights that it was unaware it held. Her friend the writer and editor Barry Callaghan would later say: "There was a courtliness to Gwen, and she loved ritual. When she read your Tarot, it was as if the cards gave her an occasion courteously to shatter the glass people usually erect to protect themselves."[3] She also kept a deck of ESP cards, developed by the Parapsychology Laboratory at Duke University for the testing of extra-sensory perception. There was a "psychic" side to Gwen, which several people saw, but which she took for granted.

Gwendolyn wrote to Al Purdy as *Saturnalia* progressed. Purdy offered himself as her buddy, rough-cut, unpretentious, but knowing his own brilliance of mind. She could play the precocious kid, which freed her from any sexual claims her provocativeness might have invited. Her novel, she told him gaily, would be "hilarious, tragic and obscene.... No one else in Canada is equipped to write this thing except me. Ego? Hell no—simple deduction."[4] Ego, she thought, was "someone else's way of describing one of the most correct and human states." She was already dealing with people who thought that, particularly for a woman of twenty-two, she took herself too seriously. Purdy consoled her: "Why the hell not take yourself seriously. I admire your self possession incidentally."[5]

She told Purdy that she was writing *Saturnalia* among the rock piles on the beach at Ward's Island, wading knee-deep among the lovers who slipped over to the island. "I set up my gleaming machine on a rock and begin to type SATURNALIA. They disperse, thinking I am coldly recording their passion. Maybe I am. Last night it was full moon, when my blood is at high tide. I walked with my cat in the rocks. Lucifer, I said, tonight I am your Whore, and by God I was. Whole regiments of demons escaped, only half-alive, from my thighs. But what a book."[6]

Mallory had obviously awakened a sexual self that had been dormant with Milton. Gwen was now going to take on female sexuality, to reinvent it in its full power. She wouldn't be afraid of the word "whore." She would throw it in the world's face.

Gwendolyn decided to write her Womb poem. It's hard to remember that a point of discussion in the sixties was whether a woman could write with a womb. It wasn't just that reconciling a career and children was thought to be difficult. It was more Victorian than that—a woman's creative energies were sapped by the mere fact of having a womb. Creativity was phallic.

In the revolutionary sixties in America, the women writers still had to fight for space. Iconographic status was accorded to books like Jack Kerouac's *On the Road*, Hubert Selby, Jr.'s *Last Exit to Brooklyn*, and to Norman Mailer and Henry Miller. Having stabbed his second wife, Mailer was famous for his remark that it took a great deal of love to do it with a knife. Ironically, the so-called sexual revolution never even confronted the issue of sexual politics. Looked back at, women can be found where they had always been found—as the artist's moll, as the objects in the free-love game. Despite all the rhetoric, most women were still what Gwendolyn called "passive verbs," and the feminist revolution, as opposed to the free-love revolution that had come with the invention of the birth-control pill, would not begin to make an impact until the end of the sixties.

Gwendolyn was in uncharted territory. She was beginning to feel the flex of her own poetic muscles. She wanted a potent female sexuality, such as she imagined to be found in the old fertility cults in which female sexuality was the dread mystery. Among all the goddesses available to her, she had chosen Kali, the terrifying Indian goddess of creation and destruction, to be her female personification in *Saturnalia*. Gwen was a myth-maker—she was much more interested in power, including the dark side, than in powerlessness. She wanted to construct an aesthetic of female erotic power. In her Womb poem, she meant to be flip and amusing and so she used the casual voice:

> WOMBS: SOME THOUGHTS AND OBSERVATIONS
> 1
> She had this little red bean with 10 ivory animals in it
> carved in India. 'Isn't it marvellous, Gwen,' she said,
> '10 ivory elephants inside this little red bean?'
>
> and the bean was like, you know what, yes, like a womb,
> that's what I said, a womb with 10 ivory elephants in it,
> and I thought I wouldn't mind 10 ivory elephants
> in mine, if it came down to that, I wouldn't mind it at all,
> I'd enjoy it in fact—
>
> now I've become rather over-selective,
> I seek the lover who can accomplish this exacting act.
>
> 2
> Salome the Immortal has a lab in Argentina
> where she seeks to free women from the tyranny of the
> Moon,
> yet I fear that all this Menstrual Research is a front,
> for men are seen to enter Salome's private room. Besides,
> they come and go in cycles, like eternal tides.[7]

Gwen was amusing herself, but there was a barb in this poem. She didn't want to be freed from the tyranny of the moon, to abandon female sexuality as a weakness, to degender women and make them men. She wanted power. Could she get it?

In the early sixties, there were few female models to define a course for women writers, and Gwen felt those few who existed had missed the point. She was already aware of Gertrude Stein, but to her Stein was sexist: she described her to Purdy as a woman who "kept a little woman in her Paris apartment who used to sit and knit doilies.... Stein would point to this dame, saying: 'She's for the wives to talk to.' Then Stein would converse with the men. Christ."[8] She disliked the new woman, embodied in Simone de Beauvoir, because she herself did not think her sex was a stumbling block. De Beauvoir approached "art and intellect from the start as romantic martyrdom and [claimed] the lack of genius lies in it being discouraged and stunted by the male! My God!"[9] And, though Gwen had missed the sociological context of the argument, it has become clear that there was something of romantic martyrdom in de Beauvoir's abdication of her talent to Sartre's greater genius.

Gwen wrote to Irving Layton: "No woman yet has poetically celebrated sex with the honesty and stamina of conscious flesh, conscious being ... The only real women I know are women who have something of the man in them ... and the only real men are those who have something of the woman."[10] She was writing this to the man who had invented himself as Canada's priapic poet, but in those days few women penetrated the implicit misogyny of that stance. For now, Gwen seems to have felt that the problem lay with women not celebrating their own sexuality. Like many young women in the first half of the sixties, she bought into the illusion that if that happened everything could be solved.

Gwen did not anticipate the slow burgeoning of feminism as, say, her friend Margaret Atwood was beginning to do, but she did see herself as a political being, and was deeply interested in the anti-war movement of the mid-sixties. In 1965, American draft dodgers had begun crossing the border into Canada, bringing with them their political activism. Those who came to Toronto often found their way to Ward's Island to one or other of the local communal houses. Gwendolyn believed deeply in their cause and tried to incorporate it into *Saturnalia*. In a strange narrative, she invents a man in a Toronto movie-house watching a film about Vietnam that has a sizzling sex plot. He comes out of the film not appalled by the violence but rather aroused:

> You have left the hot lush vegetation of bloodsoaked Vietnam. Now you step into the seething streets and you want someone to go to bed with. You notice that every time you see a war film you want sex afterwards. It's the idea that fleshiness and earthiness and bloodsoaked vegetation all go together. Sex, after all, is an atrocity too, not real but very realistic. You go to a bar, pick up a redhead who's fleshy and earthy like you, take her to a hotel, strip, and carry off the whole thing rather well, considering ... But you'd like to see her breasts exposed amidst the bloodsoaked vegetation of Vietnam, but instead they're there as always between clinical sheets and you feel cheated....[11]

She was attempting to link war, violence, and sexual machismo, but it wasn't working. Gwendolyn, however deeply she felt, could never write a straightforwardly political work. The novel was becoming completely unwieldy, and she abandoned it in disgust.

There was a social and implicitly political side to Gwendolyn's writing, but her invective had to be personal, directed against a modern society that took too many casualties. She was best when writing portraits of the broken, the misfits, those whom society had rejected as peripheral. She was always drawn to the outsiders, to hide her "loneliness in their deeper loneliness."

One such was the black sailor she had met on a train from Fredericton to Halifax when she was giving poetry readings in the Maritimes. His conversation was half-mad. He had just gotten out of what he called "the hospitality" and told her about his life as a sailor. "I'm not scared to cross the Great Atitude, Miss," he said. "They say the Atlantic, but I know it's the attitude, cause you go down the Longitude to reach the Atitude, you follow me?" She claimed only to have extrapolated his conversation in the poem she wrote to him:

> ... "Look now, you be always at the centre,
> even in a big Congomeration of people,
> and all the words you talk here
> go down to the sea, and the tide
> brings 'em back tomorrow morning.
> I tell you this so you won't fear
> and you always know just where you stand
> and how you're turning."
>
> He turned the old German compass
> over and over in his sure black hands.
> "I had this fifteen years," he said,
> "but I give it to you now so you
> can get ahead in life,
> and learn the Longitudes and the Atitudes
> and figure out just where you stand."...[12]

All she could think to give him was her book of poems. He told her he too was writing "to get ahead in life," and showed her a battered notebook where he'd written in "big scared lines" the first few letters of the alphabet. He was obviously illiterate and learning to write. But Gwen would turn this into a mythic statement—the letters of the alphabet are "scary" when you think of the implications of words. Yet there was a danger in these identifications: empathy can shift easily into sentimentality—she could radically underestimate how extraordinary and exceptional she was. Identifying with the broken, she could fail to identify the people who could match her strength.

There was, of course, an immediate reason for Gwendolyn's identification with those on society's periphery. Her mother was still very much a part of her story. Between bouts in the hospital, Elsie moved from one boarding-house to another, according to a predictable pattern. At first she would be happy, but then she would become "complaintive." In one home, for instance, run by a Mrs. Brown who was a friend of one of Elsie's long-lost sisters in London, Elsie was welcomed and fussed over. The family would take her driving, but then Elsie would expect to travel with them everywhere. She resented there being other roomers in the house. She moved.

On and off Elsie worked at Eaton's as a saleslady. The work would go well, but then her paranoia would take over. She would write letters to her manager, a Mr. Randall, complaining that disreputable characters were always approaching her counter to steal from her and there was a dope ring functioning in the store. She felt that the drug traffickers could recognize her instability; they were attempting to seduce her into addiction and prostitution. Sometimes she thought they were sent by former patients from the hospital on whom she had tattled to the staff. Paranoia is really a pseudo-rational way of imposing an order on events when the world seems out of control. One could see the logic to Elsie's paranoia. She was taking at various times and in varying doses: lithium, Tofranil, Sparine, amphetamine, Amytal, Parnate, Stelazine, Elavil, Largactil; someone *was* seducing her into addiction.

On another occasion Elsie had a vision of a leering, horrible face at her counter—it was the face of a former disturbed patient she had watched from her window at the Manitoba Psychiatric Hospital. But this was not what a store manager wanted to hear. Elsie would be let go and told that she would need a doctor's approval before she could be rehired. That she was rehired, however, says much for her kindly manager. She was caught in a familiar cycle. She would try to quit her drugs as an experiment and fall into depression, which only more drugs could relieve. The doctors spoke of her repressed hostility and rage. They also recognized she was anxiously reaching out for help. Beginning in 1960, she spent an average of seven months of the year at the Queen Street Mental Health Centre until November 4, 1963, when she entered and stayed, with only a brief interlude of two months, until December 2, 1965. She had become a permanent resident.

The poet Margaret Avison remembers Elsie at the Queen Street Mental Health Centre. "If you visit Queen Street," she told me, "you get to be very comfortable with the patients. Unlike the staff, they have no masks."[13] Avison was working as a social worker for the Presbyterian Church Mission down the street. The Mission organized picnics and outings on weekends when the patients were otherwise left to their own devices. "There was a lot of suicide over the weekends," she remembers. "That was our entrée. There was a wonderful doctor there who welcomed outsiders doing things. Elsie was great on those picnics. She loved coming back to the hospital and playing hostess. I used that the minute I spotted it. She poured the tea and encouraged the shy ones."

Avison knew Gwen was grateful for the little bit of social life she could provide Elsie. She recalls having tea with Elsie and Gwen across from the hospital. "In all Gwen's responses to her mother you would never know that intellectual sophistication was in her nature. It was this lovely simple accepting human being, a little embarrassed at her mother's pride in her. I remember the two of them. She met her mother as though Elsie were the young woman she must have been in her youth. She could be very hard on Gwen—on anybody. Gwen knew that. It bothered her not to be able to provide for her mother."

In the long and painful year of 1962 during her trysts with Milton, Gwen wrote a poem of love to her mother.

> ... wary we speak from a fringe of meanings,
> each tongue censored with love and its
> cat-paw circling
>   ,now foetal in the world's wide womb
>   ,now known in my own rebellious belly
>   the stuff to people further days
>   ,now forced by some grim reason

>   to hark down the bonds of the blood
>   ,can still remember from that womb walking,
>   sideways out of that womb,
>   glorious from that womb, bent and insolent.
>
> —morning laughter with your young daughter—
> smile at the pen she picks, armed to bring light
> into terrible focus
> and the paper builds worlds but makes
> no prodigal ...
>
> who would erase the scribbled slate
> of gone years, their jumbled algebra,
> their rude designs
> junked under a rainbow, all blood and bone
> that links the mother and the morning daughter—
> and acknowledge now, armed and still insolent
> that what is housed in the fragile skull
> —light or learning or verbal innocence—
> grows from the woman somehow who housed the whole body,
> who first fed the vessels, the flesh and the sense.[14]

It is a moving statement of courage, which Gwen stuck by. She had grown somehow from that woman and her suffering, and she would always acknowledge her. For one of her readings in the Ontario schools, she made notes on her manuscript to explain the poem: "It is a celebration of the only origin we can be sure of. If we cannot first accept the reality of our own bodies, the humility there, then what *are* we able to accept."[15] It is of course a public explanation for the poem. She would not have told the students her mother lived at the Queen Street Mental Health Centre.

She also now wrote the only poem she would write to her father:

>   ... you
> were classic somewhere in Canada on sunday
> touching trees where old apples fall and birds occur—
>
> (give us that particular cruelty necessary
> to take it, your life, a second time, ...[16]

She had repeatedly dreamed of burying her father. Here she seems to ask that the burial be finished.

Gwen longed to help her mother. Once, standing at her mother's hospital window watching a crane in the harbour, she wrote in her notebook: "Mother I have found a god for you, but your world is the world of parnate pills." "Mother, if only I could get you to LOOK at the damn thing sitting there in the harbour like a bored giraffe, if only you could come and SEE it, then you would *believe* in you, then you would forget parnate."[17] This was a note, of course, that it would do no good to send. She felt her mother's despair had most to do with her complete lack of a sense of self, and she traced that back to her personal history. For years Gwen had walked down dusty hospital corridors smelling of sickly sweet drugs; she had seen many people put there to have what she called "the wide wound" made by life stitched together. She believed in the wound.

> ... the imponderable agony
> of *being* here, of having
> to have a shape, a foot, an ugly face,
> a mind, a fit upon the floor
> when the soul breaks out of the screeching teeth
> and every nerve and muscle is screaming for release....[18]
>   "A Dance at the Mental Hospital"

Against this backdrop of personal tragedy, the pragmatic Gwen was working aggressively on her writing career. Her publisher, Macmillan, wanted her to promote her novel *Julian the Magician*. "It's selling OK," she wrote to Al Purdy, but "it needs a push like me with pigtails appearing in Weekend magazine or something to get it going better." "I'm waiting for some semi-intelligent newsman to discover that I'm a child prodigy and do a big Weekly flash, and give the book some limelight. Hell, [Marie-Claire] Blais got it on the basis of being 19, and I wasn't any older when I wrote it." They talked of Purdy writing an article: "You could say I'm bravely facing the elements in a small cottage or something, you know, introverted and alienated from society and all that nonsense.... To make the article really hot, dwell on the fact that a lot of my writing was done in my TEENS and early twenties; now I'm an old 22."[19] Purdy wrote back: "Please don't alibi yourself by saying you're brilliantly precocious. It ought to be enough to be the authentic you which requires no explanation."[20]

In the spring of 1964, Robert Weaver accepted five poems for *The Tamarack Review*. Weaver remembered that when he hand-delivered the order to Eaton's—the magazine was run on a shoestring and he delivered the issues himself—he was confronted by one of the saleswomen: "You're the *Tamarack* man."[21] He was asked to wait while Elsie was called; she had told everyone her daughter's poems were in the magazine. Elsie came forward to greet Weaver, beaming her pleasure.

Gwen was struggling for money. Thoughts of visiting Purdy and his wife were on hold because she didn't have the "dough." She told him she was waiting to hear if, by "some miracle," the CBC would come through with a contract for her to do a broadcast. It would be five hundred dollars: "one programme of this kind will pay all my bills, plus some ... what a break."

In the fall Gwen was sent on a poetry tour with Irving Layton and Leonard Cohen. (When I spoke to Cohen, he said Gwen was charming, but he remembered no details. He was not good at memories. "There's ten years of my life I don't remember and I don't want to remember," he explained.)[22]

That winter, *The Atlantic Monthly* did a supplement on Canada, including articles like: "Why Young Men Leave" and "The Trouble with Quebec" and a section on poetry. There was a poem each by Anne Hébert, Earle Birney, James Reaney, George Bowering, and Gwendolyn MacEwen.[23] When Gwen was interviewed in "The Women's *Globe and Mail*" section of *The*

Globe and Mail, she said she was delighted to be in the *Atlantic* issue. It suggested she might eventually become a writer who could live off her writing.

Sometime in early 1965, Gwen's personal life took a new direction. The relationship with Bob Mallory finally ended. In Mallory's memory, the parting was gentle; he went on to a new lover. For Gwendolyn it seems to have been much more complicated. She had become afraid. She finally recognized that in living with Mallory she was herself courting madness. She had a dream of Mallory in which he phoned and said: "Hello Gwendolyn, the weather is fine, I sliced off the top of my skull and used it for a bowl to put my brains in (whimsically, as though you were talking about an avocado)."[24] There was a part of Gwendolyn that wanted to play with powers that could destroy one, hoping that there actually existed powers that could destroy. "I do not fear that I will go mad/but that I may not, and the shadows of my sanity/blacken out your burning."[25] But she was coming too close to danger and could lose herself. She believed we all exist on the soul's shoreline; the way she put it was that we live at that point where "the soul eases up upon the beach of the brain." Mallory was folding in upon himself like a wave, folding under. She had thought she could come to know Mallory, while guarding herself against his madness. She had wanted to watch what she called the "savage flower of the mind unfolding naturally," but she discovered that the greatest danger to ourselves can be ourselves. For Mallory's equilibrium and for her own she had to pull back. Finding an apartment in the city, she left the island, and Mallory, to save herself.

In one poem of that time, she writes about suicide:

> The Choice
>
> and so we have a choice of several deaths.
>
> death one, the catapult farflung wish
> > from the stomach or the skullcave
> > shot like a bat out of belfries

> or various hells, like a horse
> through a landscape of cardboard
> calendars.
>
> death two, it is lovely, it is lovely
> > the second death, you
> > do not even know it, you
> > just fold up on a subway
> > like yesterday's newspaper
> > until someone picks you up
> > not bothering to read you.
>
> death three, it is dirty, dirty
> > the third death because
> > you plan it. it offends
> > people, it is offensive, a car
> > from a cliff, a hole behind
> > the eyes, a drug dream.
>
> and so we have a choice of several deaths
> and that in itself is a consolation.
> so go to it love, go to it:
> the red of the flower your fingers are holding,
> the green in the speech of your mouth;
> drive it, drive the horse through landscapes
> like calendars of cardboard, or nonsense mosaics
> for we are great statements in our days
>
> and on the basis of that we can expect small audiences.26

Gwendolyn even frightened herself with this poem. She spoke of it afterwards almost apologetically: "It's about death, but not about real death."[27]

For five or six years Gwendolyn and Mallory continued to have Christmas dinners together. David Mason remembers that Gwen always spoke of Mallory the way one talks of someone one cares for very much. Years later, she would still seek out Mason in his bookstore—she thought of him as one of Mallory's defenders. It occurs to him now that never once did they talk of Mallory's mental illness. "It was just two people talking about Bob and I realize now, thinking about it, how it was immensely flattering to me. She knew I understood that nothing needed to be said." "There's something in my character," he tells me, "that makes what I call the outsider, the people who don't belong, sympathetic." And of course it seems obvious: our characters, our human allegiances to the insider, the outsider, are dictated less by ideology than by the pressure of our whole history. Gwendolyn, like Mason, would always choose the outsider.

Sometime in the late sixties, the city sent in bulldozers and flattened Mallory's house, probably for non-payment of taxes and land rent. Most likely Mallory had not paid the rent for years—Mason thinks he would not have known how, and the landlord had abandoned the property. The city was threatening to kick the islanders out of their homes, and their only defence was to insist they were a friendly little family community. The loss of a house that was a fire hazard lived in by a crazy man would not have been missed. The house went, and Mason believes the paintings that were probably in it went too. His deepest regret is that he didn't have the sense to save the paintings. Mallory stopped painting sometime in the sixties, and not a single canvas survives. Bob Mallory's paranoia about the controllers, the "They" who intruded on his life, was, on this occasion, justified.

Homeless, Mallory must have turned to Gwen. She wrote to David Mason in March 1970:

> Dear Dave,
> We've been out of touch regarding the island situation, and I imagine you've been as busy as I. I'm writing this because I know you'd like to know what I intend to do after all this time has elapsed.

It's taken me a long while to come around to this decision, but—well, I'm not going to do anything further. Since Bob's been in the city, I've seen him regularly and done pretty well all I could to help him out financially. He seems better to be off the island, and I think that the move has been accomplished in that direction. I kept thinking of phoning you and making plans—but I kept getting sidetracked with work—plus—and this is harder to define—the idea kept gnawing away at me that maybe more and more *material* help is not going to do any real good—I mean, Bob tends to become more and more dependent on his friends doing things he should try to do—that dependency is never stated but it's always present—and I'm beginning to admit to a real weariness and tension after so many years of "helping"—(I use the word advisedly, because I'm also admitting a kind of failure as a friend—) no point going into greater detail here, Dave, but I wanted you to know that I'll continue doing what I can in the city—but regret I really can't face the island again.

Hope you'll understand (and excuse)....

Best wishes,
Gwendolyn.[28]

How extraordinarily guilty Gwen sounds in this letter. For years she had been taking care of Mallory, and yet she had failed as a friend. Gwendolyn had been set up for this. Her mother always manipulated her with a dependency never stated—but searingly felt. It had been her fault not to have saved her father. It was her fault, according to Milton, that their marriage had failed. It was always her fault. Gwendolyn never expected that love gave something to you. It only took. The cost of turning her back on anyone, even for their own good, was enormous. How complexly it worked, because, of course, Gwen also needed to feel indispensable if she was to feel safe. The tragedy of her family had taught her that was the only love she could get.

13
FALLING IN LOVE WITH ARABIC

In early 1965, Gwen moved into her own apartment at 1512 King Street West, on the edge of Parkdale. The building, a four-storey stucco structure decorated with pseudo-Tudor slats, was on the north side just where King Street curved up towards Roncesvalles Avenue and the houses on the south side disappeared. From her apartment window she would have had an unobstructed view of the lake, and whenever she stepped out of her front door, could still believe she lived on a harbour. She was not far from her old neighbourhood, only a short walk from the lower end of High Park.

Toronto was changing. The counter-cultural wave of the sixties was beginning to swell, though the hippie phenomenon that would hit like a cyclone and turn Toronto's Yorkville, north of Bloor Street, into a hallucinatory version of San Francisco's Haight-Ashbury, was still two years in the future. In 1965 two young Canadians were making an impact on the city's poetry scene: Margaret Atwood and Gwendolyn MacEwen. Atwood was writing the poems that would make up her first book, *The Circle Game*, which would win the Governor General's Award in 1966, and Gwendolyn was working on A *Breakfast for Barbarians*.

Now there was no longer a venue where the poets regularly gathered. The Bohemian Embassy had long since lost its status as a focal centre and would only survive another year. But when Gwen did read at the occasional benefit, or in the local clubs like the Soft Cell on King Street, run by Liz Woods, or at the Village Book Store, where Marty Ahvenus hosted readings from time to time, she would have been typecast as a Beat poet.

> my friends, my sweet barbarians,
> there is that hunger which is not for food—
> but an eye at the navel turns the appetite
> round
> with visions of some fabulous sandwich,
> the brain's golden breakfast
> > eaten with beasts
> > with books on plates
>
> let us make an anthology of recipes,
> let us edit for breakfast
> our most unspeakable appetites—
> let us pool spoons, knives
> and all cutlery in a cosmic cuisine,
> let us answer hunger
> with boiled chimera
> and apocalyptic tea,
> an arcane salad of spiced bibles,
> tossed dictionaries—
> > (O my barbarians
> > we will consume our mysteries)
>
> and can we, can we slake the gaping eye of our desires?
> we will sit around our hewn wood table

> until our hair is long and our eyes are feeble,
> eating, my people, O my insatiates,
> eating until we are no more able
> to jack up the jaws any longer—
>
> to no more complain of the soul's vulgar cavities,
> to gaze at each other over the rust-heap of cutlery
> drinking a coffee that takes an eternity—
> till, bursting, bleary,
> we laugh, barbarians, and rock the universe—
> and exclaim to each other over the table
> over the table of bones and scrap metal
> over the gigantic junk-heaped table:
>
> by God that was a meal[1]

The new audiences were devotees of the Beats and sixties folk music. Many would have been early draft dodgers, and suburban kids escaping the shackles of the bourgeoisie. They would have shouted and laughed and banged their chairs as she read "A Breakfast for Barbarians"—her outrageous humour was exactly what they meant. She had caught their metaphor of appetite: "Eat!" she cried. "The universe fits."

In the mid-sixties, poetry aficionados went to the Village Book Store, where they could count on finding copies of all Jack Kerouac's limited signed editions. Ahvenus would get books from the small presses in the U.S. or from the Turret Book Shop in England. From the time it opened in 1961, the local poets had adopted the store, since Ahvenus bought their books and chapbooks, or if money was short, took them on consignment, and actually displayed them in the window where people could see them. Poets used the store as a place to send mail, since it usually provided a more permanent address than their own shifting lives.[2]

But when Gwen became a regular at Ahvenus's, she was not buying the Beat poets, she was accumulating a library of Egyptology. Though

"A Breakfast for Barbarians" might sound bohemian, Gwen was not a Beat poet. She was too private, too secretive, and perhaps too intellectually serious. She complained that the Beats in the U.S. were only concerned with style. While she was deeply aware of technique, she insisted she was far more concerned with content.[3] Beneath her poem were longings and admissions of a sophisticated sense of impoverishment—what she referred to as "the soul's vulgar cavities"—that had little to do with bohemian notions of freedom.

Calling herself an exile in place and time, Gwen always went her own way, apart from trends or movements. Now her imagination returned to the deserts of ancient Egypt, an obsession from the age of fourteen when she had evoked Nefertiti in the desert, longing for the father. Egypt was exotic, more compelling than her present, and matched the archetypal space she entered so easily in her dreaming mind. It was vestigial, closer to the beginning of human time, closer to that vast reservoir of myths and mysteries that she felt was her real subject.

Now she began a serious study of modern Arabic and of Egyptian hieroglyphics. Perhaps it was a compensation impulse. Canada, she complained, was "so quaint, so naive, so hopeless"[4]; she required a richer historical and cultural fabric from which to work. But it seems curious that each time she began a new phase in her life, Gwen learned a new language. At eighteen she had learned Hebrew. Now, with Ward's Island and its mad magician behind her, she turned to the Arabic language and to hieroglyphics. It was as if the ordered structure of a new language gave her a way to fine-tune her mind, gave her mind a structure to hold on to.

Gwen began to read the world-renowned philologist Sir Alan Gardiner. The spine of her copy of his historical study *Egypt of the Pharaohs*[5] is broken from hundreds of consultations. Her manuscripts of this time are filled with hieroglyphic drawings as she learned the twenty-four-lettered alphabet, discovering how the language evolved from a combination of ideograms (picture signs) and phonograms (sound signs), and the mysterious miniature signs released their meanings. The language would have satisfied her eye as well as her mind, awakening the painter in her. Her knowledge became sophisticated enough that she could write her own poems in hieroglyphics, publishing several in *Prism International* along with English translations. She also bought the 1964 two-volume *A Grammar of the Arabic Language* by W. Wright, *An Elementary Classical Reader* by M.C. Lyons, and *Colloquial Arabic* by T.F. Mitchell.

And then, that spring of 1965, Gwendolyn met a young Egyptian called Salah.

Gwen always seemed to live her life in separate pockets, but by the time she moved into the apartment on King Street, she became even more secretive. She took to using her sister's address for most of her professional correspondence, because, she said, she needed to guard her private life very closely. If she offered a friend her personal address, it was a sign of intimacy.

To those who knew Gwendolyn, her Egyptian friend, Salah, remained only a shadow. Her sister, Carol, and Margaret Atwood remembered only a handsome young foreigner they noted in passing. No one remembered his last name. Only Bob Mallory offered a description of him. He recounted seeing Salah for the first time when Gwendolyn brought him to Ward's Island: "Tears of abstract joy or grief came to my eyes as I saw him approaching from a distance. I knew immediately he was the man invented for Gwendolyn."[6] From Mallory, it is a formulation that seems perfectly appropriate.

Salah was one of the most important figures in Gwendolyn's life. Years later, when she was angrily countering misperceptions about her marriage to Milton Acorn, insisting that her "brief marriage" to Milton had only lasted a few months, she added: "If anyone's interested, I lived with an Egyptian engineer for six years."[7] Twenty years after she met him, she could write in "Letter to an Old Lover"—"Salah, I have not forgotten you." She imagined him lost in another life somewhere in Cairo.

I began my search for Salah knowing only his first name and having heard a vague story that he had been studying for an M.A. in chemistry at McGill University sometime between 1966 and 1968; but such is our shared compulsion to solve mysteries that this meagre information would prove enough. I phoned McGill's Graduate Programme in Chemistry, only to be told that most of the old records from the sixties had been burned in a fire. Then I found a female administrator who was willing to search for a lost lover with an exotic first name. Her enthusiasm for the search had something to do with nostalgia—we have all had lost lovers—and with the fascination we feel for the mystery of memory, for recovering broken-off pieces of the past.

I phoned the Egyptian Embassy in Ottawa with a list of likely Arab names of former McGill students, and again the elusiveness of a lost love proved compelling, this time to a male communications officer, who, unable to provide any leads, gave me the addresses of Cairo newspapers in which to advertise. But serendipitously, the woman at McGill was able to locate Salah in a Montreal directory. He had not returned to Cairo as Gwen had imagined, but, all these years, had been living a parallel life in Montreal. I reflected—who was I to walk into his life carrying a piece of his past that had gone missing?—and yet, when I had gathered my nerve, I phoned. To my question of whether he was the Salah who had known Gwendolyn MacEwen, there was a shocked silence, and then he agreed to meet me, enabling me to pick up the narrative of Gwendolyn's life.

In 1965, Salah was twenty-four. A young Egyptian from a sophisticated, upper-middle-class family, he seemed to have stepped out of a Lawrence Durrell novel. He was extremely handsome and had that peculiar Cairene erudition that could run from Egyptian mythology, to mechanical science, to the poetry of Rilke. He had abandoned his native Cairo in disgust at the military government of Abdel Nasser, knowing that if he stayed he would have to serve in Nasser's army. As a possible destination, he did not consider the U.S.—it was involved in Vietnam. Europe was too familiar, and Australia had been branded with Second World War anecdotes of Aussie soldiers cleaning their guns with bread while starving Egyptian children looked on. He thought of Canada as neutral, a strange emptiness of snow. With one spare shirt and jacket, Salah set out for Canada to learn English. He immediately found work and was then accepted by the University of Toronto to complete his B.Sc. degree. He was a romantic nationalist, embroiled in Middle-Eastern politics—like many young Egyptians he had fantasies of blowing up either his corrupt native government or Israel. Yet he believed longingly in the *old* imagination of his people: the mental geography of desert and sun that defined the polarities of their being. The last thing he was prepared for when he arrived in Toronto was to walk into the arms of a young Canadian poet, beautiful, sensual, who could read hieroglyphics, and was consumed by his own Egyptian mysteries. Soon he moved into Gwendolyn's apartment on King Street, and began what felt like a magical existence. He met some of Gwendolyn's friends—he vaguely remembered Margaret Atwood—but always briefly. He did not speak much English. "It was like being in a glass alembic; we were autonomous, the only two people in the world," he said.[8] Salah was never involved in her professional life. That was something apart.

In 1965, Gwen was at the height of her confidence as a writer. While Margaret Atwood had gone to Radcliffe to do an M.A. in 1961, believing she could never survive as a writer in Canada, never live off poetry, and that she would have to teach, Gwen was sure she could make it. She was pulling in just enough money to live from poetry-reading tours. Michael Ondaatje remembered how important it had been to the young writing community at Queen's University when Gwen came to read in 1965. She was the poet people most wanted to hear.[9]

She had now begun to think of translation as a way of making some money. Her French was good; she would start with French. She wrote to Marie-Claire Blais, whose novel *La Belle Bête* she deeply admired—she thought of Blais as a kind of half-sister—and suggested she might translate some of her poems. Blais found her translations "impressive," and suggested: "Maybe, during the spring, when I would have translate

[sic] some of yours (je n'ai pas très confiance en moi, mais je sens assez bien ce que vous écrivez, it is the same dreary and real world, do you think, but you are more rigorous than I about language, often I me perds dans l'image), maybe in spring I could meet you."[10] They did not meet. Blais moved to the United States, where her career was encouraged by the American critic Edmund Wilson, to whom Blais introduced Gwen's work, though nothing seems to have come of this contact.

Gwen was also earning some money reading manuscripts for her publisher, Macmillan, and, since late 1963, she had, at the invitation of Robert Weaver, begun to do the occasional broadcasts for the CBC. Weaver produced the programme "Anthology," and, in 1964, asked her to write original verse plays for him. She wrote *Terror and Erebus*, a dramatization of the Franklin expedition in search of the North West Passage, and, in 1966, a play called *Tesla*, based on Nikola Tesla, the original inventor of electricity. She also read her own poetry on "Anthology." Two decades later, Weaver remembered apologizing to Gwen because he could only pay $150 for each programme; but she patted his arm and replied: "That would have kept me in Kraft Dinners for three or four months."[11]

Living with Salah, Gwen continued her study of Arabic, but he insists she pursued it on her own. "She learned Arabic in a vacuum because I wasn't helping her. She got a book, she read, she'd spend hours studying the words." Within several months she had mastered the language enough to speak her own version of it—a rather wonderful and original combination of high literary Arabic and Cairo street dialect. She made grammatical and idiomatic errors, of course, but she used to say that she could pick up languages so easily because she didn't take the whole process very seriously and went about it in a rather haphazard way, bearing in mind that "language is nothing more than a bunch of sounds coming out of the mouth," and that she was a parrot, with a good ear for the rhythms of speech. That was her characteristic modesty. In fact she loved the very idea of words—watching as the ornate Arabic script of incomprehensible circles, dashes, and curlicues with sudden hooks transformed itself from an alien code into comprehensible meaning. She wrote to Margaret Atwood in June 1965:

> Have not been writing all spring, but studying Arabic instead. A beautiful and infuriating language, ludicrously illogical in all aspects. 6 declensions of nouns and adjs. plus irregular plurals for every noun, depending on the sense you want. My first grammar was terribly classical and I was learning things like "The Caliph is the shadow of God on the earth." Now I have a modern grammar and am learning somewhat more useful things.
>
> Picking up vast vocabularies is fairly easy; I find myself relating English sound-equivalents to words. e.g. to be busy is "mush-ghew-lun" which sounds like mushroom. Are you free tonight? No sorry, I'm frightfully mushroomed just now.
>
> And so on. It is a beautiful language, and I've been promising myself for years that I would tackle it; glad to find myself with the time and inclination to do so. Have an Egyptian friend who helps me in pronunciation.[12]

The previous fall of 1964, before she had met Salah, she had applied to The Canada Council for a writer's grant to pursue a new project; she had decided she wanted to write a biographical novel about Akhenaton, the heretic Pharaoh of the Eighteenth Dynasty. She had applied once before for a grant and been turned down, so she was shocked and somewhat overwhelmed to discover she had been awarded one. She wrote to Margaret of the delight she felt at the prospect of a year's security, and told her the project was "a whopper." "When I think of it I turn pale blue all over." She knew that there had been a resurgence of interest in Akhenaton, "but to my knowledge no comprehensive and meaty historical novel has been done on him."[13] (She would only later discover Mika Waltari's novel *The Egyptian*.) She was ambitious. She wanted her novel to join the ranks of books like Robert Graves's *I Claudius*, Gore Vidal's *Julian*, and Mary Renault's *The King Must Die*. "That's the kind of thing I like best of all," she wrote Al Purdy. She wanted it to be "bulky, readable, and not overly mysterious. Working monomaniacally (duomaniacally?) on Akhenaton and Arabic grammar."[14]

Ever confident, she thought she could enter the international élite of historical novelists—she could write novels and make enough money to sustain the poetry. She had once said: "I don't call myself a poet, I call myself a writer. There is no justification for the person who just writes poetry, the one who lies on his bed and finds a line every hour and gets so precious he can't go out to work. No, I don't think the poet should be subsidized, the world doesn't owe him a living. I like to work for what I get. In a recent *Atlantic* there's a Canadian section and they published one of my poems. That's how I'd like to get paid all the time."[15]

Gwen's research on her novel was thorough. She collected a library of twenty-one Egyptologists specializing in the Amarna period, subscribed to the *Archaeological Review*, and wrote letters to American, British, German, and Egyptian museums, searching for photographs of the mummies of her characters, to one letter getting the amusing response: "The mummy about which you have inquired is in Cairo."[16] She spent weeks at the Royal Ontario Museum scouring their Egyptian collection with her friend the sculptor and painter Mac Reynolds. She overlooked no detail. She wrote flippantly to Jane Rule in Vancouver that she was particularly interested in Egyptian dental problems, a moot point maybe, but "a *moot point* is a molar root, or didn't you know?"

In the fall of 1965, perhaps influenced by Salah's academic ambitions and thinking a degree might, after all, mean financial security, Gwen applied to the University of Toronto to take an undergraduate degree in Middle Eastern Studies. She could claim to speak Hebrew and Arabic, and list three books of poetry and a novel to her credit. She was turned down on the grounds that she hadn't completed her high-school matriculation. But in January, the university, seemingly on its own initiative, reviewed her application and accepted her on her own merits.

The prospect set her in a panic. "Am I nuts," she asked Margaret, "that I actually regret the idea of ceasing to write after 4 (altogether) books published and me 24? that I have cold chills thinking about no writing if I go into this course? that I fear I will run screaming from the campus on the second day, since I am no longer able to exist in any sort of 'group' environment like a university?"[17] She couldn't imagine the loss of freedom and the commitment to a project that was not writing. She asked Margaret, who had been through universities, for a "kind, or better still, a useful word." But Gwen kept her humour. She wrote again: "Are you summering in Toronto by any chance? I am summering in Toronto, alas, and probably Falling and Wintering as well, after briefly Marching in Cairo. Oh well." She described her rigid schedule:

> As well as writing the book, I've been drawing maps of ancient Asia, and plotting various military campaigns with Hittites etc. (One has to be nuts to do this).... If you have any Hittite or Mitannian problems in the course of your studies, don't hesitate to contact me; I'll send you maps and a selected bibliography of Rare Hittitania (the new wave of Hittite poetry. The cuneiform record reveals that circa 1375 BC they were awfully worried about the breath-line and heart-beat technique in their poetry, at a time when the Habiru invaders were still hung up on their local bard Tas Eliot). I'd better close as it is evident that the rubber band I use to hold my brain together is going to snap any day.[18]

From the beginning of her relationship with Salah, Gwen found herself deeply in love and there was a new imperative—she was still married to Milton and she wanted a divorce. In the mid-sixties, to obtain a divorce one had to sue for adultery. She wrote carefully to Milton in Vancouver, saying she had saved a few hundred dollars and would be willing to pay all legal expenses, explaining that the process shouldn't be very complicated since they both had sufficient grounds; it all seemed quite silly. She must have anticipated an explosion, since she realized Milton was still in love with her. He had written to her the previous August.

August 30, 1965.

Dear Gwen;
    ... I've done a lot of writing in the last three years, tho little of it has gone out to editors. There seems little point and little use in it when my own love was cast off and thrown away, as if it was of no account or meaning. All my life I've stood against the cheats, the kibitzers, the cynics. They won. They couldn't write poetry like me but they could steal my happiness ... even tho they could make nothing of it themselves.
    God how I loved you! How proud I was that you loved me. Yet I did little writing. I was entirely absorbed in you and what you were doing. I thought I was thru writing, but separation from you opened up entire new areas of experience. It also drove me crazy ... perhaps the two are connected. Lying with you in bed at night I used to talk as I never talked to any person before or since. You understood me, and I was beginning to understand you more deeply. I couldn't tell you but I was beginning to know how to play your moods. It was people you needed, a relationship with real people doing real things. It is this real communication between human beings that is needed ... not the dizzy bed-hopping game. I wished I could have told you that, but I couldn't. There are some things that just can't be said. Now I suppose you look on my love for people with amused contempt, an unforgivable softness in a world where people need to be hard ... where there is no honor, no justice, no truth; and those who believe in them are pitiful weaklings.[19]

Sadly, Milton still seemed to be nurturing the hope that, despite everything, Gwen would one day return to him. When he thought back nostalgically on their love, he felt he had been the only one able to give her solid ground to stand on. He may even have been right, in part, but only briefly. The ground under Milton was never solid for very long. His belief in the mutuality of their relationship was sadly mistaken, since Gwen knew the anger that surfaced whenever he was opposed. He would never accept her version of their breakup: that she had been too young and needed to confront the world on her own terms. Beneath this tender letter, she could read his egocentricity: he was still the only one who stood for honor, justice, truth. This must have been a difficult letter to receive, since it would have awakened her guilt.

To her request for a divorce, Milton responded quickly and vindictively: he pointedly refused to co-operate. He wanted to know why she had married him in the first place; why hadn't she just offered him "a piece of pie"? He, who had fought for love and freedom, was "no Don Quixote." He insisted that she had no chance of suing him—she couldn't prove adultery—and he wouldn't sue her.[20]

His belligerence turned her life into an agony. The only solution was that she must "entrap him." She wrote to Margaret, seemingly the only confidante she could trust:

> I have no end to agonizing problems just now. Here's another gruesome question for you. Do you know, or can you find out, any ANY ANY details of Milton's last summer affair with the 18 year old girl? Needless to say I have severe necessity for this. Acorn refuses me a divorce and I'm afraid I'm going to have to go thru the whole grisly mess to divorce him. Thot I'd ask you, you may know time, place, name of girl, name of street where lived, name of hospital where taken, name of anybody, anybody.

> Needless to say Peggy, this is all as secret as the big icicle on your window pane ... I'll have to start this whole ghastly investigation, unless Milt decides to divorce me himself (infinitely easier, as you can imagine).[21]

In February of 1966, leaving Salah in Toronto, Gwen headed to the West Coast for her "cloak and dagger" gathering of evidence. On Atwood's advice she sought "safe haven" with the writer Jane Rule. The first Rule knew of her coming was when Gwen phoned from the airport. It was the middle of an Arts Festival at UBC and Rule had the American poet Robert Duncan and his lover, the American painter Jess Collins, staying with her. Also staying was the American electronic composer Pauline Oliveros. Still, there was a free bed in Rule's study. They were in the middle of a dinner party with the composer John Cage when Gwen arrived. "At the moment Gwen phoned," Rule explains, "Pauline and John had decided to record the flushing of our main floor toilet because of the inordinate time it took to refill, and they had microphones in the toilet, wires stretched to the tape recorder across the hall in the living room." "What will Gwen make of all this?" she asked her partner, Helen. "If it bewilders her, she's in the wrong house" was the reply.[22] But Gwen took the chaos in stride, excusing herself early, still on Toronto time.

Because she didn't want Milton to know she was in town, Gwen had insisted Rule never use her name, but Rule knew Robert Duncan admired Gwen's writing, and could not bear the thought of their sitting at the same table meal after meal without his knowing who she was. She swore him to secrecy and he was able to talk enthusiastically to Gwen about her work. Amusingly, Gwen spent hours talking to this certain "Robert" and only when she returned to Toronto did she realize he was Robert Duncan. It was characteristic. She must have been distraught by the whole Milton affair, yet that she could remain "clueless and in the dark," as she put it, several times almost making the "ghastly blunder of asking 'Do you write?'" was consistent with Gwen. She was shy in all encounters, and without guile in cultivating other writers. Margaret Atwood would add to this that she often lived like a "sleep walker," missing what to others was obvious.[23]

After several days, Gwen had collected the information she needed on Milton without having to betray her secret to the literary circles and become a subject of gossip. She wrote to Margaret: "I would ask now only that you continue your Vow of Silence indefinitely, for things are by no means over and any leakage could be disastrous."[24]

Gwen did get her divorce. When she informed Milton by letter of her intentions, he wrote back scathingly, accusing her of being "the Great North American Castrator"; she had "tried to cut [his] nuts out" and had almost managed it.[25] On the 19th of April, with Al Purdy as a witness, Gwen sued Milton for divorce on the grounds of his having committed adultery. The marriage was officially dissolved on the 17th of June, 1966, four years after its brief five months of life. Purdy said simply: "I was best man at their wedding and worst man at their divorce. I agonized. I was friends of both. But I said to myself some such cliché: 'No man ought to hold on to a woman who doesn't want to be held on to.' The bottom line was Milton wouldn't give Gwen a divorce."[26]

In fact, even after the divorce, Gwendolyn would continue to be plagued by what she felt was Milton's shadow. The literary community would always tie her to him, perhaps because the relationship, typed as Beauty and the Beast, had seemed so incongruous. She felt it unfair— no one else was tied irrevocably to a man she had married for five months. To the end of her life she always felt she was made responsible for Milton.

14
TO CAIRO

While waiting for her divorce, Gwen set out in March on her first and only trip to Egypt. Salah was attending classes at the University of Toronto and was not free to accompany her, though she would visit his brother in Cairo. Her ostensible purpose was to research her novel on Akhenaton, but she had obviously been anticipating this trip for years—she had absorbed historical Egypt in her bones. She was not prepared, however, for the culture shock of modern Cairo.

Gwendolyn would have landed in that exotic city with her usual presumption that, even as a woman alone, she could get along. But the tourist boom that would sweep Egypt in the early seventies had not yet begun, and Egypt had little experience of tourists; in those days, the only hotel to stay in was the Nile Hilton. The city would have been filled with soldiers, already preparing for the war Egypt would wage against Israel in 1967. Landing in Cairo airport, Gwen would have been an anomaly. What was this slight, solitary woman doing in Egypt on her own? Even today, a woman rarely goes on her own to Egypt. Alone, she is an ambiguous entity, her motives for being there seemingly mysterious.

Gwen booked into the Hilton on Cornishe al-Nil Boulevard in the Midan Tahrir district of Cairo, a good hotel overlooking the Nile and across the square from the Egyptian Museum. The hotel has been upgraded since then, but the bar has remained the same—an exact replica of a British pub, as in a time warp, where the coasters lining the tables advertise McEwans ale. Perhaps Gwen would have sat there alone gathering her nerve to make her assault on Cairo. She headed out at 9:00 a.m. that first day, across Cleopatra Street, through the museum sculpture garden, past the papyrus swamp, and up the steps of the tattered old building that housed some of Egypt's greatest treasures. (Built in 1900, it would get a facelift before being presentable to tourists.)

Among her books, I have the 220-page guidebook she bought at the kiosk. Entering, she would have been shocked. The place resembled a cavernous mausoleum or storehouse, rambling and disorganized, so packed was it with artifacts. The catalogue detailed exhibits by number; there were 6,366 of them. She would have headed for the New Kingdom collection, containing artifacts from the Eighteenth-Dynasty Kings. She turned down the catalogue's pages detailing those objects that would surface in her novel: a statue of King Akhenaton holding his child, who is reaching up for a kiss; a sculptor's unfinished model of Akhenaton's daughters with their strange elongated skulls; armchairs; cushions of linen and pigeon feathers; all the domestic details of her characters' lives. But one object seems to have particularly moved her, the plaster pavement from the floor of Akhenaton's Amarna palace, discovered in 1891. It is exquisite: water lilies, birds, and fish float on the floor's surface as if they were alive. In her novel, Akhenaton's daughter Meritaton recalls playing on that floor, its marshes so real that she is sure she cannot be seen.

> I feel I am eight years old again, and I am falling, falling onto the magical floor in the palace of Horizon. My big turquoise ball rolls across the pavement, over the animals and birds, the painted cranes standing one-legged in their painted marshes. It rolls over the flat papyrus

> thickets, the herons and flamingos and kingfishers and ducks. How I loved that floor—the green zigzags on the plaster, the tall reeds and flat faces of the captives of Khor! ... I couldn't understand how anybody could just walk over it to get somewhere, without getting lost in it, or lying flat upon it like I did....
>
> The big turquoise ball went plop into the pond and I lay back imagining that I was painted onto the floor. Father would come and be unable to find me; he'd walk all over me and I'd just scream with laughter. Then he'd look down and see that his princess no longer lived in the world of men. They'd bring me my food and I'd still have to continue my writing lessons, but it would all be so much more tolerable. How silly everyone would look—giving advice to the floor, scolding it, taking orders from it![1]

Inside the museum, ancient Egypt was alive and resonant, but when Gwen stepped out into the city, Cairo was overwhelming. She found herself constantly harassed by prurient guards, stimulated by the presence of a solitary woman. She managed to visit Giza, to see the Sphinx and the pyramid complex, though to do so she would have had to battle opportunistic taxi drivers, camel drivers, and hawkers. The magic she had hoped for of course occurred as she climbed the hundreds of ramped steps to the interior of Cheops's Great Pyramid, and felt the weight of its history on her head. She visited Salah's family, only to find their reception cool, which she explained to herself as their not quite approving her casual Western style.

Gwen had gone to Egypt with the intention of staying two months, but suddenly, precipitously, after only eleven days, she decided she had had enough. She packed her bags and headed back to Toronto. She had become frightened and disoriented. She wrote, with some embarrassment, to Margaret in Massachusetts:

Dear Peggy,

The excuse for this letter lies mainly in the envelope, which you will notice is genuine El Amarna Period envelope, straight from the Nile Hilton hotel in Cairo. Alas, yes, I am back already in Toronto after a trip lasting 11 days. Quite mad, all that distance purely to see the Cairo Museum, but really Egypt is a country in Very Bad Shape, and the population of Cairo is staggering. I got no further than the pyramids and the museum, after which I was so exhausted I felt the only thing was to return. A strange air of pure tension hangs over Egypt, and affects one's psychological state very badly, if one is prone to that sort of thing, and I suppose I was....

The museum [was] very fine, except very dirty.... The El Amarna Floor, which I have been dreaming about for months, turned out to be covered with a thick layer of Egyptian dust. I began to seriously think about asking the officials if they would mind if I scrubbed it clean in order to study it. Also, if they would let me take some Ajax cleanser to the Akhenaton room in order to peer better into its murky cases. But a fabulous museum indeed, and the only person there who was wholly Clean was Tutankhamon, that spoiled brat whom I never liked anyway and he's getting his own back in my novel. Meanwhile, Akhenaton stands, lean and leering in his little el amarna room, and the only people who come here to see him are nuts like myself. A short, short trip, and no doubt I will regret all that money and distance, yet I didn't feel I would survive long in that Cairo tension, or anywhere else. I dreaded Thebes, and felt my own picture of it much cleaner than the actuality, once again. A most curious experience, but perhaps one's impressions are preserved more strongly if one takes off

quickly from somewhere, a little too quickly, allowing
the regret to keep the image forever moving in the mind.
O well....2

In retrospect, Gwen would be deeply upset at her panic. Though she tried to return to Egypt on at least two occasions, she never made it back. In her letter she puts up a brave front, but what was the source of her panic that made her feel she couldn't "survive long in the Cairo tension, or anywhere," that made her dread the trip to ancient Thebes and the Karnak Temple complex, where Akhenaton had erected his first palace, which she clearly longed to see, already knowing it by heart from her research? Certainly Cairo must have seemed alien, overpopulated, inaccessible, with no door into it. The military's perpetual presence might have added to her sense of tension. She must have missed Salah deeply. And yet, though she had been lonely in Jerusalem, she had managed that city.

Gwen rarely spoke of her trip to Egypt, but she did mention to friends her bitterness at the scrutiny of the male guides at the sites, of the male attendants at the museum, and how deeply unnerving it was. She felt they viewed her as fair prey, a Western female on the hunt. In her novel *Noman's Land*, her character Kali describes Egypt:

> ... It's even worse there for a woman to walk around alone. When I went every day to the museum in Cairo because there was so much to see, the guards thought I must have been playing some really sexy game with them; it was inconceivable that I would go alone to a museum every day—why? What was my real reason? I could not possibly have travelled half way around the world to stare at statues and mummies of the dead lords of Egypt, the gold of Tutankhamon, the most exquisite sculpture imaginable. No, I was indeed a tart, a slut, a whore. So they kept plying me with sugary tea and cigarettes, and they smiled and joked among themselves, and

when I didn't want more sugary tea they offered me *Misra-Cola*, and more cigarettes and endless offers of escorted tours around Cairo. Within a few days I had acquired a reputation of being one of the loosest women in the city, a tramp, an easy lay; and of course each one of them boasted to the others of his conquest of this piece of garbage, this foreigner.[3]

Gwen's anger at the Cairene guards is palpable, but she ends the scene with a humorous, if poignant, moment that, she told her sister, Carol, literally occurred. While in Cairo, Gwen saw a King Street tram lumbering down the street, still coloured dark red and yellow and still bearing its King Street sign above the windshield. (Apparently, Canada donated its old streetcars to Egypt.) Looming down on her, it looked like some "great fabulous beast" from a "distant mythic land" coming to save her. She ran towards it as if she were running home.

Gwen's anger at the sexual attention she was receiving is understandable; but that it might send her in flight from the country seems extraordinary, unless one looks carefully at her confusion. Though it might seem trivial, this was the same trap she was always falling into. Why did she have to be friendly? Why couldn't she just refuse the tea and cigarettes and dismiss the guards from her mind? She always found herself manipulated into the play. There was, clearly, something much more destructive going on for Gwen.

After her return, Gwen recorded in her notebook a dream that occurred while she was in Egypt. She must have felt it was deeply disturbing because she obviously spent time analysing it (when is not clear). She has circled words and added hand-written marginal comments (here identified in square brackets with the circled words underlined). The ellipses and numbers are hers:

[While I was in Egypt]

1966—A boy with <u>knives</u> and the <u>death</u> [defloration?] of a woman [mother?] in childbirth.   [sister—2nd death]

Together in a dark room and mother enters, carrying food, not noticing us there.

<u>It</u> [what? intercourse] was moving down and up a hill helped by the branch of a <u>tree</u>[1] which he fixated to the ground at one end, allowing himself and the upper part to <u>swing around</u> the <u>motionless part</u> ... the road was full of the chips from the <u>cutting</u> [defloration?] <u>of the tree along the sides</u> ... but the long branch <u>broke</u> into two extremely short halves, and he had to walk around the curve of the hill between <u>savages lying in huts and he was terrified, moved slowly for fear of being seen</u> [for what misadventure] ... walked on until light of moon <u>pierced</u> [defloration?] <u>a hole</u> in the shell of his <u>fear</u>, and on the hilltop where[2] the <u>last tree</u> was lying on its side <u>suffering</u> from the <u>hatch</u>, and its branches soft and alive like octopus arms just drawn from the ocean ... and when the tree was <u>pushed to fall</u> by a <u>savage</u> and his <u>son</u>, its arms stretched and its (ventricles) sucked each other and the tree rolled along the hill like a solid cylinder <u>whose trunk was bleeding</u> [defloration?] ... the top of the hill became green with grass and he saw a <u>huge tree</u>[3] isolated in the midst of the place and it was the <u>vengeance</u> tree where the spirits of the [2] tree which <u>had suffered</u> was <u>resurrected</u> and there was yellow sand around it and a great wind from the sea ... he saw her coming and the <u>wind</u> was blowing, and she was looking for her shoe beside a new growing tree, and this was the tree of forgetfulness.

> defloration 4 references
> castration
> fear
> vengeance—punishment tree
> "I cannot forgive." Means "I cannot be forgiven?"
> Blood 1 reference
>
> There was something I just remembered—it happened long ago. But better to forget it.[4]

Were it not for Gwen's own comments explaining the dream, it might seem merely enigmatic, but her comments suggest that this is a dream of some early sexual trauma. The mother-nurturer is present in the dream but unobservant and of no help. The dreamer is split—into the *he* who walks through this terrifying landscape of dismembered phalluses and the *she* at the end. The images that one might first think are castration images—the tree on its side and suffering, its branches soft and alive like octopus arms—Gwen associates with defloration.

The dreamer desires vengeance, and yet the dream ends with a desperate defeat—while the spirits of the "vengeance tree" suffer, what grows is the "tree of forgetfulness." The legacy of the dream is shame and guilt: "I cannot forgive" becomes "I cannot be forgiven." "There was something I just remembered.... better to forget it." This is as close to the buried memory as she would allow herself to come.

Were it not for that last phrase, one might conclude the sexual metaphors could be a substitution for other fears, but as it stands, with Gwen's references to defloration, it seems impossible not to conclude that the dream refers to early sexual violation.

I have not wanted to face it before, leaping, with a biographer's presumption, to unfounded conclusions, but it seems that on the list of terrors from Gwen's childhood, one must consider sexual violation. Does this dream hold the last key to what Gwen called her "peculiar psyche," to her proneness to physical terrors, to the habit of secrecy, the need to safeguard herself and keep hidden? As I think back to the young Marion Lyons in her attic room at 38 Keele Street, confronted by the nocturnal visits of Uncle Charlie, I wonder was this what happened to Gwendolyn? There was at least one other foster child, a girl called Donna, who told Marion that Charlie had "felt her up the leg," but Gwen's sister, Carol, is very clear that she never experienced Charlie's advances and she did not believe Charlie would have approached Gwendolyn or that Gwen would not have told her had he done so. It is entirely possible that Charlie reserved his attention for the foster children. After all they were not blood, like his nieces. Perhaps in his mind he could violate the taboos with unwanted children. And yet, Gwendolyn was eight years younger than Carol, so much more exposed and vulnerable, a much easier prey than her more self-contained sister. Was it this that happened long ago that was better to forget? Or was it perhaps someone else, not Charlie at all, and something more extreme? It is impossible to know.

Sexual violation in childhood would make sense of the "death beg," the longing for oblivion—to withdraw back into the hole of self—that Gwen wrote about in her early stories. It would account for the strange "lumpy sexless child frozen between fear and surprise" that she had seen in the child-portraits of Louis de Niverville. It could be the "counterpointal" memory that was triggered by the Arab boy's assault on Jaffa beach that caused Gwen dizziness and nausea when she realized that the "counterpoint thought" was still with her. The pattern of Gwen's life would fit, if, at core, she carried the psyche of shame and fear, the self-hatred of the violated child. Whatever the root cause of this dream, whoever the perpetrator of its pain, Gwen decided she would deal with it on her own. In 1966, there was no one easily available to whom she could turn for an explanation of the dream's trauma. The help that a young woman might find today was not available to Gwen.

And one thinks how tragically unfair it was: a woman of Gwendolyn's brilliance and courage, one part of herself scrupulously researching the novel she was writing; the other part trapped in the terror of the past, the black hole in which slept the old memory: "There was something I just remembered—it happened long ago. But better to forget it." One thinks of a child: so raw and exposed, so undefined that any hurt touches the whole of the self. As a child, Gwendolyn had never been protected, allowed to evolve in the beauty of her own nature. In Egypt, alone and without any props to support her, she felt totally exposed and manipulated. In panic she fled home, deprived of the experiences she should have had.

Why did this dream surface in Egypt? Travelling alone, she must have felt extremely vulnerable. The lascivious attention of the Cairo guards disturbed her deeply, and plunged her back into a terrifying space she usually kept at a distance. And perhaps there was something else. Perhaps the unfriendly reception she felt she'd received from Salah's relations threatened her more deeply than she knew, for she was very much in love with Salah. Her intuitions may have begun to sense that something was wrong, but it would be a while before she figured out what the problem was.

Back in Toronto, Gwen resumed work on her novel. In fact, she discovered she had learned enough from her visits to the museum and from her reading to be able to recover Akhenaton, but all summer she felt she was working under pressure. She wanted the novel finished before she started her undergraduate degree at the University of Toronto. When she finally enrolled in September, however, the whole exercise proved a disaster. She described what happened in a letter to Margaret:

> Thank you for your inspiring words; alas I fear though that they only make me more disgusted with myself and my present ghastly inability to adjust to un.[iversity] life, lectures etc. Two days have passed and I am more or less underground, having buried myself there until I can sort out my thoughts. It's *bad* to have studied things on your own; it makes you mopy, resentful, and genuinely unreceptive.... Don't know how long or even if I will last it out. Plus the fact that I'm guilty about Akhenaton—I feel I rushed it and botched it badly in an attempt to finish it

before the fall.... Plus I've been in a very odd and grisly mental state for some time now and have had devastating attacks of hitherto unknown disease called Lack of Confidence. Don't know the cause of it but it's exhausting enough.... I should be studying something I absolutely *don't* know; that way I wouldn't resent the time. However, the choice is mine and, as always, one pays one way or another for one's misjudgments or what have you ... Must go mope for a while after which I'll study the Hebrew alphabet (it is absorbing), after which God knows....[5]

Gwen quit the university after several weeks. Returning to her novel, she immediately relaxed. She explained the crisis to herself as the fact that she could not live without writing. It was not worth studying for a degree at university when she already knew the material she was studying. But she had been in a "grisly" state of mind for several months. Her confidence had been sabotaged, and she believed she could not survive in any institutional setting.

Gwen was always hard on herself. It did not occur to her that for years she had been out of the routine and structure of academic life and the transition back would inevitably prove rocky. More importantly, she was also not fully acknowledging the trauma her trip to Egypt had unearthed. But deciding not to go to university would prove costly. It meant that she would be increasingly isolated, thrown back entirely on herself. The age had passed when a poet could live adequately on his or her writing and have contact with a public world because the work was valued.

What is also clear from her letter to Margaret is that Gwen's life had taken a new direction. Up to now she had bashed forward with energy and astonishing confidence, evident to anyone reading *A Breakfast for Barbarians*, but the frenetic energy that had thrust her forward was suddenly dammed up. She had now plunged into an equally astonishing crisis of self-doubt.

15
LETTER TO AN OLD LOVER

In 1987, more than two decades after she met him, Gwen wrote a love poem to Salah:

>> Letter to an Old Lover
>
> Salah, I have not forgotten you.
>
> It was you who claimed my only real virginity, you
> who deflowered my mind ...
>
> I remember the taste of Egypt in your mouth—
> mint tea and mangoes.
>
> And the nights pouring in, the winter nights
> pouring in, the magenta nights
> pouring in,
> the lake, the smell of your
> far flowers.

Salah, are you sitting now on the roof of your house in Giza
under virginal moonlight, a lean and handsome man
                                      approaching fifty
with a wife and many children numb with sleep after playing tag
all day in the blazing courtyard?

Habibi, you are still my life, I murmur in that backwards tongue
as I climb the many stairs of midnight to encounter you,
habibi, do you hear the roar of this northern lake, this
far country.

Do you hear the wail of the water,
the roar of our love, the old nights
pouring in …?[1]

Salah had not gone back to Egypt; he had been living in Montreal for the past two decades, but neither he nor Gwendolyn had attempted to find each other. Their love affair had been the kind that is of such intensity that it can never be translated into friendship.

When I located Salah in Montreal, he invited me to visit him at home with his wife, to whom he had been married for twenty-five years. She had obviously been told a great deal about the young Canadian poet her husband had encountered when he first arrived from Egypt, and seemed unthreatened by this invasion of a phantom from the past. She seemed to be fascinated by Gwen as an extraordinary conundrum. We sat in the suburban living room by the fire, Egyptian artifacts giving the otherwise conventional room an exotic air of dislocation; Middle Eastern music played in the background of our conversation.

The Salah I met was an erudite, reflective man. Still handsome, there was about him an intensity that Gwendolyn would have found irresistible. He would be happy to talk with me about the past, he said, but he reminded me that, writing my book, I was probably making two assumptions: Firstly, that one can know the past. "How can one translate what one knows *now* into the real past? How does one remove all the filters of the years that have come since?"[2] His second warning was that one can take from the past only a few "apparent things." One can never recover the totality of what went on, or the totality of another human being, the core of Gwen.

He spoke in a rich Egyptian accent, and his command of English was initially tentative, the only sign I had that this archaeology of his life with Gwen was discomforting. "A big part of that past was love," he explained. "How could you describe this? You could be in a landscape that is completely desolate and one person is there. And there are not even two persons, and yet it's the image that comes." His image of Gwen was poignantly accurate: a woman, alone, in a desolate desert; an image of love.

Salah was one of the first of the wave of Arab immigrants who came to Toronto in 1964. He lived with Gwen for about one and a half years at 1512 King Street, until he moved to Montreal. (Gwen in her memory had stretched this to six years, which must have been the psychological length of the relationship for her.) "It had no relation to reality," he said. "The whole thing. Because we were almost completely enclosed. Even though I was studying at the University of Toronto, the outside world didn't exist. It was completely inside. It was the first time I spoke English.

"You can let your imagination go," he added, as if still astonished by the fact, "and it won't even touch the real. Whatever you think, whatever comes into your mind, she will encompass it. You could even say she was mad in a way, but that was part of her genius."

This is how he translated the Gwen he knew:

> Gwen wanted to believe she could live in the mythic imagination. That is why Egypt was so powerful for her. She had a grasp of the genius of the land. Even though I had grown up in Egypt, only once did I have an actual glimpse of the genius of the land. I was on the beach and the sun was rising in the morning and I suddenly understood what the sun meant. There is something to worship

about the sun. Here in Canada it is a disk in the sky. There it has a mythological meaning. It is mysterious. You feel the age of the sun. The truth of Egypt is desert and water. It is not allegorical but a literal truth. Gwen saw this. That is what distinguished her. She saw the whole, natural thing. She was trying to live in a primordial language, where meanings were not through words, even though words were beautiful. She was like the desert mystics—so open that everything merged with their being. They were insignificant compared to their surroundings. They saw this and lived through it. It's exactly this emptiness.

For me it was a matter of probing, getting closer to the essence of what she was, what a woman was. And she wanting to know me, to know the other, the male. But then I realized how vulnerable she was. I saw the crack. She couldn't take the probing and so I became more careful and spontaneity was lost. I thought nothing could destroy it, but it was destroyed.

Salah was a twenty-four-year-old youth fresh from Egypt. He was "living for impressions." Great happiness, great sorrow, it didn't matter as long as it was a great emotion. Living for this, he had found a "gold mine in Gwen."

There was a meeting of minds. We would stay up till 3 or 4 in the morning. Talking. Making love. There were no limitations to time. Living with the total being of the other person. It was a perfect fit. I got addicted in a sense. There was always this response from her. I wanted to impersonate what she was. I wanted to go into her relationships, to live through that. But then suddenly things changed. It was not in reality what I took it to be. I could see she was hurt. But to me hurting her was not important. It was part of the bigger game being played for its own sake. But then Gwen would say I don't want this. Gwen didn't want to lose what we had, what we'd gotten, and she felt this probing would destroy it. I cannot explain. Like I would tell her I wanted to pickle her, by which I meant freezing a beautiful moment, but she would get very scared. I thought nothing could destroy us, but she became afraid. There was a secret compartment she had to keep closed.

I wanted to know what Salah meant by the "crack." Did he know of her childhood? I asked. She had talked of her father and his death. It was a special relationship, one that Salah felt Gwen always tried to re-create: a one-to-one relationship where she didn't need the outside world. He had met Elsie and Carol. Sociologists, he believed, might be able to explain these two women, but not Gwen. But there was this crack—he felt it was her fear of going mad. In retrospect he realizes that when he was young he had felt there was nothing one could not get over. One could do with one's life whatever one wanted, since fate was totally random; one was not tied to one's own biographical fate. She would talk about her mother and the dilemma of her madness, but it did not register at all. Now that he is older, he feels perhaps there are things that break you, things you cannot get over. His own childhood had been simple—his mother had been everything to him. When he sees a child now who is not protected in this way, he asks himself: "Could I have survived without love? No." I asked him whether it ever occurred to him that there might have been childhood molestation in Gwen's past, but he was nonplussed. The idea did not register.

"I was running from protection, and she wanted to be protected," he continued. Then, he had been interested neither in her childhood nor in her future. He had loved the way he could create the world with Gwen. In this Egyptian youth, Gwen had found someone who wanted to live as mythically as she.

"Were you living a myth?" I asked.

He replied: "Do you remember the figure of Lilith? Gwen said: 'I am Lilith.' I said: 'OK *be* Lilith. Be evil. But don't put any limits.'" For him it had been a game. He was experimenting: "I didn't even know words. I never spoke them. I invented them."

"But why Lilith?" I asked.

"Because she feared the destructive in herself and she wanted to go into that fear. Most people live in a reduced intensity in order to survive. She wanted to go beyond that. She wanted to probe it. To live naked."

He looked at me sadly. "Perhaps Gwen never met a man who was as advanced as she, who was up to her. Perhaps none of us were up to her. The closest thing to Gwen was the Sufi. She wanted to live and at the same time derive all the meanings from everyday acts. But you cannot live in this intensity all the time. You can only live there for short periods. The whole period we were together was too intense, and it had to be destroyed in a way. You can go mad by enclosing yourself for a year.

"Gwen had no sense of time. What is twenty human years, forty-six. One thousand years is no time to the universe. She was always looking to concentrate her life in a moment of perfection. You encounter the One in a moment of intense beauty, of love. Why come down from that? There is no more to achieve. It's fulfilment. It's self-destruction."

And then Salah told me a Sufi parable that seemed to sum up Gwen in his mind:

> A butterfly was sent to know what fire is. It returned and said: "Fire is a glow of red." And it was told: "No. Get more." The second one went and it said: "It's also very hot." And it was told to go and get more. The third one went and was consumed in the fire. And the Sufi master said: "This is the meaning. It is to be consumed in the fire."

Salah said that he remembered many times making love at three or four o'clock in the morning and "that was it"—the moment of intense fulfilment, of tremendous beauty, felt like death. "What's left? What else to see? I'm satisfied. But you postpone it. You have children. You go back through the cycle again. And this is how I survived. I had to protect myself against that intensity. But the ultimate moment of intense identification with this beauty is when you are fulfilled."

"Must you not keep a foot in the real world?" I asked. Salah responded: "Yes, that is what Gwen wanted. She wanted children, a complete life, but without losing her idealism, her genius, her art."

I began to realize that, as always, when I spoke of Gwen, I was falling into the same paradox: Salah and I were circling in a vocabulary of abstractions, in the realm of ideas, but it was as if we had kicked ourselves free from normal life. I was afraid of Salah's absolutes, of his notion of death as fulfilment, of his Sufi parable. He may have been playing at what he called "the bigger game," but then he could pull back to save himself. But what about Gwen? She was deadly serious.

I began to wonder whether Gwen was so powerful that Salah had been afraid of losing himself. The symbiosis she created in love was so total, the identification with herself so complete, that one could plunge in and lose oneself.

In a brief story, "The Oarsman and the Seamstress," in which the narrator recounts watching her lover sleep, Gwen described that longing for total identification that one sometimes finds in obsessive love:

> [He] was still asleep, and she hoped the rustling of the paper pattern wouldn't wake him. She loved to watch him while he slept, perhaps because in his sleep he no longer possessed himself, he was a lost being, a kind of orphan, suspended in another time and connected only by the thinnest of threads to his own consciousness. She loved to watch him while he slept, perhaps because it was then that she could enjoy the illusion of actually knowing him. Knowing him in his otherness, his state of being other than her. His sleep alienated her and paradoxically, drew her closer to him.... as always when she saw him like this, she ran her hand lightly down the strong lyrical line of his side, beginning just under the

arm and ending at the bone on his ankle, which jutted
out like a wing. He was turned away from her so she
couldn't watch his breathing nor see the intricate pattern of his ribs and the muscles of his abdomen, an
anatomy so breathtakingly different from her own.3

The narrator in the story climbs into the lover's dream, to know him completely, to be the other. There is something rather terrifying about this will to possess, this rebellion against the human truth that we can never know the other, that in most ways we remain strangers who have only a nodding acquaintance in the dark spaces of each other's minds. When I spoke of this to Salah, he reminded me that there was no boundary for Gwen between myth and reality. "If, in a poem, you think she is writing allegorically," he warned, "you would be wrong. For her it was all very real."

Is there a clue in Gwen's choosing Lilith as her myth? Gwen would have known that in Jewish tradition, Lilith is a female demon who pre-dated Eve, and is regarded as Adam's first wife. The Zohar describes Lilith as "a hot fiery female who at first cohabited with man" but when Eve was created "flew to the cities of the sea coast where she is still try-ing to ensnare mankind." In the Zohar most demons are mortal, but Lilith is eternal. In the Cabala she is the demon of Friday and is repre-sented as a naked woman whose body terminates in a serpent's tail. She is in fact drawn from *lili*, female demonic spirits in Mesopotamian demonology known as *ardat lili*. In medieval lore, Lilith and Sammael (Satan) are said to have "emanated from beneath the throne of Divine Glory, the legs of which were somewhat shaken by their joint activity."4

Gwen wanted to impersonate Lilith—the anarchic sexualized vengeful female. In a note among her jottings of ideas for poems, she wrote: "If women were unleashed, they would rock the world. The man God knows this. So do men."5 Gwen's versions of Lilith was as woman in her full sexual power rocking the throne of the patriarchal god with her sexual appetite.

But acted out in her relationship with Salah, what was Lilith? A fantasy many women have is that they could be completely themselves with a man—not the edited version the culture has constructed for woman as the sexual partner, beautiful, attentive, submissive; but that a man could also accord them the freedom to test the dark self, unbeautiful, outrageous, powerful. Was this what Gwen hoped? That she could live through this archetype and that Salah would still be there?

There were times, Salah said, that Gwen raged at what she felt was the subjugation of women in Eastern culture. But of course it was more than this. There was that dream that invaded her mind while she was in Egypt. Did she want at last to be released from the desire for vengeance—"I cannot forgive"—that was consuming her? An unbearable rage? This is the persona she accords the figure of Lilith in her poem by that name:

Lilith

Have no doubt that one day she will be reborn
horrendous, with coiling horns,
pubis a blaze of black stars
and armpits a swampy nest for dinosaurs.
But meanwhile
she lurks in her most impenetrable disguise—
as me—
trying to make holes in my brain
or come forth from my eyes.
And I have felt
her mindless mind within my mind
urging me to call down heaven with a word,
avenge some ancient wrong against her kind
or be the crazed Salome who danced for blood.
Ah God, her seasons kill
the sickly moon, and all my fine achievements
fall beneath her feet like skulls.
And I would claim

> I cannot answer for my deeds; it is *her time*.
> But when I try
> to prove she is assailing me
> there comes instead an awful cry
> which is her protest and her song of victory.
> See you in my *dreams*,
> Whore of Babylon, Theodora,
> utterly unquiet fiend, thou
> Scream.[6]

Lilith occupied the deepest level of Gwen's psyche—bloodthirsty, angry, vengeful for the mother, for the child. But how was she to exorcise her without destroying everything? Gwen kept her inside and paid terribly. In their correspondence, Margaret Atwood and Gwen often talked of dreams and the Tarot, and on one occasion Margaret cast Gwen's horoscope. Gwen found it amazingly accurate except on one point: that she was "hot-tempered." "Temper, in general, [is] what I most lack, in fact I am usually unable even to get *angry*—not a good way to be."[7] The rage she expresses in the poem is so profound that, were it ever released, it would spill like acid over the world.

In the fall of 1967, Salah moved to Montreal to undertake an M.Sc. at McGill University. For him it meant that his relationship with Gwen was over, though he said it had taken him another three years to untie himself psychologically from her. As far as he was concerned he had begun a new life, signalled by his becoming involved in a new relationship with a Spanish girl, with whom he was soon living. But for Gwen, the relationship had been too profound for her to give up so easily.

She travelled weekends to Montreal to visit, and her presence became a tempestuous element, not least for Salah's new girlfriend. Gwen began to write Margaret Atwood of what she called "our own Middle Eastern War."

Without telling Salah (who insisted to me that he had no idea Gwen was ever living in Montreal), she moved secretly to that city in the spring of 1968 and found her own apartment. Margaret Atwood had accepted an appointment in Montreal to teach at Sir George Williams University, and her husband at that time, Jim Polk, remembers them visiting Gwen:

> I was dazzled by the Canadian literary life, all these people who wrote poetry and were artists. It wasn't like anything I knew from my mid-western U.S. background, the doctor's son. And there was this exotic, sly creature, Gwendolyn MacEwen, trading amusements with Peggy about the poetry scene. I remember clearly how much we laughed.
>
> Gwen was living in Montreal in a very inaccessible place that had no windows. She was, Peggy told me, hiding from her Egyptian friend. It was like entering an enchanted forest: passing through all these doors, we came to this windowless room with her carved chest and her Oriental objects; and she was getting that Oriental way of looking. She was learning Coptic, so that she could read the Coptic Bible, and it looked fascinating. By then I had read the poetry and thought this was really a major person and obviously an eccentric genius, an oddity in every way, and beautiful besides. And, again, funny! Once she put on a tape she'd saved of a CBC production about Lorca, talking about duende and what duende is. There was this CBC 1950s voice going on about the dark passion of duende and the clattering this and the deep profound that, with Spanish stuff going on in the background, as this CBC guy doggedly went through Spanish passion.
>
> Gwen became a kind of fixture there in Montreal. We were never to tell anybody that she was in the city or to let on, adding to her mystery. That evening, I remember the weirdness of it, the beauty of it. The room had candles, and the Coptic Bible made a deep impression. And the

laughter. Another evening she told my fortune with the Tarot cards. I had gotten a job in Edmonton and she said, "I remember Edmonton, it was all red." It was a nightmare disaster from hell. Everything upside down. Towers of destruction, death, you name it—And all of this really turned out to be the story of Edmonton. Dead on. She was embarrassed that this should be so. She was mystical, she was from another plane; I thought she was wonderful.[8]

After several months, Gwen hastily left Montreal. She wrote to Margaret in May of 1968: "My exit from Montreal was swift and sure, so much so that I never did get around to calling you beforehand. Toronto looks as good as it will ever look, which is of course not saying much."[9]

Back in Toronto, Gwen had not freed herself from Salah. As they continued to exchange letters, Gwen recorded her psychic life in her dream journal:

May 1968 [Voice in dream] It's not the thing itself I fear. It's not doing it, not leading up to it, I fear only losing it, it not being done & therefore lost.

June 1968 Mother drives bus, it loses control & slips down gravelly hill—somewhere stops—she points to a hole in her foot where it went through the pedal or brake—many people on the bus.

August 1968 Father dies again, everything same as before: I say to Mum "That's how it happened last time" as though I wouldn't be tricked again.[10]

Gwen's relationship with Salah was churning up the ghosts from her past: her fear that she might, like her mother, lose control, her guilt at her father's death. She had written to Margaret: "Am reading (at last)

Jung's *Symbols of Transformation* and ask myself as I did with Graves, how have I survived so long *without*."[11] She was using Jung as best she could to map her own psyche.

In romantic obsession, it always seems that love is only a code language hiding another story, and *that* story has entirely to do with oneself. Gwen seemed to be dancing with her own shadow, lost to any sense of the objective world. Perhaps ironically, obsessive love, ostensibly directed to another, is rather a psychological crisis needed to confront the self since everything we are seems suddenly on the line. The passion Gwen required from life would not have been easily found, and she had found it in Salah. He became the catalyst for the plunge downward and inward into her own psyche. Her dreams had been telling her this all along: "*Winter 1967* The kingdom of the Rey & I go underwater to find him—underwater explosions and sea civilization is threatened by earth. N.B. Salah simultaneously dreams of me as a mermaid." Gwen could not give up Salah, because he touched her deeply enough that he became the occasion to do battle with herself.

But in the real world, he had become an elusive phantom. Gwendolyn saved only six letters from Salah. Though undated, it seems from the details that most were written in 1968 as the relationship ended. They are not the letters of a man in love. They are curiously, perhaps strategically, impersonal. Yet in these letters she could find enough hope to believe that the relationship was not irrevocably over.

When Salah wrote to Gwen in Arabic, his letters began: "You, Juanna."[12] One explanation for this is that it is difficult to write Gwendolyn in Arabic and Salah used an approximate: "Juanna" (the envelopes were, of course, addressed in English to Gwendolyn McEwen [sic]). Perhaps they had agreed on this. But in one of the letters she has actually translated the salutation in her own handwriting. Did it possibly shock her? Oddly it reminds me of those letters from her mother written to Wendy McEwen. Who was she now? More telling is the impersonal "You." Normally Egyptians use the salutation "Dear." Using "You" would have to have been a deliberate signal of distance.

Salah's letters are primarily about his work—descriptions of his exams, his marks, his long hours of study. He has written a computer programme, the programme is excellent, his friends overwhelmed. "I am Salah the big one," he records them saying and laughs. He is guaranteed an A. He asks what she is doing, if she's happy. The letters end without a salutation or signature.

Only occasionally does a barb enter these perfunctory letters to hook Gwendolyn. He can report, as if in an aside, that he is working hard and being unhappy because he is not used to loneliness, that she is always on his mind, and that he wants to give her the whole world, but the world is too small for her. Then his talk of work and work projects resumes.

He does offer his support, insisting there is nothing too big for Juanna. He is reading her poems; "Arcana for the King" is extraordinary. No one has ever written like this and no one in future will write like this. Juanna is big and great. And then he tells her he is being interviewed for a job by Boeing and will probably move to the States for a while to learn from their technology, before resuming his doctorate.

There is only one letter, undated, that is personal. It seems that he may be speaking of his Spanish girlfriend, who has returned to her husband in Europe and who is very unhappy. He says that he would be happy if things happened as Gwen predicted, but he has no idea what course his life will take. He asks Gwen to understand that she [the Spanish friend?] will return with a lot of hope. He asks Gwen not to build fantasies in her mind. He doesn't respect anyone else's thinking as he does Gwen's, but she must understand that, because she [the Spanish girlfriend?] is in pain, he will be in pain to the end of his lifetime. He makes no plans. He prefers destiny to take its own course. The future is enigmatic, but if he and she [the Spanish girlfriend?] are happy, he hopes Gwen will be happy too. If he and Gwen are to continue there must be no secrets between them. He asks Gwen to send the translation of the Arabic novel she is working on. He wants to read it since he knows she will understand Egypt. He will be with her every time she wants.

Gwen carefully circled the resonant words of this letter, words like *mystery*, *pain*, *loneliness*, as if she believed the letter were written in code, and its meaning lay underneath, and not on its cool surface. She could not rise in rage at its tone of rejection, demanding her rights or turning her back. I think suddenly of those long-ago letters from her father, promising a birthday present after the fact and explaining why a birthday phone call would never come. Love was always a longing that could never be fulfilled because Gwen believed there was a flaw in herself. Trained to expect less than she deserved, she could always be manipulated. She could not see that Salah was deliberately keeping her at a distance. He claimed to be the one who suffered. She could not believe that he, an ambitious young man with a future, was probably afraid of involvement with someone as complex as she. It's astonishing how such letters can seem transparent to everyone but the woman receiving them. But perhaps that is because she was the one who had been loved.

Gwen's rage could only surface surreptitiously in dreams. That September of 1968, she recorded a dream that makes it clear one part of her felt that she was the destructive element. Gwen's psychological inheritance was based on a law of fear: the fear, always, that she was somehow at fault. But the anger in this dream is also unbearable:

> *Sept.12/68* I hold Salah in my arms. He is in bad shape weeping & ill and crumples in his jacket & becomes small baby animal like pig or cat—I take him to nurse at counter & say "he must be fed" & he is put on floor to lick fallen milk—there is something about the first such animal having died—before this Susan tells me it's awful how I lead him to doom when he comes gentle to touch my nose & I lead him to destruction—later I order food in some hospital restaurant & on menu which is book cover there is a "human animal" and pictures of small human things, as food delicacy & medical study—I point

to picture and order to eat—then I ask that they don't
serve the little one, Salah—since he is human & special—they bring me something like fried chicken legs &
wings & it is human flesh—the tiny human animal.[13]

The relationship with Salah and its ending was devastating but it
was offering Gwen a challenge. Could she free herself of her need for
Salah, knowing that without him she would not be destroyed? But
Gwen had such a history of self-doubt and fear that constructing an
autonomous self would cost her enormously. She plunged into dreams
of masks, impersonations, and longing for vision.

May 23/69 On a strange bus ride which has been set up
as a kind of spy experiment—I and another enter bus
w/[ith] no fare, I just flop the offprints of *Shadow Maker*
at him. Others on bus are nervous knowing the trip has
been rigged up somehow.

June 1/69 I in prison on death row awaiting execution,
minutes tick by. I prepare some last words to give
Salah—but someone hands me a book to read the first
pages—at last moment I realize I am dying for nothing—
so frantically leaf through phone book looking for
Lawrence Stone—lawyer [Stone was the young lawyer
who frequented The Bohemian Embassy and published
The Sheet].

July 22/69 I am dangling a dark-haired woman from a
coat hanger, desperately keeping her *away* from me as
tho she is contaminated or very dangerous like a cat. I
carry her downstairs & into several places—a beer parlour where Pat & Carol are and a car. Great anxiety she
will escape.

> *August 4/69* Before leaving Montreal I see Time magazine article and photo of me sitting w.[ith] 2 other people. Hard to distinguish myself at first for I am divided in 2— the left half is me while the right half wears round sunglasses. I show it to Salah & say *please* look at this.

All the dreams confirm that, despite her many achievements, Gwendolyn always carried a sense of her own inauthenticity. The new book she was working on, *The Shadow-Maker*, was "rigged." At core was a "dark-haired woman" dangling from a coat hanger whom she had desperately to keep at a distance.

Gwendolyn could not let go of the relationship with Salah. She kept thinking things could be sorted out. She had written to Margaret that April that matters between her and Salah were resolving themselves:

> Perhaps the best news I have (and should let you know since you've followed so patiently the unfolding of the Middle East saga) is that at long last the Egyptian Alliance has been liquidated, never having been realized, by means of a simple document sent which frees all parties in question. Rather frighteningly simple. What new developments and horrors wait around the corner I dare not guess at present, and leave all things in the hands of Allah the All-Knowing and All-Merciful.[14]

Gwen had now convinced herself that her problems with Salah stemmed not from his Spanish girlfriend, who was by this time no longer a factor, but from the fact that his parents had made an arranged marriage for him with a childhood friend in Egypt (she refers to this elliptically as the Egyptian alliance), and that they were demanding he honour it. Salah insisted that there was no such arrangement, though he adds that Gwen may have believed there was. Indeed, she seems to have believed he had been married in Egypt under his family's coercion. The plot may have been in Gwen's mind, but one has to wonder if, for the young Salah, it provided an irrevocable ending to their relationship that would let her down easily. How could Gwen challenge an arranged marriage or question the traditions of another culture? The "Egyptian alliance" is tangled, too tangled for me to unravel.

When a relationship has been as intense as the one between Salah and Gwen, there will always, of course, be evasion, subterfuge, retreat, and headlong compulsion—too intense to hold on to, too powerful to let go. The only thing that can end it is exhaustion. Salah too, in his elliptical way, was holding on, not prepared entirely to give up Gwendolyn. Perhaps it was only the mature man who recognized in retrospect that he was dealing with someone who was breakable, with a psyche like fine porcelain.

Gwen wrote to Margaret on August 10, 1969. She had spent most of July in Montreal:

> Wrote you an anguished letter a while ago which I never mailed because it seemed pointless. On the one hand the Middle East crisis really is a hundred percent clearer, saner and better (beyond wildest dreams). However there are a few attendant and excruciating *details* which have sprung up which are just not to be believed. Rather more truly 'tragic,' I think, and 'Painful' than anything else ... Perhaps the most immediate concern (with me) is that he's off to Egypt in a week or two after finishing Master's thesis, and this happens to be one of the most perilous summers since the 67 war; hasn't got citizenship yet (Canadian) which would be protection against being snapped up into possible war and never heard tell of again. Oh well.[15]

Margaret advised Gwen not to worry. Salah seemed surely to be protected by an "aura of invulnerability, considering what he'd come through so far."¹⁶ Even Gwen knew that she had explained nothing, and wrote again at the end of September to a mystified Margaret:

> It's occurred to me how insane things must look from the outside (the Middle East situation I mean), and quite incomprehensible without the various details which I never got around to mentioning. I may as well mention them since you've been good enough to listen to the plot up to now—(nobody else knows anything, too complicated to explain, and it goes without saying it's all Top Secret). Anyway seems I was led to believe for some months that a divorce had taken place, but it hadn't. Was then led to believe that a letter was written stating the position, but it wasn't (merely a note to a member of the family, confidential). Was *then* informed that what complicates matters is the fact that the lady is no longer *une vierge*. This is devastating beyond comprehension since being Undone while married but not *living* with spouse is worse than being Undone while unmarried (?!) What this all means in a nutshell is that for her honour to be secure, she *must* at some point live with him; otherwise if she is divorced now, a future husband is liable to divorce her again on finding out she is Undone. In short, her life is ruined and unless he takes her to live with him, at which point he must consider it a lifelong venture, or do it for honour, which will make him miserable. At any rate, I was informed that if he actually divorces her *now*, he will feel so wretched that he couldn't allow himself to see me anymore (logical enough) and on the other hand, if he leaves it hanging, I can't really see *him* since I feel wretched about *her* position. It would seem the only answer is for nobody to see anybody. Too horrible for words really; and now I totter

on the verge of somehow bowing out of this whole thing, or bowing out long enough for it all to somehow dissolve. There *are* reasons behind these incredible actions, I'm well aware of them, but unfortunately knowing the reasons doesn't help matters in the least. Will probably lurk in the background for sometime lending support etc. and see what gives. I tend to minimize things usually, which is why I often claim things are Fine when they are hopeless (a trick to make myself believe it). Would be so nice if once all the clocks in the world would stop long enough for one to have a good look at how they work; trouble is, the cosmic clocks would probably go on ticking.[17]

Margaret wrote back rather shrewdly on September 24th:

As for Plot—why can't (she said, with her tidy mind) *he* live with *her*—like, in the same house—for a respectable length of time (say, six months); or even just transport her to Canada for that length of time—and *then* divorce her? That seems awfully cold-blooded, but at least it would circumvent an absolute *impasse*, save her face (unless there are yet other taboos I don't know about) and extricate him. The real tragicomedy would occur of course if he *did* all that & then you decided to take off for parts unknown. I suppose the crucial question is who Undid Her? If it was him, I agree he has a responsibility; if not, his responsibility is of a different kind.[18]

Gwen had managed to get herself into a baroque plot and it seems that Margaret felt it just as likely Gwen was as much attached to the plot as to the man. If Gwen won this one, would she just take off? There was certainly a paradox in Gwen's attitude. There was probably a part of her, as there is in all romantic sensibilities, that dreaded happiness. It would remove the exotic, it would reduce her to normalcy, and then where would the poems come from? But there was an equally urgent impulse to locate a kind of peace that might give her ground to stand on.

In any case, Gwen was left to her unhappiness. To Margaret she wrote: "Yes, the Undoing was Undone by him as you might have suspected, and it's all a shame, but I find as Autumn sets in and the air gets tingly again, everything seems so much sharper and more well-defined (summer makes everything blurry)."[19] She told Margaret she was not writing anything for a while, but was thinking up schemes for extravagant and impossible clothing—a forest-green velvet ankle-length cape completely lined with rabbit fur with an enormous hood. The idea was you got inside and were lost to the world.

16
THE SHADOW MAKER

When Gwen returned to Toronto in the summer of 1968, she had moved into the house of her sister, Carol, and her five children on Locust Street near Eglinton and Keele, north of their old neighbourhood. She had thought she might be able to assist Carol by being there, since Carol's life had taken a tragic turn. Her first marriage had terminated years before and in the interim she had fallen in love with another man. They had begun a good life, but within six months he was diagnosed with terminal cancer. After four and a half years together and the birth of Carol's fifth child, he died in 1967. Gwen had offered to join the family, thinking she could help out with expenses.

For Carol's children it was wonderful to have their strange and gentle aunt living with them, but for her the arrangement was difficult. That first summer she had lived on the screened-in back porch with only a simple bed and a small table for her typewriter. She told Margaret Atwood she was daily occupied with trying to find a corner in the house in which to write, spending half of her time carrying coffee, cigarettes, and paper up and down stairs or out onto the back porch as the various spaces she had found were overrun by children who wanted to play with her typewriter.

Toronto, she lamented to Margaret, was the same as it had always been, but in fact she was wrong. The city had suddenly turned into a wild and exotic place. The rumours of cultural revolution that had been filtering from San Francisco and Vancouver had materialized like a hot wind in Toronto the previous summer of 1967. Hippies flooded Yorkville, and the notorious Rochdale College, the high-rise students' residence, had begun its bizarre career that would end in a nightmarish paradise of drugs and violence. The poet Dennis Lee, co-founder of Rochdale, was talking of hiring Gwen and the poet John Newlove to organize the writing programme in 1968, though the job never materialized. Gwen was too caught up in her own obsessions for this social scene, which normally would have fascinated her, to have made much impact.

As if in an inverse mirror, the chaos of Gwendolyn's private life was almost proportionately matched by the increasing authority and clarity of her writing. It seems almost a law. The writer's intelligence affords no advantage in solving his or her own life. Indeed, one wonders if the chaos of one is sometimes needed to sustain the other. In the midst of personal psychological upheavals, the momentum of Gwen's professional life was building. In early 1969, she had good news. Macmillan had agreed to bring out her novel on Akhenaton, and Ryerson Press was interested in a collection of children's stories. She told Margaret Atwood it was an interesting exercise writing for children, trying not to write *down* to the child. "Keep trying to recall what *did* I think about when I was ten years old and then my mind recoils when I remember."[1]

She was giving a great number of poetry readings all over the country—six readings in ten days in the Maritimes, travelling on the 5 a.m. Halifax train in a snowstorm. The gold, she said happily, was dribbling in. The interviewers came, one from *Time* magazine, and universities invited her to give classes.

Soon she began to be more active. She was loosely associated with Vietnam War protesters in 1969, and wrote Margaret of her disappointment when Vietnam didn't take up the offer of Toronto as a site for the

Vietnam peace talks. With the arrival of Pierre Trudeau on the scene, she believed Canada was improving. He had, as she put it, "snuck into the Canadian psyche in such a way as to produce a marked change."

Her capacity for work had not diminished. In fact, one could say it increased. In January 1969, she had begun what would prove to be a lifelong correspondence (much of it in Arabic) with a young Syrian poet, Samar Attar, whose name had been given to her by Professor D.P. Varma, whom she had met during one of her poetry readings at Dalhousie University. It was not surprising she had looked up Varma. A world specialist in Gothic romance and a connoisseur of vampire lore, he had taught for years in Syria but had been expelled from the country in 1961 for dramatic productions he had mounted there. He had known Attar as a young poet and actress (she had starred as Desdemona in his *Othello*). She was his favourite student, and he had arranged for her to study at Dalhousie in 1965, though she had since moved to the U.S. In love with the Middle East and everything Arabic, Gwen wrote to Attar, explaining that she was translating a novel by the Egyptian novelist Taha Hussein, and was collecting poems for a radio programme on Arabic poetry. She suggested that they might collaborate on some translation projects. She was also writing her own poetry in Arabic.

While she was involved with Salah, she produced two major works: her novel *King of Egypt, King of Dreams*, about the Pharaoh Akhenaton, and a book of poems, *The Shadow-Maker*.

Gwen secretly hoped that her novel would have a tremendous impact. Akhenaton, credited as the first figure in history to have invented the intellectual concept of monotheism, was a man whom contemporary historians were only beginning to understand. Long before the Jewish or Christian religions, Akhenaton had imposed on his people the worship of Aton, the sun-god, described as an abstract concept of energy and light symbolized by a sun-disk. For Gwen, he was, like Julian the magician, one more human being filled with the god-lust. But while deeply fascinated by his metaphysical longings, and brilliantly entering his mind, her portrait is essentially critical because, in his monotheism, in his pursuit of an inhuman perfection, Akhenaton destroyed the dark gods, the polytheistic hierophany of Egypt. He became a dictatorial figure, one-sided, a man who reduced his people to war and destruction in his own egocentric pursuit of the light.

In her novel, Gwen conceived of Akhenaton as an invalid child—because of the abnormalities of his head and body, it is speculated that he was a hydrocephalic—growing up in the isolation of the royal palace, tyrannized by his father, Amenhotep, and manipulated by his ambitious mother, Tiy. From his sickbed, his childhood world had been bifurcated into a nightmare darkness and a world of light; as a man he turned the light into his god. Challenging the hegemony of a politicized priesthood, he imposed his new heretical religion on his reluctant people. As background to her novel, Gwen accurately reproduced the geography, military campaigns, political and religious intrigue, cultural customs, including those of childbirth, all the details necessary to bring that world alive.

Gwen made the crisis of her novel occur when Akhenaton turns his back on his wife, Nefertiti, alienating himself from woman in his pursuit of the *logos*, of so-called reason. Neter Ay, Akhenaton's exasperated father-in-law, relates the meaning of the narrative:

> It is a lie to assume there is only light, only goodness. Behind the tales of creation and the doings of the gods are strange and dark meanings which perhaps only the gods themselves can fathom.... the holy and the obscene exist side by side; beneath Heaven is the Duat, and beneath the bright heart of man is the dark underworld of his soul. But Wanre [Akhenaton] never permitted himself to reveal that underworld full of the creeping crawling things like violence or bitterness which all men must contain. He distorted those evils and let them build up within him until they emerged in grotesque, insane disguises.[2]

Her friend the poet Tom Marshall remembered Gwen talking of her book. It was meant as a cautionary tale. "Akhenaton's monotheism," she said, "was too abstract, too masculine."[3] She made him go to his death dressed as a woman because he had given himself too exclusively to his male ideal. Polytheism—the plurality of gods—is a truer version of the human psyche, of the multifarious forces in the universe.

Being a poet Gwen could not leave it at this. How, she wanted to know, was this insight to be brought into the modern world? Akhenaton's psychosis of denial is our psychosis, she insisted. In a poem about the holocausts that have characterized this century, she suggests, as had Jung when examining Nazism, that collective psychosis erupts in grotesque insane disguises when we locate the dark outside ourselves.

The Left Hand and Hiroshima

asked once why I fanned my fingers before my eyes
to screen the strange scream of them, I, sinister, replied:
Recently I dropped a bomb upon Hiroshima.

as for the mad dialectics of my tooth-chewed hands
I knew nothing; the left one was responsible and
abominably strong, bombed the flower of Hiroshima.

only because my poems are lies do they earn the right
to be true, like the lie of the left hand at night
in the cockpit of a sad plane trailing God in its wake.

all the left hands of your bodies, your loud thumbs
did accomplice me! men women children at the proud womb,
we have accomplished Hell. Woe Hiroshima ...

> you have the jekyll hand you have the hyde hand
> my people, and you are abominable; but now I am proud
> and
> in uttering love I occur four-fingered and garbed
> in a broken gardener's glove over the barbed
> >> garden
> >>> of Hiroshima ...[4]

She insists that we are all accomplices, with our jekyll and hyde hands, in Hiroshima. The use of the atomic bomb was, after all, not an aberration but a human evil rationalized as the necessary termination to war. At the end of the poem, the poet becomes the terrifying animal, the demonic gardener we have created as we destroy ourselves.

"I want to construct a myth," Gwen said, to counter the drive towards death.[5] Only in the world of Jung did she find a confirmation of what she meant. In what she called "the holy waters" lapping at the mind's circumference, the unconscious world of archetypes that can be both destructive and life-healing, lay her material. The thrust of the poems became the downward quest:

Dark Pines Under Water

> This land like a mirror turns you inward
> And you become a forest in a furtive lake;
> The dark pines of your mind reach downward,
> You dream in the green of your time,
> Your memory is a row of sinking pines.
>
> Explorer, you tell yourself this is not what you came for
> Although it is good here, and green;
> You had meant to move with a kind of largeness,
> You had planned a heavy grace, an anguished dream.

> But the dark pines of your mind dip deeper
> And you are sinking, sinking, sleeper
> In an elementary world;
>
> There is something down there and you want it told.[6]

Into the wilderness, the mystery of the land, into the dream. Gwen felt we underestimate our own complexity. As moderns we are too literal minded and the spirit is dead. She needed to go back in time to the ancient myths, both beautiful and terrifying, that we have lost at our peril. Other poets like Robert Graves had led the way. There was a truth in the ancient myths we had missed.

Gwendolyn did not believe in time. Whatever time is, the commonsense everyday version of it as linear, marching from left to right, from the past through the present to the future, is either nonsense or a trivial version of the truth. And the millennial expanse of evolutionary human time is only a flash in the dark. "We are our ancestors!" she said. When she thought of the idea that man evolved from animal instinct, she stood on a beach and saw creatures crawling up from the sea and asked, what cost human consciousness? What happened when the "animal soul" eased up upon the beach of the brain? We run in terror from the dark reaches within ourselves and yet the real mysteries are interior.

Gwen began to write poems about dreams: sometimes they were literal transcriptions of the dreams she had had: a strange child turning perpetually on a unicycle that she recognized as having her face—the eternally innocent child in the always nascent self; or fierce beasts roaming in the forests of the unconscious that she sought to tame. The poems grew like arcana in emblem books—mysterious and evocative. She knew some of their meaning: she would tell Margaret as they traded their dreams in letters that animals represent the instincts in general, the laws governing life. The guise of animal figures in the unconscious depends on the attitude of the conscious mind: the animals will be fierce and terrifying if the attitude towards the unconscious is negative; if positive, animals appear as the helpful creatures of fairy tale or legend.[7] She was paraphrasing Jung. As did he, she believed the unconscious is a repository of life energies or forces that direct us into life. Its language expressed in dreams is not verbal but imagistic and what these images describe are our fears and longings, from the mundane to the metaphysical. She would call her book *The Shadow-Maker*. We must enter the fearful but healing dark of our own minds.

It is the inflation of our sense of ourselves that leaves us alone in the universe, Gwen insisted. She believed that, paradoxically, we must recover a prayerful attitude of humility towards the universe, acknowledging our limited place within it.

> ... Look, I have told myself I am the sea
> sustained by the silver limits within me,
> far beaches, far shores, struck with light
> and what I take from pain is mine
> and what you take is yours
> > (we are the wild heart of stars
> > and life is the dark song descending
> > unbidden and unending,
> > and we are warned of dangers like
> > the falling of the sky
> > and know we will die
> > a thousand times;
> > though loverough hands bear us
> from perfect dark to light, there is
> no end, really, to the night).
>
> And beyond the freest reaches of our sight
> are sterner seas with birds and waves, dark
> stars, which we cannot contain, which
> are not ours; and then the shores of pain
> are all too sharply drawn
> and also the awful circle of the sun.[8]

Gwendolyn suspected that the universe may be alien; it is possible that there may be no human meaning beyond the human. But this did not preclude the human need to worship. What is to be worshipped? The mystery itself, without pretence of understanding it. In *The Shadow-Maker*, Gwen writes a poem to the god she locates within the self.

Poem

It is not lost, it is moving forward always,
Shrewd, and huge as thunder, equally dark.
Soft paws kiss its continents, it walks
Between lava avenues, it does not tire.

It is not lost, tell me how can I lose it?
Can you lose the shadow which stalks the sun?
It feeds on mountains, it feeds on seas,
It loves you when you are most alone.

Do not deny it, do not blaspheme it,
Do not light matches on the dark of its shores.
It will breathe you out, it will recede from you.
What is here, what is with you now, is yours.[9]

How difficult it is to speak the language of the unconscious.

One thinks of Gwen living in a dream landscape of terrifying images of self-loathing: "I am dangling a dark-haired woman from a coat hanger, desperately keeping her *away* from me as tho she is contaminated or very dangerous like a cat." But there was another image of wholeness and strength, the sphinx figure, the half-animal, half-divine self, image of autonomy and power that she also housed. She speaks to herself: "It is yours."

How archetypal images function in the mind is complex and personal. As Gwen said: "Dreams are either accurate or nuts." But almost everyone has awoken with a startling sense of well-being after experiencing dream images that seem entirely enigmatic. It is not that the images effect a change, but rather that the images express a psychological process that seems to be moving autonomously. Our minds are more resonant than we imagine, and move with a rhythm larger than the merely conscious mind. Perhaps that is an act of faith, but certainly one Gwendolyn had made. "All things," she wrote, "are plotting to make us whole/All things conspire to make us one."[10] If she could house that strength she would be fine. Poems are expressions of the synthesis the poet is aspiring to. Gwen was now twenty-seven; she had come far in her vision—she called it with a wonderful presumption: "plotting the birth of a more accurate world." But she still had to live in the world as it was.

During 1968 and 1969, she wrote one of her finest sequences, "The Nine Arcana of the Kings," the poems that she had sent to Salah to read. They are among the strangest love poems ever written. One reader called them "an Egyptian dream theatre"; they have the ritualistic impact of casting a spell.[11] The narrator, an Egyptian princess, describes the death of her brother/lover; through her invocations of occult practices, she attempts to resurrect him from the land of the dead. The characters seem to be, at least in part, the historical Akhenaton, his daughter Meritaton, and her husband, Akhenaton's successor, Smenkhare, who may have been Akhenaton's own son or brother (Egyptian dynastic successions were often based on incestual lineages). But out of this material Gwen has created a personal myth.

The characters are symbols, mythic entities, and the reader moves in a Jungian phantasmagoria of longing. The brother/sister seem like halves of the divided self seeking wholeness or completeness; the poet like Isis, using her magic spells to revive the dead lover, lost self, the male muse within. The poems are love poems to the elusive other who exists both within and beyond the self.

In the summer of 1969, Gwen found herself a basement apartment on Weston Road north of High Park. She had bad news about her Akhenaton novel. Macmillan would not bring it out unless they found a foreign co-publisher and three publishers in New York and London had turned it down. It seemed she would need to rewrite. She was willing, she joked, to turn it into a Broadway musical starring Julie Andrews and Yul Brynner if she had to. She wanted it published. It was supposed to make her financially independent. But when a British agent told her he was delighted with it and wanted to represent it, but that, for commercial reasons, she would have to cut it, she thought of suggesting a microscopic edition like the miniature Bibles that people read with magnifying glasses.

She was also having trouble finding a publisher for *Call of the Lark*, her translation of the Taha Hussein novel. She had gotten Robert Graves's address from the poet Jay Macpherson, and had written to Graves for advice, but he replied that he couldn't remember Hussein, and besides his sympathies were with Israel. Macmillan was interested in this book too, but they needed a co-publisher in the Middle East who would share the costs.

There was also a printer's strike, which held up the printing of *The Shadow-Maker*. Gwen wrote to Tom Marshall: "You'll be delighted to learn that ... the printers are back to work. *However,* [the books] will just get to the binders in time for a *binding strike* due in a couple of weeks.... I can visualize unimaginable chain reactions. Next will be a booksellers strike, followed by a reader's strike, followed of course by a poet's strike, which in turn will trigger off a new printer's strike. Ultimately the academics will strike and indeed the world will be quite striken."[12]

Gwen kept her spirits up. That September, Margaret Atwood sent her her newly released *Edible Woman*. She devoured it in a day and wrote back excitedly: "Thank God, I muttered to myself as I read it, somebody is writing something accurate about Woman for once."[13]

Alone in her basement apartment, she was babysitting a friend's fourteen-month-old child. She found it the most incredible experience, utterly exhausting and exhilarating. "His sense of *time* is so different from mine," she wrote to Margaret. "Five minutes are no different than a day really—also the exhausting and somehow frightening *happiness* that makes one see too clearly one's own acquired darkness. I wonder how all that light gets lost."[14]

17
SIGN OF THE FISH

In October of 1969, Gwen wrote to Margaret Atwood that Salah had taken up with a French Canadian girl "as a distraction against the imponderables," and that her own life had also taken a new turn. She had begun to study a new language, always a sign that she was leaving a past behind: "It's a snap.... Greek (modern that is) seems very logical and painless once you're past the horrible pronouns; there are a million words one can almost *guess*.... What fun—after Arabic, any language must be a cinch."[1]

She was frequenting a Greek taverna on Yonge Street called Zorba's, where, she reported, one could drink retsina until dawn and reminisce with Fernando, a Portuguese hunter who had spent years tracking down "Hibexes and Hantelopes." She liked it because you could disappear into the walls and listen to the "Song." Like Salah, she too had found a casual lover, whom she often took with her on her forays to Zorba's.

His name was Douglas Fetherling. He was eight years younger than she, a handsome, young twenty-year-old who had fled the United States in disgust at the Vietnam War. Fascinated by Canada, he was determined to transplant himself as thoroughly as he could. On his arrival in 1967, he had sought out the young writers Dennis Lee and Dave Godfrey, who had just founded House of Anansi Press, the "apotheosis of underground," in Godfrey's basement on Spadina Avenue. This was the press that set out to change writing in Canada forever, and succeeded. It was nationalistic, urban, and savvy, and soon the national newspapers were doing full-page stories on these young bohemians. Fetherling was living on a cot in the cellar next to the office. An autodidact like Gwen, he had developed a gift for hunting down whatever was of cultural interest in the city. Gwen fascinated him. She was a literary star, but she stood apart—there was something magic about Gwen. Fetherling described her in a personal memoir:

> She was petite, as people then said, and had large sad eyes under striking black brows, and wore her hair in a flip. The clothes she was partial to were first of all simple. She once admitted a liking for a particular type of lisle stockings which, she said, could only be bought at some virtually clandestine shop which catered to Roman Catholic nuns. But her clothes were dramatic as well, with flowing sleeves and silk here, brocade there. Of her appearance, I should say that she was totally up-to-the-minute by virtue of being indebted, in some vague but absolutely unmistakable way, to a much earlier time. All this made her inadvertently stylish, as she knew but wouldn't deign to acknowledge.[2]

She wasn't the sort of person to reminisce, he insists. She never mentioned her father, though once she did take him to visit Elsie at the Elmwood Girls' Hotel, a hostel on Elm Street for indigent women and ex-psychiatric patients. Elsie had taken up residence there in 1965 and would stay, with recurrent and sometimes extended periods at the Queen Street Mental Health Centre, until 1975.

Gwendolyn never spoke of her own unusual talents. Fetherling discovered them gradually. At a party, Gwen picked up a guitar, and though she began by holding it across her lap like a dulcimer, by the time they left she was playing it easily. He learned casually that she had studied violin. He discovered by chance that she still painted occasionally and had done a roomful of interesting work. He was surprised that she spoke Arabic, while her rudimentary Greek surfaced at the tavernas they visited. He followed her work—the evocative verse plays she wrote for the CBC when she needed money—and went to her poetry readings, where she would dramatically recite the poems from memory and used the book in her hand only as a prop. "She had genuine psychic ability," he adds. "Once I was sitting silently, trying to remember the title of a movie I had seen based on an H.P. Lovecraft story.... I hadn't spoken aloud about this, not so much as a word, when Gwen came into the room and said matter-of-factly, 'The name on the mail-box is Tierney.' I almost fell off my chair, for this was a line of dialogue on which the horror plot turned."[3]

Fetherling accompanied Gwen when Marie-Claire Blais invited her to Ottawa that winter to attend the Governor General's Awards ceremony as her guest. Blais had won the fiction award for her novel *Les manuscrits de Pauline Archange*. Though their correspondence had been intermittent at best, Blais considered Gwen the most interesting poet in English Canada. To make the occasion theatrical, Fetherling said they decided to dress in a "high Victorian manner, appropriate to the general air of pomposity. Gwen more or less chickened out, but I wore a frock coat and also a top hat, which I delighted to hand to an attendant as we entered." It was Gwen's first meeting with Blais, and she found her, with her luminous yellow eyes, delightful. She also met Prime Minister Pierre Trudeau. She wrote to Margaret Atwood: "He's very small and nice, and came to meet the writers; seems he published poems in college days." When she told him she was writing about Akhenaton, he raised his eyebrows a little: "indicated something, knowledge of Egypt perhaps."[4] Fetherling thought he was very attentive to Gwen "with that dry-ice charm of his."

Gwen and Fetherling briefly became lovers. Once, while in bed together, he asked her if she would mind a personal question: "If not now, I don't know when," she replied. "What's the story on you and Milt?"

Fetherling could not have known that he was awakening old nightmares. He was curious. Everyone on the Toronto scene had stories of the disastrous marriage of Gwen and Acorn, the foul-smelling proletarian poet. People had told him how the two had danced naked in their garden on Ward's Island like William and Catherine Blake. Gwen explained that it was the mistake of her life; she had been a teenager; it hadn't even lasted a year. She made it "sound like a whim that turned into tragedy" and he understood, between the lines as it were, that she had feared her talent being trampled by living with a man who was dictatorial and unstable. But Gwen was becoming more and more aware that she was the subject of gossip and, being so private, it was deeply unpleasant. In fact, Acorn continued to nurse his bitterness towards her in vituperative lyrics, and indeed, having discovered her affair with Fetherling, he wrote to her disparaging her new lover. When the affair ended after a few months, it is not surprising that Gwen found the anonymous community of Greek exiles at Zorba's more comfortable.

One of these exiles was a young musician called Nikos Tsingos. It was customary for Toronto's Greek cafés to scour Greece for musicians to play on short-term contracts in Canada, and the owner of Zorba's had sent his daughters to the Kypseli district of Athens to hunt for musicians. Tsingos arrived in Toronto in May 1969 on a six-month contract. Charismatic, handsome, a guitarist with a mellifluous voice, he spoke absolutely no English.

It was easy for Tsingos to disappear into the community of Greek immigrants, those who had come to Canada steadily since 1950, usually as economic refugees, but for the most part he found the community conservative. As he put it, he was somewhat heretical, interested in politics and fiercely against the military dictatorship then in power in Greece. He felt the majority of Greeks in Toronto remained "sealed in their houses,"[5] living a nostalgic version of Greek nationalism, not interested in what was really happening there. There were, of course, exceptions; Toronto was the headquarters of PAC, the opposition-in-exile, headed by

Andreas Papandreou, who taught at York University and, after the junta's demise, would return to assume the Greek presidency. Tsingos read the poetry of Yannis Ritsos, sang the protest songs of Theodorakis, and composed his own music in a similar mode, but he longed to make contact with this new and mysterious country he had arrived in. He did not yet know he had arrived in a triple exile, from Greece, from the Greek Canadian community, and from Canadian culture, which, despite the best entrée, he would never really succeed in penetrating.

Five months after his arrival he remembers sitting in Zorba's and watching a young woman enter with the owner's bohemian son, Thanasis Steryannis, an aspiring writer. Tsingos recalled that as she walked up the stairs she had blue lights in her face, rather than eyes. He said he fell in love at that moment, she was "so fresh, so beautiful." They met the next day in High Park, speaking with the aid of the dictionaries in their back pockets, and she gave him a copy of *A Breakfast for Barbarians*. A week later, he moved into Gwen's apartment.

Gwendolyn recorded that first encounter. They had sat without language, stumbling through a conversation about Greece with the few words they shared in each other's vocabulary. He had drawn the sign of the fish and "ICHTHYS" on a napkin. She had recently seen a film about early Christians, and the scene of their secret meetings in the catacombs under the city of Rome had stayed with her; their code sign was the fish. The synchronicity intrigued her. Nikos's drawing may have been a casual gesture, but for her it must have meant that though they did not yet share a verbal language, they could enter her world of myths together. She was right. In the seven years of their relationship, they would translate the poetry of Yannis Ritsos, *The Trojan Women* by Euripides, and write a television script on the lost Atlantis. He would become a catalyst to many of her books and poems.

In Nikos she had found a new lover and a muse. In a letter to Gwen, Margaret Atwood wondered whether the muse had to come each time bearing a new alphabet.[6] It seemed almost as if the lover had to be a complete mystery, to be discovered slowly as she unlayered his language. It is clear that Gwendolyn always found the language before she found the man.

To Margaret's comment she replied: "Yes, not only the new alphabet but the landscape as well; also seems imperative that he be in *exile* from that landscape.... In *The Caravan* he can no more get back to that landscape than can I."[7] She was always fascinated and sometimes confused at how her "myth" folded into life. Was she encountering a man or her idea of him?

The Caravan

> precede me into this elusive country,
> travel the tracks of my old laughter,
> tame this landscape, and I will follow after ...
> O love elude me, this recurring journey
> darkens my speech, disorients me
> forever from my natural country
> while the orient eye decides geography....
>
> (once, during an eclipse
> the polarities of my body argued me out
> from an arctic dream
> and I journeyed east, and south,
> to enter the final africa of your mouth)[8]

To be exiled. Gwendolyn was emotionally and imaginatively exiled, always in rebellion against the ordinary. Life had always to be other. To accept life as it was would have been horrible. Nikos was literally in exile, from another place. Surely for him this was exciting: Canada was a "strange exotic place, fraught with possibilities," he said. It required humour, adventurousness. He may have felt vulnerable and disoriented at times, but he had a persona to fall back on: the musician that people came to listen to each night at Zorba's, throwing money at his feet.

Gwendolyn kept a brief journal of their first encounters. They were a perfect erotic match. She writes about that state of absolute erotic desire, when the body stops and focuses and the mind dissolves. That kind of desire makes sex a mystery, a state of enchantment or enthralment, and the body seems life's best gift, ringing on the strings of its own nerve ends, the mind no longer divided against itself looking back at its own face in the mirror. Desire—probable origin: *de sideris*, from the stars.

Gwen had not lived with a man since Salah's departure for Montreal two years earlier, which had turned their relationship into a phantom obsession. It must have been a relief to love again. She refers to nights and days of love that left her drained and happy. What shocked her was that, for the first time, she was experiencing "not a *tragic* passion," but happiness. "How we love once with a joy and intensity that is unparalleled for each of us & I can say now nothing more beautiful has occurred to me."[9] They made love tenderly, they laughed at themselves, they played.

Nikos delighted in Gwendolyn's love of games.

> We always played games—with words, with the siamese cats we had called Constantine, Katerina and Caligula. That first winter we played games in the snow—making candles and angels. I would try to write my name in the snow. I fell down and messed up the letters and said: "I didn't speak English even in snow." We used to write our dreams. She kept a record in a book she had.

And Gwendolyn wrote stories, like "Snow," where the literal moment of their play is exaggerated to a level of magic-realism and the snow enters their dreams like "mana," like a "heavenly confetti."

This capacity for games may have been one of Gwendolyn's most fascinating gifts. To a game she could give her total focus and concentration. That first Christmas she bought them an archery set and wrote to Margaret about it:

I got the *one* thing I've wanted for years for Xmas, a very good archery set. Strange how one decides one is an expert after 24 hours with some new thing. First day I had it Nikos and I spent two hours trying to string the bow; kept doing it backwards and wondering why it looked so funny, screaming at each other meanwhile in Pigeon Greek until we got it right. To string it needs Herculean strength. First shot he drew was a dead-on bull's-eye (never shot a bow before but then he's a Sagittarian). Subsequent shots (all this going on at 4 a.m. by the way, indoors) left Swiss Cheese holes all over the wall, and I thought how I'd have to explain this somehow to the landlord and offer to pay for repairs. But 24 hours later during the second target practice session the whole thing had become deadly serious.... Blistered hands, aching wrists, callouses on the right forefinger ... I tell you I had no idea an archery set could be so absorbing; today I spent hours gluing back the feathers that fell off, adding a strip of wood on the bridge so the arrow would sit better, designing a pair of archery gloves for people with only three fingers, wondering how one might strap the left wrist for support and protect the valley between left thumb and forefinger where the arrow whizzes along the skin and leaves wounds.... You wouldn't have a pattern for a quiver in your sewing gear, would you?[10]

It must have been a strange sight to see them practising in the park near Weston Road, usually around 3 a.m., under street lamps, in the snow. Nikos said they staged championships, and bought a bronze cup for the winner.

He also remembered how once, during a cold spell, they had begun to use the fireplace in their apartment. Gwendolyn came up with a game: what would it have been like to be the first pioneers in this country, alone in the wilderness and totally dependent on fire, "fire that consumes everything and yet gives life." Soon they were burning old books, papers, old clothes in the fireplace. The incident provided the basis for her story called "Fire," only a slight step on in the chain of the game "what if."[11] Nikos loved the games. He said: "I remember thinking she was like someone from the stars—an alien—she seemed so wise, to know already things that experts had to study to know. And yet, she was also a child. I felt the need to protect her."

While Gwendolyn was happy, her own mind would give her no peace. In the intensity of erotic passion it is all very well to imagine ourselves exiles newly invented, unnamed amnesiacs in a new landscape, but we carry the baggage of our entire history. The slow process of de-mystification brings us down and into the world again.

Almost from the first, Nikos was aware of fears in Gwen. He could not understand it: "What do you fear," she records him asking in her notebook of their encounter. "You are very smart & smart people don't have to fear anything—only ignorant people are afraid."[12] He told her he feared the dark side in her.

The relationship with Salah had taken a greater toll than was at first apparent. In those last years when she was living in Toronto and he in Montreal, and perhaps during those few months when she moved to Montreal without telling him, she had begun to drink. She had always avoided alcohol, frightened of the precedent her father's fate had set, but by the time she met Nikos, she could spend a night drinking retsina or brandy. She would say: "You can't become an alcoholic on brandy."

She also developed another serious illness. She began to suffer from asthma attacks. Asthma is a disease that is attributed to a combination of genetic and environmental factors, often exacerbated by emotional stress. Gwen had never been asthmatic in childhood, and there was no asthma in the family. Still, the Great Lakes Basin is notorious for pollens, and asthma can develop in adulthood. Gwen's attacks were traumatic. Nikos remembered picking her up and carrying her to the open window in the dead of winter and watching her attempt to take the icy air into her lungs. Her friend Joe Rosenblatt also remembers what it was like standing helplessly by. Once he had been sure Gwen was dying.[13]

In one of her stories, Gwen wrote of what it was like to experience such an attack, ascribing it to her character Noman:

> ... one could die like this, I thought with terror, with everything going black before the eye, a black cloak lowered before the eyes. Was it not terrible to be drowning without water?...
>
> It is as though the storm outside is also inside ... The white folds in around you, it has become dry ice which imprisons you.... Then it begins, the stone on the chest and the fear, and the stone growing into a concrete slab ... you are trapped in the cave of your own lungs, and you sit upright pulling your chest up and down and praying *breathe, breathe* ... You want to weep but the effort would kill you, so you pray and work. Your soul goes screaming through tunnels of white mucous and slime, horrible corridors, and the pain of breathing makes each breath and each exhalation a small death.[14]

The bronchial attacks came intermittently, several a year, but so dramatic was Gwen's suffering that Nikos thought of this fear, the fear of asphyxiation, as being the root of all her fears. He may have been right. In the case of molested children, particularly when molestation is suffered in early childhood, this experience of asphyxiation, surfacing as asthma, can be a trace memory of the early violation. It is impossible to know if this was behind the stress Gwendolyn experienced. The doctor who treated Gwen for asthma no longer had files on her case.[15] He remembered only a lonely young woman who had given him some of her poems to read. He had found them morbid.

Gwen tried to cope. She did exercises to expand her lungs, though she continued to smoke, unable to quit finally until 1976. But she also developed a strange phobia that was more sinister. She found herself increasingly unable to bear plane flights. Margaret Atwood had taken up a teaching job at the University of Alberta in the fall of 1969 and invited Gwen to Edmonton to read at the end of October, but the prospect of the plane flight proved too much. At the last minute, Gwen lost her nerve. She phoned and then wrote apologetically to explain that she had just finished the eighth or ninth poetry reading of the month, when it dawned on her that she was mentally and physically exhausted, "*plus* the plane ... I *must* get over this phobia." This was not a mild phobia. After a train trip to Ottawa, Gwen wrote despairingly to Margaret:

> ... discovered to my horror that I now have to add *trains* to my list of frightening things—(before it was only cars, planes and subways). The train I was on was particularly fast, and I spent five hours with clutched fists and sinking nerves. Is there any *logic* in one having a phobia about moving vehicles, or speed in general? I'd really like to know, because my movement is seriously hampered by the fact that I'm in paroxysms of terror whenever I'm in a swift moving *thing*. It's a sickening sensation which drains me of all strength, and it's now reached mammoth proportions (can't get into a subway unless it's absolutely *necessary*, etc). Wish very much people could travel places on horseback or small sailing boats as in days of yore. But it does worry me, because I find myself unable to do simple things which I'd very much like to do, such as whipping around here and there giving readings and making money.[16]

"Yes, there were fears in Gwen," Nikos tells me. He remembered her talking of her childhood, a time in Winnipeg when her mother and father had separated. She was alone and had nightmares of tiny brown horses: "She loved horses but these were terrifying. Gwen was afraid of many things, yes, afraid of flying. But I thought her fears were real. She was afraid of things most of us can get by because we ignore them. She always went the whole way. Never half a cigarette, but the whole cigarette. I used to say: 'Gwendolyn, not the whole cigarette!'"

Gwendolyn was deeply in love with Nikos, but the world he brought her, the world of Zorba's, was complex. When one walked off Yonge Street into Zorba's, one entered a transplanted piece of the Mediterranean, drinking retsina till dawn and listening to the sounds of bouzouki and guitar re-create a lost landscape. If you were Greek, you would know everyone there: you would gossip, talk politics, complain of love affairs, family problems, jobs. As the evening stretched, someone would get up to dance the *zembekiko*, a dance performed only by men turning slowly and hypnotically on their own bodies as people threw money at their feet. Plates might fly as the enthusiasm built, though the plates were cheap and you bought them specifically to break them.

It might seem exotic, but underneath, it had the usual elements of human mendacity. Lonely people came there on the hunt. There was that sexual dynamic that could be found wherever musicians play music; the running joke among the musicians was that people came to order coffee and a Greek to go. The musicians knew they were the objects of projected fantasies—even in this small world they had their female groupies and part of their job was to be flattered. It was, in fact, a macho world with an undercurrent of sexual predation, and many wives, soon bored, stayed home.

The environment was set to activate all Gwen's insecurities and she, so brilliant, so gifted, walked easily into its trap. But it was the territory assigned her if she was to love Nikos, and she had to deal with it.

Nikos was thirty-two years old. He had lived the improvised life of a popular musician. There had been many women; in fact, one was still calling from Greece. Women are, in a sense, the booty of a male musician's life, the ones willing to credit him with charisma, since there's usually not much money in the work. What the women are up to is unclear—one could be cruel: sexual titillation, entertainment, a parasitical longing for a creativity that can't be located in the self; or simply a fantasy of emotional range in the man that seems to express itself in the music. But it's a tiresome game, and Nikos, when he met Gwendolyn, was ready for it to be over.

Still, building trust is a long and painful process. He was shocked, Gwendolyn wrote in her notebook, to discover he had been with her, with the same woman, for fifty nights. It had never happened before. He asked continually if she loved him, spoke tentatively of marriage, and occasionally his word "*agape*" (love) would be replaced with the puzzling "*apate*" (illusion). Certainly it must have been hard for him to believe that this beautiful young woman, whom he considered a famous poet— there were the books, the admiring fans—was in love with him. He wanted to know of former lovers, how many, and he didn't want to know. When she travelled for her readings, he said his mind understood that she was a writer and must go, but his heart was another matter. If they were married ... He began to fear Gwendolyn's past, the instability of his own work—he was only on a six-month contract—and his cultural difference, which he knew would occasion misunderstandings.

This, of course, is the volatile territory of passion. Four months into the relationship, nothing of its intensity had abated. But Gwendolyn began to dislike the atmosphere of Zorba's, where it was difficult for her to deal with jealousy. At the club she felt a dancer was in pursuit of Nikos. She writes: "Monday I go to the club & see the dancer—O how silly—she follows me downstairs "Then ine tipote [It's nothing]."[17] Gwen had the scenario clear in her own mind—to this girl, she was a poacher trapping the new singer from Greece, whom the dancer saw as her territory.

Her paranoia built: Nikos phoned twice to say "*S'agapo*" [I love you], and arrived home as usual at 4 a.m. when the club closed, in what to Gwen seemed like a nervous mood. She explained that what she saw at Zorba's was killing her, how she couldn't bear to live as she had done before with Salah. He assured her she had misunderstood.

Nikos tried to explain the atmosphere of the club to her. It was his job to flatter the women clientele. When they sent him drinks he had to go to their table to thank them. He had to dance the exotic *zembekiko*. He was a performer, an actor. She complained that he shouldn't have to change his character for the sake of the audience. She would accuse him of being a peacock, a flamboyant puppet. All that money thrown at his feet.

Nikos never acquired the reputation of a womanizer in the Greek community, where gossip files were kept on everyone. He was always thought of as slightly apart: private, dignified, responsible. When I first met him in 1979 at The Trojan Horse café playing with the group Compañeros, I was impressed by his quiet self-containedness and his gentleness, impressions that never altered. This did not belie a fierce resilience, rooted in his music and his own writing; his ambition and pride were located in the art. But he would not have been one to fight the conventions. He would do what was asked of him in the long years of a musician's labour in the sweat shops of the Greek cafés. Everything in his character makes it seem clear that he was faithful to Gwen. Those who were around, like Gwendolyn's sister, Carol, believed Gwendolyn's fears were self-generated.

Gwendolyn herself saw this. But it was the psychological territory of insecurity in which she lived her private, as opposed to her artistic, life. During the first months of their love—from August to April—she recorded her dreams. After a night of loving she warns herself: "The small girl in the dream, my awful rival, I realized as I looked at N.[ikos], was *me* & I have nothing to fear from her."

Gwendolyn's dreams are like a narrative of her expectations. Her first dream of Nikos on September 20, 1969, their first encounter, brings her only tremendous peace, but the dreams that followed sent her back into the psychological territory charged by the mother, where she could only lose.

> Nov 1/69: Taxi with Nikos to Keele-Bloor where old house of my childhood stands. I am horrified to go in alone & tell him so. He says he often goes alone into houses. Why can't I? *There's something inside* I whisper, &

as I look up, it is my own presence which lurks within—large Ryerson picture of me on wall.

Jan 16/70: I carry a child on my shoulders across busy street—a woman tells me it's OK to go *now*—but as I dash through the traffic we are almost hit by a car. On the other side I angrily berate the woman for giving a wrong signal, saying that the child might have died. Later the child turns into a cat & then there are many cats, very small which I am trying to carry upstairs to my place—first I must empty mailbox (#20) of B's mail. Upstairs I put the cats down so I can open door, but to my horror the smallest one walks into a hideous patch of slime or quicksand & falls right through. I go downstairs & weep together with the girl downstairs, who says some of the cats died when falling down to her place, but I see one or 2 are still moving around.

Later I am having a strenuous contest with a strong heavy man—I am pushing him away with great effort. At one point I compliment him on his strength & he in turn congratulates me.

Feb 23/70: Walking into a film which shows an actress in oriental costume—walking through a fantastic Japanese garden which had hundreds of multi-coloured birds (utterly tame)—as I walked the birds did not fly away but gently moved aside—one had to be careful not to step on them, they were so tame—I thought, or someone said, There in Japan the sound of human beings does not frighten birds or make them wild.

End of March/70: See shadows on the wall of old home on Keele St. There are children which scare me. I think they are Peter Pan's children.

These were the dreams of 38 Keele Street, where Gwen was still Peter Pan's Wendy, caught in a world where the children could not grow up. There was a crucial part of Gwendolyn still trapped in that childhood. Not unexpectedly, many of her dreams were about her mother. Gwendolyn would have feared that her mother's madness would surface in herself were her control ever to weaken:

> End of March/70: The child M [Mallory?] is being cared for in a basement centre below florist shop on Elm St. A lovely blue cord (umbilical!) stretches from there to the Hostel where Mother used to live—the cord is for the purpose of ringing the bell to the nursery when at a distance. I go down and see M, who has a large outsized head (triangular) and whose body is so small he can scarcely stand.
>
> April 9: With 2 or 3 other people in snowy field—I seem to be demonstrating how to manoeuvre in snow (the way animals can't).... Later Mom & I in bed—I consciously think—this is the phallic woman, for we seem to be joined by a long phallus—I regret it is not a man or a lover—I see 2 water wings suspended above & she mentions I should have sea-wings.
>
> April 18/70:—with mother to England. Problems at airport when I rush around with her in wheelchair. She accuses me of not handling things well enough. Then in her old house in London where I talk to aunts in a room that turns over like a water wheel—I ask to stop because I don't like the sensation—later making tea (house is cramped & dark)—& Mom says water is not pure, may have been used before for soaking girdles (!) N. is coming to England & this thought pervades dream.

—a hand makes a tin toy of child come to life—the thing becomes evil & wages war against *babies*—stands over corpse or sick baby & talks about how it has made a slow death from cancer—miles & miles inside.[18]

Gwen was tied, umbilically, to her mother. Tragically, her childhood had been so terrible, yet there was a part of her that had to stay there, stuck, petrified; as if until that childhood was somehow resolved, it would never release her. Did she feel she could not abandon the child's world, because the child knew from experience that the world outside was terrifying? Or was the molested child, unacknowledged, still trapped there? Nikos was asking her to leave that space. Like her character of long ago, Gabriela, was Gwen saying: "How do you know I want to get out? I'm getting used to it down here." The battle was extreme, its issue always in question.

In her dreams, Nikos received the projection of that part of herself, for and against which she was fighting, that wanted to undergo the painful cauterizing of that past:

Nov 1/69: Nikos (Nike Necropolis) is master of his own small Necropolis—(I was reading about this same night)—where I find him gaily rinsing out white skulls in a basin & hanging them from the ceiling to dry.

End of March/70: N (?) reveals his genitals which are several rows of small [unreadable] like penises—as though asking which I choose (!) I carefully select 2— one which enters the vagina & one higher up which simultaneously enters a passage below the clitoris. Intense sexual excitement.

End of March/70: See N. and someone else preparing a strange ceremony down the lane. I recall that N said when others start killing he *has* to join in. I go to them and N looks sad at what he *must* do to me. Gives a bowl of something to his assistant, a large man who is also reluctant. Before painting the stuff on me he first paints his own head, as though to show me he will suffer the same. Stuff is a kind of acid. He paints down both sides of his face, then mine. N applies a yellowish foam to my hair & I realize the ritual is designed to destroy all my hair. I cry out No, please, I want my own hair—but N tries to console me by showing me wigs I can have. However, I am inconsolable. (image inspired by seeing wig shop on Yonge St)

It is possible that a part of Gwen's dreaming mind had to demonize Nikos, that part of her that wanted to stay, comfortless, in her dark world.

But Gwen was also a writer and that dark world was the source of her gift; the immediacy of her connection with it gave her access to things others did not know about. But it made living in the world increasingly painful:

October/69: Old house on King Street—I float over it; in front is middle-aged female singer (very bad)—farther back, a writer—& at the very back everything is pitch black & many trees & here is where *Glenn* Gould (Gwen) lives like a Necromantist, in utter darkness, tending the coffin-shrine in the garden which is a large black guitar case w.[ith] a wreath on it.

The source of her genius was that dark garden. One could look for explanations of this macabre dream—she was always tending her father's coffin; one could also see it as a description of the mystery and the cost of her particular imagination.

18
MEMOIRS OF A MAD COOK

No matter what was going on, Gwen's capacity to write, to order the chaos of her experience into lucid, crystalline poems, never faltered. Writing was a necessity, a way of being. She felt she could not live if she did not write. She was writing poems for a collection that would be called *The Armies of the Moon*, stimulated by her enthralment as she had watched the first human beings walking on the moon in the summer of 1968. When she finished the book, she planned to make the cover a photograph of herself in a space suit.

She was also preparing programmes for Robert Weaver's "Anthology," and the CBC had bought rights to a long poem called "The Carnival," commissioned by Ron Collier and entered in the Detroit Freedom Festival of Music, where it was performed by the Ron Collier Orchestra. She had good news about a radio drama she had written in 1967 called *The World of Neshiah*, a science fiction story based on the premise of a world in which the inhabitants had no short-term memory. It had been entered in the "Prix Italia" competition, and in 1970 was to be broadcast by Radio Televisione Italiana, Trieste, in a Serbo-Croatian translation.

She was still trying to find a British co-publisher for *King of Egypt, King of Dreams*, to satisfy her Canadian publisher, Macmillan, and it was rejected by yet another agent. Jane Rule wrote to console her, saying that "*Desert* was rejected twenty-three times."

She and Nikos were still living in the apartment on Weston Road in the downstairs basement of a laundromat. Her nephews and nieces, who had begun to visit regularly, remembered how she had managed to make it exotic. Furniture was scarce, but Gwen had placed pillows everywhere. One day the curtains would be the bedspread, and then they'd be back on the windows, and the following day they would serve as a tablecloth. She'd hung her Greek posters on the wall. They remembered her cats, and her beat-up bicycle, the kind that folded up so she could carry it on the bus. She told them where the apartment key was hidden in case they needed to come and hang out, and often they would drop by with school friends. There would be candles and Greek music, and "exotic" Greek food. The friends, frightened by her black kohl eyes, the large necklaces, the Cleopatra look, would refuse to return, something Gwen's nieces and nephews could never understand since, to them, their gentle-voiced aunt was always so "neat." Unlike most adults, she seemed genuinely interested in what they were doing. "She always made you feel important. She was sweet and really loved us," they assure me.[1]

Their memories went back as far as Uncle Acorn, a big, burly man who had been so kind to them; they could hardly believe his public persona, which they learned about only as adults. They remembered the times when their step-father had been ill in hospital with cancer, and Gwen had come to look after them at their house on Locust Street. "It was always a riot." Gwen couldn't cook. She would grind the steaklets into meatloaf, which had been "gross," but also funny; she had been so serious about it.

Carol's son David remembered the way she trusted you as a child. Once, when he was twelve, she had asked him to pick up a cheque from her publishers. It was for a huge amount, perhaps $10,000. He had set out on his bike feeling "all wimpy. Could I do it?" When he delivered it to her, she was delighted. "To me it was a big deal. There was never a question that a twelve-year-old couldn't handle that kind of responsibility, and it mattered to me in a big way."

Patti, Carol's child by her second husband, remembered their trips to the zoo at High Park. She had been six or seven and it was like being with another kid, Gwen more excited by the pink flamingoes and the buffaloes than she was. Her Auntie Gwen had been crucial in her childhood. Because her father had died in her infancy, those times in school when you were expected to make Father's Day cards were horrible. The teachers didn't understand. Once Gwen asked her why she was so unhappy, and she had explained how hard it was because she didn't have a father. Gwen had said immediately: "You can have Uncle Nick." After that Patti made all her father's cards and gifts for Uncle Nick and Gwen hung them on her kitchen walls. It had mattered enormously.

In school their principal, Mrs. Green, would tell them Gwen was an extremely important poet, one of her favourite in the world, and it came as a shock. Who knew Auntie Gwen? However, when Gwen invited Carol's oldest daughter, Carol Anne, then eighteen, to accompany her to a reading at Carleton University in Ottawa, and the audience was full, everyone seeming to flatter and faun over her aunt, and the CBC footed the bill at the Chateau Laurier, she realized her aunt was someone important.

To Carol's youngest son, Michael, Gwen was magic. She provided a place he could go, where one didn't have to talk. One could sit quietly, be taken seriously. When he began to write poetry and turned to painting, she was the mentor he conjured in his mind.[2]

By the spring of 1970, Nikos's English was improving, and he watched, fascinated, as the poems accumulated. He always knew what Gwen was working on. He was always interested, he said, because he loved poetry. She was writing what she called her sewing and cooking poems. With her particular kind of macabre humour, she wrote to Margaret Atwood asking for her recipe for health cereal. "I'm half-starved, not because I'm broke, but because I'm sick of all kinds of food, and everything turns my stomach (also, can't cook).... If you give me the recipe, I'll tell you about a Greek caviar salad which I can't make, but which is delicious."[3] She got the recipe and claims to have made a ten-year supply of cereal, meanwhile returning the caviar recipe with the proviso that it was given to her by a Greek woman who didn't speak English and was to be used impressionistically. She also reported she was sewing extraordinary clothes while drunk. "Have you ever sewn while drunk? It's quite an experience" and offered advice about The Textile Clearing House, outside Kensington Market, where material was cheap and the place had soul. She didn't have the money to buy her clothes retail.

All experience could be turned into poems. That was where the pain surfaced:

Memoirs of a Mad Cook

There's no point kidding myself any longer,
I just can't get the knack of it; I suspect
there's a secret society which meets
in dark cafeterias to pass on the art
from one member to another.
Besides,
it's so *personal* preparing food for someone's
insides, what can I possible *know*
about someone's insides, how can I presume
to invade your blood?
I'll try, God knows I'll try
but if anyone watches me I'll *scream*
because maybe I'm handling a tomato wrong,
how can I *know* if I'm handling a tomato wrong?

something is eating away at me
with splendid teeth

Wistfully I stand in my difficult kitchen
and imagine the fantastic salads and soufflés
that will never be.
Everyone seems to grow thin with me
and their eyes grow black as hunters' eyes
and search my face for sustenance.
All my friends are dying of hunger,
there is some basic dish I cannot offer,
and you my love are almost as lean
as the splendid wolf I must keep always
at my door.

or

Meditations of a Seamstress

When it's all too much to handle
and the green seams of the world start fraying,
I drink white wine and sew
like it was going out of style;
        curtains become dresses, dresses
become pillowcovers, clothes
I've worn forever get taken in or out.
Now I can't explain exactly
what comes over me, but when the phone rings
I tell people I'm indisposed;
I refuse to answer the door, I even
neglect my mail.
        (Something vital is at stake,
the Lost Stitch or the Ultimate Armhole,
I don't know what) and hour after hour
on the venerable Singer
I make strong strong seams for my dresses
and my world.

> The wine possesses me
> and I sew like a fiend, forgetting to use
> the right colours of threads, unable to make
> a single straight line;
> I know somehow I'm fighting time
> and if it's not all done by nightfall
> everything will come apart again;
> continental shelves will slowly drift into the sea
> and earthquakes will tear wide open
> the worn-out patches of Asia.
>
> Dusk, a dark needle, stabs the city
> and I get visions of chasing fiery spools of thread
> mile after mile over highways and fields
> until I inhabit some place at the hem of the world
> where all the long blue draperies
> of skies and rivers wind;
>   spiders' webs describe
> the circling of their frail thoughts forever;
> everything fits at last and someone has lined
> the thin fabric of the world with grass.[4]

The poems were raw and immediate. The mythological extremism, the black tragic humour, was a mask Gwen knew intimately. Another poem, bleak and with the humour removed, makes it clear the despair she could feel:

It Comes Upon You

> It comes upon you suddenly that this is its moment,
> This is what it's all been for, the secret
> That you held in store like a juggler always allowing for
> The ball that is not there.

> It comes upon you suddenly that to sit here
> With cold coffee and the day's penultimate cigarette
> Is the sum total of all the painful becoming
> And the Hell. If you can't see it now you never will.
>
> It comes upon you suddenly that you must wear
> The many selves you gathered and regrew
> With a kind of pride and poise that falsifies their weight
> With cool deceptive ease
>
> Or else cry forever as once before you cried
> On a high hill overlooking everything; God
> Withdraw my fingers from your hair and break my eyes![5]

It is that last image—she with her fingers in God's hair—breaking the poem wide open, that breaks the heart.

Other poems spread her despair back into the objective world, which, she felt, if one stopped long enough to look, is a very brutal place. She wrote a poem about the famous portrait of the young boy in the Warsaw ghetto dancing for his Nazi guards:

> there's no way I'm going to write about
> the child dancing in the Warsaw ghetto
> in his body of rags
>
> there were only two corpses
> on the pavement that day
> and the child I will not write about
> had a face as pale and trusting
> as the moon ...
>
> the child who danced
> in the Warsaw ghetto

> to some music no one else could hear
> had moon-eyes, no
> green horror and no fear
> but something worse
>
> a simple desire to please
> the people who stayed
> to watch him shuffle back and forth,
> his feet wrapped in the newspapers
> of another ordinary day[6]

Gwendolyn did not often write "social protest" poems. "When I consider writing poems," she said, "which are protests against the evils of the world and social injustice, I become very much aware that these evils are embodied in each of us separately and in myself, and I don't feel we can cure the world until we have first cured ourselves."[7] She wrote "The Other Underground" to explain how our fantasy that evil is somehow something that happens apocalyptically, outside ourselves, is an illusion. The darkness is located in all of us.

> ... the midnights lit by warlight, scarlet stars,
> the sheer hallucination of our wars
> have grown from small hurts, symbolic
> murders,
> and the tyranny is with us everyday
> in our small cruel lies,
> in our turning away from love,
> and the Enemy is where he always was—
> in the bleak lunar landscapes of our mirrors.
>
> I'm so far underground you cannot find me,
> hating the untellable which must get told,
> trying to read the monthly Morse-code of the moon,
> these urgent letters to the world.[8]

That October, she would be appalled to find the psychosis of war active in Canada. During the October Crisis of 1970, when Pierre Laporte, a federal minister, was kidnapped and killed and the federal government invoked the War Measures Act to mobilize troops on the streets of Quebec, she wrote to Margaret Atwood, who was living in England: "The last weeks since the Laporte murder have been *bleak*. One shouldn't be surprised, of course, but something went Thud in my stomach on Oct. 17, and there's an awful taste in my mouth which I can't get rid of. Really a horrible time all around."[9]

Gwen's reputation as a poet had been building for years. Now it was confirmed. In May 1970, she was awarded the Governor General's Award for her book *The Shadow-Maker* and received $2,500; she shared the prize with George Bowering for his books *Rocky Mountain Foot* and *The Gangs of Kosmos*. Clearly the jury had been unable to decide between their works. Friends wrote letters of congratulation, and she and Nikos went to Ottawa for the ceremony, staying at the Chateau Laurier. It was wonderful to win, but like most things that came to Gwendolyn, there was a shadow side that few understood.

Milton Acorn also had a new collection of poems out in 1969 called *I've Tasted My Blood*; it was probably the best book that he ever produced and Gwen admired it. When the short-list of prospective winners appeared in *The Globe and Mail*, Milton's name was on it. Gwen had heard that two authors in the category of fiction or poetry would share the award, and she was in a terrible quandary. There was no telling whether she herself had won, nor if Milton had, but the prospect that she might share the prize with him was too devastating. She wrote privately to Robert Weaver, who was involved in the adjudication of the prize, to say that if she and Milton proved to be joint winners, she would prefer to withdraw her name:

> I don't know how to put this, but I trust that you will take it in the most confidential way possible. In order to explain what I have to say, I first have to mention that I've had some rather bad and disturbing communications

from Milton over the past number of years, and these have left me quite fearful and nervous. Consequently I have tried to avoid unnecessary encounters etc. You might guess now what I am coming to. If, in the event that two poets were chosen, and if in the remote event that they were Milton and myself, I would be quite unable to cope with the situation.

This, as you can imagine, is a very embarrassing letter to have to write, and it may be quite unnecessary ... I felt I had to tell someone in confidence that I would not be able to accept an award if Milton were also receiving one (which would mean facing the necessary encounters, as well as even slight publicity). In writing you now my main idea is ... to avoid a situation where I might have to turn down an award *after* it was offered.... I would rather I were left out of it altogether and no award were offered to me.[10]

She stressed that her desire for confidentiality was based on the fact that if Milton knew of her request, he would misinterpret it as "professional jealousy or arrogance—and I'm already frightened enough, not to want to provoke further diatribes from him." Gwen was not exaggerating. Many people were aware that Acorn nursed an incredible hatred towards her, but no one knew that he had started to write to her again in February of 1969. What provoked him is not clear, but the letters began in a similar tone. He might accuse her of being a capitalist bent on destroying him, and could add that she had used him to ignite her "small talent". She had always acted like a whore, using sex to get ahead. He wanted her "off [his] turf"; Toronto was his town, and he didn't want to have to see her "smirking" face, reminding him of her treachery. She had failed in her "mission of destruction"; laughing, he would watch her "twist and scream".[11]

At the end of July, having obviously come down somewhat from his manic high, he wrote to apologize: "You were not the only one to get a hate letter when I was in Saskatoon and you're not the only one to get an apology. I've come to the decision that I can't go on all my life hating you. It's very damaging to my psyche." But this was not much of a consolation, since the letter continued with a rant about how modern women were living in a misogynistic age; all men had a homosexual's contempt for women and he had been punished for opposing such hatred. He wanted to know why she had failed her talent, since she had written one good line: "To wear the whole cosmos like a conical hat," even if the poem wasn't good and the line was derivative of his work. She shouldn't have worried about intruding on his territory. Comparing other puny modern poets to him was like comparing finitude and infinity. The letter ended with the assurance: "I hated you, and have hated you since—which means I suppose that I still love you."[12]

As it turned out, Gwen's letter to Robert Weaver proved unnecessary. The jury had already selected Bowering as her co-winner. Milton was outraged in any case, but his bitterness was deflected onto Bowering, the Canadian establishment, and the GGA committee, who were the enemies. So angry was he that literary friends took up his cause, and proposed to organize an alternative award for "The People's Poet." The gala was held at Grossman's Tavern on Spadina, one of his favourite haunts down the street from the Waverley, a cheap hotel where he had taken up residence. He was toasted and feted and presented with his medallion in an uproarious party. Decorum was not Milton's strong point, and he managed to lose the cheque that came with the medal—it was found on the bar-room floor the next day. But the evening did bring a kind of fame to what was an important book of poetry. At a distance, Milton could be entertaining and outrageous, but for a woman who got too close, and Gwendolyn was not the only one, an encounter with Milton could be appalling. Milton never posed a physical threat—he himself was repelled by physical violence—but verbal violence was his trade. Nothing was more terrifying to Gwen; her mother, a master of that art in her manic moods, had already left too many scars.

Nikos's contract at Zorba's taverna, which had been extended another six months, was to be over in June of 1970, but by April, a new prospect surfaced. He was offered a six-month contract at a Greek club in Sacramento, California. Gwen was excited at the idea of living in a new place—it was only travelling to it that was difficult. Her friend Samar Attar, with whom she had been corresponding in Arabic for several years, would be nearby, teaching at a local university in San Diego. Earlier Gwen had written to Attar in Arabic: "Everyday you change your place like the wind, while I am a tree which dreams of travelling but does nothing."[13] "Wish I could travel as easily as you," she complained, "jumping onto planes without a worry in the world. It's very strange that with so many great fears in life, I still worry about stupid things like machines that go too fast! I would be very happy in the 15th century ..."

At the last minute, however, Nikos was refused an American visa. This was strange, since Greek musicians regularly crossed the border to work in the U.S.; the only explanation that seemed plausible was that he was being blackballed for his songs against the Greek dictatorship. It was deeply disappointing. Instead he found a summer job at a local club in Kitchener, and he and Gwen moved there, staying in the house of friends, with Gwen given access to the basement for her typing. Soon they rented a small house of their own, and Nikos remembers this as an ideal summer. They camped and swam in the local lakes, and Gwen was able to work on her collection of short stories.

In the fall they moved back to Toronto, settling in an apartment at 13 Browning Avenue in the Danforth area. Danforth Avenue is a major east-west thoroughfare that runs for ninety-one blocks from the Don River Valley, which bifurcates the city's east side, to Kingston Road in the suburban municipality of Scarborough. But "the Danforth" refers to the Greek neighbourhood that stretches from the Don for about fifteen blocks to Pape Avenue. By 1950 Greek immigrants had settled in, slowly transforming the district into a Little Greece, with the street signs written in English and Greek. The Danforth came alive at night—with strings of cafés with names like Odyssey and

Astoria, featuring Greek musicians and occasional belly dancers, where the souvlaki was cooked on an open grill and patrons went into the kitchen to choose their meal. The vegetable shops opened twenty-four hours, lambs hung in the butcher-shop windows, and the travel agents spread their windows with posters of Hydra and Delphi. Sundays, three generations of families paraded in their finest after church service, as they had once done in Greece. The street closed twice a year to celebrate Greek Independence Day and the defeat of the Fascists in the Second World War.

Gwendolyn loved the Danforth. Her Greek was by now very good, and she came to know many of the Danforth's characters. What she most liked about the Greeks was their uninhibitedness, their exuberance. They seemed transparent; in what they said or did there seemed no hidden agenda. They had a particular kind of insanity she admired: "You live life; you think you know what you're doing; but you look at it from another perspective and it's all suddenly absurd."[14] But there was still a chauvinism to contend with. In its public persona at least, this was a male world.

Her old friend from the Toronto Island days the sculptor Mac Reynolds remembers visiting one of the nightclubs with Gwen. When the strains of the *zembekiko* began to play, Gwen got up to dance. She danced with a brilliant fierceness, playing intricate variations with her body on the strict and complex rhythm of the music. She loved the dance: it was, she said, "both a fight against gravity and a kind of flirtation with the earth." She danced it defiantly. On the sidewalk afterwards, Reynolds remembers a fierce argument, entirely in Greek, with one of the men who had followed Gwen out. She had violated their tradition.[15] In 1970, the *zembekiko* was still a dance danced only by men.

And Gwen remained fiercely Canadian. On the Danforth it was a practice of the Greek café owners to keep the passports of visiting Greek musicians during their tenure in Canada. This outraged Gwen: "They may be able to do that in Greece," she would tell the musicians, "but in Canada they have no right to keep your passport." When Nikos was expected to

Gwendolyn and Nikos Tsingos at Delina Tavern, Danforth Avenue, 1971.

Gwendolyn practising archery in her Browning Avenue apartment, 1970.

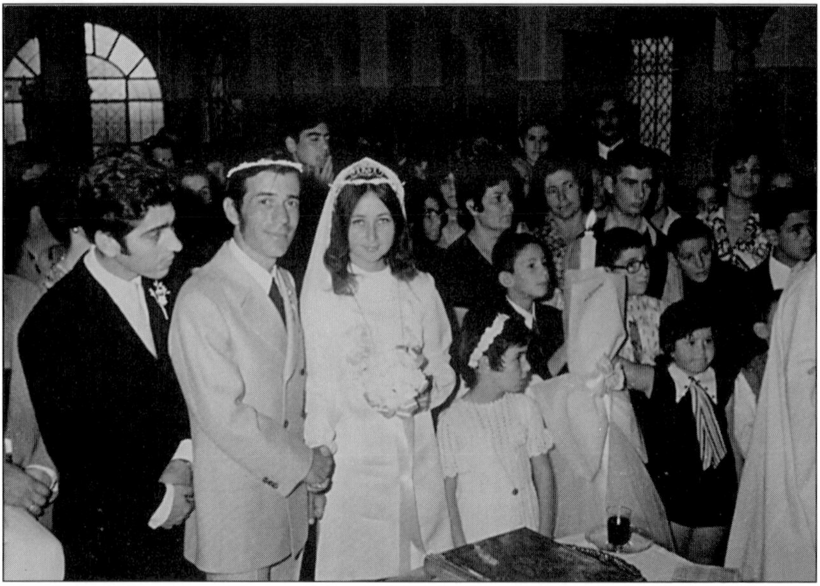

Nikos Tsingos

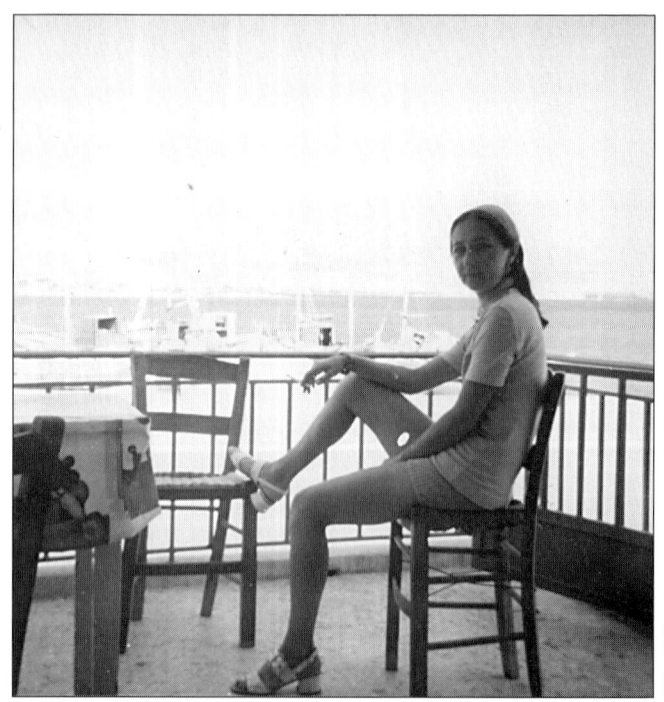

Wedding of Gwendolyn and Nikos Tsingos at St. Thomas of Kypseli, Athens, 3 October 1971.

Nikos Tsingos

Gwendolyn at Mandelena Motel in Antiparos, 1971.

(Left) *Nikos Tsingos in the town square of Antiparos, 1976.*

(Below) *An oil painting by Gwendolyn of Nikos Tsingos. This is the only example of her painting that has survived.*

John McCombe Reynolds

Photograph of Gwendolyn in a "space suit" taken by Mac Reynolds for the cover of her 1972 book, Armies of the Moon. *(The photograph was not used.)*

Barry Callaghan

Launch of Barry Callaghan's The Hogg Poems and Drawings, Isaacs Gallery, *1978. From left to right: Stephen Williams, Gwendolyn, Timothy Findley, and William Whitehead.*

Robert Weaver

Celebration of the 30th anniversary of CBC Radio's "Anthology" series and the publication of The Anthology Anthology, St. Michael's College, University of Toronto, 31 October 1984. Back row from left to right: Glenn Witmer, George Bowering, Matt Cohen, Margaret Lyons, Joyce Marshall, Helen Weinzweig, Marian Engel, Alice Munro, Robert Weaver. Front row from left to right: Norman Levine, Gwendolyn MacEwen, Morley Callaghan.

John McCombe Reynolds

The sculptor Ruben Zellermeyer, in 1987.

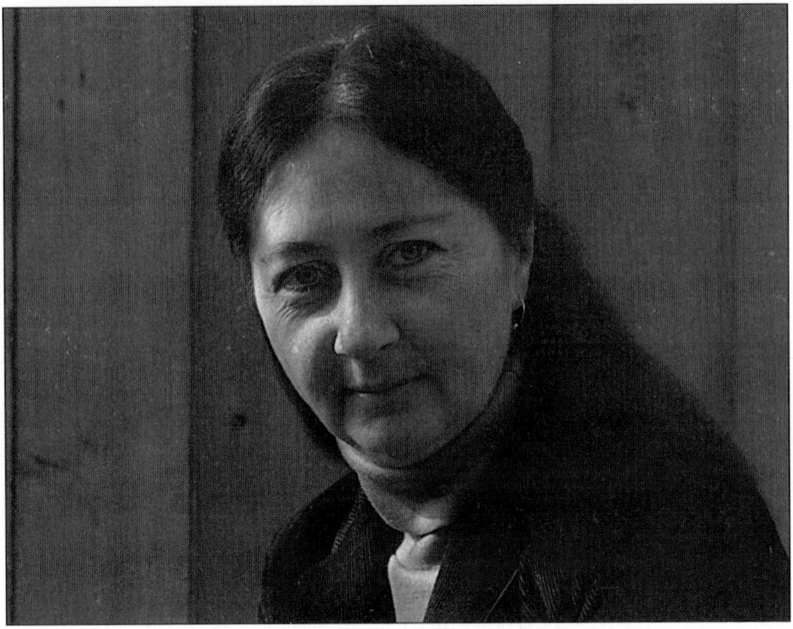

John McCombe Reynolds

(Above) *Gwendolyn in 1987, the spring before she died.*

(Below) *Carving of Hathor, goddess of love, fertility and joy, on a capital of the Temple of Denderra, Qina, Egypt. The resemblance between the face of the goddess and Gwendolyn's face is uncanny.*

Rosemary Sullivan

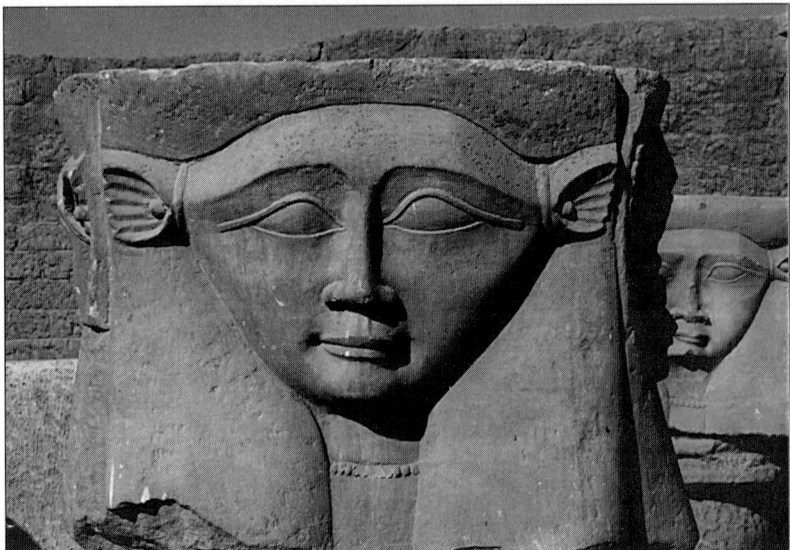

play six nights a week for little pay, she would march in to tell his boss that he was being exploited. This, of course, could never sit well with Nikos. She was intruding. She did not understand that she would only make his life harder. He could easily be blackballed by café owners if he did not play by their rules—there was no musicians' union on the Danforth.

It was curious how naïve Gwen was about the double standard that was to be found not only on the Danforth but in Canadian society as well. She wrote to Margaret, who was then living in England:

> My editor at Macmillan has a book jacket on the wall which reads (title), I LIKED IT BETTER WHEN I WAS A VIRGIN, SHE SAID, and although I haven't read the book, I have read the title, which intrigues me. Everything was so much easier when one was a *girl*, strolling through the quagmires, picking dandelions, billowy skirts fluttering in the wind, etc. But being a woman is *vletch*, and after 30 years of blissful innocence I'm just beginning to discover that I am being exploited ... or not me, everyone. How come there's no topless gogo places featuring *men*, so I can go and watch? How come all the sex films spend hours trailing their cameras down *female* flesh, so it's fun for everybody except us? No fair. Are we supposed to identify with all those heaps of thighs and somehow get our kicks from them? *Blahh*. Would a man feel comfortable sitting in a theatre and watching a member of his sex slowly strip to the ultimate X.... I don't know if I mentioned before that POWER POLITICS is a stunning book.[16]

One wonders how Margaret responded to this letter. Feminism was a new movement about to take hold. Perhaps she found it poignant that Gwen, with her history, her fear of her mother and her father-longing, had sustained her blissful innocence so long. She kept silent.

In their correspondence they did not talk of feminism. Gwen was deeply uncomfortable with any movements, so that feminist analyses of the roots of sexism were not available to her.

At Browning Avenue, Gwen kept her address secret and when she met people, she often met them elsewhere. She told Samar Attar that she preferred it like this—it was the only way she could get any work done, and there were only a few people she wanted to see. She was writing a book of animal poems, which she intended to call "Magic Animals" and which was to end with a poem about the Loch Ness monster. She took to visiting the Toronto zoo for ideas and wrote to Margaret:

> Do you have any special ideas on the Loch Ness monster and other sea-beasts? I heard a strange biologist on TV recently who wrote a book called THINGS; he claims the L.N. monster is a giant eel; apparently eel larvae have been found which are gigantic. He also related some incredible things about a queen ant in S. America who can teleport herself out of a sealed shell and into another one! Not to mention a certain species of spider which 'die' when their water is taken away, and come to life again after months and months when the water is put back. Not to mention flying stones which can turn corners and change direction in mid-air. At the moment I'm more interested in the Loch Ness monster, tho.[17]

Gwen envied animals. She had developed the idea that they lived the "conscience of the flesh." When vicious, their viciousness was innocent. She envied their joy of movement, their conviction of direction. She wanted to find a language as visceral, as clean as theirs. In her zoo she imagined animals watching man from their cages, "holding [his] immortal soul in trust"[18]—by which she meant that what we do to the animals we do, ultimately, to ourselves. She felt that we were destroying nature. She hoped the animals would outlast us.

Despite everything, Gwen was essentially affirmative about life. There was in her that quality of "hope" that would always astound her friends. She would complain that the only criticism she had of modern poetry was that it tended to be an exploration of pain, a kind of dwelling on one's wounds and scars. She insisted that poetry should also heal; it should "seam up" some of the wounds that life opens. Amazingly, Gwen never lost her humour. That summer she met the Maritime poet Alden Nowlan on one of his trips through Toronto and she was amused when he made her vice-president of the Canadian chapter of the Flat Earth Society, which he had just founded. Her job was to find new members since, at the moment, there were only three. She wrote to Margaret Atwood: "One of our immediate aims is to approach the United Nations with the request that a large fence be built around the Edge of the earth to save people from falling off into the Abysmal Chasm, and also to discourage possible suicides. If you feel, then, that you are more or less On the Brink, you must join the club."[19] The writer Ray Fraser did a radio interview in Montreal in which he insisted that the moon landing of 1969 had been faked in Newfoundland. The Flat Earth Society's current project was a response to the concern that a good deal of racial discrimination could be attributed to the convention that North is always placed at the top of the globe and South at the bottom. Even assuming that the world is round, this was an arbitrary placement. The Flat Earthers committed themselves to placing all continents on the same footing. Meanwhile, they would hang all their maps of the world upside-down.

Gwen spent the year of 1971 working on her book *Noman*. While parts of it came from her early abandoned manuscript *Saturnalia*, most of it was essentially new. She had written to Margaret back in 1968:

> Was recently in Ottawa, reading, and drove on a thunderstormy night to Kingsmere in the Gatineau (Mackenzie King's odd estate grounds—saw for the second time those incongruous old pillars and arches that he imported from Greece and Italy—had (also for the

second time) an absolutely cold, shivery experience while approaching one particular arch. Wind was gusty, night was black, lightning etc ... but as I approached the arch I was seized with absolute creeping horror, froze in my tracks and couldn't go a step farther; that arch radiated some sort of anti-magnetism; at any rate it definitely didn't want to be visited. This in itself is nothing much to speak of, but the interesting thing was my companion (a sensible person in the business world, but one who does not have psychic leanings) stopped short just before I did, also unable to budge from the spot.

There are, I gather, funny tales about Kingsmere ... it burned down once, also something about King watching the parliament bldgs. burn through that particular arch(?). I don't know the details; will have to find out. All I know is Kingsmere is absolutely haunted. Anyway the thing begins to obsess me.[20]

Out of that obsession she crafted Noman, multi-lingual, Canadian, who discovers that his country is exotic, as mysterious as any country in the world. When she read it, Margaret wrote of her delight at the game Gwen was playing:

I've just read NOMAN. Sorry again it took me so long, but I kept waiting for a quiet moment ... It's fascinating ... the thing that holds it together, for me, is the attempt to find a place for the mythical, the magical, in Kanada ... with the movement from myth to the city in the first story, and the reverse movement in the last ... from everyday out through the arch. Seems to me an exploration of ways of fitting together the mythic East of the poems with the eggs & bacon present of Kanada (in the poems too) and it's enormously suggestive ... for instance, that Noman is really a Kanadian but manages to fool the rest, that Julian ends up in burlesque houses and nobody understands/appreciates his magic ... also the death-in-the-snow thing, & the fact that the second death in the snow isn't real ... I think it would be great fun to write something about this, putting it together with the other magic/Canadian figure I know, namely the hypnotist in Davies' Fifth Business, also a Kanadian in disguise ... (both of them have to assume a false European identity in order to impress the natives!) Do you know of any others? ... I've sworn not to write any more criticism but know this is a swear that will probably fall by the wayside. (*just one thought—Charlotte Shade is a magician/charlatan too, but a bad one.) (Reaney's play.) Hope all is going well.[21]

The "swear" did fall by the wayside. Margaret wrote an essay dealing with Gwen's work: "Canadian Monsters: Some Aspects of the Supernatural in Canadian Fiction." Gwen responded to this letter by saying that Margaret had gotten her point exactly. It delighted her that someone, out there in the silence, was listening and had understood.

19
THE TROJAN HORSE

In the summer of 1971, Gwendolyn and Nikos decided to marry. For her, it was not an easy decision. She wrote to Samar Attar in June to congratulate her on her own recent marriage, glad there was someone else in the world with the courage to have done what she was about to do. She worried about the loss of personal freedom that marriage entailed: "It's so difficult to understand the self, and to come to terms with conflicting desires in life. I used to think that personal freedom was important until I realized that freedom is the most frightening thing of all, and perhaps we are only truly free within the confines of a pattern or system.... I still don't know the truth of anything, and the only thing to do is go ahead and jump, and trust the future. Life is so damnably short, there is no time to do half of what one wants."[1] She had made such a disastrous first marriage, it would take courage to try the institution again.

Gwendolyn and Nikos decided to go to Greece for the wedding, which was to be in Athens on October 3rd. As soon as they arrived in Greece, Gwen was consumed by its light, its architecture, its people and their history. As any poet would, she kept a journal of her days, which would eventually become the travelogue *Mermaids and Ikons*.

She records in her journal that they landed on August 10th, and plunged immediately into modern Greece. They spent fifteen days in Athens among Nikos's family and relatives, as he pursued his contacts in the music business. Gwen found herself playing the part of the bride-to-be, which was both amusing and trying. Nikos remarked to me that he remembered the difficulty she had with his mother's attentions in particular. His mother would prepare eggs in the morning and then want to feed Gwendolyn, actually putting the spoon to her mouth. It angered Gwen, and Nikos, trying to find the middle ground, would say: "You have more imagination than my mother. Please let her love you in her way."[2]

But mostly, Gwen was fascinated by her initiation into domestic life. She must be the only traveller to begin her account of her trip to the Acropolis with a knitting party of women sitting in an Athenian kitchen wielding their weapons of domesticity (she quite inadequately), while the Acropolis and its temples hovered in the high wind just beyond the windows. "What is history when you live *in* it, and are not time's tourist?" she asks in her travelogue.[3] These women, "knitting past and future into the gaudy and complex patterns of the living moment," were not to be condescended to—their domestic rituals, their visitors bearing gifts of flowers, their whoops of admiration: *apithano* (wonderful). Gwendolyn loved what she felt was their fervent or even ferocious involvement in the present moment. It was there in their language, with its impossible declensions and accompanying gesticulations, a language so suited to haggling and nagging. The temperament of these women fascinated her, their sheer effort to create occasions for excitement and their passionate and possessive devotion to family, layered as it was over a recent past that had seen brutal war, Fascist occupation, mass starvation, and a current military dictatorship.

She and Nikos spent days in the Acropolis, the Agora, and the many small Byzantine churches. She was intrigued in particular by the excavations at the ancient necropolis, the Keramikos. In her journal, she carefully recorded and translated an inscription she found on the sarcophagus of a grandmother and child: "When I lived we beheld the light, now I hold her dead, being dead myself."[4] She spent hours in the markets buying trinkets, thrilled to discover her talent for bargaining; drinking the vendor's wine, pretending to be Greek Canadian, she could get the price down by half. "She was so pleased at herself. It was as if she'd bought the world," Nikos explained. But it was their trip to Paros and its sister island of Antiparos, where Nikos was born, that was, for Gwen, the essence of Greece.

They landed in the port town of Parikia, on Paros, where all the ferries docked. "Paros all gold and white, Paros the white dove," as Lawrence Durrell called it in his Greek travelogue; every writer fell in love with Paros.[5] Durrell described approaching the island, the sea like a prism of colours shifting from nacre to saffron, lilac to rose, with flying fish and dolphins swirling across the bow of his boat. Paros was also the favourite island of the Greek poet George Seferis, the loveliest, he said, of all the Cyclades. The organization of its streets and squares "aspired to the condition of music."[6]

But for Gwen, the island of Antiparos was even more resonant. She and Nikos took the motorboat across the green translucent sea to the small port of Antiparos, jammed with fishing boats, the saffron nets of the fishermen laid out on the docks to dry.

> The island is shy and exuberant, savage and fair, bold yet self-effacing. It is a woman in heat, a man in despair, a blonde horse at sunset, a riot of fog trees, a flaking white salt bed, an arid garden of thyme and oregano, a hundred clotheslines full of octopi hung up to dry, a warm night of fireflies and tiny shrimps with burning eyes.... Suddenly you know you have been here forever.[7]

Nikos conjures their days for me. They stayed on the main street of the village in the one-room house where he was born, with its stone floor and white stucco walls, still without electricity and running water.

The village was now home to old women and children, the men having left for jobs in the city.

Gwen met the villagers and recorded their stories: the old woman who forgot her from day to day so that each day she had to introduce herself as if for the first time and who warned her that, while it is good to swim—the sea heals all wounds—she must never swim with jewellery—the sea steals your gold. Nikos introduced her to the doctor, the mayor, and the chief of police, for whom they proposed to invent Sherlock Holmes mysteries to relieve his boredom. The island had its characters: Christos, who, terrified of banks, had kept his money in the wall of his house, only to find it eaten by mice. Her favourite villager was a man called Agamemnon, the forty-year-old shoemaker and village fool.[8] He had the mind of a ten-year-old, and had lost a leg, but was so dynamic and exuberant that Gwen loved him. He was the butt of everyone's jokes because he was absolutely credulous. If he was told a beautiful woman from Tripoli was coming to marry him, he could be found waiting on the dock for days. He expected Nikos and Gwen to find him a *gorgona* (mermaid) when they went fishing. When they would turn up each day empty handed he would laugh, "Promises, promises," and hobble away. She loved his view of the world. When he was warned people were making a fool of him, he only smiled and said men were not that cruel; they only tried to have fun.

She was delighted by the island's churches, each with its votive saint and icons, amused when she found detergent and dust cloth tucked in behind an icon of the Virgin Mary. In such churches the Holy Altar is always separated by an *ikonostasi*, or wooden partition, making it out of bounds to women. Once when alone, she decided to violate that male sanctuary. Behind the partition was a small altar covered in white linen, and, to her astonishment, there was nothing there except a flat wooden carving of a crucifix. So crudely was it done that she turned it over to discover that it was made from a piece of wood from a Coca-Cola crate. Leaving the sanctuary, she managed to hit her head on the votive lamp hanging from the ceiling, and the burning oil trickled into her hair. God was not displeased at her invasion of the Holy of Holies, she reported; rather, she had been anointed.

Nikos remembered taking her to visit the old blind priest, Papa Stephanos, over eighty, who lived with his thirty-one-year-old daughter in the Castro, the circular core of the village dating back to the thirteenth century. They would join him at night to drink ouzo and talk of the village: of how, for instance, Agamemnon's mother had once threatened to commit suicide over a rejecting lover, but when she approached the sea and stooped to take off her shoes and socks, everyone had laughed—"You want to die, but you don't want to ruin your shoes." The crisis was immediately diffused and she returned with the villagers, convinced that life was good after all.

Nikos explained that Papa Stephanos had taught him Byzantine music and saved his family during the war when the Fascists occupied the island and the children had had to steal potato peelings from the garbage cans behind the houses occupied by the German soldiers. He remembered how Papa Stephanos would bring the children pieces of bread from the communion wafers and feed them what crumbs he could, as if they were birds. Now he and Gwen would sing him *rebetiko* (these he describes as a popular form of music with vulgar lyrics about someone in jail who couldn't sleep) like lullabies to put him to sleep at night. Most would have thought it a form of disrespect, but the old priest loved them.

One day they attended the funeral of a villager and Gwen was moved by the self-conscious grief of the three teenaged daughters who paraded in black mourning through the village, as the women followed, wailing and ululating in screeching cadences. She thought of her own childhood training "to hide ... emotions, to keep a stiff upper lip, even if it means a lifetime of repressions and neurosis," and envied them their dramatic grief. "You let it all hang out—birth, death, everything. If necessary, you overplay emotions; you do not understate, you do not conceal. It is the only way," she wrote in her travelogue.[9]

Nikos, island-born, was amphibious, and on this trip he taught Gwen to snorkel and to use a spear to fish. The corals around the island are justifiably famous, the underwater visibility seemingly limitless. They spent days hunting shrimp for bait, catching octopi and frying their catch on the beach. Once Nikos remembered they saw a lone white horse playing in the surf. Gwen made a poster of the photo Nikos took—she loved the colours and the serenity of the scene—and then wrote the poem "The White Horse."

The White Horse

This is the first horse to come into the world;
It heaved itself out of the sea to stand now
In a field of dizzy sunlight,
Its eyes huge with joy and wisdom,
Its head turned towards you, wondering
                why you are wondering

And how it comes about that you are here, where
Shrapnel from wars whose causes are forgotten
Has invaded the soft legs and bellies of children
And phosphorus bombs have made burnt ivory
                of the limbs of lovers
In Ireland and Lebanon and all the broken countries
Of the universe where this horse has never been.

You reach out your hand to touch it, and
This is the first time you have ever seen
                your hand, as it is also
The first time you have smelled the blue fire
Within a stone, or tasted blue air, or
Heard what the sea says when it talks in its sleep.

But hasn't the brilliant end come, you wonder,
And isn't the world still burning?

> Go and tell this: It is morning,
> And this horse with a mane the colour of seafoam
> Is the first horse that the world has ever seen,
> The white horse which stands now watching you
> Across this field of endless sunlight.[10]

Of the photos Nikos showed me of their trip, one in particular holds my attention. It is a long-distance shot of Gwen standing at the end of a beach against the rockface. She has removed the upper part of her bathing suit and has the body of a boy. On her head she wears her towel tied into an Arab *koffia*. Nikos explained that she told him she was "Lawrence of Antiparos"—already, I think, T.E. Lawrence, already in possession of what would be her greatest myth in the poems she would write in his name ten years later.

Antiparos was hard to leave, since Gwen had completely absorbed the island imaginatively. In the boat as the island receded, she wrote in her journal: "It is as though we are not leaving it at all—it is leaving us." For Nikos it was as if Gwen had given him back his island; seeing it through her eyes, it had never been so resonant with history.

Back in Athens, on the 22nd of September they attended the funeral of the Greek poet George Seferis. The funeral was a national event; the entire city seemed in mourning. The body of the poet had lain for a day surrounded by flowers in a small local church, and Gwen and Nikos followed the procession to view the coffin, everyone in a haze of tears. Later they climbed the hill to the Acropolis, remembering Seferis's lines: "A little further, let us rise a little higher." His death was a shock. Gwen had been hoping to meet Seferis. She was also envious of the pomp of his funeral: this was how Greece treated its poets.

Now Gwen found herself bogged down in wedding preparations. Theirs was to be a traditional ceremony and all the relatives had been invited. Soon she was longing to have a moment, an hour, to herself and was angered that she should have to apologize for this feeling. She hated the Greek Orthodox religion, thinking of it as a "horrendous system."

Asking the priest why they would not be permitted to have two women as witnesses at the wedding, she was told that "the Bishop does not believe in the word of women."[11]

They were married on the 3rd of October in a Greek Orthodox ceremony at the Holy Church of St. Thomas of Kypseli. On the marriage certificate, Nikos is listed as a musician, "in first wedlock"; she as a writer, "in first wedlock" as well. Gwen must have thought Milton was none of their business and would have bristled at the forensic metaphor—she wasn't about to be locked in.

But it was a wonderful day. Gwen wrote in her journal: "A beautiful wedding—ourselves thoroughly enjoying our 'prototype' appearance—surprised to find the ceremony which we both looked forward to with trepidation was actually most tender and real." She had a flash vision of the man she was about to marry and suddenly realized "how very elegant in spirit and body he is." She was dressed in a traditional white wedding gown with veil, and, on their heads, both she and Nikos wore wreaths of gardenias connected by a long silk ribbon meant to symbolize the delicate but irrevocable bond between them. Papa Stephanos, who was to marry them, was late; the younger priests were still trying to put his robes on him as he came running down the isle. The wedding guests crushed in behind, singing the wedding chants into which they wove Gwen's and Nikos's names, and Papa Stephanos led them in a strange blind dance around the altar. Gwen loved the beautiful chaos of it all.

As a kind of honeymoon, they set out to visit the historical ruins in the Peloponnese—Corinth, Sparta, Olympia, Mycenae, Mystras, about which Gwen would write. It would not have been easy to write yet one more travelogue on Greece, but she was not a conventional tourist: "Everything demands attention; there is nothing subtle about Greece.... I wanted everything; I wanted to be enormous and overwhelming, yawning and expansive like the light."[12]

For Gwen the past was not the past. It was immediate and accessible. On the plains of Sparta, she had an eerie experience of *déjà vu*—that moment when a foreign place seems utterly familiar, as if one has been there before. She hadn't expected this on the narrow Arcadian plain with its sheep and goats and red earth. In the freezing rain, they approached Mystras, "the phantom city, dark with tragic history," "absolute panic of beauty as I entered the gates." Mystras, skeletal, abandoned, wound up the mountain in a steep maze. It seemed to her "some incredible thing, beast or plant, all in fragments and clinging to the mountainside the way a nightmare clings to the mind of a sleeper. It was ghastly green with rain, tragic with history, unspeakably Byzantine."[13]

As she and Nikos approached a small nondescript church with rain beating on the courtyard stones, she had an "absolutely stunning" experience: a sudden visible image of King Constantine, the Byzantine emperor who had come to Mystras to be crowned as his empire died around him, stood at a slight distance. She wrote in her journal that he looked like a playing-card figure entering the chapel to pray for the protection of Mystras, followed by his retinue of guards in their soaked velvet clothes.[14] In her vision he was crowned by gilded priests. Accident, or miracle? she asked herself. She took it in stride, as she did all telepathic or extra-sensory experience, even amused by her vision of the "playing card king," though she was intrigued to learn later that they had stumbled without knowing it onto the small nondescript church Constantine had selected for his coronation. On the second day of her visit, she saw the "playing card king" again.

Mystras overwhelmed her:

> The chill in our bones was the chill of history, the endless sieges of Mystras, assassinations, slaughters. I began to see children's eyes staring out from vaulted doorways, and black-robed women clutching icons of the Virgin to their breasts, praying for the relief of the city. I imagined the aristocracy up on the higher safe slopes, perhaps under the protection of the palace or castle, while the poor got butchered in their flimsy homes or in the streets by invading armies. I kept seeing the rain of war falling,

falling. History like a great mud-slide; human beings, snails, donkeys, plants all clutching the mountainside for dear life.[15]

But this was the dark, shadow side of Greece. There was also Olympia, a world of pure sunlight, golden and seductive, with its temple of Zeus. She could not get over finally seeing the famous "Hermes of Praxiteles," in the flesh as it were, a sculpture so perfect that she could almost see the muscles, sinews, and veins just under the skin. She loved the back of Hermes' knees: "They were the most interesting and sexy back-of-the-knees imaginable." She wanted a word for them and called them "knoves." The statue made her think of the beauty that seems to exist in "another time/ space dimension" entirely in its own terms, a beauty so perfect one is forced "to re-think reality, or to weep, or to die."

Gwen and Nikos returned from Greece on the 28th of October. She wrote to Samar Attar that Greece was fantastic, apart from the noise and confusion of Athens, and that the wedding had been very moving. She then exacted a promise from Attar not to tell anyone in the literary world that she was married. Apart from her family and a few close friends, no one was to know: "It's difficult to keep a balance between my public self as a writer and my home life. I think you will understand."[16] (I wonder if, in particular, she wanted to keep the secret from Milton.) To try to capture some sense of how evocative the trip had been, she began her travelogue *Mermaids and Ikons*, but would only complete it after a second journey to Greece in 1976.

On her return, her Akhenaton novel, *King of Egypt, King of Dreams*, finally came out, and, as she always did, she madly sent out copies to all her friends. The reviews were good. Christopher Xerxes Ringrose wrote in *Books in Review* of the novel's "starkly brilliant opening pages." "By the end of the novel we come to register it as genuinely tragic that this glorious vision of God should be enveloped in night."[17] But Gwen had warned Margaret Atwood in a letter that she would be back from Greece "just in time to watch KING OF EGYPT ETC plummet into oblivion, which I have no doubt it will immediately do."[18] After the initial small flurry of reviews, that's exactly what happened, though two decades later, the novelist Timothy Findley would say: "It's the kind of book where you stay with every word. It's really like entering a dream. Beautifully sad. Every bit of that book is marvellous."[19]

The Armies of the Moon and the collection of stories, *Noman*, came out in the spring (the former won the A.J.M. Smith Award for Poetry) and a reading was arranged in the Town Hall at the St. Lawrence Centre. The journalist covering it for *The Toronto Star* was overwhelmed at the enormous crowd who showed up: "Gwendolyn MacEwen is clothed in a flowing robe of wine-dark velvet trimmed with gold braid and she leans on the grand piano.... Just think, a small dark woman can fill Town Hall, St. Lawrence Centre by simply standing there and reciting her poems ... Perhaps it's a return to soul and simplicity.... But for a woman alone to do this and arouse a crowd to demand curtain calls at the end is something else."[20] Michael Ondaatje remembers being in the audience, listening to Gwen "reciting from *Armies of the Moon* by heart. It was the first time I had a sense of the poet as a public person," he recalls. "She was giving herself to the public. It was the voice of the bard. She was the last of the bardic poets, the poet who took all risks for poetry."[21] In 1972, Gwen was one of the writers who was changing the cultural map.

After three years together, Gwen and Nikos were still trying that often impossible task of fitting two lives together. The problems were ordinary. Nikos, to make any money, had to work at night, often till 4 a.m. Gwen had always used the days to create, but now she tried to fit herself to Nikos's schedule. She began to complain in letters to Margaret Atwood that, sleeping all day, the world had shut down by the time she was ready to use it. When she didn't go to the club, she spent the night alone and the temptation was to drink. She could write to Margaret that she'd made a batch of rum eggnog and when no one came by, ended up drinking it alone, crawling into bed "completely cut."[22] At such times, there were not many distractions from the dark spaces in her own imagination.

And her problems with jealousy continued. One evening, not long after their return from Greece, she and Nikos invited Elsie and Carol's family to Orestes, a restaurant on the Danforth where Nikos was working. As usual, after his song a young woman sent a drink to the stage. He nodded his thanks. As he turned back to his own table, Gwen stood up. Without saying a word, she took the edge of the tablecloth and yanked. With the dishes flying in all directions, she marched out. Nikos ran after her, and they shouted at each other all the way down the stairs and into the streets. So outrageous was their mutual screaming that a policeman stopped to intervene. Gwen assured him everything was fine and then the two, much calmer, returned to their Browning Avenue apartment. The night ended in gentleness, but Nikos had been unnerved at his own explosion.

In 1972, Carol remembered many long, incoherent phone calls from Gwen late at night, when she had obviously been drinking, in a despair of jealousy. Carol tried to reassure her—Nikos wasn't like that—but it rarely worked.

A solution seemed to present itself. Nikos wanted to get out of the exhausting nightclub business and an obvious idea seemed to be to open their own coffee-house. Nikos explained to me that they thought it might also solve their financial problems. In late spring they began to hunt for a place on the Danforth. The Victory Fruit Market at 179 Danforth Avenue had just closed down. In a sketch she would eventually write about setting up the club, Gwen remembered peering in through the dusty window at a man packing Del Monte peas in the dim recesses, wondering if it would work.[23] After much anxiety and many doubts—neither she nor Nikos had owned a business before—a lease was signed and the place was theirs. They would call it The Trojan Horse—were they not bringing a new phalanx of music to transform the Danforth, assaulting Toronto's gates? On the Danforth, clubs were still playing the music of the forties and fifties, but the cultural revolution in Greece, inspired by the composer Mikis Theodorakis in protest against the ruling military junta, had not yet made many inroads.

The Trojan Horse would be a *boîte* on the French model, a place you could go, as Gwen wrote, "to forget what nightclubs did to you," where you could talk to friends and "solve the problems of the universe." The renovations began. There were endless permits to be gotten from city hall, and fire and plumbing regulations to conform to. Gwen and Nikos rolled up their sleeves, stripping ancient wallpaper and plastering a thousand holes with Polyfilla. They had to install a kitchen and two washrooms in the basement, but thankfully, their friend Lefteris took over the plumbing and Gyprocking. Gwen loved Sundays best, when the guys in the basement sang Byzantine hymns to the accompaniment of electric saws, and lunch break was squatting amidst the sawdust with olives and feta cheese. She had the hardware detail—and loved the language of the trade: in her navy-blue jumpsuit caked with Gyprock dust, marching into the local hardware to ask for number eight four-inch butterfly screws with rawl plugs—the old walls were so porous nothing else would hold. She spent three days on her back varnishing the low cedar tables they had built, whistling and chuckling to herself until the urethane overcame her and she had to rush, gasping, into the alleyway.

For months, Nikos remembered, they had gone over the decor in their minds, down to the colour of the ashtrays. The colours were to be those of pre-classical Greece: three colours and three colours only—terracotta, black, and ochre, the colours of the early Greek amphoras. There would be no travel posters of the Acropolis. Gwen invited her old friend Mac Reynolds to paint the large wall panels with Greek images. She wrote of him wedging himself into a corner of the chaos and commenting on the strange foreshortening of limbs in archaic Greek art and puzzling over the gender of the first Trojan horse.

Gwen hired Carol's sons, Donnie and David, to help out with the renovations. They were delighted, not only to be paid but because of the trust her invitation demonstrated. Downstairs, Donnie painted a cartoon of a huge wooden elephant before the walls of Troy, soldiers pouring from its belly, as those on the ramparts looked on: "Not to worry. They said it would be a horse."

After six weeks of work, The Trojan Horse opened in early September, flanked by the Titania Theatre on one side, the Tea Room on the other, with Medusa Hair Stylists across the street. It seemed half the Greek population of the Danforth poured in to see what was up that night. Gwen also invited all her Canadian friends. The young Greg Gatenby loyally showed up, with the novelist M.T. Kelly. Gatenby had been told to come at nine, and like a good Canadian he arrived on time. He remembered the café as exotic—low cedar tables, corduroy cushions on the floor, Greek coffee, but the show didn't start until twelve, by which time he was tired and didn't hang around long.[24] Gwen wanted The Horse to be a place where Canadians and Greeks would meet. And people did begin to come: Marian Engel, Margaret Atwood, Tom Marshall, Howard Engel, even Bob Mallory came several times. Nikos remembered Barry Callaghan skulking in a corner—he had just published his interview with Golda Meir and had been threatened with severe violence for his report about being in the Black September war. Gwen was amused when, one night, the famous stripper Xaviera Hollander mistook her for the hat-check girl and, as she obligingly handed over her mink, pressed a quarter into Gwen's hand. Douglas Fetherling described The Horse as full of music, food, and old friends, "a kind of salon and she was in her element—the perfect backdrop to the antiquarian side of her personality."[25]

The Horse was open seven nights a week from 9:00 p.m. to 3:00 a.m. Nikos sang, accompanied by a second guitar and a pianist called Sylvia Mitler. It was never a restaurant, but they served a hefty seafood plate called "The Trojan War," taramasalata, yogurt, and pastries. Drinks were "Bloody Helens"— Bloody Marys without the vodka; they had no liquor licence—and Greek coffee. Ironically Gwen, who hated cooking, ended up in the kitchen, and they had so little help that, after playing, Nikos would rush in to help her crack the crab's legs. She invited her mother to help with the washing up; Elsie proudly reported to her doctors that she was assisting her daughter in opening her new restaurant.

There were many good times. Once Gwen took it into her head that, living in Canada, the Greeks must learn to skate. She had bought herself and Nikos skates and with the other musicians, the waiter, and their wives, a small troupe set out from The Horse for Withrow Park, just south of Danforth Avenue. She herself hadn't been on skates in years and fell flat on her face, but everyone was determined to learn, some having only one skate and a boot and dangling their pom-pommed toques for balance. They stuck to it for hours in the Canadian cold.

But after ten months, Gwen and Nikos were disheartened. Selling only coffee, they were losing money. People came and stayed for hours nursing a single coffee. The work was too much and Gwen was giving all her time to the business. Her health was deteriorating: the smoke-filled atmosphere exacerbated her asthma and she was drinking from a plastic flask of alcohol she kept hidden in her purse. They had put $12,000 into buying and renovating The Horse; when they sold the business at the beginning of July, Nikos reported they only got $5,000 for it, which didn't even cover their debts. The contract, done precipitously, included all the club's contents. When the new owners, who had been friends, took over, Gwen was furious to discover Nikos wasn't even allowed to retrieve the two copper wall-hangings that had been a gift from his brother. She told one of the owners that if he didn't at least return the guest book that contained comments of visitors to the club, she would punch him. He ripped the book in half, keeping the blank pages for future use, while Gwen cursed him roundly in Greek.

Nikos continued to play music at The Trojan Horse, though their venture into entrepreneurship was over. But as usual, Gwen had left the city a major legacy. Greek musicians began to drop by. Mikis Theodorakis, playing downtown at Massey Hall, came one night and sat there smiling: "I like this." Sovopoulos and Zenakis, while in concert in Toronto, came too. The future president of Greece, Papandreou visited. The Horse was slowly becoming a centre of the new Greek culture. Eventually the club would provide a refuge for exiles from Pinochet's dictatorship when Latin American musicians arrived in the city and joined the Greek musicians at The Horse to form the group called *Compañeros*. Those who would make an impact on Canadian immigration law like Barbara Jackman or Lorne Waldman, or in medicine like

Phil Berger, spent much of their youth at The Trojan Horse as it continued its precarious existence well into the 1980s.

Money was always a problem for Gwen and Nikos. And Nikos had begun to feel that Gwen needed to get out of Canada, that the long nights at The Horse, and some of the people she met there, sapped her strength. He wanted them to collaborate on a project that would take them to Greece. Gwen proposed that they do a TV documentary on Greece. Who knew it better than they? She was intrigued by the work of a Dr. Spiros Marinatos, a professor at the University of Athens who was pursuing a theory that the ancient Minoan civilization on the island of Thera was the Atlantis alluded to by Plato, and had been destroyed by a cataclysmic volcanic eruption. They decided to propose a documentary on the Cyclades Islands that would include Marinatos's theory of Atlantis. Gwen wrote to Robert Weaver, and to George Jonas, producer of TV drama at the CBC. Jonas was enthusiastic but preoccupied with another project and sent them on to another producer. In her outline, which included a brief draft and hints at a cheap budget—they could hire the cameramen in Greece—she explained that they wanted a "gutsy" look at Byzantine Greece, with "such phantom cities as Mystras and weird monastic areas such as Meteora" as the focus. Archaic Greece (Minoan-Mycenean) and post-classical Greece (Byzantine Greece) had been overlooked while classical Greece had been "done to death."[26] The proposal was greeted enthusiastically and died. The idea of the artist, like Peter Ustinov or Glenn Gould, documenting a culture had not yet come. Gwen, as usual, was ahead of her time.

Now Nikos began to realize that Gwen's drinking had developed into a very serious problem. In the space of a few brief years, she had become a closet alcoholic, though to outsiders, she remained the same Gwen. Since 1973, she had had a contract giving a summer course in Toronto in the Annual Summer Writers' Workshop, run by Gerald Lampert. His wife, Arlene Lampert, was then executive director of the League of Canadian Poets: "No one realized Gwen was drinking. At parties she refused alcohol and would take only soft drinks. She always gave her classes and was loved by her students, but when it came to the public readings in which she was scheduled to participate, she was often unreliable. She just wouldn't show up."[27] Lampert was very taken with Gwen. She remembered particularly one night when Gwen had stayed after the others left, and they had spent a hilarious time composing limericks based on Milton's *Paradise Lost*: "There once was a fellow called Adam ..." But her unreliability was puzzling. No one knew of the plastic flask of vodka in her purse.

Aware of the black despair that overtook Gwen when she was drinking, Nikos grew increasingly concerned. He thought that if only their financial problems were solved, things would improve. He proposed that they approach the poet Yannis Ritsos, who, nominated for the Nobel Prize three times, had an international reputation, and offer to translate some of his poems into English. Gwen wrote Ritsos in her elegant Greek, sending him a few of their early translations. He was very enthusiastic in his replies, but it would take several years to sort out their role with his publishers. Eventually they would translate many of his poems, including the remarkable sequence "Helen," published by Barry Callaghan in *Exile* magazine and Exile Editions,[28] as well as in the collection of Ritsos's poetry, *Fifty Years of Yannis Ritsos*. It turned out, of course, that there was little financial reward in such work, but Gwen was thrilled when she could write to Samar Attar in 1975 that, while she was forgetting her Arabic (would she one day forget English?), the Greek poet Yannis Ritsos "has acknowledged us as his foremost translators in English."[29]

Looking back on 1974, Nikos explained to me: "It was a hard time, but we still had hopes. We had problems, of course, but there was still a balance." There was, at least, their mutually shared fantasy that one day they would somehow manage to live part-time in Greece.

20
DESOLATE LANDSCAPE

Money does not create happiness, but its absence can destroy freedom. Musicians playing seven nights a week at The Trojan Horse could expect eighty dollars at the end of it. It is intriguing that we can speak of the hazardous professions—a fireman, a policeman place themselves at risk by the nature of their work. We do not speak of art as a hazardous profession. In fact, we rarely speak of it as a profession at all because we have accumulated so many myths about it. The romantic notion of the artist as a solitary genius born with his or her eccentric talent is a brutal myth because it leaves artists essentially alone, consigned to their attic-space, confronting a society that accepts no responsibility for art. Curiously, the myth leaves the art valueless, with little place for art in the culture. It takes extraordinary luck and stamina for the artist to survive in modern culture. Art is not a safe profession.

In the long incarnation of The Trojan Horse, there were several musicians who died prematurely, from suicide or alcohol. Nikos knew the pressures of surviving as a musician on the Danforth, the cruel stamina it took. There were jobs, but he had been finding it increasingly hard to get ones that paid decently, or where the audience was responsive to the kind of music he played. And Gwen herself seemed to be losing heart. Nikos began to feel that the despair that surfaced when she was drinking would suffocate him. He too felt infected by her blackness. His own anger that night in 1972 shortly after their marriage, when she had ripped the tablecloth from the table, sending the dishes crashing, had frightened him, because there had been a part of him that admired the aggression of her act. He began to fear that he might be precipitated into that anger again. In the spring of 1975, he was offered a job playing at a club in Montreal, and, because it paid decently, he decided to take it. The plan was that he would commute to Toronto on his days off.

Gwen was devastated. She thought that their relationship was disintegrating and that she had failed again. She had written in "Memoirs of a Mad Cook": "All my friends are dying of hunger/there is some basic dish I cannot offer/And you my love are as lean/as the splendid wolf I must keep always/at my door." The syntax was deliberate. She had to *keep* the wolf there, though she couldn't fathom why. In those months when Nikos was in Montreal and she was essentially alone, her mood must have been desperate. Her early dream had been that she would live as an artist, she would write those novels that would make her lots of money and enable her to write the poetry. She would find the love she needed in the world. It must have felt like falling into her own nightmare. Few had worked as hard as she. She had put every ounce of her being into the work: not to be poor, not to be alcoholic, not to be mad, and now she watched those things rushing up at her and she seemed unable to do anything to stop it. Nikos was leaving her.

With the financial strain of trying to survive alone, Gwen moved to a basement apartment on Chester Hill Road, north of Danforth Avenue. Nikos visited once or twice a month. By September she was staying with her poet friend Stephanie Nynych because she had stopped being able to take care of herself, something she was not particularly good at anyway. Her drinking had reached a half-bottle of vodka a day and she had developed an excruciatingly painful kidney infection, as well as hyperthyroidism. On the afternoon of the twenty-first she had a dream of assassins invading the house to kill her, but it seemed so real she panicked. Deeply distressed at her condition, Nynych talked things over with Gwen's friends, including a psychiatric nurse called Maureen Wright, and together they persuaded her that she should go to the Clark Institute, which had an addiction research programme.

After an examination, however, the Clark determined she was well enough to return home. Seemingly calmer, she slept through the night, but the next morning, after preparing her a bath, Nynych found her kneeling beside the tub grasping at air. Gwen said she was trying to catch the bloodied babies as they fell. Nynych called a psychiatrist she knew, Dr. Frank Sommers, who advised her to return to Emergency at the Clark. Gwen could be admitted on his authority as a voluntary patient.

I turn again to hospital charts that uncannily mirror Elsie's charts, as if Elsie's shadow had finally occupied Gwen. Gwen was diagnosed as a hysterical personality. The sheets of diagnosis accumulate:

> *Mental Status Examination*: 34 yrs old woman looking about 45 yrs old. Fairly well groomed. Facial expression was anxious and twitching. She had some stammering. She walked slowly and her gait was a little unsteady but no significant thought disorder. She denied any hallucinations or delusions. The sensorium was clear except for a poor concentration. Abstraction functioned quite well. Hysterical personality. Meds.: valium.[1]

The hospital found her guarded but co-operative. I read the edited history of her life that she offered to doctors:

> Personal History: The patient was born in Toronto, the second child of a family of two siblings.... early life unremarkable.... began school at the usual age and finished without any academic difficulty at the age of 17....

describes her early life in terms almost solely related to her school and her homework.... on graduating from high school, she felt she did not want to go to university, and decided to pursue a career as a writer. At the age of 19, one year following her father's death, she married a man who was in his middle thirties ... [whom] she had met at a poetry reading session.... marriage lasted only a few months: the patient giving as a reason for the break up the fact that they both realized the impossibility of a continued relationship in a situation where there was such a discrepancy with respect to age. Her interests at this time became totally centred around her writing, and she became quite well-known in the literary circle in this country....

The patient met her husband approximately six years ago and they subsequently married. He is a Greek folk singer and up until about one year ago, found steady employment in this city. She describes her relationship in relatively rosy terms, but one suspects, as has been confirmed by some of the patient's friends, that there has been some marital discord, especially over the last year....

On admission, the patient complained of financial difficulties stemming from the breakup of her relationship with her husband and the subsequent attempted maintenance of her own apartment. There are no children.

There is no family history of any mental or nervous disease. The mother is alive and well, and the patient has one sister older than she, who is married with children of her own.[2]

In the sanitized history she was offering, there are only a few statements that are completely direct. Petrified that she and Nikos were separating, she had been binge-drinking. The dissolution of The Trojan Horse had left her and Nikos in debt. In fact the sum was only five hundred dollars, but money is a metaphor. Gwen, with her history, was appalled to be indebted to anyone and to her at the moment that was an insurmountable sum. Furthermore, the failure of The Horse was a symbol of the failure of her marriage.

The doctors did learn her true history from Stephanie Nynych, who described this anonymous woman to them as a shy, quiet, kind, intelligent person. She told them what she knew: that Gwen's father had been an alcoholic, and that her mother had been hospitalized "at least once" for her emotional problems.[3] Gwen was brilliant: she had received the Governor General's Award at age twenty-seven, and taught herself Arabic and Greek. "Gwen is said to be the best Canadian female poetess," the social worker records.

Gwen stayed at the Clarke for one week. It must have been terrible to find herself there. The nurses reported that she did not make use of the hospital's "social activities," but only watched from the periphery. She knew those "activities" from her mother's world. As soon as he was aware of the crisis, Nikos returned immediately from Montreal and told her he would move back to Toronto and somehow find work. On the 29th, when antibiotics had cured her kidney infection, Gwen checked herself out of the hospital against the doctors' advice. In her chart I note the laconic remark: "Not a suicide risk." Gwen was not psychotic like her mother.

Her recovery was remarkable. Nynych believed this was because Nikos had returned to her. Abandoning the appalling basement apartment in the east end, they moved to 149 St. George Street. But Gwen had refused to undergo therapy with Dr. Sommers, so that the underlying causes of her despair had not been probed, and that was dangerous. Yet she bounced back, picking up her work immediately and finishing a new collection called *The Fire-Eaters*. She had long planned to turn her notes on her trip to Greece into a book, and applied for a Canada Council grant. When she was awarded three thousand dollars, she and Nikos decided that the best plan was to return to Antiparos, where she had been so happy. Both of them knew it would be an attempt to put their marriage back together.

Nikos left for Greece in July while she waited behind for the money to arrive. She wrote to Samar Attar: "My husband Nikos is at the moment somewhere in the middle of the Aegean Sea, where he waits for me to join him ... which I will do when I get some last minute bits of work cleared up, and also some money. Damn money!"[4] Gwen followed in mid-August. Nikos remembered her arriving at the Athens airport in her wide-brimmed hat and polka-dot dress, completely drunk. She looked so vulnerable. He knew she had had to drink to get through the flight.

For Gwen, the highlight of their two-month stay was her encounter with Yannis Ritsos. In her travelogue *Mermaids and Ikons*, she describes meeting the sixty-seven-year-old poet, "the greatest living European poet," in his tiny Athens apartment, its floors, tables, shelves, and mantelpieces covered with the small stones he was famous for painting with images. "My work keeps me alive," she quotes him as saying. "In creating, I am affirming my place in the universe, I am making a statement against death."[5] He was working on his long poem about Pablo Neruda, and spoke of his own "political detention" in prison on the island of Leros under the military junta. She and Nikos had brought him two stones from Antiparos, which, with sepia-coloured India ink, he converted into Poseidon and a pair of lovers. They talked of politics, of music and art, of cats, and left at 4 a.m. The next day Gwen wrote a poem for Ritsos:

Stones and Angels

for Yannis Ritsos

I tried to find a stone for you to paint on, Yanni,
    and I found that
Stones are lost sheep in golden dust
Stones are the blind eyes of lost gods
Stones are stars that failed and fell here
Stones are the faces of watches without hands,

Stones are the masters of time.

And we would become the masters of time, Yanni,
> in the great loneliness which is God,
In the mad, dynamic silence poems and ikons adore.

We would paint the universe the colours of our minds
> and flirt with death, but
Whether we dance or faint or kneel we fall
On stones.

Stones are old money with which we rent the world,
> forgetting that the landscape borrows us
For its own time and its own reason.

The way is open, it is paved with stones;
They are the fallen eyes of angels.

Antiparos, Greece, 1976.[6]

Gwen and Nikos's effort to put their marriage back together did not work. They simply could not live together. How does one explain this, since the love was there? Does such a question even have an answer? Perhaps the most direct explanation would be that Gwen would not face that she had become an alcoholic. She could not give up drinking, and Nikos could not bear her black despair. All he could tell me when I asked him was that he felt, when her despair surfaced, he too was suffocating in its darkness.[7] She did not know how to let him help her. And I think, she could not afford to let herself be fully known even by Nikos. There were still too many secrets Gwen had to keep, even from herself.

When they returned to Canada, they lived separately, but Nikos was always someone Gwen could count on. When things got very tough, he was the first one she turned to.

Her devastation at her loss leaked into her dreams:

> N & I are in museum which is To library. Exhibit of reconstruction of a Greek temple of Apollo, v.[ery] important, etc. First of its kind. Recent excavation. 2 gods as statues. Apollo is large and hermaphroditic. 2nd god is an animal—wolf or large dog. I approach. The quicksilver eyes of the dog Apollo move around & fasten on me. A high keening cosmic music. Feeling is ecstasy. The MC puts me in another stage—: You stay here, you make the god move!" Apollo walks, etc. Dog-god threatens me. Later "Apollo" as an actor ironically asks me *who he is*. I say, I don't know, but I used to.[8]

Gwendolyn had so saturated herself in Robert Graves's *White Goddess* (a book that she called one of the two most important in her life) that her subconscious seems to have lifted this dream directly from his pages, pages that, in her copy of the book, Gwen had underscored several times. Graves describes Apollo not as the Sun God, but as a more primitive oracular hero. "The poetic meaning of the dog," he writes, "is 'Guard of the Secret,' the prime secret on which the sovereignty of the sacred king depends."[9] Curiously, on the same page, Graves relates this with a similar contingent Welsh legend in which a boy Gwern, after being crowned king, is beheaded or burned to death.

How Gwen was reordering these details to fit her own psychic history is impossible to recover. All that is clear to the outsider is that there was still a terrible secret to be kept. And that Gwen knew she had lost Nikos, and she couldn't explain why. She also believed she had lost a magic connection within herself. Nothing she had lost so far could have felt so important.

Gwendolyn wrote to Samar Attar that spring of 1977. Attar herself had obviously been very depressed, seemingly about her isolation as a Syrian in Australia, and the strains it was making on her life. Gwen wrote to console her:

Dear Samar,

How wonderful and unexpected to hear from you again after so long a time, and across so much space! I thank you for being less lazy than myself, in terms of keeping our communication alive; I think of you often, yet my own state of mind is usually so complex (and often bleak), that I hesitate to write to you. Months pass, and a million things happen, and I am at a loss as to where to begin when I finally do get down to writing you. I retain a strong memory of a lady wearing black and gold, visiting my rather abysmal basement apartment in Toronto in 1969. That's eight years ago, and yet I feel that you are one of the few people I can think of as a friend.

Your letter touched me deeply ... especially at a time in my own life when I am experiencing very similar feelings of loss and personal alienation. I know also, Samar, that "the source of all unhappiness or all misery lies within us".... and I know how deceptively easy it is to express and believe the truth of this, while meanwhile, we grapple with the ever present demons of despair, of emptiness.

However, my close yet distant friend—I am full of positive thoughts this evening as I write to you. (No doubt they are all clichés, but then, clichés get to *be* clichés because they are always maddeningly correct). I want to say—Hang ON!—and yet I think to myself, Good God, *I* don't know what Australia's like, although I do remember the bleakness of Halifax ... and I also remember the last couple of winters in Toronto which have been in some ways like nightmares in disguise. They were not black (for black is pure), but grey, which is the colour of limbo. Nikos and I have had several temporary separations, and yet we are still essentially together. He seems to be in search of some elusive corner of his soul, and I am often obliged to give him the gift of my absence, rather than my presence, in order that he may find peace. Love between two conscious, well-meaning people, can be a tremendous test. (Another cliché).

As I develop and progress as a writer, I find that each word, each idea, becomes increasingly painful, demanding a purity and an honesty which I sometimes think is beyond my capacities. Yet the words emerge, take shape, demand even more purity and honesty. I'm finishing a book about Greece right now, and in the summer I will begin to write a new novel based on the ideas of NOMAN, an earlier book of mine.

My intimate friends at the moment are: my magic cat, 'Dingbat', who spends most of her time inventing dreams, and studying an invisible spot on the ceiling— my skinny and frightened squirrels who I try to fatten up with peanuts, and a few wild-eyed pigeons.

When Nikos and I were in Greece in October, we met the great poet Yannis Ritsos in Athens. We have translated some of his work. He too knows about the emptiness of the soul, the tremendous burden of our sheer humanity which we must carry as long as we choose to be conscious beings. When I spoke with him, I knew that he could only reinforce the bitter, yet clean truths which we must live by. His face, though, was a study in the sort of beauty which is sculpted by pain. He moved with a slow grace, a gentle and ironic lyricism. He was at one with himself—neither accepting nor rejecting the human condition ... at the age of 67, he could have been 50—or a thousand! I saw him as a child of the universe (as we all are); I saw him as one of the few human beings we have among us ... because he was *conscious*.

I could ramble on for pages, Samar, about the details

of things I've seen and known since I wrote you last—and probably if we met together, we'd go on talking for days on end, non-stop! What concerns me now is the sense of isolation and despair I found in your letter. I can't say—NO, it's not like that! (because I know it is) but I *can* say this, and I know it is true: you are in no way alone. You pay for the gift of your vision, your sensitivity ... but you are in no way alone. (I say this, knowing full well that I am also talking to myself as I talk to you, knowing that I speak in clichés).

Write soon, even if the next time I hear from you, it's from Alaska or Timbuctoo!
Gwendolyn[10]

Gwen continued to dream of Nikos:

A castle in a desolate landscape—Romania, Yugoslavia, Transalvania. N and I are getting married again. Teresa Stratas is there, plus members of Nikos's family & Carol. In dressing room I lose bridal costume, go on tour of castle to find clothes, and up in sacred room, church, taboo place of ancient oracles, no lights, dust etc., of ancient illusions. Most important is string to move mask of the *white head*—from depths of audience to stage. I explain to N and everybody how illusion works—like an elastic band—and everyone is satisfied—I also say that if we turn the lights out, the luminous head will still glow in the dark. Later, when everyone is gone—I open great locked doors of the castle & sunlight flows in.[11]

Though she longed for it, the remarriage would not take place. To her the white mask of her dream was the Magus, the great magician. Part of her mind saw how she manipulated the mask. Part chose to stay with her magic illusions, where the writing came from. Alone, she could walk out into the sunlight, but the landscape would always be desolate.

In May of 1977, Gwen was contacted by Leon Major, the artistic director of the St. Lawrence Centre, who had run both the complex and the theatre it housed since 1970. He wanted to mount a Greek tragedy and asked her to do a new translation. He remembered Gwen as being extraordinarily humble, insisting that she was a poet and had little knowledge of theatre. He told her not to worry; it was the language that was essential in Greek tragedy. He would make the drama work. He does not remember how they settled on *The Trojan Women*, but he found her a wonderful colleague: "She worked very hard and took no remark flippantly. If I asked for something, she thought long and hard before she made her decision, but once she had agreed, that was it. She also had a great sense of humour though it was often hard to reach it."[12] Her humility about her dramatic gifts was totally unfounded. He discovered she had a natural instinct for the theatre.

As she worked on her translation, Gwen wrote to Major that her focus in the play would be the idea of women trapped in a social/historical bind, unconscious of their own powers. She saw the theme of the play as the idea that women carry war in them as much as men.

> Hecuba's agony is [the] result of this step by step realization, i.e. women are as responsible as men. The play *is* Hecuba's discovery and consequent agony/breakdown. Hecuba must *see through* each woman in turn, beginning with her own daughter.... Are we, at this point in the play, getting curious about Helen? Curious *enough*? Do we have inklings at this point that the play will have something to say about the nature of female sexuality—with respect to power-struggles? (Men turn to war; women become insufferable bitches and liars). Thinking aloud, I write: the *misdirected* forces of both male and

female sexuality.... Is Hecuba the only woman to rise above all this rot?[13]

Major remembers her attending only a few rehearsals to listen to the actors in order to determine if her language was working. He believed she felt she couldn't contribute. In fact Gwen was delighted to be involved. She told an interviewer for *Writer's Quarterly* that she enjoyed writing for the theatre because it was less solitary than other writing: "Most writers will do anything for company, given half a chance. Most writers are dying for someone to interrupt them."[14]

Gwen left the production up to Major. She had confidence in him, and in particular, thought his choice of set would work. He and his set designer, Murray Laufer, had come up with the idea for the set as they drove along Toronto's waterfront where a construction company was in the process of dismantling three huge grain silos. The silos stood with their reinforcing steel rods exposed, large pieces of concrete dangling in the air. This would be the backdrop for *The Trojan Women*. The chorus of women lived in that wall, emerging from it like carrion crows. Centre stage was a huge hole, down which the actors descended. When Gwen had finished the translation—she was brilliant with deadlines, she kept them—her last letter to Major, dated December 30th, read: "Dear Leon, It's all yours. I look forward to hearing from you in due time."[15]

A totally modern adaptation with a jazz score by Phil Nimmons, the play opened at the St. Lawrence Centre on November 20, 1978. Ken Adachi, always the most perceptive critic of Canadian theatre and writing, wrote in *The Toronto Star* that no one was more appropriate than Gwen to "tackle the complexities of Euripides' classic tragedy. Her credentials, both literary and personal, are almost impeccable."[16] Referring to her amazing productivity: ten "well-praised" books, six collections of poetry, two novels, a book of short stories, her Greek memoir, and her translations of Yannis Ritsos, he described her as one of Canada's major poets.

In his review/interview Adachi had asked her what the play was about. "About war, its insanity and ugly aftermath," she had said. The play did have a message: she had explained to Leon Major that it was not Helen's face that had launched the Trojan War. It was "human duplicity, as the Greeks understood it ... Not exactly hubris, but something more closely related to Poe's idea of the 'Imp of Perversity.' Human intelligence at odds with itself."[17] The small wars within the individual "erupt into the Troys, Hiroshimas, and Vietnams." "The real tyranny," she told Adachi, "lies in the bleak lunar landscapes of our mirrors. We're tied up in ourselves in the wrong way, with specific daily pains."[18]

Thinking back, Leon Major remarks: "I wasn't smart enough then to say what I'd say to Gwen now. 'Let's make a project. Let's do a cycle of plays from the Greek.' It would have been wonderful. She would have got stronger and stronger in her understanding of theatre. She was so good at it." It would have been difficult to convince his board of directors, though he believes he could have done it. When he had gone to them with the idea of doing a play by Euripides, translated by Gwendolyn MacEwen, his board had asked him who they were. He had explained that the play was a Greek tragedy, and one board member replied: "How many Greeks in Toronto do you think will come to see the show?" "They were working on that level," he says, still astonished. "The St. Lawrence Centre was a mixed bag." Working on *The Trojan Women* was one of the six truly rewarding experiences of Major's tenure there.

Major suggested a second project to Gwen. Once when he had been talking casually about the experience of his parents as immigrants to Toronto, Gwen had spoken of her knowledge of the Greek community. He realized she had an exact grasp of the syndrome of exile. She was herself in exile, haunted by the absence of a sense of place. She wrote *The Scissors-Grinder*, about the life of immigrants on the Danforth, for Major. He thought it a wonderful play, but when he proposed the script to CBC television it was rejected. In the early eighties, he again turned to Gwen: "Let's do *The Scissors-Grinder* as an opera," but she threw up her hands and said she'd had enough. She wasn't prepared to go through another series of rejections, and the invitation had come too late, at a time when her life was spiralling downward.

21
THE GWENNESS GONE

In 1977, Gwendolyn's search for a publisher for her Greek memoir, *Mermaids and Ikons*, brought with it a lucky accident. It was the occasion for the renewal of her old friendship with Jim Polk, whom Gwen had known in the sixties when he was married to Margaret Atwood. He was from Montana, though his style was that of an Easterner, with an amusingly ironic disposition masking a fierce mind. A trained classical pianist with a Ph.D. in English, he had taught at university, published a book on Canadian animal stories, and was finishing a novel for Houghton-Mifflin. He and Margaret had separated in the early seventies, and he was the editorial director at the House of Anansi, then in its heyday as a pioneering publisher of the best new Canadian writing. He admired Gwen as a poet and was delighted when she decided to send Anansi the manuscript of her Greek memoir. "We thought it a great book," he says, "but it was short, we wanted more."[1] He took on the role of editor, but soon found that trying to edit Gwen was not easy. "Getting a word changed was a whole other thing." She was stubborn; nothing could be changed without a great deal of thought. He discovered she was a perfectionist, uncertain about anything she had written, which, given the authority that was so evident in the writing, came as a surprise.

Eventually he took to visiting her at her apartment at 149 St. George Street. As in that windowless apartment in Montreal in 1967, she had created an exotic space. There was the carved chest in which she kept the favoured books, and her Egyptian and Coptic bronze sculptures. He came to think of it as her "invention of the self." He felt she wanted to become "an artifact or an artifice or something that would remove her from her terrifying childhood."

Soon they began to "step out" as a couple. It was a wonderful time. She knew all the inexpensive restaurants along Bloor Street. They'd often go to the Cretan ones; Gwen would speak to the staff in Greek and they'd be dazzled. But she professed she was through with things Greek after her separation from Nikos—no more exotic, she'd done with the Middle East. Now she was just plain Gwen. Work proceeded on her manuscript, though the end result of Polk's editing was to get her to choose a few more anecdotes and to polish some already well-wrought phrases.

Over that year, the relationship intensified. Polk remembered it had begun like a game of mirrors: they were both born on the same day in September, two years apart. They were both asthmatic. Sometimes it felt as though they were "lost children together. Let's have some fun. Let's laugh a lot. Let's play. I loved it and so did she." She'd kept her sense of humour. He remembered she wrote parodies of exotic Eastern love poetry that all started "Oh Lily!" She told him his Toyota looked like a Chiclet (it did) and that his novel read like popcorn popping. Her humour was "rooted in parody and voices and quick verbal assessments." He learned, little by little, about her childhood. She showed him photographs her father had taken for Kodak, and spoke of him as "an artist, an art photographer who had introduced new techniques to Kodak, but then was such a drunk he lost his position"; she remembered him "as a failed sad figure drinking himself to death." "I looked at the pictures," Polk recalls. "I thought they were beautiful. There was something of

Gwen's own aesthetic in them, but I couldn't explain that in words. There was a forties look to them. They were very dramatic.... trees, water, Canadian landscapes. They were very precise and perfect in the way that some of her best work is."

Gwen also talked of her mother, how she had been manic-depressive since her early twenties. Between 1977 and 1978, Elsie went through several admissions at the Queen Street Mental Health Centre, only to be discharged to a variety of group homes. Whenever she was in a group home with access to a telephone, she would frantically call Gwen. Gwen explained to Jim that Elsie was in her manic phase. When she was depressive, she didn't phone and was actually a reasonable sort of person. Her manic calls were abusive. "I saw you last night under the lamp post," she would say to Gwen, and "I knew what you were doing. You're a whore. You are giving yourself to men for money, and I saw you do this." Polk answered the phone a couple of times and the voice was "quite enraged, angry, cutting, coarse, hoarse." Gwen always said very little on those phone calls, but she would go to visit Elsie. She told Polk that Carol refused to speak to their mother. "Why do you?" he would ask. "Why do you take this?" She would only reply that someone had to look after Elsie; she was stuck with her loyalty. She told him that Carol had managed to abscond from her childhood, had cut herself loose from it, and that she admired her sister for the courage it took to do this.

But she kept going back, as if she felt she might get from Elsie the thing she had always missed—the simple affirmation of maternal attention. Once, in casting Gwen's horoscope, Margaret Atwood had requested the time and weekday of her birth. When Gwen asked Elsie, she explained to Margaret: "I was referred by my mother to my aunt! Also I might add, and this is strictly off the record, it was apparently one of those odd births where neither parent remembered having done anything which would result in me, so to speak—(at least so I am told by my mother who still hasn't quite figured out what happened)!"[2] The balance between humour and pain was characteristic. In a casual entry in her journal, she noted the strange constellation of females who had presided over her birth: Elsie, Aunt Margaret, Aunt Maud. These were, as she put it, her female muses. Only Aunt Maud, in a correspondence that had lasted until her death, had affirmed her niece's gifts as a writer.

Gwen seemed to be attempting to take care of her health. On doctor's orders, she had finally managed to quit smoking by eating endless sunflower seeds. At the end of a session of writing, there would be a small mountain of seed husks piled beside her desk. She didn't seem to be drinking much. Polk would occasionally bring her aqua vitae— Gwen favoured vodka and aqua vitae because they were white and had no calories—but there was always a small shot glass nearby, or a tiny wineglass with a little clear liquid in it, and Polk noticed that these glasses seemed to "extrapolate" themselves more and more.

In the spring of 1978, Gwen moved from her St. George Street apartment to the bottom flat of an old house at 73 Albany Avenue. Polk remembered the apartment as having no light—Gwen kept the drapes drawn. He muses: "There seemed no place to go. There was many an evening in candlelight. What am I trying to say? An atmosphere was being created in this place, but it was even more unreal than it had to be. And we seemed to be drinking a lot." Gwen had no money and he marvelled at how she kept going. She did readings, she did "Artists in the Schools" programmes, she somehow managed to pay the rent, but her books weren't making any money. Though she had finally found a British agent, Anne McDermid of David Higham Associates, who was willing to represent her work and had hopes at least for *King of Egypt, King of Dreams*, the agent hadn't been able to sell anything. Polk suggested Gwen try to get the Royal Ontario Museum to sell her Akhenaton novel in its Egyptian exhibit, but they were unresponsive.

"There was a sort of refugee centre going on at her place," Polk explained. Gwen entertained Greeks who were passing through and had heard about her. Nikos would often come by to see that she was all right. She was working on her new novel, *Noman's Land*, which was to pick up where her last story of Noman had left off in 1972, but it wasn't going well.

Polk speaks carefully, trying to be precise:

> There was a sense in that period that Gwen seemed more and more uncertain and timorous. We would have little—they weren't really fights, but quibbles over wording. She would get very, not angry, but frightened. Our relationship was not going particularly badly, but it seemed that there was something really—it was concerning me that this kind of other creature underneath the assured poet was there. It seemed we were drinking more. Years later I once said to her: "I didn't know you had a drinking problem," and she laughed and said: "That's because you were drunk. But you went home and you didn't do it the next day. I just kept on drinking."
>
> It was just me being stupid. I didn't really note this until some really bad times—I'd say the spring of 1978—where Gwen would be sort of wailing and the eyes looking at me weren't anybody's I knew. Some fear or terror. And I didn't know what this was and I couldn't seem to talk my way back to the person I knew. I mentioned going to a shrink because she did not seem to be happy. She seemed to be quite alien to me, although I'd go over there, and stay. But there were so many people there, and she seemed out of sorts, and the phone would be ringing, and the novel wasn't going well—it was a jarring, alien sort of time.
>
> But she still had those wonderful dreams. Everything was colour, she was flying, there were whole civilizations and cities rising. This too was part of the constructing of this whole beautiful reality in which she was—even her unconscious was busy doing it. Very seldom did we go anywhere. Very seldom was there any direct light in the room. It was like going into the unconscious or into a dream. The Middle Eastern music, which I liked, would

be in the background, and there would be little glasses of whatever.

Yet she was frantic. She was losing the sense of what kept it going. Why, I don't know. I'd been to a shrink and I said: "Maybe you don't need one yourself, but you might go and talk about your mother." No, no, she wouldn't have that, she knew about shrinks, they were evil and bad, and would destroy her creativity. I just thought it might help her to get some take on what the problem was. I assumed it was her mother harassing her, and maybe her fear that she was going to end up like her mother. Which was very real.

Polk also remembered a conversation that disturbed him. He once asked her: "Did you ever have a brother?" She replied: "Jim, if I had a brother, I would never write, I would never need to do anything." "What did she mean by that?" I asked. "She was looking for an other." I recounted details of the photograph of Gwen Nikos had taken on the island of Antiparos, the one in which Gwen had removed the top of her bathing suit and wound her towel around her head like an Arab headdress, looking like a young boy, impersonating "Lawrence of Antiparos."

"Yes," says Jim:

> Maybe with some truly creative people, there's a need to create yourself in both sexes. Both Gwen's father and her mother had failed—that's unfair but ... if you are androgynous and self-contained, you are your own world. It's like the dream: You're your own civilization ... you are male and female and beautiful. She's ... "unique" is the word that leaps out at you. This is what she staked it on. I will create my own universe. And she did. But there was another one. What struck me in her most drunken state was this wasn't Gwen. It was, I would say, her mother, if I

was a pop psychologist. This coarse, braying and terrified person, who was not subject to any kind of rational ... the Gwenness had gone into the other room. That person was on hold for a while.

Polk's role in the latter phase seemed to be "Mr. Sensible." She didn't want to hear that from him, when she was terrified she was turning into her mother. Ultimately, it was very clear that the relationship was not going anywhere, and she broke it off. She said she'd found somebody else. "I don't know if that was true," he tells me, "but it didn't matter. I couldn't do anything for her. Now I've wondered what should have been done. What could have been done, if anything."

It wasn't that Gwen wasn't trying. She wrote to Samar Attar in January 1978:

> Things are fine between Nikos and me, which means that we are very good friends, and although we no longer live together, we see each other every day. We all live and die alone, Samar—as you said—and I am learning slowly to take life somewhat more practically than before. One of my main goals at present is to become healthy, for I have realized that I neglected my health for many years. It's a slow and interesting process, like training the self to recognize and acknowledge life, always....
>
> I wonder ... is there such a thing, perhaps, as a continent of the mind? An ideal landscape? Or, perhaps, a comfortable back-garden in some delightful country? Probably not, my friend—but maybe there are other comforts. Since we last communicated the world has gotten neither gooder or worser (pardon my English) and I do not really expect it to evolve in any fabulous directions in *my* lifetime. *But* ... in March, I have a new

book coming out, one which I'm sure you'll like; it's a prose narrative (travel etc) about Greece, and it's called *Mermaids and Ikons*.[3]

Mermaids and Ikons came out in March of 1978. The book that Polk had in mind, and that Gwen had in mind, was not there. The cover was a disaster. It was supposed to be glowing and golden, but was a flat mustard colour with barely legible graphics. Neither Gwen nor Polk was pleased.

Mermaids and Ikons got respectful but patronizing reviews and didn't sell very well. "I still think it's a beautiful little book," Polk says. But the fact that it didn't sell added to Gwen's panic. "She wasn't making any money. And the mother, and the drinking. Give her a break. Who wouldn't have panicked?"

In September 1978, she received a letter with the vice-regal seal inviting her to dinner at Rideau Hall. On the occasion of the 25th anniversary of the accession of Her Majesty to the throne, Gwendolyn had been awarded the Queen's Silver Jubilee Medal "for worthy and devoted service to the improvement and enlargement of life as we know it." Apparently her name had been submitted by the premier of Ontario. Unfortunately it was misspelled "MacEwan."[4]

That autumn, a lovely interlude did occur to lift Gwen's spirits. Victor Braun, a Windsor-born baritone who had made his debut at the Frankfurt Opera House, and had sung at La Scala, Covent Garden, and the San Francisco Opera under the direction of conductors like Klemperer, Solti, and Ozawa, approached Gwen with a commission. He had fallen in love with the poems from *The Shadow-Maker* and had asked the Dutch composer Rudi van Dijk to set them to music. Van Dijk, who had taught at the Royal Conservatory of Music in Toronto in the early seventies before moving to Boston, had been delighted with the idea.

"The Shadowmaker: Four Pieces For Baritone Voice and Orchestra" was performed by the Toronto Symphony under the direction of Mario Bernardi on three evenings in October 1978. The poems were printed in the programme and van Dijk wrote an accompanying note: "What attracted me to the poetry was the substance behind the subject matter—namely the dream. The poetry attempts, it seems to me, to lift the veil of 'maya' (illusion). Is our sensuous experience reality or illusion? MacEwen has something in common with Strindberg and D.H. Lawrence, as an explorer of these dark corners of the soul that most of us shut out conveniently, in order to create a safe but illusory reality."[5]

Gwen was invited to the opening performance. Her friend Mac Reynolds, who attended, remembered her sitting by herself in the balcony. At the end of the performance, the composer, van Dijk, was called up from the audience for the curtain call—the moment turned somewhat humorous when he tripped trying to climb onto the stage. No mention was made of the author of the poems sitting in the balcony. Reynolds felt Gwen must have been disappointed.

In 1979, perhaps to shore up her sagging finances, Gwen wrote a children's book, *The Chocolate Moose*, and approached her friend the painter Charles Pachter, already famous for his moose paintings, to ask if he would illustrate it. He declined since the idea seemed rather coy—he felt his own moose imagery was more ponderous and ethereal—but concluding that Gwen was feeling isolated and wanted to plug into a community, he invited her to join his Artists' Alliance.

In 1973, Pachter had bought a building at 24 Ryerson Avenue, with a down payment given him by Margaret Atwood, and, until 1982, it was a focus of artistic activity. Pachter lived in a loft on the top floor; the second floor was writers' and artists' studios; and the first was an art gallery called Artery. "Twenty-four Ryerson was a sort of filter," Pachter says. "Many interesting people came through." His photos of the parties from those days include painters and writers like Gwen, Joyce Wieland, Jay Macpherson, Allan Sparrow, Barbara Hall, and Susan Crean.

Pachter and Gwen would go to Emil's on Queen Street and have perogies, or they'd go to Rooneem's. And he painted her. It never occurred to him that she had a drinking problem. He found her astute and pragmatic about her work.

> Gwen was brilliantly organized. She would often call me for advice about an opening or a launch: where should she have it, how should she do it, any of that kind of thing. To me Gwen was a sprite. We were pals. She saw something of the artist in me that I didn't quite see. I remember the lucidity and the curiosity. I was glad she considered me part of her universe. She always had a very distinct sense of herself. She never masked her fascinations. Whatever fascinated her, she was right out front with it, and she would draw you into it with her. Even if you were momentarily preoccupied, she would somehow find a way to make you change what you were thinking about to go along with this scenario. She was fascinating that way. Like music: get this, listen to this sound, and this taste, and everything was like a sensual treat. There was an otherworldliness, an enormous sensitivity and vulnerability to Gwen.[6]

They talked of art. She must have been working on her projected second book about Noman, for she wrote to Charlie about the fantastic surreal material she was working with:

> The disturbing vision of monstrous and meaningless happenings make quite other demands on the power of the artist than do the experiences in the foreground of life. The vision is not something divided or secondary, and it is not a symptom of something else. It is a true symbolic expression; that is, the expression of something existent in its own right, but imperfectly known. The artist is not a person endowed with free will, but one who allows art to realize its purpose through him. It is not Goethe who creates Faust but Faust who creates Goethe. His personal career may be inevitable and interesting but it does not explain the past. Regards, Gwendolyn.[7]

Gwen was wrestling with disturbing visions and was asking: are these simply the product of a personal past—the product of personal neurosis, as the psychiatrist might insist—or are they the expression of a true aspect of mental experience? She believed that the psychiatrist would be reductive, explaining away loneliness and despair as maladjustment, not as the inevitable consequences of seeing the human world with too penetrating a vision.

But Pachter noted that Gwen was looking unwell. He began to feel that she was building what he called "a case against herself." He couldn't understand it. "It couldn't have been career: she was widely known and respected. I visited her in her apartment. To end up in a place that was unheated, with too little money to eat. What was that all about? It makes you susceptible to self-contempt. You must have got it wrong somehow."

In the late seventies, there were many other friends, but the closest were a constellation of powerful women writers: Joyce Marshall, Marian Engel, and Judith Merril. Joyce Marshall was a novelist and short-story writer who had worked for years as a freelance editor for publishers and the CBC; she was also an important translator of French historical and fictional works, and had recently won the Governor General's Translation Prize for her translation of a novel by Gabrielle Roy. Marian Engel had had a *succès de scandale* in 1976 with her novel *Bear*, a fable about a woman enamoured of a bear, which had also won a Governor General's Award. And Judy Merril was a well-known science fiction writer. She had been the first woman to crash the gates, as it were, of that exclusively male genre in 1948 when she published her story "That Only a Mother," and had become a dominant figure in the American SF community before she left the United States abruptly in 1968 in disgust at the Vietnam War.

Merril remembered her first meeting with Gwen in the late seventies at a party at Marian Engel's house. They talked for two hours and then returned to Gwen's and talked all night. "We discovered," says Merril, "that we lived in parallel universes." The universe that Merril had walked into was the "science fiction" part of Gwen's mind that had produced *The World of Neshiah*[8] and was writing *Noman's Land*, that speculative facility that matched Merril's own capacity to build a universe on the premise of "what if." "We were aware of the same quasi-realities. It was precisely like falling in love." Merril was astonished by Gwen's intellectual acumen. "One doesn't expect this incredible intelligence from a poet—emotion, intuition perhaps—but most people with that kind of intellectual rigor don't write poetry." What seems to have most moved Merril about Gwen was her subversiveness and her political astuteness. She understood human nature, how society functions in terms of power structures, and she wanted that changed, knowing full well that this was impossible.

Merril was aware of an element of sadness in Gwen. From the time she first knew her, she felt Gwen was being torn apart by her yearning for Nikos. Gwen kept imagining she and Nikos would get back together, and when it was quite clear that this wouldn't happen, she was broken-hearted. "Sometimes she would do things—get ill and only Nikos could take care of her. One felt after a while that the point of the illness was that Nikos would have to come."[9]

For years after their separation, Gwen mourned Nikos; she could not achieve a separation in her mind. When she wrote to Samar Attar she always spoke of him. In May 1978, she sent her a letter about the upcoming production of *The Trojan Women* and added that Nikos was in Greece for six months, and she was considering going at the end of the summer to rest and recuperate. "Although we do not live together anymore, we are the best of friends ... (a good arrangement)."[10] She wrote in October 1979 to say that she had been commissioned by the St. Lawrence Centre to write a play on the modern immigrant in Canada.

> Which brings me to Nikos ... we are still very much together in spirit after ten years ... although we don't live together, we see each other every day; it's an unusual situation! Recently he has been ill with a nervous condition

that flares up in his stomach; he's worried about his work, and is tired of performing, but finds that there's little else to do. It worries me too, so we are both at the moment somewhat nervous wrecks. I am lucky to have my work to take my mind off things; he has no such outlet.[11]

She also wrote to Margaret Atwood that fall: "Nikos and I (we don't live together but are still very much together) were supposed to go to Greece in Sept., but he got sick instead ... a flare-up of an old ulcer operation, not serious. Also he's having a sort of mid-life crisis; it seems to go on and on. Eek. When we're both eighty-five, we'll live happily ever after, the whole two weeks of it."[12]

Gwen was trying to convince herself that the root of their problem was simply the mechanics of their lives: it was impossible to put two artists' lives together—they had lived at separate ends of the day, she hated the nightclub scene, and so forth—but reconciliation was fantasy. Nikos would be there as a friend to help, but he had clearly begun a new life. She was desperately lonely. She again started to binge-drink secretly, and could not face the fact that her drinking was getting completely out of hand.

Neither Marian Engel nor Judy Merril had any clue that Gwen was drinking until December 11, 1980, when she phoned Marian to say she was very ill and needed help to get to the hospital. Engel took her to the emergency ward at Mount Sinai Hospital. While they were in the waiting room, Engel phoned Merril. When Merril arrived, she found Gwen incredibly disoriented—she couldn't find her health card and was fumbling and confused. After Gwen disappeared into the consulting room, the doctor returned to say: "It looks like the DTs." They were incredulous, and stammered that that was impossible, their friend did not drink, but when they looked in Gwen's purse they found the small plastic flask of vodka.

It was astonishing that she could have kept her drinking so hidden; they had each been seeing a lot of her. But apparently her drinking was a constant small tippling, so that she had a high alcohol content in her system, although she was never quite drunk.

Gwen was released from hospital after only two days, and returned home. She was admitted again two months later in February. It is impossible to ascertain how long she stayed,[13] but it is clear that this was a severe bout. Gwen, it turned out, had her father's constitution. Though some people can drink heavily for a lifetime, he had deteriorated in ten years. His daughter's health had been dangerously compromised in the same span of time.

Her friends were trying to help. Marian Engel decided that Gwen must meet Aasta Levene, a classical pianist at the Royal Conservatory of Music, because Aasta too had grown up with a mother who suffered serious mental illness. As Engel put it, "they needed each other: two women who had grown up with that terrible background; how do you survive it?" Gwen was working on a small article about the Elmwood Girls' Hotel, where Elsie had been living, when Engel brought the two of them together over her kitchen table.

I met Aasta Levene in the rooftop café of the Park Plaza Hotel. She was a woman in her late fifties, still beautiful, with a thin, articulate face and remarkable eyes. Strangers, we watched the winter city frozen beneath us in the thinning twilight and spoke carefully. But then I asked what she and Gwen talked about, and the need to explain her understanding of what it must have been like to be Gwen brought an urgency to her voice:

> We talked about our mothers. I will tell you what it is like. You live most of your life in pain. You have watched your mother lose control. No one who has not experienced it knows what this means at the most intimate level. I, for instance, at a very young age lived with people coming to subdue my mother, putting her in an actual white straitjacket, taking her away. You see what complete lack of control is. Drawing on walls. I think Gwen knew that. I

think as a child a person of Gwen's sensibilities is aware of almost everything, and it's just how you deal with it.14

Levene explained that the legacy of such a childhood is terror, a terror at the loss of control. Conscious that madness is in the family, you learn to impose an extraordinary control over yourself, but you are also constantly aware of what Levene called "the black hole there behind the shadows ready to come out." Gwen must always have felt that if she was not careful, she too could break down. Doubts must have plagued her. Could she not have communicated better with her mother, might she not have helped in some way? "With a psyche like Gwen's," Levene explained, "somehow you are always at fault." The horrendous stigma that mental illness carries leads you to feel that people look at you differently. All Gwen needed to do was to go overboard once and people would know the whole thing. She had to be secretive. How deeply she was devastated by her mother's illness is clear from her decision never to have a child. She believed that madness skips a generation and that any child she might have would be born mad.

As she spoke, I watched Levene's eyes become suddenly backlit with sadness:

> Gwen worked so hard to be strong. One's reactions are so complex—there is the terrible fear, the terrible hatred, the embarrassment, humiliation and all the rest of it—I don't know how to describe it—it tears at your psyche ... you can never fill up, you're empty inside in some way, and then there's the search to fill again, and that's where one can start drinking ... to fill oneself up, the holes that you've cut away from yourself ... that have been cut away by others when you were too young to do anything about it.

Levene felt that Gwen came closer to that edge than most people because, as a writer, she dared to enter that territory. She had enormous courage, but the legacy of her childhood meant that she would always have been afraid of loss. Most tragically, Levene thought that Gwen would not have believed happiness was possible; she might even have sabotaged anything that would be happiness in her life. Yet, what Levene found most astonishing about Gwen was her sensitivity—her antennae were out in every situation.

> I reverberate to that. You so seldom see it. When you see a person so exquisitely sensitive and acutely aware, you know how painful it must be for them to go through life like this. And yet you want to be near that person because you think, this is what is real. Everything else is so totally artificial and superficial. People go through their whole lives without examination. Gwen examined.

When Gwen and Marian Engel became friends in 1979, Engel had already been diagnosed with the lymphoma that would kill her six years later. The cancer took its toll intermittently. Whenever Engel was bedridden, Gwen would drive on the new moped she had bought to Engel's house on Marchmount Road north of Davenport Road, and for hours they would sit and talk of Greece. Engel had lived for a time in Cyprus, and loved the culture. They would speak a little Greek and put Greek records on the stereo, and sometimes they would dance. They would talk of cats, gardens, writing, and gossip about friends. No one had any money in those days and they talked of how the marvellous Robert Weaver, at the CBC, kept everyone alive. Marian would complain about the stupid travel things she had to write to get extra cash. Sometimes Gwen would speak of her childhood, the visits she had made to insane asylums in Toronto to visit her mother, and the need she had felt to re-create herself because she had had to grow up so quickly.[15]

Engel's young daughter, Charlotte, who was then fourteen, remembered Gwen driving up on her moped, looking exotic with those kohl-lined sapphire eyes; she was convinced she was Egyptian. Gwen always had a way of reaching a child. At the parties at Marchmount, adults would invariably greet Charlotte and her brother with some version of: "I haven't seen you since you were this high, boring stuff, but Gwen would never treat you as anything other than what you were," she tells me. Gwen seemed ethereal, and yet so incredibly friendly and funny. She was one of Charlotte's favourite people.

But even the child was aware that emergencies surrounded Gwen. There seemed to be a "phone dynamic." Charlotte understood that Gwen would be suddenly "sick" and "we" had to do something about it. "People came and did stuff right away. It happened incredibly fast."

Jim Polk remembers Gwen that spring of 1981. She had called to ask him to meet her. She had done this before and then would cancel, but this time they settled on the Rajput Restaurant on Bloor Street at 4:30 in the afternoon. When he arrived, the restaurant was empty except for a middle-aged woman in a kerchief. He sat, nursing a beer, and waited, until he realized with a start that the woman was Gwen. As he approached, she looked frightened, and asked who he was. He reminded her how they'd arranged an early dinner and sat down. Her voice seemed somehow all wrong to him and conversation was difficult. She requested vodka; she did not want to eat. Polk was horrified by her appearance and, not knowing what to do, asked: "How have you been? I've never seen you like this." She was wearing a cap under the scarf and lifted it to show him marks where her hair had been cut away: "They put things on my scalp to test the waves," she explained. "It's been a rough winter." He tried to comfort her: "I'm sorry you've been through this," but it was no use. This wasn't Gwen. "The problem was her voice. There were two voices: the sophisticated, amused, intense one, and then this rough, monosyllabic, unfocused thing."

Almost immediately Gwen decided she wanted to leave. Polk offered to walk her back to her apartment, but she said that was impossible: didn't he have his car? He explained that he'd sold it. Though she only lived three blocks away, she seemed at a loss as to how she would get home. She had counted on the car. He suggested a taxi, but no, she couldn't do that. Eventually he walked her to the bottom of her street, but she would not allow him to go any farther. By then he felt bits of the real Gwen were appearing in the conversation. When he reached home he phoned, but she did not answer. Several days later, the real Gwen phoned him and did not allude to that afternoon. It was a very funny phone call about some poet who wanted to meet Polk, but she would be nameless. He replied: "If she's nameless, she's got a problem being a poet," and they both cracked up. It was not much of a joke, but it was a relief to be laughing.

There were several phone calls over the months and when Polk saw her riding her bicycle, she was the Gwen he knew. She told him: "I've licked myself. I'm off the sauce. I'll do fine." Then he would see her at a party or a reading again and she was still the real Gwen, but he could tell she'd been drinking. "She was slipping. She couldn't make it work. She just couldn't choreograph the two Gwens." When people who didn't know her would say "Oh, Gwen's just a drunk," Polk would feel his blood starting to boil and insist, "No, she's not. It's not like that. That's not what's going on at all."

22
REACHING FOR LIFE

Since 1978, Gwen had been living at 73 Albany Avenue in the district of Toronto affectionately called the Annex. The Annex got its definition from the University of Toronto, which sat on its eastern perimeter. It was the kind of place that used to be found in any urban university area. Miscellaneous shops dealing in used books, vintage objects, vintage clothes were laced through the side streets. The occasional small publishing house like Coach House Press could be found in its back lanes. There was a European feel to the Annex; it was tolerant of heterogeneity and it was possible to live there relatively cheaply and gracefully. The university owned much of the area through bequests from alumni and, with a view to expansion, maintained houses as cheap student residences, letting them run down. There were frat houses and rooming houses dating back to the turn of the century, shared among students, artists, and the working poor.

The Annex was defined against the mainstream, with places like Other Books, Other Travel, and the Poor Alex Theatre (so named in friendly opposition to the Royal Alex on King Street, which catered to the up-scale crowd). Along Bloor Street one could find inexpensive Hungarian restaurants like L'Europe, where one lifted a curtain and entered to the romantic strains of a gypsy guitar, or the Blue Cellar behind it, where students sat in the semi-darkness and, over gingham tablecloths, discussed art and life with little disturbance from the overworked waitresses who were glad to leave them unmolested. The Annex had flair. It felt like a downtown cross-section where several worlds met. One could sense a slow transformation as the rooming-houses were being bought up by the renovating middle class, but it was still a good place to be and Gwen enjoyed her daily cycles through it.

In 1980, she met a young sculptor, Ruben Zellermeyer, who lived in a basement apartment next door to her flat on Albany. Ruben would then have been thirty-one. Born in Israel, he had moved to Canada with his parents at the age of eight. The last thing his parents wanted in the family was an artist, but he had rebelled, going off to Berlin at twenty-two to study casting methods at the Noack Foundry. When he met Gwen he was swept away. They became lovers, then friends.

The first time I met Ruben, I visited him at his studio. As I entered he was standing on a stool, dishevelled but with an almost rabbinical look to his bearded face, totally absorbed in putting the last touches to one of his gigantic etiolated bronzes. A man obviously clumsy in his body, he stumbled from his perch and offered me a shy smile. The studio was large, filled with light, and the broken torsos of animals and humanoid creatures with their split profiles and staring eyes affronted with an archaic, primitive power. He was another myth-maker. I could see that he was nervous, mistrustful; he kept the door to the street ajar as we sat.

I was immediately astonished by his inarticulateness—he had to punch out his words with an aggressive energy that was disconcerting, but I remembered—Gwen never required language from her men. With wine, he did not exactly relax; rather his frustration at his own inarticulateness mounted with his excitement, but his shyness disappeared.

On the wall behind us were the cut-out magazine photos of Egyptian artifacts that Gwen had once pinned to her walls; he has kept, like amulets, the typewriter spools of ribbon with which she typed her last manuscript. Clearly he revered her. To this day he cannot make himself go down the street on which she died. Like so many of her friends, he feels guilty: "I encouraged her to go out there alone," he almost cries.[1] Now he knows that no one is strong enough to survive alone.

I think, curiously, that in Ruben, Gwen had found a kind of Milton, a man of evident talent, but who was not good at negotiating his way through the world. The relationship would have been imbalanced, she imposing herself between the world and his need. Her life had come full circle. There is something antediluvian about him, a rough-hewn primitivism. Whatever else he is, there is nothing inauthentic about Ruben. He is an absolutely essential outsider, totally raw.

But again the man I meet is not the figure Gwen's friends reported him to be in the past. Since those early days with Gwen, the world has given Ruben financial stability and some attention. Money has come from a small inheritance from a dead relative, providing a studio to live and work in. His sculptures can be found in a number of locations around Toronto, including the Village by the Grange near the Art Gallery of Ontario and the Holocaust Museum on Bathurst Street. He talks, with delight and a certain humility, of exhibitions in Toronto and even one in South America. Gwen's confidence in the artist was correctly placed.

He was not an easy figure for Gwendolyn's friends, who were so deeply concerned about her health. They thought him dependent, someone whose own drinking would have weighed on Gwendolyn. When she lived on Albany, she had offered him her backyard to work in. He was always out there, hammering, cutting, sawing, chiselling away at his sculptures. To her friends, he was just a friendless, penniless, woebegone guy that Gwen had decided to take care of. Gwen would sometimes complain of his jealous possessiveness; he intruded on her friendships. Once when she had brought a male friend home, he'd gone crazy, pounding on the windows from outside the house. Sometimes it seemed almost impossible to have a private conversation with Gwen because he was always there.

But Ruben had his defenders. Judy Merril found him very gentle and caring towards Gwen, not someone she particularly liked but whom she respected. Jane Jacobs, the brilliant social and urban theorist, was Gwen's close neighbour on Albany. She only met Gwen in passing, but she was fond of Ruben. When Gwen's landlord objected to Ruben working in the backyard of 73 Albany—all that hammering in stone bothered the neighbours—Jacobs had offered him working space at the back of her driveway. She marvelled at the discipline and skill of his workmanship, and thought him very talented. As she sat at her window working on her own books, she often found herself typing to the rhythms of his hammer, thinking how similar their arts were: he tapping to release the figure from stone; she tapping to release the idea from the page.[2]

Mac Reynolds thought of Ruben affectionately as a naïve primitive, an original. Gwen and Ruben would come to visit at his schoolhouse studio near Collingwood north of Toronto, and he saw that Ruben was passionately in love with her, although he also felt that he was, like Acorn, whom Reynolds had known, a kind of Quasimodo figure, one of society's outcasts, whom Gwen protected. "She was matching up her self-image, the secret terrible self-image that lay underneath all that need for alcohol, of being an essential outsider, rejected by the world."[3]

Ruben, however, was someone from whom Gwen didn't have to hide the dark side of her life when she was drinking. He felt she was the Queen of Egypt. "What can happen to someone who is the Queen of Egypt in Toronto?" he asks me, quite seriously, and it *is* a serious question, to which the answer is not much that is good. Gwen and Ruben never lived together, but she shared her Toronto with him—they would ride their bicycles through the city after breakfasting at The Mug on Bloor Street, or walk the Annex to see what was happening on the streets, and she would point out a small clapboard house and say how nice it would have been to own it. It would be *hers*, a working space. He remembers their going to the University of Toronto one night and pulling up plants for her yard, laughing as they looked around anxiously for the plant police.

The world he presents is straightforward: Gwen getting two newspapers every day, *The Globe and Mail* and *The Toronto Star*; working on her new T.E. Lawrence sequence, talking about the gelignite Lawrence used to blow up trains; suffering from asthma attacks—she used an inhaler regularly and refused to take the doctors' advice that she not keep cats. Sometimes when they walked past the Queen Street Mental Health Centre, she would point out the rooms Elsie had stayed in. She occasionally played the violin for him. It fascinated him the way she held it lovingly and tightened the strings with hard wax. "In another life she would have been a violinist." She talked of her father: the rabbits he had saved from the Banting Institute experiments; the shadows on the wall at night that frightened her and that her father assured her were angels; the photo he'd taken of her under the wishing tree in High Park; that long-ago train trip when she had been kidnapped by the social worker and her father had rushed into the station as the train pulled out, crying "Don't let them make you forget me." "She *knew* who she was," he almost shouts. "She was a total giver."

Ruben found it too difficult to talk about her drinking, but he insisted there was one mistake people made about Gwen. She wasn't destitute. She was proud of the fact that she earned her own living, even if it was frugal. "When she had her head together, everything was OK." He learned from Gwendolyn: "If I got angry at someone, she'd say: 'Think of them alone in bed at night, confronted with life, death. Whenever you are angry, think of them that way. We are all vulnerable.'" Or "Once on a bus I was getting *self-conscious*. She would say: 'Don't be like that, look at their faces. Two thousand years old. That same face was there in those times. The distance is not great.' She was always asking me to think in a larger way." He remembered driving to a memorial exhibition of the paintings of Barker Fairley. "I was looking at the rocks. I was getting stuck. She said: 'Look this way—the sun, the lake, the boats.' She turned my head. She was right."

Gwen took on the task of Ruben. To her friends' annoyance, she promoted his work, constantly asking them to buy his jewellery and sculpture.

The writers Leon Whiteson and Aviva Layton were living around the corner from Gwen on Howland Avenue. Layton had known Gwen from the very early days when, as a teenager, Gwen had stopped in Montreal to visit her and her then husband, Irving Layton. In 1981, Gwen would sometimes turn to them in her need. Layton remembers her as the most alone of people. "Every writer constructs some kind of safety net," she remarks, "either a stable relationship or a stable financial base. Nobody can exist, nobody can endure, without a safety net." She adds emphatically: "Gwen had no safety net." To explain Gwendolyn to herself she returns to an earlier memory of her as a sixteen-year-old schoolgirl, a very "little thing, shy and probably sexually terrified. Good God, she really was a raving beauty."

> I remember we had supper one night, and it was just Irving and myself and Gwen, and obviously Gwen was there because of Irving. And Leonard [Cohen] came. We had a hilarious evening. I don't have a clue what we were talking about, and it ended with Leonard chasing Gwen around the table. We were screaming with laughter. It was all very funny until we noticed that Gwendolyn was genuinely terrified and burst into tears. She must have thought that she had fallen into a den of iniquity in which we were going to watch while this rampaging beast Leonard Cohen was going to rape her on the dining room table amid the spaghetti bolognese.
>
> I felt terrible, we all felt terrible, because Leonard was playing being a demon. He was hilarious, and sending himself up, as he is always sending himself up. When I look back on it, it was terribly cruel, but we were doing it with affection. We were playing. I remember her bursting into tears, and her face, which was always white, becoming absolutely ashen with fear. Did she run out of the front door screaming and never come back? I

can't remember. Anyway that is my first memory of Gwen. I think I understood that under that exotic person there really was a fragile person. I don't mean that as any putdown. She was also tough as nails. She and Leonard went on tour together years later and I'm sure they laughed about it.[4]

In 1981, Gwen's finances were in an absolute mess. Sometimes she did not even have food. Friends like Margaret Atwood would invite her to dinner; she would accept but not show up. There were only a very few people to whom she would turn for financial help. The poet and novelist Barry Callaghan had been a longstanding friend since the days when they met to discuss the Middle East, and he had consistently published her work in his magazine *Exile*. He only discovered how poor she was when he dropped by unexpectedly. She was in the kitchen making her supper with a jug-sized glass of vodka beside her. When she invited him to eat, he discovered the meal was two fried green peppers. "Gwendolyn, you cannot eat and drink like that," he told her. With a certain dignity, for someone who was quite drunk, she replied: "I'm broke." "I had talked to her about money before," he explains, "but I had never felt—it was like a stone was dropped—how close the relationship was between often not having a nickel in her life, the despair of loneliness, and the dive into the bottle. She was such a courtly, rare woman, and I saw destruction written everywhere. Luckily, the reason I had dropped by was that I was bringing her money as a payment for something in *Exile*. It saved her embarrassment."[5]

The poet Karen Mulhallen, editor of *Descant*, would, whenever she could find money through her magazine, allocate some small amount for Gwen. One of the very few people Gwen would actually ask directly was Aviva Layton. Layton remembers those phone calls: "She'd just phone up and say I need twenty bucks, or I need groceries. I'd give her money, or latterly, I'd bring a whole pile of groceries to her place to make sure she was eating and not just drinking. She didn't have any of that idiotic sense of shame or anything, but still, I knew it was hard for her to ask. She simply acknowledged that she was needy at the time and she did it with great dignity." Gwen might explain that she was waiting for payments for public readings from The Canada Council. When they were late, she'd say: "What they don't realize is that that's where my next meal comes from. And the rent doesn't get paid. It's my bread and butter." She was living from hand to mouth.

Leon Whiteson, Layton's husband, remembers another side of Gwen. At night he'd often wander into the doughnut shop at the corner of Bloor Street and Walmer Road, where one could sit into the small hours of the morning. One met all kinds there: people buying doughnuts, street people, the police, writers, the edgy and the desperate seeking refuge. Under the harsh fluorescent lighting, Whiteson would find Gwen sitting alone in a far back corner. Something of the black Celt would come out in Gwen. She would watch as people entered and find the comment that cut to the bone. She was never cruel but rather relentless. In the tone of the words and the hardness of her eyes, it was as if she were looking up from a black pit and seeing the absurdity of the whole human comedy. To Whiteson's mind would come the words of the Spanish poet Calderón: "the greatest crime is to have been born." "It was as if she was the only one who understood how dreadful this whole human business is and at the same time how comic. It was absolutely black. A completely unsentimental view of the sort of idiocy of being alive. Nobody escaped. Everyone wallowing in self-pity."[6]

Living more and more in that black vision, Gwendolyn could not give up alcohol. Twice more she was taken to Mount Sinai Hospital. On June 14, 1981, she was admitted to Emergency suffering from alcoholic withdrawal. In her ordeal, there was a period when she was tied to her hospital bed. As she recovered, the hospital wanted her to remain for tests, but after four days she refused to stay. Since her clothes had been confiscated, she marched home in her nightgown. When she was admitted again on October 6th, her doctors told her that if she continued to drink she would be courting death.

Her friend Mac Reynolds visited her in hospital. He knew a great deal about the secretive disease of alcoholism, having once suffered from it. "Alcoholism is not a stimulant, it is an anaesthetic," he explains, "because you can't face something. You need alcohol to numb yourself. Denial is the alcoholic's defence. It protects you. To have to give it up is terrifying because there is nothing between you and your fear."[7] But the battle one wages with oneself is soul-destroying: "Inside the drunk is another person inside another person inside another person. But at core is the sober person with a conscience to whom the drunk must always justify himself." He had been trying for a long time to get Gwen to go with him to AA, but the memories of those early visits with her father in her childhood had turned her against the organization.

The first day he visited at Mount Sinai Hospital, he had made his argument that Gwen had to stop drinking—she owed it to those who thought of her as a fine poet. She had looked at him blankly and said: "Thank you for coming." But on his second visit she had suddenly said: "You're right." He understood this to mean that she accepted the pact between them. She had accepted that she must stop. This time, when she left hospital eight days after her admission, she really meant to quit.

23

THE CHOSEN TWIN

After leaving Mount Sinai Hospital in June, Gwen began a programme of health: she swam daily, she practised yoga, and paid attention to her diet. Her will, as always, was monumentally strong and she succeeded in stopping the drinking. However, as a concession to her friends, and particularly to Mac, who insisted she could not solve the disease of alcoholism on her own, she presented herself that October at Intake at the Addiction Research Foundation on Russell Street, a short bicycle ride from the Annex.

When she began her consultations, Gwen was ambivalent. She made light of the whole matter, telling the doctors she merely wanted a few exploratory sessions, without making a long-term commitment. She did not feel she had a serious problem and had come to make her friends happy. She agreed to sessions with a therapist at the centre called Barbara Bruce. Bruce was unusual in that she was blind and was always accompanied by her seeing-eye dog, which would have mattered to Gwen—Bruce was a woman who had obviously faced and surmounted her own suffering.

Gwen began to visit ARF on a weekly basis. I was never able to talk personally to Bruce, who was bound by rules of doctor/patient confidentiality, but, as a biographer, I was able to obtain from the centre its summary files of admittance that gave a running narrative of Gwen's experience there.

At the beginning of Gwen's treatment, October 27, 1981, Bruce noted in the file: "Gwen is always feeling that she is unimportant and taking up too much of my time."[1] Although her whole history anticipates this statement, it is still startling to read that Gwen, whom everyone considered brilliant, unique, would apologize for occupying a professional's time.

In the course of her initial visits, Gwen told the therapist she believed her birth had not been planned and that she felt she had never been wanted, ironically, of course, echoing her mother's belief about her own birth. She insisted that her mother never wanted either of her daughters. A foundational layer to Gwen's psyche was clearly the self-contempt and guilt symptomatic of the motherless child. What, one asks oneself desperately, does it take to erase that "unwanting"? Whether Gwen ever spoke of her dream of "defloration," of the young girl who told herself: "There was something I just remembered ... better to forget it." "'I cannot forgive.' Means 'I cannot be forgiven,'" I cannot know. No such reference appears in the files. But Gwen did describe a black hole of emptiness within that could not be filled up. Forming relationships with people, finding anyone with whom she had something in common, she explained, was always a struggle. There seemed so many barriers to surmount; how was that magic act achieved?—reaching beyond the self, trusting another.

According to the reports, Gwen attended ARF for six sessions, before beginning a pattern that would establish itself. She would cancel one week and then return the next. She saw her therapist a total of fourteen times, before she ended the therapy at the beginning of May 1982, when she told Bruce that she would no longer need appointments at ARF. There were more "needy" people than she who required Bruce's time. She would only come "if there were relatively few people in the waiting room when she dropped by."

How far Bruce penetrated the dark secrets Gwen housed cannot be known. In November Gwen made an appointment in order to report to Bruce that she had not taken any alcohol for a year. She brought Bruce a box of chocolates to celebrate her sobriety, and continued to send her newspaper clippings indicating how well her literary career was going. In December she could tell Bruce that she was grateful for her survival, glad to be alive. Bruce was disappointed that the sessions could go no further. She felt that Gwen failed to recognize or give herself credit for the remarkable way she had gotten back on her feet after being so ill for so long.

The bravery that had always sustained Gwen, that had sent her into the midst of danger, for instance, on her lonely expeditions to the Middle East, was now a hazard. She layered over the history that had forced her spiralling downward. She quit drinking and kept her secrets, deciding to work on them alone, as she had always done, through her writing. She turned back to writing her T.E. Lawrence sequence, which she had begun back in early 1981. Lawrence was obviously one of those figures in whose loneliness she could hide her own darker loneliness.

There is a computer programme called "Morphing." You can take pictures of two people, as long as they are of similar size, and by a process of innumerable mathematically precise calculations made by the computer, you can watch as one face metamorphoses into the other. It's fascinating to watch as a face turns slowly to the left and dissolves and reshapes into another face: female becomes male, animal becomes human. I have taken a photograph of Gwen and watched her metamorphose into a photograph of her chosen twin, T.E. Lawrence. The faces fit: the eyes have the same guarded and desperate intensity and the mouths the same delicacy. They are both intensely androgynous.

Gwen had been fascinated by Lawrence since she was a teenager. In 1962, at the Hotel Zion in Tiberias on that long-ago trip to Israel, the tall white-haired proprietor had invited her downstairs one evening to take tea. He had noticed her making endless jottings in her notebook and took her to be a writer. He showed her a room hung with sepia photos of camel riders in the desert, among whom she recognized T.E. Lawrence—her host had ridden with Lawrence in one of his campaigns. In Greece she had invented herself as Lawrence of Antiparos, imitating the Arab headdress. She did not know it yet, but she would find out that her Aunt Maud and a girlfriend, whose family was in the diamond business, had met T.E. Lawrence (or Ned as they called him), and had spent several evenings at his Dorset cottage, "Clouds," before he became Lawrence of Arabia. When her aunt told her this after reading her Lawrence poems, it amused her that there was a "family connection."

In 1981, Gwen had told her friend Mac Reynolds that she was writing of T.E. Lawrence. Reynolds was someone she respected and trusted. He had started out as a painter in 1936, and sustained his career as a "passionate amateur" by working for years as a producer in the CBC newsroom. He had entertaining stories to tell about his youthful days in England visiting Leonard Woolf near his aunt's home in Rodmell, or later, as an artist, hobnobbing at the Chelsea Arts Club, picking the brains of the ancient academicians in the sumptuous gardens. He had been to Norman Bethune's parties in the 1930s and had heard his famous Massey Hall speech on his departure for Spain in 1937. An amusing experience for a socialist, he had sculpted the Queen at Buckingham Palace.

When Gwen told him she was writing her *T.E. Lawrence Poems*, he had thought it a "pretty nutty proposition." Why write of such an exotic? What could Lawrence have to do with her, or even with the contemporary world? But as they discussed it over lunch, he saw that she was preoccupied with Arab cultures, and it began to seem a reasonable proposition. Gwen had never really lost her passionate involvement in the Middle East. She had written to Samar Attar that she believed the Western world was in decline and the future would be decided in the Middle East. As each scene of the long, drawn-out Middle Eastern war that had begun in 1967 played itself out, she had written telegrams of condolence to Samar; for instance, to Damascus, Syria in 1973: "I send my hope for peace for your people. I am with you. Gwendolyn."[2] Attar was in Algeria at the time, but remembered how very moved her sister Raja had been to receive Gwen's gesture in the midst of the war.

What most struck Reynolds is that Gwen was writing the poems before she gave up drinking and she completed them in sobriety after she had quit, and there was no difference in the poems.

The same had happened to him in the long-ago days when he had been drinking. He had once done a portrait, sculpting it in a blackout, and then found there was no difference in terms of quality between it and the ones he did later when sober. "So I think that the artist doesn't get drunk, ever," he tells me.

> The artist stays sober while the worldly part of one disintegrates into drink. Alcohol is like an anaesthetic; it anaesthetizes certain parts of the brain and perhaps there is part of the brain that is not affected, until later on, when unconsciousness takes over. Artists who have been alcoholic have in some cases even improved when they were drinking, when the rest of the brain was not getting in the way and the creativity department was able to function fully. Nobody knows about these things. I suppose it's possible that the part of the brain that was the poet and was therefore liberated when Gwen was half-drunk was where she wanted to be. Because the act of picking up a drink is an order to change, to make yourself fit the circumstances that exist. To be half-dead is the goal sometimes. Although I desperately wanted her to stop drinking—I thought it could kill her—I empathized, in a way, with Gwen's desire to live in that sort of netherworld that is half-drunkenness, when passing out is really a relief. Trying to achieve a sort of non-existence. To be released.[3]

In the dark year of 1981, as her despair grew in the long months of illness, she had turned to Lawrence. As a teenager reading *Seven Pillars of Wisdom*, she must have been thrilled by the heroic Lawrence, by the story of a man who, having fallen in love with the desert, had metamorphosed himself from a staid Englishman into the Lawrentian knight of Arabia, the saviour of an alien race. When she turned to him in 1981, however, it was to find a man haunted by his own loneliness, driven by a ravaging sense of emptiness, exiled from both his own and from Arab culture. Lawrence acknowledged that his Arabness was an affectation only, but it was deep enough to leave him disenchanted with everything his own culture stood for. He had written in the first chapter of *Seven Pillars of Wisdom*: "I had dropped one form and not taken on the other, and was become like Mohammed's coffin in our legend, with a resultant feeling of intense loneliness in life, and a contempt, not for other men, but for all they do.... Sometimes these selves would converse in the void; and then madness was very near."[4] Gwendolyn found in Lawrence precisely the persona she needed to explore what she herself had been through. One of the last poems in her *T.E. Lawrence Poems* is called "There is No Place to Hide."

> ... No. What I am really doing is standing in an unlit room
> Holding a court martial upon myself. Shaw tells me
>   that to live under a cloud
>   is to defame God. I can neither reveal myself
>   nor hide. No matter what I do, I am naked.
> I can clothe myself in silk or chain mail, and I
>   am naked; everything shows through
>   and yet no one can see me.
>
> Can you imagine that posterity will call me wonderful
>   on the basis of a few pencil sketches,
>   a revolt in the desert,
>   and my irresistably foul soul?
> Outside my window, a small tit bird bashes itself
>   against the glass. At first I thought
>   it was admiring itself in the window.
>   Now I know it's mad.[5]

Gwen's poems are written in that unlit room, in Lawrence/Shaw's voice (so disgusted had Lawrence been at the legend of "Lawrence of Arabia," he changed his name to Shaw in 1921) as he holds a "court martial" over himself. Gwen needed a voice to hurl her invective at the world at a time when her vision had become so black that being human didn't seem worth the trouble. She found it in Lawrence, the "hero" in a colonial war.

Seven Pillars is an extraordinarily raw, humanly naked book. Gwen scoured it carefully, finding many of her poems in specific incidents Lawrence recorded. Her sequence becomes his confession. T.E. Lawrence's ambition from childhood had been to secure a generalship and knighthood by the time he was thirty. He achieved this, but his morbid sincerity, his self-castigating honesty, led him to write up his war as almost no other person has done. Beneath the images of heroism in his book is the schizophrenic war in his own "foul soul." He insisted on acknowledging it, though like most human beings, including Gwendolyn, he could not solve it. Gwen's brilliance as a writer was that she could *see*, but the seeing did not bring resolution. This is the puzzle of the writer's life. Gwendolyn might release Lawrence from his ghosts, but that did not mean she could exorcise her own.

After her poems were published, Gwen explained in a letter to her friend Samar Attar why she was drawn to Lawrence:

> It has always been my conviction that in order to understand the nature of aggression and war, we must first examine the enemy within—the darkness and ambivalence of our inner selves—the self-deceit and lies, all of it.... I find the real enemy where he always was—in our mirrors—only in understanding the hidden horrors and truths within ourselves can we begin to understand the monstrous realities in the history of this world.[6]

Gwen found in Lawrence an embodiment of the schizophrenia of his culture. Lawrence was addicted to war, to its theory and philosophy; he was brilliant at it, manipulating its physical, technical, and metaphysical components. He was uniting the Arabs as a fighting force in the name of an idea: Freedom. Death was immaterial. "Civilization has always paid the mind from the body's funds" was his sanitary way of putting it. And yet the other side of his mind *knew* absolutely that it was all a sham, a "mind-sickness," he called it. Still, he stayed in war after the First World War was over, joining the RAF in the 1920s and serving as an airman. As if there were nothing else but war. War was a nihilism he could not escape.

The Peace Conference

After prostituting myself in the service of an alien race,
    I was too mangled for politics; the world
    swirled around me and I was its still center.
Old men crawled out of the woodwork and seized upon
    our victory, to re-shape it at their will.
We stammered that we had worked a new heaven and
    a new earth. They thanked us kindly, and
    made their peace....

Everything sickened me; I had been betrayed from the moment
    I was born. I betrayed the Arabs;
    Everything betrays everything....[7]

Lawrence had no illusion that his Arab war, spent in his white "Shaffir" costume, dressed like "a theatre knight," "a wedding cake," as he himself put it, was a monumental lie. He was telling the Arab nations that he was leading them to freedom when he knew the British and French intended to carve up their territory among themselves after the war was over. "I exploited their highest ideals and made their love of freedom one more tool to help England win.... Rankling fraudulence had to be my mind's habit ... I feared to be alone, lest the winds of circumstance, or power, or lust, blow my empty soul away."[8] Lawrence had no doubt about the hypocrisy of imperialism. While the Englishmen pretended they were pushing struggling humanity up its road, their prejudice glittered like mica; they dismissed Arab nationalism when it reared its ugly head as grotesquely "ungrateful."

But even Lawrence was trapped in this schizophrenia. He loved the metaphysical art of war; yet, in its indescribable cruelty, he knew war was indefensible. He was loyal to England, and hated the British, with their hypocritical superiority and stunted imaginations, imperialists playing the world's vicarious policemen. He loved the Arabs and was tired to death of them. He was fighting the Germans as the enemy and yet he was proud of their militarism; in their endurance in defeat they were more glorious than any other nation. What could explain Lawrence?

What explained Lawrence to Gwen was his self-hatred, his monumental self-disgust, the legacy that his "civilization" had given him. For Lawrence the world was bifurcated into instinct and reason; he had been taught to loathe the body, the animal self. *Seven Pillars* has as its foundation a loathing of the body, and therefore of the world, so extreme that he must immolate both. Gwendolyn would have read Lawrence's words:

> I was busy compartmenting-up my mind, finding instinct and reason as ever at strong war. Instinct said 'Die,' but reason said that was only to cut the mind's tether, and loose it into freedom: better to seek some mental death, some slow wasting of the brain to sink it below these puzzlements.[9]

> We Westerners of this complex age, monks in our bodies' cells, who searched for something to fill us beyond speech and sense, were, by the mere effort of the search, shut from it forever.... We racked ourselves with inherited remorse for the flesh-indulgence of our gross birth, striving to pay for it through a lifetime of misery; meeting happiness, life's overdraft, by a compensating hell.[10]

To Gwen, this was madness, of course, sheer incomprehensible madness, but it is what Lawrence's culture had taught him—the alienation from the body so profound that the sick mind sees death as the longed-for consummation. The first *world* war, the very concept was ludicrous, the world engaged in a grotesque dance of death, and Lawrence's was a good war—he would never, ever be as happy again.

Gwen did not believe that Lawrence's nihilism was personal; it was a cultural symptom. She turned to his childhood. Because the poems are written in the first person, one can almost hear Gwen speaking of herself:

The Parents

Frightened people, they stared into cameras
        and their souls came out in sepiatone.
I can't imagine them doing anything with passion,
But if it is true that the fault of birth rests somehow
        with the child, and I believe it is so,
        then I was the one that lead them on to bear me;
I was responsible for all that tossing and heaving,
I the unborn one caused their flesh to itch and burn.

I was the bed on which they lay; their shy and awkward crimes
        were once committed in my name.
Their necessary dark did not deceive me, their furtive
        Victorian midnights did not deceive me.
I was the place they sold their souls in, and now I pay
For every breath I draw with the memory of their shame.

Now it is I who must give birth to them, redeem them
        and restore them to a kind of grace,
        for I carry them around within me endlessly.
Father and Mother, be born in me.[11]

It is a powerful poetic idea: the desire of life in the unborn child causes it to be born, the drive of one sperm defeating the millions of others to penetrate the egg and create its life. And the world this child walked into was fraught with puritanical guilt about sex—those "furtive Victorian midnights." Lawrence was his parents' sin. Gwen knew his history: that he was born to upper-class parents, his father a dilettante until "converted" by his mother; his mother an Irish Catholic whom Lawrence called "The Holy Viper." His father had left an earlier marriage to live with his mother, which meant that the children were "illegitimate," that brutally quaint word. His mother would expiate her sin by eventually becoming a missionary in China. The presumption of it—that she would export her version of her guilt and repression as something that could redeem "the pagan," exporting her sickness, forcing others to believe in her God.

It was that childhood that created Lawrence, sent him in quest of another culture to escape the impossible one into which he had been born. In other poems Lawrence/Gwendolyn describes his childhood: "Let them find something else to devour besides/their own children."... "I was a standing civil war for as long as I remember." Ignored by the father, possessed by the mother, Lawrence was driven to escape by creating himself. His childhood visions became heroic. He would be the crusading knight in the brass rubbing he kept over his bed: the legitimate prince, "All colours admired him, God/admired him, God how I longed to become him." Dreaming of saving millions of people, of rescuing a whole people from tyranny, the "tender, obscene visions" of his childhood.

Often in the poems, Gwendolyn's own voice comes crashing through that of her Lawrence persona:

The Child and the Cathedral

It was in the white light of a dreadful afternoon
that I saw the child. She wore a bright

White dress and was playing with a ball in front
Of the cathedral. I knew
                           she was animal; in my hatred
Of animals I began to balance her
                      against the cathedral.

If I had to sacrifice one of them, I asked myself—
         which would it be?
                    I knew it was
The cathedral. I would destroy it to save her.

Another time I swerved at sixty miles an hour
To save some damned little bird that dashed itself out
         against my side-car. Why did it have to
Kill itself against *me*, for God's sake, why *me*?

Don't they know their existence wounds me, don't
They know I am a victim of such loveliness
         I want to die in it and cannot?
Don't they know the hatred and fear and pity go on and on
And turn into love, horrible love that bashes
         its brains out against the light?[12]

    She has built the poem on Lawrence's obsession: the "animal spirits" that he was trying to transcend. Lawrence loathed the body, yet it was the only place he truly loved. He loved the empty desert he so brilliantly described, the people he called more instinctive. He loved life in the midst of war. Indeed, he said that the real motive that kept him going throughout the war and that he could never mention was his love for the young Arab boy Dahoum, the love that could not be named. What a horrible paradox: he was bashing his brains out against the light that said he was fighting for civilization, that stone cathedral of an idea. His military training and culture had beaten out of Lawrence "the insolence of simply being." But in the poem, the last phrase "horrible love" resonates with Gwen's voice; she whose love had always been bashing its brains out.

The crisis of Lawrence's war, at the centre of his book, is his rape at Deraa, described as if this degradation were the expression of the worst the war could do to a human being. Gwendolyn recreates it:

Deraa

I started to write something like:
The citadels of my integrity were lost, or
    quo vadis from here Lawrence?
        How pathetic.
I may as well tell you that as a boy my best castle
    was besieged and overcome by my brothers.

What happened of course was that I was raped at Deraa,
    beaten and whipped and reduced to shreds
    by Turks with lice in their hair, and VD,
    a gift from their officers, crawling all over
    their bodies.
        I had thought that the Arabs were
Bad enough. Slicing the soles of a prisoner's feet
    so that when they let him return to his men,
    he went very, very slowly;
        but they were merciful.

Imagine, I could never bear to be touched by anybody;
I considered myself a sort of flamboyant monk, awfully
    intact, yet colorful.
        Inviolable is the word.
But everything is shameful, you know; to have a body
    is a cruel joke. It is shameful to be under

> an obligation to anything, even an animal;
> life is shameful; I am shameful. There.
> So what part of me lusted after death, as they smashed
> knees into my groin and turned a small knife
> between my ribs? Did I cry out or not when
> they held my legs apart and one of them rode
> upon me, laughing, and splitting open
> a bloody pathway through my soul?
> I don't remember.
> They beat me until something, some
> primal slime spilled out of me, and fire
> shot to my brain.
> On a razor edge of reality,
> I knew I would come out of this, bleeding and broken,
> and singing.[13]

In his book, Lawrence tells this anecdote graphically. The chapter begins with a reference to his "corroding sense of my accessory deceitfulness towards the Arabs." He then describes being abducted by a Turkish garrison and raped. His 1993 biographer, Lawrence James, insists that Lawrence could not have been in Deraa when he said this incident occurred. The incident is invented. But if he made up the incident itself, Lawrence knew this cruelty on other occasions, including a first assault he described as occurring in his British public school. This image of rape becomes the logical consummation of war, loathed and longed for—perfect: the animal body degraded as war dictated it must be. "There seemed a certainty in final degradation, a safety," Lawrence had written. And he rises "bleeding and broken and singing." Gwen has caught his voice exactly.

The lust for death, the thrill of war, the destruction of the body. This was the horrible, ordinary armageddon of it all. This was the evil potential in every human soul.

Tafas

We came to the village after the Turks. Everyone was
                                                    dead,
Except a little girl who came out of the shadows with
A fibrous hole gaping where her neck and body joined;
                                                    she
Cried *don't hit me, Baba*, then hobbled away and fell
Down in a little heap.
                    And then, I think, she died.
Death's little silver cock was stuck
                            between her mother's legs;
She sat on the tip of a saw
                    bayonet. And a pregnant woman
Was bent over a sheepfold,
                        the hilt of Hell's sword
Sticking up from where
                    the fetus was, into the air.
                                            And others
Were pinned by legs and arms to the ground like
                                            insects
Mounted by an insane collector.
                            We went after the Turks
And killed them all.
            Then we blew in the heads of the animals.
The sweet salt blood
            of the child ran out and out
                                    and on and on
All the way to Damascus.
                All this happened as I have said, and
The next day was Friday.[14]

As Gwen explained to her friend Samar Attar, she was not writing a political poem about imperialism. All were participants in the theatre of war—Lawrence and his Arab soldiers, on the road to liberating Damascus, turn a bloody armageddon of vengeance against the enemy, killing even the animals.

But Lawrence was more remarkable than the invention of him as the Prince of Mecca. He had at least seen the grotesque parody he had become. He had seen it in the desert. Gwen creates a man caught in a long dark night of the soul.

Solar Wind

It comes upon you unawares—
                              something racing out of the edge
Of your vision, as when you are staring at something
    and not staring—looking through—
A herd of white horses grazing on the periphery
Of your sight, and the afternoon
                      slanting into night—

Comes the wind that is
                  the colour of the sun, and your eyes
    which are nuggets of gold follow it
    down the barrels of the rifles, through
    the gun-cotton, and over the culverts,
Leaving everything gold, gold in its wake.

The past and the future are burning up; the present
    melts down the middle, a river of wind,
    wind from the sun, gold wind, anything—
And suddenly you know all the mysteries have been solved
    for you, all questions answered.

> You must find a god to worship or you will die
> In that unholy moment just before darkness and the sound
> Of guns.[15]

Lawrence was a huge paradox, an archetype of the human soul. Admirable, lyrical, loving, foul, sadistic, masochistic—the whole human puzzle. Gwendolyn spoke once about Lawrence on a CBC radio programme hosted by the poet Robert Sward. It was a panel called "Spirituality in Canada," involving a group of writers who were supposed to have a particular interest in mysticism. Normally Gwen disliked the word: "Mysticism means either an awful lot of things, or it means nothing," she once remarked.[16] She didn't even like the label "mythopoeic poet" usually assigned to her. (In an amusing aside on one of her work sheets she wrote: "I've been called a mythopoeic poet," she said. "Poor dear, have you had it for long. My aunt suffered from spleen.")[17] But Sward had a reputation for seriousness; she was accommodating and explained:

> Lawrence was fascinated with Arab mysticism, with Semitic mysticism. He was drawn to the desert Arabs, to the Bedouin in particular, among other things by the fact that they felt such great joy in renouncing the treasures of the world. It was almost a voluptuousness in not having anything, and the relationship to their God was a passionate one, intense and passionate. Lawrence was constantly in awe of this but he could never achieve it himself and I feel the same way. This is one of the reasons why I wrote this book in the first person, myself as Lawrence. I feel that way myself looking upon this marvellous religious phenomenon and not being able, quite, to participate in it. Knowing however what it means. I feel much more of a mystically minded person than

> Lawrence was. I feel perhaps closer to the kind of passionate fervour the desert Semites felt towards the God in this vast nothingness and a feeling of identification with the infinite, the one, the all, and the nothing, however one wants to put it. I feel that to Lawrence these were only words that fascinated him, concepts that fascinated him, but didn't quite touch him.[18]

This is the halting voice of someone thinking out loud on radio. When Sward asked whether she belonged to any group or was following any devotional practice, she replied: "Not at all. I think that life is a devotional practice in itself: consciously day by day aware of the sheer wonder, the sheer mystery of things at all times, that in itself is a perpetual prayer of some kind." In her Lawrence voice she had sounded more desperate: "God is not yet born, and we await the long scream/of His coming."

Human beings are biological and emotional filter systems. We survive because of what we can filter out through our senses and our forgetting. Were we not able to filter out most of the world, it would drive us crazy. Gwen did not have a good filter system. Wars, brutality, the violation of the living planet and its creatures were truths she found impossible to turn into something manageable. She had no protective skin, no carapace to hide in. Only her humour kept her going, but sometimes despair caught her and her anger was savage. The things that keep our filters working—family, material security, the commitment of intimacy—she had not been able to find in her world.

24
SEARCHING FOR ELSIE

In 1982, a new loss came to sabotage Gwen's carefully constructed equanimity: her mother was deteriorating quickly. Elsie had spent the summer of 1981 at the Queen Street Mental Health Centre, her twenty-fourth stay in a Canadian mental institution. The story repeats itself: "Patient—frail, elderly woman depressed and crying during the interview." She was being difficult, ordering the staff about as her "maids." When her requests for tea were not met she would scream and become "nasty." In her file, one detail is particularly disturbing. A nurse brought her a newspaper clipping with a photograph of Gwendolyn MacEwen and a write-up about one of her poetry readings. Elsie seemed momentarily interested, but then said she did not recognize the woman.

At the end of October it was determined that Elsie was well enough to be moved to a nursing home. She had told her doctors she was apprehensive about leaving Queen Street but that the move was for the better since her daughters had been afraid to visit her at the hospital; she knew they thought: "like mother, like daughter."[1] Gwen, she informed them, had been a patient at the Clarke Institute. In the taxi to Fairview Nursing Home, she told the driver she had won three million dollars. As they drove, her social worker reported, Elsie was able to identify many of the streets they passed.

Gwen visited Elsie at the Fairview Nursing Home, bringing fruit and flowers, while her friend Ruben Zellermeyer waited outside. Often when she returned, she told him she was glad she hadn't asked him to come up. Elsie was smaller and smaller; she didn't recognize her; or she was yelling: "You're a whore."[2] Gwen always said that she understood—it was the madness speaking.

On the eve of her forty-first birthday, Gwen received a phone call from Fairview. Her mother had died quietly in her sleep. Ruben remembered her sitting on her bed and holding herself. She started to cry, desperately: "It's OK. It's for the better," she said, as she rocked back and forth.

Mac Reynolds went with Gwen to the funeral parlour on Ossington Avenue where the body was taken. With Gwen, he had visited Elsie at the Queen Street Mental Health Centre a couple of times. Once she had been making a "pearly king" jacket, covering it with buttons. It was meant to be like the traditional button-covered garments, still resonant in her memory, that the cockney kings and queens had worn in the East London of her childhood. She insisted Reynolds try it on. It was so heavy he could hardly stand up in it, but she demanded that he take it.

The funeral parlour, as he remembered it, was terribly sad—"just Carol and Gwen and no one else." But at the funeral itself, Dora Lyons, one of the foster children from 38 Keele Street, came to honour Elsie, as did a number of nurses from the Queen Street Mental Health Centre. Carol attended for Gwendolyn's sake, feeling that by coming she was being a hypocrite.

Several days later, Gwen phoned the Queen Street Mental Health Centre and asked for the names and addresses of the nursing homes Elsie had recently stayed in. She told them that she was looking for figurines that had belonged to her mother, and was trying to trace the various residences where her mother had lived, in the hope of recovering them. The figurines were not valuable, she explained, but her mother had asked her to "look after" them.[3] They sent her a list of the six homes where Elsie had resided in the last six years, in between her seven stays at Queen Street. Though Gwen contacted the Public Trustee's office, where unclaimed goods of deceased patients were deposited, and a search was made of the "trunk room" at the Queen Street Mental Health Centre, she never found the figurines. She was only able to locate Elsie's wooden box with her costume jewellery, and the silver necklace and cross she herself had once given her. Of these few trinkets, what she kept was odd—Elsie's eyeglasses in their lilac cover. It was as if she could never bear to throw them out, for they were the only object, along with the twenty-eight books, that Ruben Zellermeyer gave me as the things Gwen saved. They have the disconcerting poignancy of trivial objects that have survived the life of their owner.

Elsie's death did not free Gwendolyn. Her non-life haunted her more than ever. To Ruben, she explained that she felt she had failed her mother—she should have been able to provide for her financial security, should have visited her more often. She felt a desperate need to give Elsie's life meaning in the only way she knew how: by writing about her. She began to conceive a poem called "Black Tunnel Wall," named for that tunnel in which her mother had hidden from the war as a child. But it was devastating to write because it brought her so close to her mother's tragic history.

Gwen returned to an article about Elsie that she had begun much earlier called "A Day in the Life of the Old Elmwood,"[4] the *girls'* hostel run by the YWCA on Elm Street, where Elsie had spent the early part of the seventies. The focus of the article is a figure called Wanda, whom Gwen follows through her meaningless day in the stale, overcrowded loneliness of the hostel, where "girls" from the age of sixteen to seventy, some ex-psychiatric patients, some ex-drug addicts and hookers, lived under the censorious eye of the woman at the front desk. There is no rhythm to the days of these broken lives except drug-induced sleep, but at least in this voluntary jail they feel safe from normal society. The day, spent waiting for it to be over, ends with Wanda on her balcony, looking out past the rusty railing at the shimmering city, dreaming of glamorous society ladies in luxury cars, laughing and dancing.

There was an irony in this. After the Elmwood Girls' Hotel had ceased operations, a woman called Sherry Brydson bought the building and spent several million to renovate it into the Elmwood Club, an exclusive private fitness institute for executive women. When Brydson bought the building, it had 150 work orders against it. The phantoms that Wanda had imagined had actually settled in.

There is nothing in Gwen's article to say that the Wanda she writes about was her mother. The material was still too dangerous, in the real sense of the meaning of danger, to get too close; the secret too dark to reveal publicly.

But Gwen wanted more from herself. She decided that if she was to write about her mother, she must return to her mother's beginnings. She would go to Poplar to find the relatives that could tell her Elsie's history before she herself had become part of it. She applied for a Canada Council travel grant for writers and waited.

Gwen maintained her health: she could be seen cycling on her little fold-up bicycle through the Annex, or swimming at the Y; she claimed to have an infinite tolerance for exercise. She practised her yoga and now she turned her full attention to her book *Noman's Land*, on which she had been working on and off since 1978, but, as Jim Polk remarked, the book had been fighting her even then and wouldn't get written.

In February 1978, she had found a clipping from *The Toronto Star* that had given her her character. The headline read: POLICE TRY TO IDENTIFY MAN WHO SAYS ONLY THREE WORDS.[5] The article began: "The only words John Doe has spoken in two weeks are: 'Come, follow me.'" It reported that a young man, described as being in his thirties, five feet nine, with long brown hair, beard, and moustache, had been picked up by police on Lawrence Avenue East in Scarborough. When he said, "Come, follow me," he led police to McMillan Avenue and stood staring at the tree. He had no identification or money, and was diagnosed as suffering from amnesia.

Gwen had found the reincarnation of her character Noman—this time he would be an amnesiac. She would resurrect him after his disappearance under Mackenzie King's arch at Kingsmere in her last *Noman* story. His memory wiped clean of all history, he would have to discover where he was. She intended the novel to be her meditations on Canadian identity and place. "Kanada is the most exotic country in the world," she had told a journalist who had interviewed her in those days. She believed that the country would not be loved until its writers made fiction of it. For that was what literature did: writers served as explorers who laid claim to the territory by simply naming it, bringing it within the mind. And Canada, only recently released from its colonial past, was, in the 1970s, just beginning to find its chroniclers.

But *Noman's Land* also became a distillation of her private obsessions. As often in her work, there are two voices in the novel: Kali and Noman, the female and the male self. In the female voice of Kali, Gwen found an equivalent for her long-ago myth of Lilith—Kali, the terrible consort of Lord Shiva, the creative/destructive female, wearing a necklace of skulls around her neck.[6] She is the backdrop to the novel, watching as the male Noman finally catches up with things she has known all along.

All the places and people Gwen knew in Toronto are included in this book: the Greek tavernas, the Arab falafel houses, High Park with its zoo and mineral baths, King Street at Roncesvalles Avenue, Toronto Island, the harbour, the fortune-tellers on Queen Street. How deeply Gwen knew the city, how deeply she claimed it and loved it; she had cycled every part of it. The world she created is haunted by myths and ghosts: there was magic in Kanada too.

But it took so long for Gwen to write this novel because its ending eluded her. She had to live its affirmation in her life before she could write it convincingly, something she could not do until she returned to it in 1982.

The only possible conclusion to her novel of the amnesiac Noman's search for place was that he must meet himself. To re-create this dramatically Gwen has Noman decide to swim Lake Ontario, to lay claim to his unknown country. Noman's Arab friend Ibrahim complains: "It's the kind of monstrous idea that this crazy country gives birth to. Like those madmen who walk on tightropes over Niagara Falls or fling themselves over the edge in barrels. A northern madness, a madness born of desperation."[7] But of course, it is a symbol.

Lake Ontario, beside which Gwen had lived so many years, is always there at the back of her novel: "the soft lisp of the lake articulating something which lay at the edge of their understanding." It is the mystery, the alienness, the unknown that lies beneath the world we claim to know. It is the mystery within the self.

Noman's marathon swim across the lake from the Niagara River to Toronto Harbour lasts twelve hours. In those twelve hours, the solitary swimmer is taken into his own absolute isolation, into the space between life and death, a space Gwen knew well. As the lake surges over Noman and his lungs betray him, he is certain that he is drowning. But suddenly the lake spits him out:

> What a colossal irony—he couldn't die now when he tried, he who had 'died' so many times in the past. Was it a luxury to even consider death in the midst of life, an unearned luxury? No, it was more than this—it was an error. It was as he had always known. You couldn't die....
>
> It occurred to him that since he was alive he may as well do something about it. And following upon that thought was another—that as long as one was alive, one may as well do it *right*, period. It was as simple as that; it always had been.[8]

When asked by reporters why he undertook the swim, Noman says: "It was the only way I knew to come home." Home is normality— "whatever that is supposed to mean." A life with Kali and her child. A love that involves both intimacy and failure, a love that is human.

"It was as simple as that; it always had been." Novels are not abstractions; they are distillations of one's life. Gwen had come through the hell of 1981. She had decided that death was an unearned luxury. She had chosen life. She had even attempted to contain her own presumptive longing; she wanted normality. When the novel was accepted by Coach House Press, she was warned that the title was a disaster; the book would disappear on bookstore shelves. She kept the title, dedicating *Noman's Land* "Once again, to all the strangers in Kanada."

25

THE BLACK TUNNEL WALL

In 1982, Gwen met a young classical composer called Christos Hatzis, who was to become an important friend. He had come from Greece to study music at the Eastman School of Music in Rochester and then at SUNY in Buffalo. Early in his student days, he took to crossing the border to visit the coffee-houses on the Danforth. He felt Toronto resonated; when he graduated he knew it would be the city he would choose to live in. He had met Nikos Tsingos at the Lyra Coffee House, a café on the Danforth where Nikos was then working, and they had become close friends.

When Hatzis moved to Toronto, Nikos introduced him to Gwen, who made it her business to establish him in the city. She contacted friends at Radio Drama at the CBC, and took him to meet David Jaeger, the executive producer of Contemporary Music, who, almost single-handedly, was to guide his career. Only in retrospect was Hatzis astonished at the amount of support she had offered: "She was a relatively closed person; nevertheless she went completely out of her way for me."[1] Gwen decided he must meet Glenn Gould.

Hatzis discovered that Gwen was one of the persons Gould called almost nightly towards the end of his life. The brilliant musician had long since distanced himself from his eager public. As he became increasingly ill, he suffered anxiety attacks. He would call people he knew at 3:00 or 4:00 a.m.—he had lost all sense of time—and keep them on the phone for hours. Gwen was one of those he called most frequently. She would have to relax him, to calm him down until he could sleep. She never explained to Hatzis how her friendship with Gould had started, nor what those early-morning conversations had been about, but she arranged for Hatzis to meet him. Sadly, Gould died of a stroke in October before the meeting could take place.

In 1983 the Array Music Ensemble of Toronto invited Hatzis to compose a chamber piece. It was his first commission, and he decided to write a song cycle. He had read Gwen's poems by then and knew immediately that he would use her work. His English was excellent, and there was something about her work—its immediacy, its refusal of elaborate structures so that the power came entirely from the words and the energy they released when combined—that overwhelmed him, reminding him of his favourite Greek poet, Elytis.

He selected "The Nine Arcana for the Kings," the sequence Gwen had written in the late sixties based on the same material as her Akhenaton novel and spoken in the persona of Akhenaton's daughter Meritaton after the death of her husband-brother Smenkhare. Gwen had reacted violently to the idea: "You can do anything but that. Not that. They are too personal." But after Hatzis had played the first few melodies on the piano for her, she decided to trust him; she found that he had discovered the melody that had always been implicit in the poems without her knowing it. He realized that his stubbornness in insisting on those poems and his probing to discover what lay behind them disturbed her deeply, but he never really understood why. He remembered once saying something to the effect that the poems seemed like *King of Egypt, King of Dreams*, but seen through clouds. She had looked at him starkly and said: "Not clouds. My problem is I see too clearly."

The "Arcana" received its world premiere at the Toronto Dance

Theatre in October of 1983 with Christine Frolick as soprano and Henry Kucharzky conducting the Array Music Ensemble. Gwen was present and read the poems between movements. "Arcana" was an extraordinary composition: Hatzis had caught the eroticism and elegiac intensity of the poems exactly.

At the time that they were working together, Hatzis was making a living playing music at a restaurant on Scollard Street called Aristides, named after its owner, one of those larger-than-life "Danforth" characters who orchestrated the world as if it were his own idea. The club was tiny, ten tables in a basement, but Aristides, who claimed to have a degree in archaeology, was a brilliant chef. People poured in as the place got smaller—Aristides had removed three of the ten tables to make room for a grand piano when he had hired Hatzis. Hatzis invited Gwen to hear the music, but she was so poor that she was reluctant to come. She couldn't afford to eat out. Aristides knew Gwen was a poet and he valued poetry. There was a notorious story that once, when he had needed to introduce a particular Neruda poem to a friend, he had called an acquaintance to have the poem delivered by taxi.

When Gwen came, Aristides feted her, but she felt very uncomfortable sitting by herself at a table when the place was packed and people were lined up on the sidewalk, and although Aristides was insistent—"Don't move. That's your table"—she didn't return. Eventually Aristides approached Hatzis: "Your friend Gwendolyn hasn't shown up again. Was it the food or the music she didn't like?" Hatzis explained the problem: "Poets can't afford you." Aristides responded by making a sign that read: THIS TABLE IS RESERVED FOR GWENDOLYN MACEWEN, and added, "If she doesn't come, nobody's going to sit there." When Hatzis told Gwen, she returned with Marian Engel. Several times over the next months she came to claim her table.

Hatzis was always amazed at Gwen's uncanny perceptiveness, recalling one memory in particular. When they were working on Arcana, Gwen dropped by his studio and said: "Let's go do something." The cinema across the street from the Ontario Arts Council was featuring a double bill of *Star Wars* and its sequel, and they decided to see the five-hour extravaganza, Gwen joking: "if only the Arts Council knew what we are doing with our money." After the show Hatzis invited Gwen for a drink. He still did not know she was a reformed alcoholic, realizing only in retrospect how tremendously difficult it must have been that he was always inviting her for a glass of wine, though she never drank in his presence. "It was stupid of me—I should have read her reactions."

Both of them had found the use of psychological archetypes in *Star Wars* fascinating, even if the mode was cartoonish, and fell into an argument over what the plot of Star Wars Three would be. Hatzis insisted that Darth Vader would be destroyed. "No," Gwen replied, "he will be redeemed. He will redeem himself. You haven't looked Darkness in the face. If you look you will see that Darkness too has a face." She didn't explain further. When Hatzis finally saw part three, *Return of the Jedi*, he suddenly realized something he hadn't noticed before: in the earlier films Darth Vader had had no face. His mask had seemed a bionic extension, making him an impersonal embodiment of pure evil. In the third film Vader took off the mask, revealing that Darkness is human; it has a face. "When I saw the third film, I was shocked—I got the chills—I remembered the conversation I had had with Gwen," he explained. He never had the opportunity to ask her what face darkness wore when she took off its mask.

Those who remember Gwen in the early eighties remember a life of extreme simplicity. In 1983, she moved to the ground-floor flat of a house at 240 Robert Street, still in the same area but south of Bloor Street. Her landlord, Roberta Frank, a professor at the University of Toronto who admired her writing, was pleased to have her as a tenant and kept the rent extremely low. Grateful and anxious not to be a burden, Gwen rarely turned to Frank when any of the normal disasters in an old house occurred, preferring to fix them herself. However, Frank had one memory of arriving with an electrician to check the wiring. As he opened the circuit box, Gwen was delighted to see the multi-coloured wires that carried the current. She did a riff on the rainbow of blue, green, yellow, red, and white electricity that descended from the sky into her house, while the disconcerted electrician looked on.

Even the prospect of being late with her rent would send Gwen into a panic. Later in her tenancy she would write to Frank: "I've never mentioned that I appreciate—(and am surprised) that you've never increased the rent since I've been here.... I wouldn't mind if you ever *had* to increase it."[2] Amused at being asked by her extraordinary tenant to raise the rent, Frank did not follow her suggestion.

Aviva Layton and Leon Whiteson had also moved from Albany Street, to Major Street, just around the corner from Robert Street. Layton saw Gwen regularly, and was astonished at the new incarnation—the last thing in the world she could imagine was Gwen as athletic. Gwen would try to convince her to go swimming—"Gwen in a swimming pool!"

Layton was also intrigued by Gwen's apartment, which was so spotless, so clean, so attractive. She hadn't realized that Gwen was a homemaker; she had made a "beautiful little nest" for herself. She had covered the chest, in which she kept her books, with a bit of embroidery and placed it under a shelf so that it was easy to slip books into it, but would have been hard to remove them. Gwen always insisted that she found people who displayed their books pretentious—they probably hadn't read half of them. On the white walls, she had her poster from the production of *The Trojan Women* and the broadsheet of her "Loch Ness Monster" poem, and had strategically placed her few icons. She also had a little garden out back where her old cat Dingbat—he survived until he was seventeen—roamed freely. But what most astonished Layton was Gwen's desk:

> It was about three inches by two and a half, the size of a postage stamp. I, who was doing nothing, had a desk the size of Bloor Street messed with papers and books. And there was Gwen who was turning out this marvellous stuff, and I remember saying: "Gwen, I've got a spare desk." No. She explained why she wanted that tiny desk, the pencils and pens just so, and not a crumpled paper.

There wasn't any evidence!

We had tea in her garden—little cookies, little tartlets. In a funny sort of way she did look as if she were playing—a little girl playing house. When I think of that sparse little desk, it was like the desk of a nun, and her place was a little like a nun's. Now that I think of it, Gwen *was* a nun, a passionate nun. She had such a strange generous soul. People who live that very inner life are alone. I think she was alone from the moment she was born to the moment she died. Yet, if somebody needed her she was there in a marvellous way.[3]

Gwendolyn always took younger poets under her wing: one was Mary di Michele, a Canadian of Italian extraction who had just brought out an astonishing early collection called *Mimosa and Other Poems*. Di Michele, like most people, loved Gwen deeply, but, also like many, felt she never knew her. She remembered her wonderful sense of humour: once sitting on her couch and reading the telephone book like a poem. Di Michele had written a sequence of poems about the love affair between the Mexican painters Frida Kahlo and Diego Rivera, and had talked with Gwen about the demon lover—how a man can lodge in a woman's psyche and will not depart. Di Michele recalled Gwen saying: "Mary, I *am* Nikos," knowing very well that she was paraphrasing Emily Brontë.

Di Michele also remembered that Gwen was honest enough to admit that she hated aging, feeling the body running down, beginning its disloyal rebellion that makes no sense to the mind. Once when she met her cycling down Robert Street, Gwen had dismounted in her purple shorts and said: "Mary, I've done it, I've turned forty. It's OK. But it's got to stop here." Thinking of Gwen, di Michele turns to me desperately, in a kind of *non sequitur*: "If only she'd had a house. She deserved that."[4]

In the late fall of 1983, Gwen fell in love again. His name was Antony. He was British and handsome, looking very much like T.E. Lawrence—

thin, with a long, narrow, classically pale face and brown hair, and, indeed, he claimed to be a distant relative of Lawrence. Certainly he had a Lawrentian charm and a wicked sense of humour. He seemed to be involved in theatre and video art and spent his time between Canada and Ireland, where his mother lived. How Gwen met him is unclear, but when she first knew him, he was looking for an apartment. Gwen's old friend the poet Joe Rosenblatt was visiting from Vancouver Island that November and knew of a flat in the home of a painter friend called Lynn. Antony was delighted.

Gwen told her friend Judy Merril that, in Antony, she had finally met a man who could replace Nikos: she planned to go with him to Ireland; she was ready to change her life. When Merril suggested she was being a bit impulsive, that perhaps she might go to Ireland, but should she not be a bit more cautious, Gwen only laughed. She had already turned Antony into the meaning for her life. Antony had, in fact, become essential, since she had lost Nikos. Gwen had been able to reach the point where she could accept that she and Nikos did not live together because she believed he would always return. Like Penelope, she could wait. But on November 8th of 1983, she and Nikos filed for divorce.

What is romantic love, romantic obsession, that Gwen could not live without it? It is, of course, simple to say, as psychologists would, that it is the theatre of projection: we see the "other" as an undiluted and perfect embodiment of all that we want and cannot claim in the self. And of course Gwen was smart enough to know this. But what if such love is rooted in loneliness? To find someone who could match her intensity would have been very hard for Gwen. This is the level of love she wanted:

Blue

body of improbable life
easy vessel of my death

> body which has never betrayed me
> body which will ultimately betray me
>
> body which is earthbound, snowbound,
> starbound, a spacesuit, a shell
>
> body of brilliant sorrows
> body of ecstasy beyond recall
>
> body which contains your body
> body of precious oils, body of love
>
> body of many wings, beloved,
> body of many blue wings[5]

What if, by temperament, you insist on sustaining that intensity, and will settle for nothing less? Of course the human world cannot offer this; it will always bring you crashing to earth. Romantic love is an act of will, a fantasy that the mind constructs, an insistence that life be what we make of it. Despite her affirmation of normality in *Noman's Land*, perhaps Gwen could never tolerate the fact that life was smaller than her own imagining of it.

Yet again, it is dangerous to speculate about Gwen. She had fallen for Antony. From her relationship with Nikos, she knew what a sheer battle human intimacy is. Was she simply looking for another chance to engage in that struggle with a powerful opponent? I think of her poem "November," where she plays humorously on a laconic line from the musical *Guys and Dolls*: "I loved you. So sue me." The relationship with Antony continued.

But there is something deeply disturbing here. With Antony, Gwen began, very casually, to drink again. She later told her therapist that she had had liquor in the house when her male friend visited because he enjoyed drinking, and then she had started to join him. She said, simply, that she thought she could handle it. I cannot ask Antony about this, since he has long since disappeared, but his landlord, Lynn, remembered him talking of his dinners of wine and salmon with Gwen.

Perhaps it was as simple as Gwen's refusal to tell Antony she had a drinking problem, even knowing the risk that drinking involved. "I can neither reveal myself, nor hide. No matter what I do, I am naked," she had written in her Lawrence persona. "With Gwen's history, you must be secretive," her friend Aasta Levene had said. "There is the self-doubt. You are empty inside in some way, and you can never fill up." There is no more human impulse than the impulse to fill oneself with another.

In the spring of 1984, Gwen was awarded a Canada Council grant to write "The Black Tunnel Wall." The project involved visiting England and Scotland to trace her ancestry, and she began to make her plans. Her friend Mac Reynolds insisted that she stay at the Chelsea Arts Club, where he still had many friends from his old days in London. He was worried about her flying, knowing how it terrified her, knowing that if the trauma proved too great she might weaken and find herself drinking again. Would it be possible for her to get on a plane without getting completely cut first? He suggested that, together, they make a trial flight to Ottawa just to see if she could get through it, but when he asked a few days later when they were going, she replied brightly: "I've already done it." She must have hated the self that had to lie to Reynolds, to perpetuate the charade that she had not returned to drinking. She could not have risked the humiliation of telling him the truth.

When she left for London on May 26th, her friend Ruben took her to the airport. He remembered her fear, her saying that she didn't think she could do it. But then, as people entered the turnstile, making their way to the departure lounge, a woman arrived with a baby. Gwendolyn looked at the baby and said: "If a baby can do this, I can." And laughed. All she needed was to get on the plane going. "Coming home on a plane never bothered her," Ruben explains. "Coming back was nothing."

From her jottings in her notebook, I see she tracked down her aunts

Jess and Winnie and went to visit 26 Byron Street in Poplar. That district of London was still shockingly poor, with its bleak, dreary lanes and desolate little houses with their narrow little doors. She learned about her grandmother from her Aunt Winnie. Winnie described her mother as a washerwoman, a north-country woman, extremely strong. She recalled, as children, folding the washing in blankets and delivering it. On Sunday, after chapel, they had had to drop into the pub to get their dad his ale, and had been terribly embarrassed, knowing the neighbours coming back from church would see them. It was Jess who told her that what caused Elsie's problem was that she was the last of the children and "maybe Mother had tried to take something so as not to have her."[6]

Gwen seemed to be fine. She visited museums: the Victoria and Albert, the National Gallery, and the Science Museum. She spent time with Reynolds's friend Lee Kenyon, famous for his Second World War exploits—his experience in a German P.O.W. camp during the Second World War was the basis for the film *The Great Escape*. Kenyon talked of building the tunnel out of the camp and making it to freedom. She went to visit the poet Jeni Couzyn, who had moved from Canada to London, and they had a wonderful time as they talked of poetry as a metaphysical quest. She met the diplomat and writer Charles Ritchie at Canada House, although he later remembered little of the encounter[7], and then visited Blood Axe Press. The Press was thinking of bringing out her Lawrence poems, though the idea was eventually dropped.

But there were subtle hints that Gwen's sense of security was slowly being undermined. She found herself frightened by the "literati" at the Chelsea Arts Club, intimidated by their posh British accents. Mac Reynolds had told her she would be respected and admired as a poet at the club, but she only felt alienated and alone. She hid out upstairs, eating in her spartan room with its coin-fed heater instead of in the communal dining room, where the artists met in the evenings. She was annoyed with herself that she could not find the courage to discover "who the nice ones were." Her shyness became defensive. "I feel closer to Mom's working class family than to these artists here," she wrote in her notebook. "It is false, it will pass.... I don't like what I am here in London, I don't like being a writer." She told herself that her grandmother, a washerwoman with eleven children in the slums, had more endurance than these "intellectual snobs." Feeling completely exposed, she thought longingly of the genuine admiration and respect she had at home in Canada.

On June 1st, she began to elaborate her feelings in her notebook:

> Feeling shitty, rain again & cold & stomach queasy—Westminster in morning for rubbings—then rest & read in room.
>
> A voice inside me—"I command you to be still."
>
> Evening—definitely a bad day for me—feel nauseous & lost & scared & alone—but I recall how this sort of thing used to have the power to destroy me & now I know it won't. The fear of fear, the crippling dread of something horrible about to happen—but I know what it is now & I will not succumb. All the strength & lessons I learned from my experiences of the 70's should be with me now to serve me, for me to draw from. To seek the center & be still, to know there is only this day, this hour, this minute, to get through. I am thousands of miles from home & the pit of my stomach is green—perhaps I should have made this trip shorter—(I *can* make it shorter, I can go home any minute) but now 1/3 of it is over. It is only time. The *sea* is between me & home, that's what makes it different from just being far, like B.C. Just saw Lee playing pool downstairs—I should go & talk to him—he saw me & asked "are you all right?" a little concerned.
>
> But I came here partly to define my life to myself. Now at 42, *what is important*? What really matters to me? Warmth & love, security. Someone at my side, a companion & this is

> what Ruben is, a brother. Never take this for granted. I am sure I have already told him that, & told myself. Home matters, but I never doubted that, nor did I kid myself that I "like to travel"—I knew before I left that I'd have some bad times like today, but I wanted to *know*, I have to *know* that I can ride them out. I hate to travel, to be far from home. I have always hated it. With N[ikos] in Greece it was easier, I was not alone. So I must ride this out, command myself to be still, to seek the center, the quiet, to draw from the self I have constructed & re-constructed over the years. It is not strength, it is quietness.[8]

Gwendolyn did force herself to go downstairs to talk with Kenyon and felt better. She phoned Ruben, "dear friend" she called him, and decided there was a simple solution: she would go to Glasgow to see her father's family, and then determine whether to shorten her trip. If she went home from Glasgow instead of returning to London, she consoled herself that she would still have had a two-week trip.

She wrote sketches for poems:

> It is in the Garden that you'll find
> the Enemy ...
> The world offends him, he is
> hideously sane.
> He has been in the garden
> since the beginning of time
> And will live here forever
> staring at nothing
> thinking of new ways
> to bend & break your mind.
>
> This is the most fascinating thing
> this fear of fear

it can lead you right through the garden gate
into a world where
black sun flowers grow
tall as towers.

Notebook jottings:

> This trip is about my parents—I think I know why they left—I see now the space, the freedom, the terrifying openness of Canada. But it is my country, no doubt of it now.

> I didn't come to suffer. I am *half-way home!*

> Huge thunderstorm last night & I dreamt of A(ntony) & then Mary Ellen (myself) packing bags & bags of things & escaping from some hotel—she had committed some crime, is lame (because of an abortion) & I am covering for her to owner of the hotel.

> Today the sky looks just like the sky—"the world is more benign than we think."

> Evening—so the London trip has come to an end. It's cold outside & I'm calm & tired, a little scared of what's still to come, a little sad—always homesick, but just a little more time—I'll phone Ruben from Glasgow tomorrow night.

> June 4 dream:
> Something about Salah. Then Ruben & I in Toronto, then me combing the grey wig of the "medicine man" into my own hair until it comes out even & merged, the lengths of both sides perfectly even, as I had not thought, & the old Indian's voice assuring me that this was right,

> that things did match after all. Then seeing a TV ad for the four part TV drama of Ulysses ... Back to Indian, now in jail, I in my wig decide to go in & exercise my influence in freeing him, even though he has committed no crime—Ruben asking—"what are you doing?"

Gwen left London by train. As she looked out the window from her seat in the first-class compartment, she thought of the mangy stray dog she saw on the platform and "the millions of people who dream of a trip like this & save for years." Arriving in Glasgow on June 5th, she records: "Possibly the worst day I can imagine." There is no hint as to why. She had met her father's family, and her cousin Susan. She jotted a few anecdotes of genealogy: "My great-grandfather was Alexander who ran away with table maid to America. Susie recalls stories of wild men and grandma McEwen using a rifle." She left in the fog for Edinburgh—"my spirits in the pits, my stomach churning, nervous panic coming on." The panic only subsided when she touched base and phoned Ruben in Toronto. "I must sleep now and decide what to do—ask Providence for guidance."

On the 6th, she visited the Maritime poet Fred Cogswell, editor of the magazine *Fiddlehead*, whom she had known since the sixties when he had published her early poetry, and who was then writer-in-residence at the Canadian Studies Centre in Edinburgh. She had phoned to say she was visiting relatives in London and Glasgow, and was tired to death of them. Homesick for Canada, she needed some relief. Cogswell had never spent time alone with Gwen. He found the visit pleasant and thought Gwen charming, though nothing of moment was said.[9]

That night she decided she had had enough of Scotland. "Tried to phone A[ntony] but could get no answer of course. I'll regret this when I return," she wrote, "but now I give in, my mind & nerves can't stand more."

She left Scotland on the 7th. In her day journal she recorded a single entry: an etymological reference to the poet Robert Burns's dialect, which no one spoke any more: "*dreich*: dismal (adj) the mind of a man of winter."

26
BACK ALLEY BLUES

When Gwen returned to Canada, one of the first things to greet her was the decree absolute of her divorce from Nikos. It was dated June 13, 1984. The second thing was the final clarification of her relationship with Antony.

That summer Antony left for his periodic trip to stay with his mother in Ireland and invited Gwen to follow him. Clearly, something was disturbing her. Antony was elusive—her response when she had phoned him from England was: "could get no answer of course." In a love affair, we so often participate in our own deception. She knew, and had not been admitting to herself, that Lynn, the painter whose basement apartment he rented, had become more to Antony than simply his landlady. The day after he left, she phoned Lynn to say that she and Antony were lovers, she intended to join him in Ireland. She wanted to know the nature of Lynn's relationship to him. Lynn said she too had been invited to Ireland. Gwen had better come over; they needed to talk. It was then that Gwen discovered Antony had been sleeping with both of them and they learned he also kept his former girlfriend on the hook. He had been pledging undying loyalty to all three of them.

At first, Gwen was wild with rage and pain at the discovered duplicity. It seemed to Lynn, however, that it didn't take very long for them to find themselves laughing at the ridiculousness of it all: two women caught in a plot made trivial by repetition: both in love with the same philandering man. They began to do hilarious riffs on Antony's kind of man—the one who stores his stuff in women's basements, which he collects when he is ready to move on.

Antony was soon writing desperate letters from Ireland, shamefaced notes about how he had gotten things into rather a mess and what a mix-up it all was. They read his letters to each other. Beneath it all, of course, both women had been deeply hurt and both were angry. Gwen and Lynn became friends, a friendship that would continue until Gwen's death.

Lynn invited me to her house in the northern part of the Annex, the same house in which Antony had rented the basement flat a decade ago. She is an artist in her late forties, and the house had that dishevelled feel of a life that has been improvised for years without much financial stability. Her paintings, surreal and dramatic in colour, covered the walls. Over herbal tea, she offered me a portrait of Gwen with the same painful urgency I have sensed from all Gwen's friends. One of the legacies of the love felt for Gwen is the despair of having failed her.

Lynn now looks back at Antony, still somewhat fondly, as a man who turned out to have enormous weaknesses. How then to account for his charisma? We try. In our conversation, we build a profile of such a man. "Antony was exciting to be around," Lynn tells me.[1] There was that wicked sense of humour, and a mad-cap adventurous quality about him: puckish, impish—digging up blue scillas in the luxurious gardens of Casa Loma and planting them in Lynn's garden, and no doubt in Gwen's too. What is the attraction of such a man? Is it simply that men who haven't settled have an aura of mystery about them? Or is it that Antony's kind of man reads women very well, seeming to offer a thread of connection with a woman that suggests a meeting at a profound level, an intimacy that seems immediate and unique. But, in fact, it's all a game played on the surface, offered to every woman, beneath which there's a dark labyrinth too complex to enter.

Lynn insists there was something rare about Antony, as if he belonged to another era, or came from another context—he was one of those Byronic figures who exert a very strong pull. But the funny thing is that men who appear to be larger than life usually turn out to be smaller than life. The charm is often a tool, a style, for a man in retreat from himself. There was no hint of what Antony's trouble was—he had spoken vaguely of the cruelty of the mother with whom he lived in Ireland, the woman whom his lovers were expected to join, but he was too evanescent, too much a man in perpetual movement to offer much self-reflection. For such a man it is necessary to have many women—there is safety in numbers—so that confrontation becomes impossible. But perhaps that is too kind. Perhaps it is sheer narcissism. It is too puzzling. We don't know.

"What was Antony for Gwen?" I ask. Looking back ten years, Lynn thinks Antony was ripe for Gwen's theatre of projection. He could be a mythic figure. "In fact had he been capable of monogamy, of commitment," she tells me, "he would have been perfect." There was something frugal, even monastic about Gwen, as if she'd taken a vow of poverty. Antony was also frugal. She remembers them cutting each other's hair once—they had been so gentle and humorous. When she thinks of them in retrospect, they matched in some ways—he was intelligent and funny. If only he had been up to her.

Gwen had a terrible summer. Beneath the sardonic humour, she was deeply grieved to have found that, once again, having exposed the whole of herself in love, she had been terribly self-deceived. When Antony returned from Ireland and asked to collect the few belongings he had left in her basement, she would have nothing more to do with him.

She had fantasies of revenge. Once, browsing in a second-hand shop on Dundas Street, she found a pair of red satin sheets, and bought them. She was going to invite Antony for a candle-light dinner and when he came into the bedroom, as he rolled back the red sheets, he would find her, Lynn, and his ex-girlfriend under them. Did Gwen think they would be like vengeful Thracian women tearing him to shreds? She must have decided the idea was feeble. She gave the red satin sheets to her niece, Carol Anne.

That autumn she pulled herself together and took a job as writer-in-residence at the University of Western Ontario in nearby London, which meant she was living reasonably on a stipend of $18,000. It was good to feel involved in the world, to break the solitude of writing, since such solitude is costly. Gwendolyn complained that she became more acutely aware of the loneliness as she got older, but that she accepted it as an inevitable part of the writer's life. "It's an intense solitude, that only a writer can understand, and it can often be excruciating, of course, but it's absolutely necessary."[2] She was working on her new book, a collection of poems she would call *Afterworlds*.

She still had hopes of achieving an international audience. Judy Merril had introduced Gwen's poetry and fiction to her American agent, Virginia Kidd. Kidd's partner and daughter, Karen Emden, was very enthusiastic about her work, but just as Gwen was expecting something to happen, she was informed in November that Emden had died of post-operation trauma at the age of twenty-six. Gwen must have felt cursed.

Throughout the fall Gwen had been preparing herself for a much deeper loss. Her close friend Marian Engel was dying. The lymphoma she had been fighting for six years had finally defeated her. When she was not commuting to London, Ontario, Gwen spent most of her free time with Judy Merril and Joyce Marshall, visiting Engel in hospital. Marian died on February 16, 1985, at the age of fifty-one. The last week had been an agony, and Gwen was glad when Marian was released from further torment. She wrote to Judy Merril, who had taken a brief vacation in Jamaica, only to be stranded there with an attack of appendicitis, to tell her about the memorial service.

Feb 27/85

Dear Judy,

Ann phoned to say you were out of hosp. and OK. GOOD! It must have been rotten for you, and even worse being down there alone with the grief of Marian's death. I told Ann I had sent clippings, etc (this is one time you might appreciate my methodical nature)—and am enclosing more things now.

The memorial service is tomorrow, and in a way this letter will help me organize my thoughts on what to say....

I think I'm going to say that Marian and I were light years apart as writers—I was never a great reader of fiction, and she didn't quite understand my poetry—so it was wonderful—we didn't have to be literary! Also, some recent memories, including you and I with her in the hospital room last summer with the awful hamburger [plastic hamburgers, silly blue food, that we declared a feast; nothing had tasted so good for ages] and the laughter and us talking about what we might have been if we hadn't become writers.

Also—she brought me a marble egg from Paris (something magical for Gwen, she had written on her shopping list)—and me visiting her at home about a week before the end saying Marian, let me do something USEFUL—so she suggested I straighten the books on the shelves (perfect job for me) and I came across the children's classic At the Back of the North Wind, which she said I should take. Marian, I said, do you realize you're always giving me *children's* books? O, O, I should watch that, she said, taking a long drag on her cigarette and giving me that wicked sideways grin. You read me so well, I told her.

Also—an amazing conversation about a month before when she said she was thinking again of finding her twin sister, but didn't really want to ... and I said (God help me)

> Marian, I think the sister you're looking for and don't want to meet is your celestial twin, your spiritual twin, your *ka*, your soul ... Another long puff on the cigarette, then, with absolutely no malice or sarcasm [considering the impertinence and PRESUMPTION of my remark]—O Gwen, you're so smart.
>
> Then I guess I'll end my piece tomorrow night with the poem (enclosed) and hope to hell all I've said will hit the right note, the right tone, and be a proper tribute to our brilliant and gutsy and much-to-be-missed friend.
>
> What else to say? I know if you were here you'd make a far better job of it than I will ... but I thought you'd like to know that I'll mention you in the course of things, and I know you'll be there in spirit. Tiff and several others are going to speak ...
>
> Take care, write if you can or want to—I guess it won't be long til you're back. Gwen.[3]

Engel's daughter, Charlotte, remembered the blue food. "Gwen had these little devices to take your mind off your troubles. She'd say silly things like: 'Why is there no blue food?' Berries didn't count. And she'd get us going. My mom was bedridden and we all sat around her room, trying to think of what things could be blue food. It was hilarious. When I see something now that might be blue food, I always think of Gwen."[4]

At Engel's memorial service, Gwen read the poem she'd written for her, "The Yellow House." Engel had often fantasized about a house she planned to buy on Cape Traverse, Prince Edward Island, but had been much too sick ever to go look at it. On one of her reading tours, Gwen had stopped by to see the yellow house and had made a drawing of it, which she brought back to hang in Marian's hospital room so that she could fantasize her escape. At the service, she spoke of the great courage with which her friend had faced death. She had felt that Marian was not just leaving, she was going somewhere.

Marian had told Gwen to take the flowers from her garden after she died; they would need a new home. Gwen required a car to transport the plants and asked her friend Aasta Levene to accompany her. As they dug up the bulbs and shrubs in the drizzling rain and planted them in Gwen's tiny, sunless backyard that had turned into a mud flat, Levene remembered Gwen hovering over the plants: "They're going to grow," she said. Her almost "child-like optimism" astonished Levene. It was so "exquisite." Those same bulbs would eventually be taken from Gwen's backyard and replanted in the Marian Engel Memorial Garden at the Metro Toronto Public Library. When the library was renovated, the bulbs were thrown out.

In October 1985, Nikos finally married a Greek Canadian woman whom he had met years earlier. Gwen knew of her and could recognize that she suited Nikos: she came from the same cultural background, was kind, extremely supportive, and obviously loved Nikos very much; she never questioned the sense of responsibility that he felt towards Gwen. Gwen sent her a letter with best wishes for her marriage, but of course she was devastated and her anger surfaced indirectly.

Christos Hatzis had been Nikos's best man at the wedding. Shortly after the wedding, he was offered a film project and suggested the producers also consider Gwen. When he mentioned this, she wrote a furious, snapping letter in which she accused him of using her high profile as a poet for his own advantage. He was disturbed by the unjust accusation until he realized what had motivated it. Because they were friends, she viewed his being Nikos's best man as a treasonous act.

She wrote to Hatzis in early December: "I feel I must apologize for my outburst recently; as I explained to Nikos, I had been through a terrible month, and had felt rejected and disappointed in many ways. Unfortunately I tended to take it out on everyone in sight. Cheers for the season!, Gwendolyn."[5]

Gwen, Hatzis realized, had never gotten over Nikos. "Gwen must have been a very difficult person to live with," he says. She could have the occasional, very nasty mood, and when this happened the person who was its object would be taken aback because her response seemed to have no relation to real events:

> Gwen could be very friendly and very close to people because she could always withdraw somewhere, but when you live with a person you cannot do that. The person has to be close to all sides of you. Nikos must have had a very difficult time because he also loved her. There was just a point where it was very difficult to continue. But I think I'm trying to invent explanations for everybody. There are no explanations in human relationships. They either happen or they don't happen.[6]

Hatzis understood that both Gwen and Nikos felt that the best time, the time of least friction, in their relationship had been that first winter when they had begun to live together. Nikos had been a new immigrant and the snow world of Canada had seemed magical. That things worked so well may have been due to that magic, but it was also important that they were isolated; there was no interference from other people. "Whatever insecurities they had in a crowd weren't there." It had, of course, always worked that way. Gwen had always chosen men who were isolated, without language, to whom she could be the whole world.

"I was close to Nikos, and that was good enough for Gwen," Hatzis continues. "She envied me in a sense—that I could spend time with Nikos. We could go here and there and make nothing of it. Every time she was with Nikos, she wanted it to be such an important time, and that same fact destroyed it by the very amount of importance invested in it. Nikos would meet her for breakfast, perhaps twice a week, and he really cared about her and wanted to be there, but there was always this incredible energy because it meant so much."

What few people knew was that on October 22nd, Gwen had renewed her sessions with Barbara Bruce at the Addiction Research Foundation. She had been binge-drinking and had again to face the fact that her drinking was not something she could control on her own. That must have been frightening, she who had always counted on her own strength of will; and humiliating, feeling as she did that the world was waiting for her to lose hold. Willing her own reality had been her survival mechanism throughout her life. She was deeply ashamed and deeply critical of herself for the relapse.

Again, the diagnostic charts emerge in Gwen's life. Bruce writes: "Together we started doing some problem solving around Gwen's difficulties."[7] Gwen had decided that she needed to get out of the house, where alcohol was too strong a temptation, and Bruce suggested she become involved in a swimming programme at the Crippled Children's Centre. She seemed enthusiastic at the prospect of using her skills to help someone else. An appointment was made for the end of November.

Gwen kept the appointment, but it cost her a great deal, consumed as she was by guilt. She had not been able to follow Bruce's advice, and now they talked of her becoming involved in some of the city's literacy programmes. She presented Bruce with a poem she had written for her and asked if she could dedicate it to her in her next book. Beneath its playfulness is a terrifying realization: Bruce was deflecting her from the "gates of hell." There were blind spots in her vision she could not face or fathom. She recognized that her own camouflage was so deep that not even she could penetrate it.

Seeing Eye Dogs

for Barbara

If my cat sits long enough on my typewriter
She might write something wonderful.
Meanwhile the dog stars, the sundogs, those fake suns
Blind us who are addicted to light and dark, whose eyes
Are windows often peering into nowhere,
Into the phony houses of our lives,

While you and your black all-seeing dog
Lying in the corner of your room deflect me
From the gates of hell, then he
Leads you through the streets of this shady city.

Already I perceive the holes in my vision, the blind spots
I dare not face, I and my fellow fools
Glancing through day and night, dancing, adoring
The glare of our darkness.

Last night on TV Sherlock Holmes got into a carriage
Led by a horse with blinkers, and Sherlock's eyes
Went prancing, reflecting clues and theories
And focusing, finally, on the fact (surmise)
That the world was just as mad as he was.

And went home and shot up on something from the boredom
The boredom of it all.

Then I watched this fish with the craziest camouflage ever—
A phony eye at his tail so his enemies couldn't tell
If he was coming or going or what the hell
He thought he was doing.

So when I turn away from you I have eyes at the back of
my head
Which allow me to see a world I've left behind—
And the dear creature who is your eyes
Lies regarding me with horror and surprise,
That I might glimpse reality perhaps once in a lifetime,

Or if my cat sits long enough on my typewriter
She might write something wonderful, sublime.[8]

Is there also an implicit despair, that while the seeing-eye dog, "that dear creature," saw her clearly, she doubted that Bruce, indeed that anyone, could help? The charts continue. Gwen, Bruce discovered, felt herself cut off; dealing with people was difficult. Her reputation as a writer kept people at a distance; they thought of her on a pedestal, not as a "human being." Gwen left the office without making another appointment.

Despair had caught Gwen again and her anger was almost savage. She was losing the strength to keep it all going. Life resisted her on too many levels. The kind of love and intimacy she wanted she had not found. She was also deeply angry that after all her work, and few worked harder, she still could not survive directly from her books. She might have had recognition in literary and academic circles—a Ph.D. thesis had been written about her work[9]—but she had to exist on grants and readings, or occasional writer-in-residencies, which, because of her shyness and habits of secrecy, she often found depleting in the extreme. She had always believed that art mattered, and indeed was treated as if it did, with an entry in the *Canadian Who's Who* and newspaper clippings calling her one of Canada's most brilliant writers, but poetry did not matter enough to contemporary culture that one could live from it.

And there was something worse. Poetry was becoming a no man's land, and not only in Toronto. Many writers, like Margaret Atwood or Michael Ondaatje, had managed to switch to fiction; they could switch easily and not lose anything in the process because their way of thinking was, in a sense, totally independent of the medium. But Gwen had a poet's vision; even her novels were *poetic* novels. And poetry was dying. Modern culture gave lip-service to poetry, but who really read it? A good book of poems would sell five hundred copies.

Gwen also hated what was happening to Toronto in the eighties, the decade of greed. It was becoming a mean city, a city that saw itself as real estate where fortunes could be made by tenant evictions and land flips. The sixties had seemed to provide some space for the artist— one could live in a cheap loft and survive on little. In the mid-eighties many of the artists and second-hand book dealers were fleeing to small towns, where one might still live an existence driven by art rather than by money.

The Annex neighbourhood was becoming a less generous place to live. Most of the streets were threaded by back alleys, usually unpaved lanes lined by fences, and the lanes were filled with stray cats and the occasional bag lady. Gwen loved cats: over the years there had been Dingbat, Prune, Constantine, Katerina, Caligula, and many more. When Prune died, she wrote a gentle elegy with the line: "Everything dies and I'll get God for that." In "Magic Cats" she had humorously described cat psychology: "Cats on the whole are loath to discuss God.... When cats grow listless (i.e. lose their lists) they cease to entertain fleas. They mumble darkly about radishes and death."[10] Cats were shrewd, occasionally nasty, but essentially sane creatures, and often better companions than human beings.

In the back alleys around Robert Street, Gwen undertook the care of the wild cats, the descendants of unwanted animals cast out by owners in the hope that they would disappear. She bought cat food and every day changed and replenished the food and water supply in Coca-Cola boxes she set out for the strays. She found there were at least two or three other people, "my shady accomplices" she called them, who were doing the same. Together they kept the stray cats fed and removed the stiff little corpses of the ones who died. Gwen also built a small shelter of several stories at the bottom of her garden for the cats, which, of course, made her unpopular with the neighbours, who wanted to be rid of the pestilence.

Ruben remembered that in 1986, Gwen was engaged in an altercation about the cats with a particular neighbour who lived near the Henry Morgenthaler Abortion Clinic on Harbord Street. Her walks through the lanes to feed the cats would take her out onto Harbord Street, among the vituperative pro-lifers singing and chanting as they picketed the centre. One night, he insists, she was threatened by a man in a car: "Don't feed the cats." Soon Gwen found that many of the cats had been poisoned.

Gwen responded angrily by writing an article for the popular magazine *Now* called "Back Alley Blues." Written in February, when her despair at human nature had taken a bad turn, it has a Swiftian quality of misanthropy to it—a hatred of human stupidity that is almost savage. Gwen was neither crusader nor eccentric. She was simply saying that how we treat animals is symptomatic of our morality as human beings. Who among the pro-lifers were marching out of concern for the unwanted children who would be born, rather than fired up with their own ideological arrogance?

> This [that she was feeding the cats] bothers certain residents of the area who say things like: "if you stop feeding them, they'll just go away!" I believe this means die, but that's the sort of word which, when uttered aloud, tends to become real. So it doesn't get uttered, and you wonder at those humans carrying their garish signs along Harbord Street who also never really say what lies in store most of the time for the world's unwanted creatures—back alleys, disease, hunger, poverty, foster homes, neglect, jail, drugs, suicide, and so on....
>
> It has been said that Canadians are far too sentimental about animals. I think it's time we realized that when we speak of animals, we speak of ourselves. For many people animals aren't really "real," any more than the starving millions of Africa and Asia are real....
>
> By all means Let Them Live—every last pathetic one of them—and if there are too many of them, we can just fling them into the lanes of the world and pretend they don't exist. Does India exist, does Bangladesh exist, does anything so unthinkable it puts the mind into a numb stupor really exist?.... Wait!—I have it, I just thought of something! *Maybe if we stop feeding them they'll just go away?*[11]

She, who had so little money, had adopted a child from El Salvador through a Save the Children programme. In one of her letters to him, she had sent a picture of herself, to make herself real; he had written back to say that she had nice eyes.

At the time she was writing her article, Ruben remembered sitting with Gwen at "The Windows," their name for the Other Cafe on Bloor Street, and a woman arrived with a baby. The way Gwen looked at the baby was so jarring it seared his memory. To him it was like watching a two-thousand-year-old woman looking at a child, so distant had she come to feel from human beings. She was like T.E. Lawrence, feeling contempt not for other men, but for all they do. It was as bad as that.

There were many reasons, and a number of them far from personal, why Gwen continued to drink. Her few close friends who were in on the secret of her drinking could see the danger and tried yet again to help. Judy Merril had been reading *Noman's Land* and wrote from Jamaica:

> 17 January 1986
>
> Dearring Gwendolyn—
>
> ... Today I love and miss you very much and as it happens—
>
> Tomorrow a friend of mine is returning to TO and will carry letters up, so I have a sense of immediacy in writing to you that is impossible with the usual anticipation of two weeks or so delay in delivery.
>
> I have been wanting to write to you not only since I arrived here, but since the last evening I saw you—when you came to pick up the stereo—which you may not remember too clearly, because you were (not uncharmingly, but) very drunk at the time.
>
> Are you still reading? Please, I hope so.

I had in fact been wondering from various familiar signs, whether you were back on the booze again, but was disinclined to ask about it, because I know how you feel people are always watching/waiting to see you Fall From Grace. Well, I don't give a shit about Grace, but I do about you, and that night you were not only acting, but smelling, drunk. So I had my answer, but it took me a while to figure out just what business I had saying anything to you about it—not to mention getting clear in my head exactly what I meant to say.

OK, with luck I've waited long enough so that you have things under control again, and all that follows is unnecessary. If so, please file this letter for next time it starts to get bad enough for you to reach for a bottle, because I might never be in just this space to say it again.

So Rainmaker's/Noman's has made that clear—while renewing ponderings about myself and the nature of my true affections. In your case, right now, you know, I love you dearly. I love your wild chatter and space-people humour and the serious giggling we do together, and having someone with whom to share some (sane? mad? irrelevant) parallax-making visions of the mad?/sane? surround. I don't want to lose all that, especially so soon after Marian....

Of course, I don't have all that when you're drunk anyhow (brace yourself this is Straight-Arrow Judy on the computer now) because (this is what I meant above, see word "familiar") you start repeating the same joke over and over and can't hear what I'm saying (DEADLY sin!). So if you drink enough to kill yourself, I lose a friend who matters a lot to me—and if you just drink enough to keep the pain fogged-out, I lose most of it.

(Note I'm not talking about what YOU lose, because that's YOUR choice, of course, and how the fuck do I know if you're losing or gaining more, in YOUR experience?) But what I realized this morning was something (more important?) silly word—anyhow)—

Flashback: I had another friend I loved very dearly indeed, and indeed still do, though I have little contact with him now, because he too is a writer whose work I also love—sometimes—and what I found out eventually with him was that the work I most want to see from him gets written ONLY WHEN HE'S DRINKING—and the person I want to be with is at home, so to speak, only when he's not. Okay this guy has an incredible constitution, and at almost-75, after 40-45 years of getting on and off the juice, he's still relatively healthy. Maybe that could work out for you if necessary—

NECESSARY? That's what I've been getting around to. I THINK Noman's and the new poems were written sober. If indeed they were written drunk, the hell with my personal loss—just keep drinking, baby, because my loss is the world's gain—and also my own. But if that IS the case, try and bear in mind that whether you've been seeing me or not, any time the booze starts to threaten your physical well-being and your ability to write, if you holler I will come and try and get you back on your feet. I mean, in your chair, at the desk.

But if my first guess was right, and you had not started secret tippling when you were doing that work ... so—if you did that writing on water and coffee (or fkrissake, Pepsi or even PERRIER!), and if you ARE still boozing now—

Pick up the phone NOW and get hold of Mac and ask him to get the hell over and help you get out of it. AND/OR

Pick up the phone NOW (or next) and get hold of the blind lady therapist and tell her you're on your way over, AND/OR
Pick up the phone next time you wake up relatively sober and phone [me] ...

Hay, maybe you'd phone even if you don't need me, just to let me know you're still speaking to me? Or send a night-letter? Or anyhow write?

Much love, dammit![12]

Gwen did not write to Merril. On the 3rd of March, 1986, all the horror of the disease that had sabotaged her in 1981 returned. When she was desperate, Gwen had always turned to her friend Joyce Marshall. That night she asked Marshall to come over because she was very ill. Marshall remembered sitting through the night on the end of her bed, "trying to soothe her while she shivered and shook."[13] In the morning, with Mac Reynolds's help, she took her to the Toronto Western Hospital, where Gwen admitted she had been drinking steadily for three months. She had quit three days prior to the admission. Such an abrupt termination caused withdrawal symptoms, fever, nausea, and, most terrifying, seizures. The effort to reach towards health on her own was dangerous. This had always been Gwen's tragedy, to be rebuffed by life when she reached for it, perhaps because she insisted on reaching for it alone.

She would not be caught in the web of health-care institutions as her mother had been. As soon as she was strong enough to walk, she signed herself out and returned home. The hospital had been dreadful, dark, and gloomy. She wanted to be surrounded by her own possessions and assured the hospital doctors she had a circle of very good friends who would stay with her. She wrote a note to Bruce: "I feel I should explain my hasty leaving from the hospital; I felt I could do better at that point at home, and in fact I now feel fine, solid, and back to the state I was in during the last years of sobriety. It was indeed a relapse, violent, but temporary. I want to thank the excellent staff...."[14] She did not see Barbara Bruce again for almost a year.

While stating that there seems to be a genetic basis to alcoholism, Joyce Marshall wrote in her memoir of Gwen: "It's human to think that there must be a reason—or reasons—that would send a person back again and again to poison." "When I asked [Gwen] why she'd begun to drink again this last time, she told me that her mind 'had become saturated.' She didn't say with what and I didn't ask." Marshall had learned to be cautious with questions about alcoholism. She did finally ask why Gwen hadn't told her about whatever it was that had saturated her mind, and Gwen had only responded: "Foolish pride." Marshall believed that Gwen's sobriety held more or less for a year, long enough to see her through the completion of *Afterworlds*, and to write her children's book *Dragon Sandwiches*, lovingly dedicated to her niece's son, Christopher.

27
AFTERWORLDS

In the fall of 1986 Gwen was appointed writer-in-residence at the University of Toronto. The prospect helped to pull her up. She, who had never completed her high-school matriculation, was being acknowledged by Canada's most prestigious institution. Ruben remembered how she had prepared herself with such excitement. That summer she wrote the university's numerous libraries to determine their holdings of her work. To Hart House, Sigmund Samuel Library, Massey College, Trinity College, University College, and Victoria College, she sent copies of the books they needed to complete their collections. Somewhat naïvely, she took the position very seriously. She was shocked to discover that the position carried little kudos within the institution, which went on under the pressure of its own momentum, barely aware of any individuals within it. There were two small ads in the student newspaper about the new writer-in-residence. She sat in her office waiting for the students who might have read it to come, and was occasionally invited to read her work in Canadian literature classes. In November, she wrote a frustrated letter to complain that students had been unable to buy her books in the university bookstore. They hadn't been ordered in time.

There were good people at New College, where Gwen was assigned an office, people she liked, such as Professor Mary Nyquist, who was teaching in the Women's Studies programme, but they always seemed to be distracted and overwhelmed with administrative work. Once Gwen stood leaning on the door to Nyquist's office and said, smiling: "I don't know how you do it."[1] Nyquist had thought it a compliment. More likely Gwen was wondering how she lived this frenzied pace that seemed to have so little to do with the real world.

Nyquist was impressed with Gwendolyn. She was always punctual—it never occurred to Nyquist that she had a drinking problem—and when the students began to drop by her office, they seemed devoted to her. Soon Gwen found herself reading endless manuscripts of poetry and fiction, and was drained by it. The students, assessing her work, would later report that she had been the best possible writer-in-residence: unfailingly generous with her time and deeply insightful. One of the things she would tell them was that young poets suffer from a sense of restraint and burden. "Better to let loose and make mistakes than not at all."[2]

That fall of 1986, in interviews with the university papers like *The Bulletin* and *The Varsity*, Gwen was looking to the future. She said that she knew the projects she would complete in the next ten years, though not in what order, and that she was also confident she would get by financially; she always had. She spoke of her current work: "I'm working on a long, very difficult poem which I am scared to death of, called 'The Black Tunnel Wall' which is about my parents in the U.K. during the First World War when they were children, and it's taking a long, long time. I have been on and off it for ages."[3] Nothing survives of "The Black Tunnel Wall." Whatever she had written, Gwen must have destroyed the manuscript.

To her student readers she explained that she had ordered her life around her art, deliberately never having children, and setting up her life in such a way that domesticity wouldn't intrude. "Biologically women have had to make sacrifices," she explained, though she added that there were women who had carried on both "sides" successfully, and she admired them. "I was a feminist all my life before the word ever came into being. It never occurred to me that I couldn't do anything I wanted to."[4]

Gwen, it was clear, now felt under a compulsion—to course through her past, to put the pieces together, to make it add up. Ruben remembered that she took him back to the old neighbourhood of Keele and Bloor. Thirty-eight Keele Street had been torn down to make room for the subway, and now there was only a naked hill where it had once stood. They visited Gwen's old high school, Western Tech. He remembered climbing the steps of that stone mausoleum and Gwen saying: "They have never invited me back. Somebody should have invited me back." She wanted to prove to them that she had become what she said she would. He also remembered she returned to Winnipeg to see the old house. For the plane trip, Ruben had made her a special amulet, with instructions to open it only when she was up in the air.

Still, Gwen kept her sense of humour and her love of self-parody. She and Aviva Layton had always had a running joke about the fact that she was absolutely besotted with the American actor, Jack Palance. From Los Angeles, where she and Leon Whiteson had relocated, Layton sent Gwen Palance's address that September, assuring her it was top secret since she had managed to ferret it out only with the greatest difficulty. Gwen had always insisted Palance was her Noman, which Layton thought perfect since he was primitive and rough hewn, somehow prehistoric, as if he were the missing link, and Gwen was obviously attracted to that strength. It wasn't quite as mad as it sounded. Palance had done some exceptional films and also published a book of poetry. Gwen replied by postcard:

October 2, 1986

My God, I have Jack Palance's ADDRESS. What will I do, what will I send, what will I say, what will I WEAR, which book should I send, or SHOULD I send a book. What about a letter, but what will I SAY, I can't handle this, I'm not ready. Do I have a photo that makes me look about 60 or does he go for young chicks in which case do I have an OLD photo, or should I even send a photo. WHAT WILL I DO?????

Love, Gwen
P.S. Hope you are well. HELP!!! Should I see a shrink? Should I have my hair done before I write the letter?[5]

Layton found Gwen's postcard absolutely hilarious. If Gwen did write to Palance, he never answered.

Much of her book *Afterworlds*, which she was now preparing for publication, is a returning, a coursing back, a summing up. There are poems to old lovers. In "Letters to Josef in Jerusalem," written in 1983, she invents letters to Josef Avisar, whom she hadn't seen in twenty-one years, poems that she called a series of statements about the nuclear terrorism into which we were plunging ourselves, and about all the little wars the world was engaged in. She wrote a love poem to Salah, whom she imagined living in Egypt, not knowing he was still in Montreal. She included the sequence "Terror and Erebus," which had been broadcast on the CBC as a verse play in 1965, when it had so moved the young Margaret Atwood that she had tried for years to get it published. It had finally appeared in *The Tamarack Review* in 1972. What is remarkable is how seamlessly it fits into the book; Gwen had been in control of her vision at the age of twenty-three.

And then there were new directions. Gwen had been reading books of modern physics, discovering that the physicists' version of reality matched her own. She wrote to a friend, Myra MacFarlane: "The world of subatomic reality, once thought to be inhabited by poets and mystics, has now finally become the domain of physicists. It delights me to know that FINALLY the real minds in science are accepting the paradoxes and mysteries of nature."[6] She turned these ideas into poetry:

... And where do all the words go?
They say that somewhere out there in space
Every word uttered by every man
Since the beginning of man
Is still sounding. Afterthoughts,

Lethal gossip of the spheres.

Dance then, dance in the city streets,
Your body a fierce illusion of flesh, of energy,
The particles of light cast off from your hair
Illumine you for this moment only.

Your afterimage claims the air
And every moment is Apocalypse—

Avatar, deathless
Anarchy.[7]

In January, a memorial evening was held for Milton Acorn, who had died on August 20th the previous year. Gwen was immediately asked if she would participate in the "wake." She was not a prime mover in the event, but was asked to write a few notes to friends like Irving Layton, Margaret Atwood, and Leonard Cohen, inviting them to participate. There was a slight mix-up with Margaret Atwood's invitation and Gwen wrote to her about her own "uneasiness" at making the invitations: "Why should *anyone* be pressured into appearing at a thing celebrating an important poet, but a man who *did* insult everyone in sight, including me." She was thinking of people being forced into saying "nice" things, rather than "real things, which Milton himself wd. have preferred."[8] Only Purdy, she added, "does wonders with hating and loving the guy, dead or alive."

The wake's organizer, the musician and actor Cedric Smith, found her curiously nervous, even paranoid about the event. It puzzled him that she seemed to think people identified her as the "villain" in Milton's life. He believed she felt there were some who insisted, "ludicrously, that he had been the love of her life."[9] Smith wondered whether Gwen was being realistic; was it possible that the "literary community" was so introverted and artificial that such gossip existed about Gwen?

One more time, she tried to set the record straight. The National Film Board made a film of the wake, in which Gwen stands at the podium, reading Acorn's poem with the lines: "Wherever you are be fearless & wherever I am I hope to know that you are moving vividly beyond me." The "you" of the poem is herself. Milton had claimed publicly that he had released her; why couldn't everyone else? She spoke of meeting Milton when she was "all of nineteen years old."

> Milton was thirty-eight. Our brief marriage in 1962 ended later that same year after I turned twenty-one. What happened was that the enormous age difference created a very odd couple to say the least. We were referred to as beauty and the beast. That wasn't fair. I was no raving beauty and Milton was not a beast.... I was glad to have been a brief part of Milt's life in those early years when he was reaching his zenith as a poet and I was much younger and coming into my own very very slowly.[10]

Perhaps Gwen was feeling so raw and exposed that everything began to feel like an assault. The pressure was to explain, to be freed, to be left in peace.

That summer of 1987, Gwen appeared fine to most friends. Only a very few knew that she was deeply in trouble. Even most of those who knew she was drinking didn't realize how serious her condition was becoming. But she was narrowing her world. A Chilean musician-architect, Ricardo Rivas, had opened a jewellery shop at Brunswick Avenue and Bloor Street called 8-3 Atelier. Gwen would stop in to buy the occasional tiny piece of lapis and they would talk about lapis lazuli, her favourite stone—how it came from only two places in the world—and discuss the differences between Afghan and Chilean lapis. Rivas had been a member of the music group *Compañeros*, and they'd talk about The Trojan Horse. It pleased her that, though she and Nikos had lost it, it had gone through the right evolution, becoming a home to Latin American exiles.

Once, she asked what happened to the paintings she and Nikos had hung on the walls of The Horse, and Rivas explained that they were stored in the basement of the old building, which had been taken over by a co-op. She asked if she could have them. Painted on cheap plywood, they were conventional Greek images—a hunter and deer, two warriors fighting, a portrait of Bacchus. Rivas brought them to Robert Street, nailing them carefully where she asked, into the mid-frames of the windows, blocking the light. It felt as though she were asking him to board up the windows with them, so that she could surround herself with the memories she loved.[11]

Some days she would go alone to a restaurant bar on Harbord Street called Henry's, a depressing club that had been renovated but hadn't caught hold. It was usually empty. Gwen would be in a corner drinking a beer, slowly, deliberately. She was always alone, guarding her secrets.

The poet David McFadden's portrait of Gwen at this time is evocative; it is the Gwen most people saw. McFadden had known Gwen for years through Coach House Press, which had published both of them:

> The last time we had lunch was at a Greek restaurant on the Danforth. I think I had a glass of retsina but she insisted on ordering soda water with her meal. She very nicely told me she had no money and I of course covered it, no problem. It was always nice to be with Gwen. As we left the place, someone had put an old sofa out on the curb for the garbage truck. Gwen eyeballed it incredulously.
>
> "That's better than the one I have at home," she finally said.
>
> "Why don't you take it?"

"Do you think I should?"

"Why not? It's obviously been discarded by the owner."

"How would I get it home?"

"How about a cab?"

She couldn't see how the sofa would fit in a cab so I hailed one over. The driver helped me put the sofa in the trunk, and though of course he couldn't close the trunk with the sofa in it he just happened to have a rope so the trunk lid wouldn't bounce up and down as he drove. As we folded up her fold-up push bike and put it in the back seat, Gwen gave me a little kiss goodbye, hopped in the front passenger seat and off she went.

I just stood there smiling at the cab heading west on the Danforth with this huge sofa sticking out of the trunk. The cab went out of view, then the next thing I knew it had made a U-turn and was heading back.

"Oh, Dave," she said. "Something I forgot." She looked terribly embarrassed. "I don't have any money."

This was the woman who once announced she wouldn't do any more readings funded by the Canada Council because it took too long to get paid. So I gave her ten bucks, and told her to offer the driver the change if he would help her into the house with the sofa. He nodded. So did she. That was the last I saw of her.[12]

One of her friends over the last years was a homeless man on Bloor Street who covered the beat at the corner of St. George Street and, later, at Bedford Road. For years McFadden had seen him at his post and always gave him subway tokens, or bought tokens from him at half-price. McFadden presumed he felt the token business was more "dignified" than asking for money, or "more interesting," since he could then provide discount tokens to people who couldn't afford the full fare. "This was a man for whom things had gone wrong from day one,"

McFadden explains. Gwen surprised him one day by remarking as they were walking along Bloor Street that this man was a close personal friend. Every so often he would phone her, which meant that "he either had a little excess money and wanted to treat her, or he was dead broke and wanted her to treat him." They were drinking buddies. Their "lunches" were always liquid lunches.

This man was like her other long-ago friend, "John the Baptist," in Jerusalem, whom she had desired to know because he "stole away my own loneliness in the presence of his own deeper, subtler loneliness and confusion." These were among the people for whom she was writing poetry. It was as simple as that:

Let Me Make This Perfectly Clear

Let me make this perfectly clear.
I have never written anything because it is a Poem.
This is a mistake you always make about me,
A dangerous mistake. I promise you
I am not writing this because it is a Poem.

You suspect this is a posture or an act.
I am sorry to tell you it is not an act.

You actually think I care if this
Poem gets off the ground or not. Well
I don't care if this poem gets off the ground or not
And neither should you.
All I have ever cared about
And all you should ever care about
Is what happens when you lift your eyes from this page.

Do not think for one minute it is the Poem that matters.
It is not the Poem that matters.

> You can shove the Poem.
> What matters is what is out there in the large dark
> And in the long light,
> Breathing.[13]

Gwen was writing poetry because the poem was the closest thing to real speech, "beautiful and lethal":

> ... Poetry has nothing to do with *poetry*.
> *Poetry* is how the air goes green before thunder,
> is the sound you make when you come, and
> why you live and how you bleed, and
>
> The sound you make or don't make when you die.[14]

That spring Gwen had travelled across Canada giving readings from *Afterworlds*. The reviews were laudatory, and her reception was enthusiastic, but the trips had exhausted her. By the summer she wanted to stay home and take care of her cats. On June 18th, she dropped in to see Barbara Bruce, whom she hadn't seen for a year, again apologizing for taking up too much of her time, and bringing her a copy of the new book. She had finished her stint as writer-in-residence at the University of Toronto. "It had been draining," she said. She felt she was slipping, "dabbling" in wine to reduce the social pressures of the last several months. She was working on another book, which she said she had already "mapped out." But when Bruce made a second appointment for her, she did not keep it.

Gwen's spiral downward that summer of 1987 was rapid. On August 7th, the painter Mieke Bevelander was visiting, as was Ruben. Mieke had been trying to get her to eat something, a sandwich at least. As she sat on the bed, Gwen started going into a seizure. She collapsed, stopped breathing, and turned completely blue. Horrified, Mieke sat her up and pounded on her back to start her breathing again, shouting at

Ruben to call 911. An ambulance arrived and she was taken to the emergency department at the Addiction Research Foundation.

At the hospital she told her doctors she had not been drinking for two days, and was suffering withdrawal seizures. Again, the seizures came because she had decided to quit, but the effort to reach towards health on her own was exceedingly dangerous. Her charts speak of a patient alert and clear minded. Under personal history is written: "Influential Canadian poet quite reluctant to have her alcoholic problem known except to close associates. This results in her not seeking medical attention until a crisis situation occurs and friends intervene."[15] This time Gwen's hiding, her terror of exposure, was proving deadly.

The doctors' goal, as the charts put it, was "to ensure a safe withdrawal." But when they inserted intravenous tubes to correct her dehydration, Gwen pulled them out. As soon as she could, she walked out of the hospital.

For the next four weeks Gwen kept a weekly appointment with Barbara Bruce in the out-patient service. On the first meeting, she was embarrassed to see Bruce, afraid that she had disappointed her by ending up in hospital in such bad shape. She had felt humiliated in the ARF ward, in particular by the doctor who had brought his students to study her like a "guinea pig." She insisted she was feeling better now, cooking and eating meals, though her back pained from all the seizures she had suffered during her withdrawal. She spoke of romantic disappointments. Finding "anyone with whom she has something in common" was impossible. But she would live quietly now, she insisted; she would work on her book.

Gwen explained over the next few weeks that she had traced her life back to her first success with abstinence from alcohol in 1981. That time there had been a "click" and everything fell into place. It had had to do with her writing, but now the writing wasn't working: she could not motivate herself. The "click" didn't come. She thought of other careers. She loved animals; perhaps she could work in the animal rights movement. A complete change might help her to kick the alcohol habit. She was thinking a great deal about her father's death from alcoholism. She was confident she could quit drinking; she just had to figure out how to cope with her feelings, to slow down her life completely, and not to allow the pressures to build within her. She was determined this would never happen to her again.

On August 27th, she left her appointment with Bruce early because she had a meeting with the loans officer at her bank. Even though she had been making adequate money from her university salary and public readings, her finances were in a mess; the daily cost of alcohol was taking its toll. She assured Bruce that she was not worried: the money would come through. But when she went to her bank, she found her request for a loan had been refused. Ruben remembered her coming home in a fury, collecting all her books, and marching back to the bank. She banged the twenty books down on the counter and said: "Here! I did these. I just want to get my money." In her small blue bankbook, the last withdrawal is dated September 11th. It was for $390.00, which left her with a final balance of $2.02.

Gwen did not keep her appointment on September 4th. On the 7th she called Judy Merril and Joyce Marshall. She was very ill and asked them to come by. They took her to Emergency at Toronto Western Hospital from where she was transferred to the Addiction Research Foundation. She had recently been on what she called a "drinking binge," and had quit for two days when she suffered a "grand mal" seizure. Again she left hospital within three days, before the test results were in.

From Gwen's descriptions of herself, a psychiatrist made the following notes:

> The patient is a successful writer, having published 20 books and having recently completed a one year position as writer in residence. She describes her writing as centred on the struggle between fantasy and boring reality, leading to a search for a super-reality through love or, artificially, through alcohol. She describes a propensity

to fall quickly and deeply in love, which transforms her world, but her affairs do not usually work out because men find her intimidating as a writer. This leads to disillusionment, depression, and another bout of drinking. She describes her depressions as associated with meaninglessness and emptiness, rather than pain, and lasting up to several days. She denies difficulties with self-care, sleep, appetite, or of ever considering suicide. She has maintained the same apartment for six years, lives off the proceeds of her writing, and states that she has supportive friends. She describes herself as independent, bored with academics, and growing weary of writing. She tends to wait for others to reach out for her rather than taking the initiative. Her only regret is her use of alcohol and she states her intention is now to quit....

Personal history reveals that she was born in Toronto, the second of two daughters. Her parents are both dead. She sees her father as having been victimized by her mother's depression and frequent suicide attempts. Her mother was invalided by this condition, while her father was driven to drink and died a broken man. She feels her mother inflicted mental cruelty on her father.[16]

Bruce tried very hard to help Gwen. She warned her that she was in danger—her liver and pancreas had been damaged by alcohol—and spoke of the need for some very intense work to reach the "bottom of her problems."

Gwen kept five appointments at the Addiction Research Foundation in September, and then cancelled a meeting on September 29th, and again on October 5th. She did not return to ARF. Bruce phoned her a number of times, but the phone would be lifted and the receiver replaced. She contacted friends, only to discover Gwen was drinking heavily. She reached Gwen once, but Gwen replied that she was busy with her publishers. A letter was sent on November 16th, to try to contact her. Bruce was waiting for Gwen to be admitted to Emergency again.

The battle Gwen was waging was brutal. The poet Janis Rapoport, who lived close by and whom Gwen often visited as she cycled through the Annex, was desperate to help. Gwen had become close to her and her family. Rapoport's favourite memory of Gwen was of once telling her off-handedly that her daughter Renata had been deeply disappointed when, having seen a wand in in a store called "The Witchy Shoppe" on Harbord Street, she had asked the owner if she could buy it, only to be told it was very expensive and much too powerful for a child of her age. When Gwen next visited she brought Renata a little glass wand filled with stars.

Now, when Rapoport tried to elicit from her some sense of what was wrong, Gwen spoke abstractly, theoretically: "She seemed, I can only say obsessed, with the battle between Thanatos and Eros. I thought she was talking about themes in poetry and only realized in retrospect that she was talking about her life."[17] It was as if she were being tossed like flotsam between those two monumental forces—the drive to life and the drive towards death. Rapoport, of course, had hoped to talk to Gwen about her drinking, but Gwen offered no opening for such a conversation. Perhaps she was ashamed. Or perhaps she was exhausted. She had been over and over the subject and there was little left to say about it.

Silly incidents happened to aggravate her. On the 18th of November, she found herself in court for trespassing on a neighbour's property. She claimed that in the late summer, she had gone into a yard to give water to two dogs that had been tied up and left in the sun. It had been very hot and the crying of the animals had made her extremely angry. Ruben went to court with her as a witness. He had raged at the judge and the whole thing had degenerated into a fiasco, with the judge yelling from the bench. Gwen's irritation was directed at Ruben.

Memory is eccentric, how we select the stories we will keep. Ruben remembered odd things from those last weeks. Gwen, he felt, was angrier than she had ever been before. Two weeks before she died she decided she was going to phone the actor Jack Palance and Ruben encouraged her. She didn't get to speak to Palance; she was told he was out riding horses, the Hollywood euphemism for making a film. Ruben recalled that last week looking with Gwen at the well-known photograph of the dead Marilyn Monroe as her body was carried from her apartment on a stretcher—her face was puffed and unrecognizable, emptied of all the beauty that had been Monroe. Gwen was incredulous. "That's how one looks. That's what death does to you," she had said. She told Ruben that if one finds a dead body, one must always remember to close the eyes.

Friends were trying desperately to help. Judith Merril remembered a conversation over lunch. They were talking about writing and Gwen's voice became suddenly serious. She said: "It's not that I can't write. I can write better than I ever did before. But I don't want to be bothered. It's not worth the trouble."[18] Like most writers, Gwen always suffered from postpartum depression after a book publication. But to Merril, this seemed different, more sinister.

Mieke Bevelander tried to discover what was causing Gwen to spiral down. "I asked her probably a hundred times, what was doing this to her. Finally she said: 'Look, Mieke, you know, I could just sit right down at that desk over there, right now, at my typewriter, and I could write another brilliant poem, but you know what it's really about. I don't want to write one more poem. It's over.' She had come to that place when you feel there's nothing left, nothing inside that compels you to create."[19]

Merril remembered her last visit to Gwen that final week. Mieke Bevelander showed up, surprised to meet her there. Bevelander hadn't known there were others also taking care of Gwen. Up to the end, Gwen kept her friends in separate pockets. Gwen had been crying desperately, insisting that she must speak to Nikos. She phoned and he came immediately. He got down on his knees and tried to comfort her. She was very distraught because someone she had considered a friend had stolen the last few dollars she had from her purse. Judy remembered how simple and gentle Nikos was with her. Gwen turned to Nikos and said: "You were the one. The only one. The decent one." There seemed to be nothing they could do for her.

In the last months, Gwen had established a relationship with a man called Frank whom she had met at the doughnut shop on the corner of Walmer Road and Bloor Street. To most of her friends he seemed the final parody of those men she chose who were totally inadequate to her, the strays who served, as Mac Reynolds felt, as her self-image, "the secret terrible self-image, that lay underneath all that need for alcohol, of being an essential outsider, rejected by the world." An unemployed drifter, he was a man who complained endlessly about his fate in life. At the end he was living in Gwen's apartment and doing odd jobs. They drank together, but some evenings Gwen would read him her poetry. He had never heard poetry before and was deeply moved.[20] Only Judy Merril saw him sympathetically. "The impression I got," Merril said, "was that he was a very decent, ordinary guy who really cared for her and who tried to cope with this incredible personality." The weekend of her death, Frank himself was in hospital. Had he been there, he might have been able to help.

The last person to see Gwen was the novelist M.T. Kelly. Earlier that month he had asked her to write a blurb for the back of his novel, and when he phoned that Sunday night to collect it, she had said it was ready. He had been reluctant to trek out on that bleak November night, it was so bitterly cold. At her door Gwen had handed him the blurb, typed beautifully on pristine paper and elegantly worded. They spoke briefly. He noticed that she seemed dazed; there was something odd or askew about her eyes. Embarrassed, she had asked if she could borrow twenty dollars. As he handed her forty dollars, she told him to wait a minute. He had watched her disappear down the dark hallway, and could just see, in the distance, the red coils of the open oven, the door of which she had left ajar to warm the freezing apartment. When she returned she handed him a small tin butterfly, its wings glazed in purple and red sparkles.[21]

Ruben had a key to Gwen's apartment. He knew she had been alone all weekend. They often had dinner together, but that weekend she had cut him off. After receiving no reply to his knock on Monday morning, November 30th, he had let himself in. He remembered the bedroom messy, the bed dishevelled. She was lying against it. He tried to wake her. He screamed "Gwen" and hit her on the back to try to start her breathing. He fumbled for the phone, which seemed to be tangled in the bedclothes; when he freed it, the cord was twisted and he couldn't get it to work. He couldn't work the living-room phone either, though he later discovered that it was in fact functioning. Frantically he ran down the street to a pay phone and called 911. Then he ran to get Joyce Marshall, who lived just around the corner. He kept babbling to her about an apple he had seen in the kitchen. Only one bite had been taken out of it, and the flesh was still white. It couldn't have been long since she'd eaten it. "She was reaching for life," he kept shouting, shaking his head. And he had forgotten after all to close her eyes.

Joyce and Ruben returned to the apartment and spent four hours with the assorted specialists—policemen, photographers, the coroner. Joyce Marshall has written of what happened: "As they were searching for what they called 'signs of foul play,' going through her papers, examining (and commenting on) her clothes, bringing me scribbled notes to see whether I could identify the names, I wasn't allowed into the bedroom and so didn't see her in death. I didn't want to, preferring to say my goodbye, in my own way, to the small, rather flat-looking covered shape as it was carried out."[22]

The weekend of Gwen's death, Mieke Bevelander had gone north to Midland to visit her father, who was dying of cancer. It was dark when she returned. As she was parking her car in her driveway, she saw Ruben, facedown on her sidewalk, howling like a wounded animal. She knew immediately that Gwen was dead.

The coroner's report on the autopsy is cryptic: "*Cause of death*: Metabolic Acidosis, resulting from a recent history of binge drinking and no food intake."[23]

But there are two details in the coroner's report that are deeply jarring:

"*Skin*: Imprint of telephone on abdomen." Had Gwen been trying to telephone someone?

"*Screening for alcohol and drugs*: negative." There was no alcohol in her system.

Had Gwendolyn, once again, been reaching for life?

The week after her death, Gwen's sister, Carol, and her son David came to empty the apartment, collecting her fold-up bicycle, her manuscripts, the letters she had left behind. No one noticed her cats. Gwen's landlord, Roberta Frank, eventually put an ad in the newspaper: "Poet's cats could use a good home."

After you die the danger is that you become the words people use to remember you and who can speak for Gwen? But Gwen had countered in her T.E. Lawrence voice: "The world can have me any way it pleases." She had left her own testament in the final poem of her last book:

The Tao of Physics

In the vast spaces of the subatomic world where
Matter has a   tendency   to exist
The lord of Life is breathing in and out,
Creating and destroying the universe
With each wave of his breath.

And my lord Siva dances in the city streets,
His body a fierce illusion of flesh, of energy,
The particles of light cast off from his hair
Invade the mighty night, the relative night, this dream.

Here where events have a   tendency   to occur
My chair and all its myriad inner worlds
Whirl around in the carousel of space; I hurl
Breathless poems against my lord Death, send these
Words, these words
Careening into the beautiful darkness.[24]

AFTERWORD

When I began this biography, my search for Gwendolyn was personal, driven by a single question: Why had she died so prematurely? Then, I had no idea what story I would find; now I see only her bravery, her stamina, and the remarkable invention she made out of herself, building on the least likely foundations. I think of Salah's image of her: a woman alone in a deserted landscape, an image of love. Gwen's is a sad story. Too much conspired to undermine her, to make her suffering unendurable.

My last act as Gwen's biographer is to sit before a pile of photographs that I have collected. I must construct a brief visual mosaic of her life. That strange, haunted, Gothic house, 38 Keele Street, with its third floor, must be there, the house that Gwen tried to escape in dreams throughout her lifetime; and the child in the wishing tree photographed by her father, so tiny, so preoccupied, already so burdened with the world's weight. Of the family photos, there are not many to choose from: only one of Alick and Elsie McEwen together with their daughters. The ones of Elsie and her sister and brother-in-law are like all family photos, conventionally posed to reveal nothing of their hidden dynamic. The only thing I notice is how quickly Elsie has aged and that Alick is absent. Gwen seems fresh, shy, expectant, waiting for life.

When Gwen becomes the solitary young magician without quick wrists, she suddenly assumes an exquisite and fragile beauty that worries me: such a delicate shell to house so fiercely original a mind. Of the men she shared her life with I can find only a few photographs: of Milton, looking much more presentable than anecdotes of him prepared me to expect; there are no photos of Mallory or of Salah. It is with Nikos that suddenly life seems to assume a normalcy—I find photos of their wedding, of dinners in restaurants, of vacations. I choose the playful one of Gwen as the archer demonstrating to someone outside the photograph how to stretch the bow in her Browning Avenue apartment. In other photos, the sun pours from Greek landscapes and Canadian snowdrifts, and Gwen looks happy.

It is the last photo of Gwen that unnerves me. It was taken in the spring of 1987, six months before she died. Her face reveals little, and so I wonder what she was holding back. The smile is constrained, ironic perhaps, and her eyes are tired. Beside it I put the other Gwen, the sculpted Hathor, goddess of joy, love, and fertility, whose face always lurked beneath Gwen's face. To everyone who knew her, she was not the product of her Scottish-English ancestry, but someone who came from elsewhere, from the place she had chosen, out of history, out of myth.

Now I wonder which photograph I should choose for the cover of this book: Gwen standing at a winter window holding her cat Dingbat, who looks out alertly at the back alley while she looks down, lost in thought, pensive and melancholy. Or Gwen posed beside a mirror so that her image seems to emerge from its still surface and her face is doubled, trapped in shadows, a Janus figure looking forward and back. Instead I choose Gwen with her outstretched arm resting against a door as if she is just about to open it. The light streams in through its window, illuminating her left side; only her right side is in shadow. She is thirty years old. She wears an Arabic shirt trimmed with triangles. As the sun turns her hair to silver, she stares out at the world with her characteristic directness, challenging the viewer. She is the Shadow Maker.

ACKNOWLEDGEMENTS

Those who loved and respected Gwendolyn MacEwen have made this biography possible. Without their memories there would be no book. I would like to thank Carol Wilson who gave me unrestricted access to her sister's literary and personal archives, while imposing no control over my interpretation of her life. She could not have been more forthright, assisting me directly in the pursuit of whatever material I determined would be helpful. Margaret Atwood gave me copies of her voluminous correspondence with Gwendolyn MacEwen, which had not been made public before, and has been extremely supportive in all aspects of the writing of this book. John McCombe Reynolds provided copies of the photographs he took of MacEwen over the years, as well as continuous anecdotes of their friendship of several decades.

Gwendolyn MacEwen was fortunate to have so many friends and admirers. I would like to thank those I interviewed, many of whom I imposed upon numerous times as I sought to thread the narrative of her life: Marty Ahvenus, Tom Arnott, Samar Attar, Margaret Avison, Mieke Bevelander, Marie-Claire Blais, George Bowering, Barry

Callaghan, Leonard Cohen, Fred Cogswell, Victor Coleman, John Robert Colombo, Gregory Cook, Don Cullen, Doug Donegani, Mary di Michele, David Donnell, Charlotte Engel, Howard Engel, Douglas Fetherling, Timothy Findley, Roberta Frank, Greg Gatenby, Peter Gzowski, Ralph Gustafson, Christos Hatzis, Jane Jacobs, D.G. Jones, M.T. Kelly, Pen Kemp, Joy Kogawa, Irving Layton, Dennis Lee, Aasta Levene, Dora Lyons, David McFadden, Leon Major, Joyce Marshall, Tom Marshall, Bob Mallory, David Mason, Judith Merril, Bruce Meyer, Karen Mulhallen, Michael Ondaatje, Charlie Pachter, Jim Polk, Marion Porter, Al Purdy, Janis Rapoport, Charles Ritchie, Ricardo Rivas, Joe Rosenblatt, Jane Rule, Salah, Robin Skelton, Cedric Smith, Lawrence Stone, Robert Sward, Nikos Tsingos, Lawrence Walker, Robert Weaver, Phyllis Webb, Aviva Layton Whiteson, and Leon Whiteson. I would also like to thank Gwendolyn MacEwen's nephews and nieces: Carol Anne, David, Patti, and Michael.

There is one person in particular to whom I must express my gratitude for the patience with which she read and reread my manuscript, with an impeccable instinct for its strengths and weaknesses. Arlene Lampert was my chosen reader long before this book found a shape. I want to thank David Layton, Richard Teleky, Marion Porter, Margaret Atwood, Carole Corbeil and Timothy Findley for reading the manuscript with shrewd insight. I am grateful to Josef Skvorecky, Deirdre Bair, and Joan Givner for their generous recommendation of my work.

Several people helped me with translations of this remarkably polyglot writer: Samar Attar and Marwan Sherif translated letters from the Arabic, and Androulla Haalboom helped me with Greek. Adam Hunt and Kim Hornburg assisted with document research and worked on tape transcriptions. Imposing on a long friendship, I asked Dr. Sharon Salloum to confirm the accuracy of medical details in the biography. Professor Donald Redford, Director of the Akhenaton Temple Project and a world expert on Amarna, helped immensely with my understanding of MacEwen's Egyptian research.

The Queen Street Mental Health Centre was very co-operative during my weeks of research there. The Addiction Research Foundation and the Clarke Institute of Psychiatry provided me with their summary files on Gwendolyn MacEwen, without compromising doctor/patient confidentiality.

I wish to acknowledge the generous support of the John Simon Guggenheim Memorial Foundation who provided me with release time from teaching to write this book, and the Canada Council and the Toronto Arts Council who assisted with the financing of my research.

I had to consult many libraries in the course of my research. Among them, I would like, in particular, to acknowledge the Queen's University Archives, the National Archives, the National Library, and the attentive staff, especially Edna Hajnal and Albert Masters, of the Thomas Fisher Rare Book Library, the University of Toronto.

Finally, I wish to share my delight in my editor Iris Tupholme whose humour and wisdom turned the process of editing into a pleasure; Mary Adachi for her unfailing precision; and Juan Opitz for his loyalty and love. He provides the still centre that makes the writing possible.

ENDNOTES

Introduction

1. The friend was the editor of *Descant* magazine, Karen Mulhallen. Interview, Toronto, 31 March 1993.
2. Letter from Samar Attar to Carol Wilson, 9 May 1988.
3. "Gwendolyn MacEwen," *The Oxford Companion to Canadian Literature*, Toronto: Oxford University Press, 1983, p. 483.

1: Thirty-eight Keele Street

1. "Notebook and additional notes: Dreams/Visions/Musings; the sixties, seventies and eighties," Gwendolyn MacEwen Papers, Thomas Fisher Rare Book Library, University of Toronto, Box 1.
2. Arthur Morrison, *Tales of Mean Streets*, Boston: Little, Brown & Company, 1895.
3. Marion Porter (née Lyons), autobiographical essay (unpublished); interview, Ottawa, 4 February 1993. The details of the portraits of the Martins are derived from Marion Porter.
4. Elsie McEwen, Clinical Record, 16 April 1934. Department of Health: Hospital Division, Queen Street Mental Health Centre.
5. McEwen, Clinical Record, 18 September 1939. Queen Street Mental Health Centre.

6. Letter of 3 July 1926, Thomas Machell & Sons, Dulcitone House, 45 Great Western Road, Glasgow. Interview with Lawrence Walker, Peterborough, 15 February 1993.
7. Letter of 27 March 1929, F.W. Harris, F.I.C., Chemical Laboratory, Tontine Buildings, 20 Trongate, Glasgow.
8. McEwen, Clinical Record, 16 April 1934, Queen Street Mental Health Centre.
9. McEwen, Clinical Record, 10 October 1936, Queen Street Mental Health Centre.
10. McEwen, Clinical Record, 10 October 1939, Queen Street Mental Health Centre.
11. McEwen, Clinical Record: Final Note, 8 July 1957, Queen Street Mental Health Centre.
12. McEwen, Conference Report, 6 February 1940, Whitby Psychiatric Hospital, Queen Street Mental Health Centre.

2: The Third Floor

1. Interview with Carol Wilson, Barrie, Ontario, 15 July 1992.
2. Letter to author from Marion Porter, 5 February 1995.
3. Interview with Dora Lyons, Toronto, 18 January 1993.
4. Church playbill, 12 May 1935. In the possession of Dora Lyons.
5. Interview with Marion Porter, Ottawa, 4 February 1993.

3: A Room in Winnipeg

1. "Notebook and additional notes: Dreams/Visions/Musings; the sixties, seventies and eighties," Gwendolyn MacEwen Papers, Thomas Fisher Rare Book Library, University of Toronto, Box 1.
2. De Niverville essay, Gwendolyn MacEwen Papers, Box 23.
3. Letter to Gail Fox, undated, Gail Fox Papers, Queen's University Archives, Kingston.
4. Letter to author from Phyllis Webb, 28 November 1993.
5. "Animal Syllables 1962-65," Gwendolyn MacEwen Papers, Box 1. Later revised as "Fragments from a Childhood," *The Fire-Eaters*, Ottawa: Oberon Press, 1976.
6. Interview with Lawrence Walker, Peterborough, Ontario, 15 February 1993.
7. McEwen, Clinical Records, Final Note, 8 July 1957. Résumé of patient's history, including Winnipeg hospitalizations, Queen Street Mental Health Centre.

8. Interview with Lynn _____, a friend of Gwendolyn's who wished to remain anonymous, Toronto, 23 March 1994.
9. "Day of Twelve Princes," *Noman*, Toronto: General Publishing Co., 1972, p. 28. Published version of a draft dated pre-1961.
10. "Day of Twelve Princes," p. 39.

4: Space Lady

1. Letter from Alick McEwen, undated, Collection of Carol Wilson.
2. Letter from Alick McEwen, 15 November 1953, Collection of Carol Wilson.
3. Letter from Alick McEwen, 31 August 1954, Collection of Carol Wilson.
4. "High School Poems, 1955-56," Gwendolyn MacEwen Papers, Thomas Fisher Rare Book Library, University of Toronto, Box 1.
5. *Westward Ho!*, March 1959, p. 78. Western Technical-Commercial School Archives.
6. "My Favourite Teacher," Recorded for CBC radio: *Dayshift*, 13 March 1987. Gwendolyn MacEwen Papers, Box 23.
7. Letter from Gwendolyn MacEwen, September 1958, Collection of Carol Wilson.
8. "Languages (2)," *Afterworlds*, Toronto: McClelland and Stewart, 1987, p. 89.
9. "My Favourite Teacher," Box 23.
10. "Nefertiti," High School Poems, 1955-56, MacEwen Papers, Box 1.
11. "The Wah Mai Café," *Afterworlds*, p. 34.
12. *The Canadian Forum*, Vol. 38, No. 455, December 1958, p. 205.
13. Letter from Gwendolyn MacEwen, 17 October [1957], Collection of Carol Wilson.
14. Letter from Alick McEwen, 22 October 1957, Collection of Carol Wilson.
15. Letter from Gwendolyn MacEwen, September 1958, Collection of Carol Wilson.
16. Letter from Alick McEwen, 12 August 1958, Collection of Carol Wilson.
17. Letter from Elsie McEwen, 14 April [no year], Collection of Carol Wilson.
18. Easter card from Elsie McEwen, undated, Collection of Carol Wilson.
19. Letter from Alick McEwen, Sunday 13th [no year], Collection of Carol Wilson.
20. Letter from Gwendolyn MacEwen, undated, Collection of Carol Wilson.
21. Letter from Alick McEwen, 10 October 1959, Collection of Carol Wilson.
22. Letter from Alick McEwen, 10 September 1959, Collection of Carol Wilson.

5: Adam's Alphabet

1. Letter to Peter Miller of Contact Press, [undated, 1963?], Gwendolyn

MacEwen Papers, Thomas Fisher Rare Book Library, University of Toronto, Box 25.
2. Interview with George Bowering, Toronto, 16 March 1994.
3. Postcard from Mrs. Kenneth Patchen, 29 May 1962, MacEwen Papers, Box 25.
4. Among her notes for 1959 Gwendolyn MacEwen has listed reading material, including *The Book of Tokens*, commentary by Paul Foster Case, 1947, and Arthur Edward Waite, *Pictorial Key to the Tarot*, 1910.
5. McEwen, Clinical Records, Final Note, 25 February 1959, Queen Street Mental Health Centre.
6. Interview with Margaret Avison, Toronto, 12 March 1993.
7. Letter to Alick McEwen, undated, Collection of Carol Wilson.
8. Ibid. Marginal note in father's handwriting in MacEwen's letter.
9. The books were given to author by Ruben Zellermeyer.
10. "Adam's Alphabet, 1959-1960," Gwendolyn MacEwen Papers, Box 1. Part of the Introduction and six of the twenty-two poems of "Adam's Alphabet" were reprinted in *The Poetry of Gwendolyn MacEwen: Volume One: The Early Years*, eds. Margaret Atwood and Barry Callaghan, Exile Editions, 1993.
11. Ibid.
12. Letter to Margaret Atwood, 1963, Collection of Margaret Atwood.
13. "Gabriela, 1959-60," p. 61, Gwendolyn MacEwen Papers, Box 1.
14. Ibid., p. 63.
15. "Uncollected Poems, 1959-60," Gwendolyn MacEwen Papers, Box 1.
16. Interview with John McCombe (Mac) Reynolds, Toronto, 21 May 1994.
17. Letter from Robert Weaver, 5 October [no year], Robert Weaver Papers, National Archives of Canada.
18. Interview with Joe Blumenthal, Toronto, 14 October 1994. The name Blumenthal is a pseudonym, since Joe requested that I not use his real name.
19. "Gabriela," p. 43.
20. "Notebook and additional notes: Dreams/Visions/Musings; the sixties, seventies and eighties," 2 October 1968, Gwendolyn MacEwen Papers, Box 1. There are several recorded variations of this dream.

6: Magicians Without Quick Wrists

1. Letter from Mario Manzini, 19 March 1966, Collection of Carol Wilson.
2. Interview with Tom Arnott, Barrie, Ontario, 2 December 1992.
3. *Julian the Magician*, Toronto: Macmillan of Canada, 1963, p. 12; published from American edition, Corinth Books, 1963.
4. "Manzini: Escape Artist," *A Breakfast for Barbarians*, Toronto: The Ryerson Press, 1966, p. 37.

5. "The Signet Ring," *Westward Ho!*, Western Technical-Commercial School, 1958, Gwendolyn MacEwen Papers, Thomas Fisher Rare Book Library, University of Toronto, Box 1.
6. *Julian the Magician*, p. 113.
7. Ibid., p. 112.
8. Ibid., pp. 114-115.
9. Ibid., pp. 115-116.
10. Letter to Irving Layton, undated, Irving Layton Papers, Concordia University Special Collections.
11. "Notebook and additional notes: Dreams/Visions/Musings; the sixties, seventies and eighties," Gwendolyn MacEwen Papers, Box 1. Dreams dated 1963-64.
12. *The Little Magazine in America: A Modern Documentary History*, eds. Elliott Anderson and Mary Kinzie, New York: Pushcart Press, 1978, p. 612.
13. "Symposium," *Occident*, Spring/Summer, 1969, p. 110.
14. Letter to Peter Miller, [undated, 1963?], Gwendolyn MacEwen Papers, Box 25.
15. Letter to Phyllis Webb, [1963], Phyllis Webb Papers, National Library of Canada.
16. Letter to J. Michael Yates, undated, J. Michael Yates Papers, National Library of Canada.

7: The Bohemian Embassy

1. Harold Town, *Albert Franck: Keeper of the Lanes*, Toronto: McClelland and Stewart, 1974, p. 19.
2. Interview with Don Cullen, Toronto, 2 March 1993.
3. Ibid.
4. Interview with Margaret Atwood, Toronto, 23 April 1993.
5. Margaret Atwood, "Isis in Darkness," *Wilderness Tips*, Seal Books, McClelland-Bantam Inc., 1991, pp. 57-58.
6. Interview with Margaret Atwood, Toronto, 3 August 1993.
7. Robert Graves, *The White Goddess*, London: Faber & Faber, 1961, p. 24.
8. Letter to Margaret Atwood, 1961, Collection of Margaret Atwood.
9. This joke comes from "Isis in Darkness." Margaret Atwood says she made it up, but it was "exactly the kind of thing Gwen would have said."
10. "Notebook and additional notes: Dreams/Visions/Musings; the sixties, seventies and eighties," Gwendolyn MacEwen Papers, Thomas Fisher Rare Book Library, University of Toronto, Box 1.
11. Interview with Margaret Atwood, Toronto, 8 August 1993.
12. *In Love and Anger: Milton Acorn, Poet*, NFB documentary, director/producer Kent Martin, 1984.

13. Interview with Richard Lemm, Toronto, 17 April 1995. Biographer of Milton Acorn.
14. Al Purdy, "Introduction" to Milton Acorn's *I've Tasted My Blood: Poems 1956-1968*, Toronto: Steel Rail Educational Publishing, 1978.
15. Interview with Cedric Smith, Toronto, 4 November 1993.
16. Interview with Tom Arnott, Barrie, Ontario, 2 December 1992.
17. Interview with Al Purdy, Toronto, 5 May 1993.
18. Letter from Al Purdy, undated, Gwendolyn MacEwen Papers, Box 25.
19. Interview with Margaret Atwood, Toronto, 23 April 1993.
20. Letter to Milton Acorn, 28 December 1960, Milton Acorn Papers, National Archives of Canada.

8: Mr. & Mrs. Acorn

1. Letter from Raymond Souster, 1 July 1960, Gwendolyn MacEwen Papers, Thomas Fisher Rare Book Library, University of Toronto, Box 25.
2. The word "selah," which refers to a musical interlude in the Book of Psalms, derives from two Hebrew roots: Sll—to lift up and praise; Slh—to bow down or bend. Note from Sarah Turvey.
3. Letter from Elsie McEwen, Saturday, 6 July [no year], Department of Health: Hospital Division, Queen Street Mental Health Centre.
4. Letter from Elsie McEwen, 25 January, Noon, Ottawa, [no year], Collection of Carol Wilson.
5. "Genesis," *Tean dadóir*, 1961, pp. 57-58. Collection of Carol Wilson.
6. *The Drunken Clock*, Toronto: Aleph Press, 1961.
7. Letter to Milton Acorn, [undated], Milton Acorn Papers, National Archives of Canada.
8. Letter to Milton Acorn, July 1961, Milton Acorn Papers, National Archives of Canada.
9. Letter from Milton Acorn, [undated], Gwendolyn MacEwen Papers, Restricted File.
10. Interview with Lawrence Walker, Peterborough, Ontario, 15 February 1993.
11. Interview with Margaret Avison, Toronto, 12 March 1993.
12. Interview with Aasta Levene, Toronto, 29 November 1992.
13. "Poems 1960-64 (unpublished and published), Work sheets and first drafts," Gwendolyn MacEwen Papers, Box 4.
14. Interview with Al Purdy, Toronto, 5 May 1993.
15. Letter to Al Purdy, [undated], Al Purdy Papers, University of Saskatchewan Library.
16. Charles Taylor, "Allan Gardens Poetry," Joe Rosenblatt Papers, Box 5, Thomas Fisher Library, University of Toronto.

17. Ken Lefolii, "If the law bans poets from reading in public parks, then the law is wrong," Joe Rosenblatt Papers, Box 5.

9: The Beach of Jaffa

1. "Notes from Israel [July 10 to August 28] 1962," Holograph notebook, Diary Notes. Gwendolyn MacEwen Papers, Thomas Fisher Rare Book Library, University of Toronto, Box 2.
2. "Israel: 1962," Typescript, Gwendolyn MacEwen Papers, Box 2.
3. "Notes from Israel [July 10 to August 28] 1962," Gwendolyn MacEwen Papers, Box 2.
4. *The Rising Fire*, Toronto: Contact Press, 1963, p. 9.
5. "Israel: 1962," Typescript, Gwendolyn MacEwen Papers, Box 2.
6. Ibid.
7. *Afterworlds*, Toronto: McClelland and Stewart, 1987, pp. 61-62.
8. *The Shadow-Maker*, Toronto: Macmillan of Canada, 1969, p. 41.

10: Breakup/Breakdown

1. "Notes from Israel [July 10 to August 28] 1962," Holograph notebook, Diary Notes, Gwendolyn MacEwen Papers, Thomas Fisher Rare Book Library, University of Toronto, Box 2.
2. Letter to Milton Acorn, [undated], Milton Acorn Papers, National Archives of Canada.
3. *The Rising Fire*, Toronto: Contact Press, 1963, pp. 3-4.
4. Interview with Al Purdy, Toronto, 5 May 1993.
5. Letter to Milton Acorn, [undated], Milton Acorn Papers, National Archives of Canada.
6. Milton Acorn's sister and literary executor, Mrs. Mary Hooper, requested that I not reproduce her brother's letters written while he was in hospital; in fairness to Acorn, he was deeply unwell when he wrote them.
7. Letter to Milton Acorn, 16 January 1963, Milton Acorn Papers, National Archives of Canada.
8. Letter to Milton Acorn, July 1963, Milton Acorn Papers, National Archives of Canada.
9. "Skulls and Drums," *The Rising Fire*, p. 23.

11: Leo and Leo Revised

1. Interview with John McCombe (Mac) Reynolds, Toronto, 10 May 1993.
2. Interview with Peter Gzowski, Toronto, 30 November 1993.

3. Interview with David Mason, Toronto, 30 September 1993.
4. Interview with Victor Coleman, Toronto, 1 November 1993.
5. Interview with Bob Mallory, Toronto, 30 September 1993.
6. "The Hand, For B.M.," *The Rising Fire*, Toronto: Contact Press, 1963, p. 55.
7. *The Rising Fire*, p. 64.
8. Letter to Irving Layton, [undated], Irving Layton Papers, Concordia Special Collections.
9. Letter to Irving Layton, [undated], Irving Layton Papers, Concordia Special Collections.

12: Saturnalia

1. Letter to Al Purdy, [undated], Al Purdy Papers, University of Saskatchewan.
2. Letter to Al Purdy, [undated], Al Purdy Papers, University of Saskatchewan.
3. Interview with Barry Callaghan, Toronto, 5 November 1993.
4. Letter to Al Purdy, [undated], Al Purdy Papers, University of Saskatchewan.
5. Letter from Al Purdy, [undated], Gwendolyn MacEwen Papers, Thomas Fisher Rare Book Library, University of Toronto, Box 25.
6. Letter to Al Purdy, [undated], Al Purdy Papers, University of Saskatchewan.
7. *A Breakfast for Barbarians*, Toronto: The Ryerson Press, 1966, p. 8.
8. Letter to Al Purdy, [undated], Al Purdy Papers, University of Saskatchewan.
9. Ibid.
10. Letter to Irving Layton, [undated], Irving Layton Papers, Concordia University Special Collections.
11. "Notes for Saturnalia," Gwendolyn MacEwen Papers, Box 4.
12. "The Compass," *The Shadow-Maker*, Toronto: Macmillan of Canada, 1969, p. 18.
13. Interview with Margaret Avison, Toronto, 12 March 1993.
14. "Morning Laughter," *The Rising Fire*, Toronto: Contact Press, 1963, p. 60.
15. "Notes for a School Reading," Gwendolyn MacEwen Papers, Box 4.
16. "For Alick MacEwen [sic]," *The Rising Fire*, p. 61.
17. "Animal Syllables, 1962-65. Drafts and Revisions, 1962," Gwendolyn MacEwen Papers, Box 1.
18. "A Dance at the Mental Hospital," *Earthlight*, Toronto: General Publishing, 1982, p. 80.
19. Letter to Al Purdy, [undated], Al Purdy Papers, University of Saskatchewan.
20. Letter from Al Purdy, [undated], Gwendolyn MacEwen Papers, Box 25.
21. Interview with Robert Weaver, Toronto, 11 June 1994.
22. Telephone interview with Leonard Cohen, 29 October 1993.
23. *The Atlantic Monthly*, Vol. CCXIV, July-December, 1964.

24. "Notebook and additional notes: Dreams/Visions/Musings; the sixties, seventies and eighties," Gwendolyn MacEwen Papers, Box 1.
25. "The Thing is Violent," *A Breakfast for Barbarians*, p. 42.
26. *The Rising Fire*, pp. 70-71.
27. "Notes for a School Reading," Gwendolyn MacEwen Papers, Box 4.
28. Letter to David Mason, March, 1970, Collection of David Mason.

13: Falling in Love with Arabic

1. *A Breakfast for Barbarians*, Toronto: The Ryerson Press, 1966, p. 1.
2. Interview with Marty Ahvenus, Toronto, 31 January 1995.
3. "The Women's *Globe and Mail*," interviewer: Linda Monk, *The Globe and Mail*, 28 January 1965.
4. Letter to Margaret Atwood, 17 July 1964, Collection of Margaret Atwood.
5. Sir Alan Gardiner, *Egypt of the Pharaohs*, Oxford: Oxford University Press, 1961. One of the twenty-eight books given to author by Ruben Zellermeyer. In *Prism International*, Summer 1966, Gwen published two poems with an English and a hieroglyphic version, and in an explanatory note called the "visual experiment" a lot of fun, though she "wanted to avoid the impression I am setting up as an Egyptologist."
6. Interview with Bob Mallory, Toronto, 15 December 1993.
7. Letter to David Lawson, ECW Press, 1 October 1985, Gwendolyn MacEwen Papers, Thomas Fisher Rare Book Library, University of Toronto, Box 25.
8. Interview with Salah, Montreal, 20 March 1994.
9. Interview with Michael Ondaatje, Eden Mills, 4 September 1993.
10. Letter from Marie-Claire Blais, 1 January 1965, Gwendolyn MacEwen Collection. Translation: I don't have much confidence in myself, but I sense very well what you write ... I often lose myself in the image.
11. Tribute to Gwendolyn MacEwen, hosted by Robert Weaver, *Centre Stage Forum*, 20 January 1988.
12. Letter to Margaret Atwood, 29 June 1965, Collection of Margaret Atwood.
13. Ibid.
14. Letter to Al Purdy, [undated], Al Purdy Papers. University of Saskatchewan.
15. "The Women's *Globe and Mail*," 28 January 1965.
16. Henry G. Fischer, Curator, Department of Egyptian Art, The Metropolitan Museum of Art, New York, 19 January 1965.
17. Letter to Margaret Atwood, 28 January 1966, Collection of Margaret Atwood.
18. Letter to Margaret Atwood, April, 1966, Collection of Margaret Atwood.
19. Letter from Milton Acorn. 30 August 1965, Milton Acorn Papers, National Archives of Canada. The ellipses are Acorn's.

20. Letter from Milton Acorn, 21 January 1966, Milton Acorn Papers, National Archives of Canada.
21. Letter to Margaret Atwood, 6 February 1966, Collection of Margaret Atwood.
22. Letter to author from Jane Rule, 22 June 1993.
23. Interview with Margaret Atwood, 8 August 1993.
24. Letter to Margaret Atwood, 17 February 1966, Collection of Margaret Atwood.
25. Letter from Milton Acorn, 22 February 1966, Milton Acorn Papers, National Archives of Canada.
26. Interview with Al Purdy, Toronto, 5 May 1993.

14: To Cairo

1. *King of Egypt, King of Dreams*, Toronto: Macmillan of Canada, 1971, pp. 262-263.
2. Letter to Margaret Atwood, 18 March 1966, Collection of Margaret Atwood.
3. *Noman's Land*, Toronto: The Coach House Press, 1985, pp. 108-109.
4. "Notebook and additional notes: Dreams/Visions/Musings; the sixties, seventies and eighties," Gwendolyn MacEwen Papers, Box 1.
5. Letter to Margaret Atwood, 22 September 1966, Collection of Margaret Atwood.

15: Letter to an Old Lover

1. *Afterworlds*, Toronto: McClelland and Stewart, 1987, pp. 113-114.
2. Interview with Salah, Montreal, 29 May 1994.
3. *Noman*, Toronto: Oberon Press, 1972; reprinted by General Publishing, 1985, pp. 47-48.
4. Gustav Davidson, *A Dictionary of Angels*, New York: The Free Press, 1967; Gareth Knight, *A Practical Guide to Qabalistic Symbolism*, New York: Samuel Weiser, 1965.
5. Gwendolyn MacEwen Papers, Thomas Fisher Rare Book Library, University of Toronto, Box 13, file 9.
6. *Magic Animals: Selected Poems Old and New*, Toronto: Macmillan of Canada, 1974, p. 95.
7. Letter to Margaret Atwood, 12 February 1969, Collection of Margaret Atwood.
8. Interview with Jim Polk, Toronto, 4 March 1993.
9. Letter to Margaret Atwood, 5 May 1968, Collection of Margaret Atwood.
10. "Notebook and additional notes: Dreams/Visions/Musings; the sixties, seventies and eighties," Gwendolyn MacEwen Papers, Box 1.
11. Letter to Margaret Atwood, 4 September 1968, Collection of Margaret Atwood.
12. Letters from Salah, [undated]. Translated by Marwan Sherif.
13. "Notebook and additional notes: Dreams/Visions/Musings; the sixties, seventies and eighties," Gwendolyn MacEwen Papers, Box 1.

14. Letter to Margaret Atwood, 5 April 1969, Collection of Margaret Atwood.
15. Letter to Margaret Atwood, 10 August 1969, Collection of Margaret Atwood.
16. Letter from Margaret Atwood, 12 August 1969, Collection of Margaret Atwood.
17. Letter to Margaret Atwood, 22 September 1969, Collection of Margaret Atwood.
18. Letter from Margaret Atwood, 24 September 1969, Collection of Margaret Atwood.
19. Letter to Margaret Atwood, 26 September 1969, Collection of Margaret Atwood.

16: The Shadow Maker

1. Letter to Margaret Atwood, 7 July 1968, Collection of Margaret Atwood.
2. *King of Egypt, King of Dreams*, Toronto: Macmillan of Canada, 1971, p. 235.
3. Interview with Tom Marshall, Toronto, 17 April 1993.
4. *A Breakfast for Barbarians*, Toronto: The Ryerson Press, 1966, p. 26.
5. Statement to Margaret Atwood reported in "MacEwen's Muse," *Second Words: Selected Critical Prose*, Toronto: Anansi, 1982, p. 76.
6. *The Shadow-Maker*, Toronto: Macmillan of Canada, 1969, p. 50.
7. Letter to Margaret Atwood, 3 January 1969, Collection of Margaret Atwood.
8. "Dark Stars," *The Shadow-Maker*, pp. 8-9.
9. *The Shadow-Maker*, p. 14.
10. "The Name of the Place," *The Shadow-Maker*, p. 16.
11. Sylvia DuVernet, *Egyptian Themes in Canadian Literature: A Review*, Toronto: Blue Chip Publications, 1987, p. 125.
12. Letter to Tom Marshall, 29 May 1969, Tom Marshall Papers, National Library of Canada.
13. Letter to Margaret Atwood, 22 September 1969, Collection of Margaret Atwood.
14. Letter to Margaret Atwood, 12 September 1969, Collection of Margaret Atwood.

17: Sign of the Fish

1. Letter to Margaret Atwood, 26 September 1969, Collection of Margaret Atwood.
2. Douglas Fetherling, *Travels by Night*, Toronto: Lester Publishing, 1994, p. 183.
3. Ibid., p. 183.
4. Letter to Margaret Atwood, 29 May 1969, Collection of Margaret Atwood.
5. Interview with Nikos Tsingos, Toronto, 16 November 1992.
6. Letter from Margaret Atwood, 24 September 1969, Collection of Margaret Atwood.

7. Letter to Margaret Atwood, [undated], Collection of Margaret Atwood.
8. *Magic Animals: Selected Poems Old and New*, Toronto: Macmillan of Canada, 1974, p. 53.
9. "Notebook and additional notes: Dreams/Visions/Musings; the sixties, seventies and eighties," Gwendolyn MacEwen Papers, Thomas Fisher Rare Book Library, University of Toronto, Box 1.
10. Letter to Margaret Atwood, 30 December 1969, Collection of Margaret Atwood.
11. *Noman*, Toronto: General Publishing, 1972, p. 18.
12. "Notebook and additional notes: Dreams/Visions/Musings; the sixties, seventies and eighties," Gwendolyn MacEwen Papers, Box 1.
13. Interview with Joe Rosenblatt, Ottawa, 18 June 1993.
14. *Noman's Land*, Toronto: The Coach House Press, 1985, pp. 96-97.
15. Telephone conversation with Doctor K. Mohan, the Albany Medical Clinic, 25 January 1993.
16. Letter to Margaret Atwood, 13 January 1971, Collection of Margaret Atwood.
17. "Notebook and additional notes: Dreams/Visions/Musings; the sixties, seventies and eighties," Gwendolyn MacEwen Papers, Box 1.
18. Ibid.

18: Memoirs of a Mad Cook

1. Interview with David, Carol Anne, and Patti, nephew and nieces of Gwendolyn MacEwen, Barrie, Ontario, 15 January 1995.
2. Letter from Michael to Carol Wilson, 28 January 1995.
3. Letter to Margaret Atwood, 4 January 1970, Collection of Margaret Atwood.
4. *The Armies of the Moon*, Toronto: Macmillan of Canada, 1972, p. 14, pp. 8-9. *The Armies of the Moon* was awarded the A.J.M. Smith Prize for Poetry in 1973.
5. Ibid., p. 40.
6. Ibid., p. 33.
7. Contemporary Poets on Tape: Dorothy Livesay and Gwendolyn MacEwen, OISE (Ontario Institute for Studies in Education), 1971.
8. *Armies of the Moon*, p. 34.
9. Letter to Margaret Atwood, October 1970, Collection of Margaret Atwood.
10. Letter to Robert Weaver, 24 March 1970, Robert Weaver Papers, National Archives of Canada.
11. Letters from Milton Acorn, ? February 1969; July 1969, Milton Acorn Papers, National Archives of Canada.
12. Letter from Milton Acorn, 22 July 1969, Milton Acorn Papers, National Archives of Canada.

13. Letter to Samar Attar, 19 August 1970, Collection of Samar Attar, Translated from the Arabic by Samar Attar.
14. Interview with Christos Hatzis, Greek friend of MacEwen, Toronto, 24 August 1994.
15. Interview with John McCombe (Mac) Reynolds, Toronto, 15 June 1994.
16. Letter to Margaret Atwood, 4 June 1971, Collection of Margaret Atwood.
17. Letter to Margaret Atwood, Spring, 1971, Collection of Margaret Atwood.
18. *Magic Animals: Selected Poems Old and New*, Toronto: Macmillan of Canada, 1974, p. 123.
19. Letter to Margaret Atwood, 13 January 1971, Collection of Margaret Atwood.
20. Letter to Margaret Atwood, 13 August 1968, Collection of Margaret Atwood.
21. Letter from Margaret Atwood, February "something," 1973, Collection of Margaret Atwood.

19: The Trojan Horse

1. Letter to Samar Attar, 28 May 1971, Collection of Samar Attar.
2. Interview with Nikos Tsingos, Toronto, 18 December 1992.
3. *Mermaids and Ikons*, Toronto: Anansi, 1978, p. 18.
4. Greek diary notes, 1971, Gwendolyn MacEwen Papers, Thomas Fisher Rare Book Library, University of Toronto, Box 14.
5. Lawrence Durrell, *The Greek Islands*, New York: Viking Press, 1978, p. 222.
6. Ibid., p. 224.
7. *Mermaids and Ikons*, p. 63.
8. In *Mermaids and Ikons* Gwendolyn identifies Agamemnon as Odysseus.
9. *Mermaids and Ikons*, p. 80.
10. *Afterworlds*, Toronto: McClelland and Stewart, 1987, p. 14.
11. Greek diary notes, 1971, Gwendolyn MacEwen Papers, Box 14.
12. *Mermaids and Ikons*, pp. 85-86.
13. Ibid., pp. 25-26.
14. Greek diary notes, 1971, Gwendolyn MacEwen Papers, Box 14.
15. *Mermaids and Ikons*, p. 40.
16. Letter to Samar Attar, 30 October 1971, Collection of Samar Attar.
17. "Printed Reviews," Gwendolyn MacEwen Papers, Box 34.
18. Letter to Margaret Atwood, 9 June 1971, Collection of Margaret Atwood.
19. Interview with Timothy Findley, Toronto, 9 March 1993.
20. Helen Worthington, "Young Poet's Recital Draws Full House," *The Toronto Sun*, 1972.
21. Interview with Michael Ondaatje, Toronto, 15 September 1993.
22. Letter to Margaret Atwood, 26 September 1972, Collection of Margaret Atwood.
23. "How to Build a Trojan Horse," 1973, Gwendolyn MacEwen Papers, Box 12.

24. Interview with Greg Gatenby, Toronto, 8 March 1993.
25. Douglas Fetherling, *Travels by Night*, Toronto: Lester Publishing, 1994, p. 194.
26. "Notes and Correspondence about a television programme on Atlantis, 1973," Gwendolyn MacEwen Papers, Box 12.
27. Interview with Arlene Lampert, Toronto, 1 August 1994.
28. "Twenty Poems," *Exile* Magazine, Vol. 2, No. 1, 1974; the translation of the long poem "Helen" was published in *Amichai and Ritsos: Two Long Poems*, Exile Editions, 1976.
29. Letter to Samar Attar, 30 December 1975, Collection of Samar Attar.

20: Desolate Landscape

1. Clarke Institute of Psychiatry: Admission Report, 21 September 1975. These are admission files and report patient's general condition.
2. Clarke Institute of Psychiatry: Final Note, 29 September 1975.
3. Interview with Stephanie Nynych, Toronto.
4. Letter to Samar Attar, 1 July 1976, Collection of Samar Attar.
5. *Mermaids and Ikons*, Toronto: Anansi, 1978, p. 103.
6. *Afterworlds*, Toronto: McClelland and Stewart, 1987, p. 23.
7. Interview with Nikos Tsingos, Toronto, 3 March 1993.
8. Loose sheets of dream notes, Gwendolyn MacEwen Papers, Thomas Fisher Rare Book Library, University of Toronto, Box 1, file 16, dated 1977.
9. Robert Graves, *The White Goddess*, London: Faber and Faber, 1961, pp. 52-53.
10. Letter to Samar Attar, 7 April 1977, Collection of Samar Attar.
11. Loose sheets of dream notes, Gwendolyn MacEwen Papers, Box 1, file 16, dated 4 December 1977.
12. Interview with Leon Major, Washington, 1 September 1994.
13. *The Trojan Women*, Revision Notes: 9 December 1977, Gwendolyn MacEwen Papers, Box 15.
14. Patricia Keeney Smith, "WQ Interview with Gwendolyn MacEwen," *Cross-Canada Writers' Quarterly*, Vol. 5, No. 1, 1983, p. 17.
15. Interview with Leon Major, Washington, 1 September 1994.
16. Ken Adachi, "Poet Trying Her Luck with Euripides Classic and Smattering of Jazz," *The Toronto Star*, 21 November 1978.
17. Letter to Leon Major, 18 June 1977, Gwendolyn MacEwen Papers, Box 15.
18. Adachi, review.

21: The Gwenness Gone

1. Interview with Jim Polk, Toronto, 4 March 1993.
2. Letter to Margaret Atwood, 3 January 1969, Collection of Margaret Atwood.

3. Letter to Samar Attar, 7 January 1978, Collection of Samar Attar.
4. Letter from Rideau Hall, Ottawa, 6 September 1978, Gwendolyn MacEwen Papers, Thomas Fisher Rare Book Library, University of Toronto, Box 27.
5. "Toronto Symphony Programme," 57th Season, October 24, 25, and 27, 1978.
6. Interview with Charles Pachter, Toronto, 18 June 1993.
7. Letter to Charles Pachter, [undated], Collection of Charles Pachter.
8. *The World of Neshiah* was written for CBC radio in 1967; it was again produced by "Earplay," WHA radio, the University of Wisconsin, 1973.
9. Interview with Judith Merril, Toronto, 10 November 1992.
10. Letter to Samar Attar, 1 May 1978, Collection of Samar Attar.
11. Letter to Samar Attar, 19 October 1979, Collection of Samar Attar.
12. Letter to Margaret Atwood, 10 October 1979, Collection of Margaret Atwood.
13. While Mount Sinai Hospital Department of Records released dates of admission, no other details were forthcoming.
14. Interview with Aasta Levene, Toronto, 29 November 1992.
15. Interview with Charlotte Engel, Toronto, 28 February 1995.

22: Reaching for Life

1. Interview with Ruben Zellermeyer, Toronto, 29 August 1993.
2. Interview with Jane Jacobs, Toronto, 5 February 1995.
3. Interview with John McCombe (Mac) Reynolds, Toronto, 12 July 1994.
4. Interview with Aviva Layton, Los Angeles, 23 August 1993.
5. Interview with Barry Callaghan, Toronto, 18 November 1992.
6. Interview with Leon Whiteson, Los Angeles, 23 August 1993.
7. Interview with John McCombe (Mac) Reynolds, Toronto, 12 July 1994.

23: The Chosen Twin

1. Clinical Institute, Addiction Research Foundation: "Calendar Entries, O.P.D. Progress Notes, Primary Care Progress Summary," 22 October 1981 to 2 November 1982. Summary files were kept on MacEwen's visit that allow me to have a sense of when she went, and what in general was discussed, without breaking doctor/patient confidentiality.
2. Letter to Samar Attar, 10 November 1983, Collection of Samar Attar.
3. Interview with John McCombe (Mac) Reynolds, Toronto, 5 May 1994.
4. T.E. Lawrence, *Seven Pillars of Wisdom*, Harmondsworth: Penguin Modern Classics, 1969, p. 30.
5. *The T.E. Lawrence Poems*, Oakville: Mosaic Press, 1982, p. 67.
6. Letter to Samar Attar, 31 March 1983, Collection of Samar Attar.

7. *The T.E. Lawrence Poems*, p. 59.
8. *Seven Pillars of Wisdom*, p. 514.
9. Ibid., p. 561.
10. Ibid., p. 521.
11. *The T.E. Lawrence Poems*, p. 4.
12. Ibid., p. 16.
13. Ibid., pp. 46-47.
14. Ibid., p. 52.
15. Ibid., p. 42.
16. "Through The Poet's Eye," Program #4, Rogers Cable Television, 28 March 1982. One-hour interview with Gwendolyn MacEwen; host: Rosemary Sullivan.
17. Notes to manuscript of *Noman*, Gwendolyn MacEwen Papers, Thomas Fisher Rare Book Library, University of Toronto, Box 19.
18. Robert Sward, "Spirituality in Canada," *Anthology*, CBC radio feature, 1983: Margaret Atwood, Earle Birney, John Robert Colombo, Joy Kogawa, Gwendolyn MacEwen.

24: Searching for Elsie

1. Clinical Record, 28 April 1981, Department of Health: Hospital Division, Queen Street Mental Health Centre.
2. Interview with Ruben Zellermeyer, Toronto, 10 September 1993.
3. Clinical Record, 9 September 1982, Department of Health: Hospital Division, Queen Street Mental Health Centre.
4. "A Day in the Life of the Old Elmwood," typescript, 1983, published in "Fanfare," *The Globe and Mail*, 12 February 1983, Other Writings, Gwendolyn MacEwen Papers, Box 23.
5. "Noman. Notes for First Draft, 1977-78," Gwendolyn MacEwen Papers, Thomas Fisher Rare Book Library, University of Toronto, Box 19.
6. In *The White Goddess*, Robert Graves offers a number of descriptions of the goddess Kali, which must have been one of Gwen's sources for the myths attached to the Indian goddess. Interestingly, he explains that the skulls that Kali wears as a necklace stand for the fifty signs of the early Sanskrit system of writing, something between an alphabet and a syllabary, which Kali allegedly invented.
7. *Noman's Land*, Toronto: The Coach House Press, 1985, p. 98.
8. Ibid., p. 135.

25: The Black Tunnel Wall

1. Interview with Christos Hatzis, Toronto, 24 August 1994.

2. Interview with Roberta Frank, Toronto, 12 February 1995; Letter to Frank, 20 March 1985.
3. Interview with Aviva Layton, Los Angeles, 23 August 1993.
4. Interview with Mary di Michele, Montreal, 17 November 1992.
5. *Afterworlds*, Toronto: McClelland and Stewart, 1987, p. 19.
6. "England—Travel Notes, 1984," Gwendolyn MacEwen Papers, Thomas Fisher Rare Book Library, University of Toronto, Box 23.
7. Interview with Charles Ritchie, Ottawa, 12 September 1992.
8. "England—Travel Notes, 1984," Gwendolyn MacEwen Papers, Box 23.
9. Letter to author from Fred Cogswell, 23 June 1993.

26: Back Alley Blues

1. Interview with Lynn, Toronto, 23 March 1994. Lynn requested to remain anonymous.
2. Interview with Phyllis Webb, 1983, Phyllis Webb Papers, National Library of Canada.
3. Letter to Judith Merril, 27 February 1985, Collection of Judith Merril. The square brackets indicate MacEwen's addenda in the margin.
4. Interview with Charlotte Engel, Toronto, 28 February 1995.
5. Letter to Christos Hatzis, 9 December 1985, Collection of Christos Hatzis.
6. Interview with Christos Hatzis, Toronto, 24 August 1994.
7. "Primary Care Progress Notes," 28 October 1985, Addiction Research Foundation.
8. *Afterworlds*, Toronto: McClelland and Stewart, 1987, p. 75.
9. Jan Bartley, *Invocations: The Poetry and Prose of Gwendolyn MacEwen*, Vancouver: University of British Columbia Press, 1983.
10. *Magic Animals: Selected Poems Old and New*, Toronto: Macmillan of Canada, 1974, p. 139, 152.
11. "Back Alley Blues," *Now Books*, January 30–February 5, 1986, p. 23. Timothy Findley was one of the people deeply moved by Gwen's campaign to save the cats. The image of Gwen feeding the cats in the back alleys of the Annex in a winter blizzard became the inspiration for his character Amy Wylie, in *Headhunter*, who fights against the extermination of birds in a plague-ridden city. For Findley, Wylie is the "embodiment of the truly civilized" in his novel. Interview, Toronto, 9 March 1993.
12. Letter from Judith Merril, 17 January 1986, Collection of Judith Merril.
13. "Remembering Gwendolyn MacEwen," *Brick: A Literary Journal*, No. 45, Winter 1993, p. 63.
14. Letter to Barbara Bruce, 13 March 1986, Addiction Research Foundation.

27: Afterworlds

1. Interview with Mary Nyquist, Toronto, 24 October 1993.
2. Interview with Karen Hoffman, *The New Edition*, 4 November 1986.
3. "Gwendolyn MacEwen: On Writing and Being Written About," Interview with Peta Gillyatt, *The Varsity*, 9 October 1986.
4. Hoffman, *The New Edition*.
5. Postcard to Aviva Layton, 2 October 1986, Collection of Aviva Layton.
6. Letter to Myra MacFarlane, 31 October 1986, MacEwen Papers.
7. *Afterworlds*, Toronto: McClelland and Stewart, 1987, p. 13.
8. Letter to Margaret Atwood, 28 October 1986, Collection of Margaret Atwood.
9. Interview with Cedric Smith, Toronto, 4 November 1993.
10. *A Wake for Milton*, NFB, Directors: Brian Pollard, Mike Mahoney, 20 August 1986.
11. Interview with Ricardo Rivas, Toronto, 3 August 1993.
12. "My Friends are Dying: Memories of Greg Curnoe, Gwendolyn MacEwen, and bp Nichol, *Canadian Notes and Queries*, No. 48, 1994: 1, pp. 6-7.
13. *Afterworlds*, p. 36.
14. Ibid., p. 35.
15. "Medical History," 7 August 1987, Addiction Research Foundation.
16. "Consultation Form," 10 September 1987, Addiction Research Foundation.
17. Interview with Janis Rapoport, Toronto, 23 May 1994.
18. Interview with Judith Merril, Toronto, 25 May 1994.
19. Interview with Mieke Bevelander, Toronto, 14 December 1993.
20. Interview with Roberta Frank, Toronto, 12 February 1995.
21. Interview with M.T. Kelly, 13 February 1995.
22. Joyce Marshall, "Remembering Gwendolyn MacEwen," p. 64.
23. Report of the Centre of Forensic Sciences, Ministry of the Solicitor General. The report elaborates: Metabolic Acidosis. Diabetic Ketoacidosis is the most common cause of metabolic acidosis. Alcoholic ketoacidosis occurs in those with chronic alcoholism and a recent history of binge drinking, little or no food intake, and recurring vomiting. There was no evidence of ingested substances in this case. [The convulsions resulting from this condition can be fatal unless there is immediate medical attention.]
24. *Afterworlds*, p. 123. *Afterworlds* won the Governor General's Award for Poetry. Gwendolyn MacEwen had been informed of this before she died. The prize was awarded posthumously in the Spring of 1988.

BIBLIOGRAPHY: GWENDOLYN MACEWEN

Poetry
Selah, Aleph Press, Toronto, 1961.
The Drunken Clock, Aleph Press, Toronto, 1961.
The Rising Fire, Contact Press, Toronto, 1963.
A Breakfast for Barbarians, The Ryerson Press, Toronto, 1966.
The Shadow-Maker, Macmillan, Toronto, 1969.
The Armies of the Moon, Macmillan, Toronto, 1972.
Magic Animals: Selected Poems Old and New, Macmillan, Toronto, 1974.
The Fire-Eaters, Oberon Press, Ottawa, 1976.
Trojan Women: The Trojan Women by Euripedes and *Helen* and *Orestes* by Yannis Ritsos; translated with Nikos Tsingos, Exile Editions, Toronto, 1981.
The T.E. Lawrence Poems, Mosaic Press, Oakville, 1982.
Earth-Light: Selected Poetry 1963–1982, General Publishing, Toronto, 1982.
Afterworlds, McClelland and Stewart, Toronto, 1987.
The Poetry of Gwendolyn MacEwen: The Early Years (Volume One), eds. Margaret Atwood and Barry Callaghan, Exile Editions, 1993.
The Poetry of Gwendolyn MacEwen: The Later Years (Volume Two), eds. Margaret Atwood and Barry Callaghan, Exile Editions, 1994.

Novels
Julian the Magician, Corinth Books, New York; Macmillan, Toronto, 1963.
King of Egypt, King of Dreams, Macmillan, Toronto, 1971.

Short Stories
Noman, Oberon Press, Ottawa, 1972.
Noman's Land, The Coach House Press, Toronto, 1985.

Travel
Mermaids and Ikons: A Greek Summer, Anansi, Toronto, 1978.

Juvenile
The Chocolate Moose, N/C Press, Toronto, 1979.
The Honey Drum, Mosaic Press, Oakville, 1983.
Dragon Sandwiches, Black Moss Press, Windsor, 1987.

Theatre
The Trojan Women, Playwrights Co-op, Toronto, 1979.
The Birds: A Modern Adaptation, Exile Editions, 1993.

INDEX

A

Acorn, Milton, 114-118, 188, 269-270
  correspondence with Gwen *see* MacEwen, Gwendolyn Margaret, LETTERS
  early friendship with Gwen, 118-122, 126-128
  forms Interpoet group, 134-135
  Gwen obtains divorce, 194-198
  Gwen's interpretation of their marriage, 188, 244-245, 397-398
  marriage to Gwen, 129-134, 151-152
  memorial evening for, 397-398
  memories of him, 117, 129, 131-132, 152, 261
  mental breakdowns, 115, 152-154
  personality, 115-116, 132-134
  as a poet, 117-118, 158, 268, 270
  reaction to breakup, 152-154, 196
  receives award as "The People's Poet", 270
Adachi, Ken, 270
"Adam's Alphabet" (MacEwen), 75-77, 146
Addiction Research Foundation, 336-337, 382, 403-405
Afterworlds (MacEwen), xii, 378, 392, 396, 402
Ahvenus, Marty, 160, 186
A.J.M. Smith Award for Poetry, 288
Akhenaton, 232-235, 240
  Gwen's novel on, see *King of Egypt, King of Dreams*

Alcoholics Anonymous (AA), 44-45, 335
Alcoholism
  and the artist, 340
  Aunt Maud, 44
  Gwen, 44-45, 169, 250, 263, 288, 292, 293-294, 295-296, 298, 300, 301, 312, 317, 321-321, 325-326, 334-335, 336-338, 340, 364, 368-369, 382-383, 388-392, 398, 402-406
  Gwen's father, 38, 39, 44-45, 62, 72, 83
Aleph Press, 123
Allan Gardens, poetry reading controversy, 134-135
Animals, 274, 304, 346-347, 403
  Gwen's care for, 386-387, 406
Annex neighbourhood, 327-328, 386
"Anthology" (CBC programme), 191, 260
Antiparos (Greek island), 280-284, 300
Anti-war movement of mid-1960s, 172
Antony, 366-369, 375-378
Arabic
  Gwen's knowledge of, 244
  Gwen writes poetry in, 233
Arabs
  Arab friend in high school, 58
  Gwen's sympathy for, 138
  T.E. Lawrence Poems, 338-353
Archetypes, 236, 239, 364
Aristides, 363
Armies of the Moon, The (MacEwen), xii, 260, 266, 288
Arnott, Tom, 91, 117, 135, 168
Artists' Alliance, 317
"Artists in the Schools" programmes, 312
Asthma, 250-251, 292
Atlantic Monthly, The, supplement on Canada (1964), 179-180
Atomic bomb, 235-236
Attar, Samar, 233, 271, 274, 302
  see also MacEwen, Gwendolyn Margaret, LETTERS, to Samar Attar
Atwood, Margaret, 76, 106, 151, 172, 184, 188, 190, 198, 252, 291, 385
  friendship with Gwen, 108-114, 219-220, 227-230, 273-276, 311, 333, 396, 397

publishes *The Edible Woman*, 241
reaction to marriage of Gwen and Milton, 129
remembers Milton Acorn, 117
see also MacEwen, Gwendolyn Margaret, LETTERS, to Margaret Atwood
Aunt Jess, 369-370
Aunt Margaret. See Martin, Margaret Mitchell
Aunt Maud. See McEwen, Maud
Aunt Winnie, 369-370
Avisar, Josef, 147-148, 396
Avison, Margaret, 73, 106, 108, 129, 176

B

"Back Alley Blues" (article by MacEwen), 386-387
Bateman, Jack, 163
Bear (Engel), 319
Beats, 186-187
Beauvoir, Simone de, 172
Ben-Shahar, Abraham, 139
Bevelander, Mieke, 402, 407, 409
Blackstone, Harry, 40, 41, 59, 72, 88
"Black Tunnel Wall, The", 16, 356, 369, 394
Blais, Marie-Claire, 113, 179, 244
Gwen translates her poems, 190-191
Blood Axe Press, 370
"Blue" (MacEwen), 367-368
Blumenthal, Joe, 81-84, 107
Boatman, The (Macpherson), 106, 112
Bohemian Embassy, 102-103, 104-108, 114, 165, 185
controversy over poetry readings, 134-135
Bowering, George, 72, 268, 270
Brain's the Target, The (Acorn), 126
Braun, Victor, 316
Breakfast for Barbarians, A (MacEwen), 185-187
Breakfast metaphor, 151
"Breakfast, The" (MacEwen), 149-150
Bruce, Barbara, 336-338, 382-385, 391, 392, 402, 403, 404, 405-406
Brydson, Sherry, 357

C

Cabala, 72, 73, 75, 90, 145, 217
Cairo, 199-204, 208
Callaghan, Barry, 169, 291, 294
memories of Gwen, 333
Call of the Lark (MacEwen translation of Hussein novel), 241
Canada Council, 334, 357, 400
grants to Gwen (1965), 192; (1976), 299; (1984), 369
Canadian Broadcasting Corporation. See CBC
Canadian Forum, The, 59, 123
"Canadian Monsters" (Atwood), 277
"Caravan, The" (MacEwen), 247
"Carnival, The" (MacEwen), 260
Cats, 170, 248, 256, 304, 331, 365, 410
Gwen cares for wild cats, 386-387
CBC (Canadian Broadcasting Corporation), 179, 191, 244, 260, 262, 293, 324, 361
"Certain Flowers" (MacEwen), 125
Chelsea Arts Club, 339, 369, 370
"Child and the Cathedral, The" (MacEwen), 346-347
Chinatown, 103
Chocolate Moose, The (children's book by MacEwen), 317
"Choice, The" (MacEwen), 180-181
Circle Game, The (Atwood), 184
Civil disobedience, Interpoet group, 134-135
Clarke Institute, 297-299
Coach House Press, 327, 360, 399
Cogswell, Fred, 374
Cohen, Leonard, 106, 112, 151, 165, 179, 332-333
Coleman, Victor, 161-162, 169
Collier, Ron, 260
Colombo, John Robert, 106
Comic books, 40, 42-43, 72
Compañeros (musical group), 255, 292, 399
"Compass, The" (MacEwen), 174
Contact Press, 99, 123, 164
Corinth Books, 98
Couzyn, Jeni, 370
Cronenberg, David, 151

Cullen, Don, 104, 105, 107, 117, 134, 152
"Cultural revolution" in 1967, 232

D

"Dance at the Mental Hospital, A" (MacEwen), 178
Danforth area of Toronto, 271-273
"Dark Pines Under Water" (MacEwen), 236-237
"Dark Stars" (MacEwen), 238
"Day in the Life of the Old Elmwood, A" (article by MacEwen), 356-357
"Day of Twelve Princes, The" (story by Gwen at age 18), 47-49, 71-72
"Death beg", 207
Déjà vu, 285
"Deraa" (MacEwen), 348-349
Dialectics of Nature (Engels), 140-141
di Michele, Mary, 366
Donnell, David, 126
Double Persephone (Atwood), 113
"Draft dodgers", 172
Dragon Sandwiches (children's book by MacEwen), 392
Dreams, 84, 85-86, 98, 144, 169, 180, 204-208, 217, 221-222, 224-226, 236, 239-240, 248, 255-259, 296, 313, 373-374
  childhood dreams, 1-2, 26, 34, 37, 95
  dream journal, 1, 34, 98, 221
  Gwen writes poems about, 237
  of her mother, 257-258
  of Nikos, 255, 258-259, 301-302, 305
  recurring nightmare of burying her father alive, 86, 156
Drunken Clock, The (MacEwen), 123, 124
Dudek, Louis, 164
Duncan, Robert, 99, 197
Dürer, Albrecht, 164
Durrell, Lawrence, 280
Dylan, Bob, 163

E

East End of London, 3-5, 357, 370-371

Edible Woman, The (Atwood), 241
Egypt, 186, 187
  Gwen's visit to (1966), 199-204, 208
  King of Egypt, King of Dreams, 199, 200-201, 232, 233-235, 240-241, 261, 287
  "Nefertiti", 57-58
Egypt of the Pharaohs (Gardiner), 187
Egyptian Museum in Cairo, 200-204
Egyptology, Gwen studies, 186-187, 193-194
Eighth Street Book Shop (New York), 98, 100
Elmwood Girls' Hotel, 243, 322, 356
Emden, Karen, 378
Engel, Charlotte, 324-325, 380
Engel, Howard, 291
Engel, Marian, 291, 319, 321, 322, 324, 363
  death, 378
  Gwen's memories of, 378-380
England, Gwen visits (1984), 369-374
Esoteric philosophy, 72, 73, 74-75, 89-91, 145
"Eternally Lost" (Gwen's story at age 13), 53
Exile, Gwen's sense of, 246, 247, 308
Exile magazine, 294, 333
Extra-sensory experience, 285-286

F

Fears, 126, 127-128, 139, 206-207, 224, 225, 250, 313-314, 323, 332
  Gwen's fear of fast travel, 252-253, 271, 300, 369
Feminism, 170-172, 273-274, 394-395
Fetherling, Douglas, 242-245
  memories of Gwen, 243, 291
Fiddlehead magazine, 374
"Filter systems", 353
Findley, Timothy, 288
"Fire" (story by MacEwen), 250
Fire Eaters, The (MacEwen), 299
First Floor Club, 84, 102
Flat Earth Society, 275
Flying
  dreams or fantasies of, 34, 42-43, 95, 98
  Gwen's fear of, 252-253, 271, 300, 369
Folk music, 103
"For Alick MacEwen" (MacEwen), 177-178

Foster children at 38 Keele Street, 24, 27-33, 207
  see also Lyons, Dora; Lyons, Marion
Franck, Albert, 103-104
Francks, Don, 103
"Frank", 408
Frank, Roberta, 364, 410
Fraser, Ray, 275
Frye, Northrop, 112
Fulford, Robert, 160

G

Gabriela (MacEwen), 77-81, 85
Gallery of Contemporary Art, 104
Gatenby, Greg, 291
Gerrard Street Village, 104
Glasgow, Gwen visits, 372-374
Globe and Mail, The, 179-180
Gnosticism, 72, 73, 90-91
God, 239, 266
  "God-lust", 233
  in Gwen's childhood imagination, 43, 44
  Gwen's concept of, 352-353
Godfrey, Dave, 243
Gould, Glenn, 361-362
Governor General's Award, 244
  awarded to Gwen for *The Shadow-Maker* (1970), 268-270
Graves, Robert, 112, 237, 241, 302
Greece
  first visit (1971), 278-287
  second visit (1976), 287, 300-301
Greek language, Gwen's knowledge of, 242, 244, 246, 272, 294, 310
Greek Orthodox religion, 284
Gzowski, Peter, 160

H

Hatzis, Christos, 361-364
  memories of Gwen, 381-382
"Helen" (MacEwen translation from Ritsos), 294
Henry's restaurant, 108, 399

"Hermes of Praxiteles", 287
Hieroglyphics, Gwen studies, 187
Hippies, 160, 184, 232
Hiroshima, 235-236
Hollander, Xaviera, 291
Homes, 130-131, 159, 184, 190, 240, 261, 271, 274, 310, 312, 327, 364-365, 399
  childhood home *see* Thirty-eight Keele Street
Horoscope, 219, 311
House of Anansi Press, 243, 309
House of Hambourg, 102

I

Interpoet, 134, 135
"Isis in Darkness" (Atwood), 108
Israel, Gwen visits (1962), 134, 135, 136-148, 149, 151-152, 338
"It Comes Upon You" (MacEwen), 265-266
I've Tasted My Blood (Acorn), 268

J

Jacobs, Jane, 330
Jaeger, David, 361
Jaffa, 137, 138
James, Lawrence, 349
"Janus" (Joe Nickell), 163
Jazz clubs in 1950s Toronto, 102
Jerusalem, 135, 136-137, 139, 140-141, 142-144, 146, 147-148
Jewish mystical tradition, Gwen studies, 72, 73, 74-75
Jonas, George, 293
Julian the Magician (novel by MacEwen), 89, 91-95, 98-100, 164, 178-179
Jung, Carl, 222, 235, 236, 238, 240

K

Kahlo, Frida, 155, 366
Kelly, M.T., 291, 408
Kenyon, Lee, 370, 371, 372
Kerouac, Jack, 186
Kidd, Virginia, 378

King of Egypt, King of Dreams (novel by MacEwen), 192-193, 199, 200-201, 208-209, 232, 233, 240-241, 261, 287-288
Kingsmere (Mackenzie King's estate), 168, 275-276, 358
Koran, The, 58, 141

L

Lampert, Arlene, 293-294
Lampert, Gerald, 293
Laporte, Pierre, 268
Last Exit to Brooklyn (Selby), 170
Lawrence, T.E. (Lawrence of Arabia), 143, 284, 331, 338-339, 340-353, 388, *see also T.E. Lawrence Poems* (MacEwen)
Layton, Aviva, 332, 333, 395, 396
   memories of Gwen, 332, 333-334, 365-366
Layton, Irving, 95, 106, 110, 128, 179
   Gwen's letters to, 95-97, 165-166, 172
Leavens, Redge, 84
Lee, Dennis, 232, 243
Lefolii, Ken, 135
Lefteris, 290
"Left Hand and Hiroshima, The" (MacEwen), 235-236
Le Hibou (Ottawa coffee house), 124
"Let Me Make This Perfectly Clear" (MacEwen), 401-402
"Letters to Josef in Jerusalem" (MacEwen), 396
"Letter to an Old Lover" (MacEwen), 188, 210-211
"Letter to Josef" (MacEwen), 147-148
Let Us Compare Mythologies (Cohen), 106, 112
Levene, Aasta
   on marriage of Gwen and Milton, 129
   memories of Gwen, 322-324, 369, 381
Lilith, 214-215, 217-219, 358
"Lilith" (MacEwen), 218-219
Loch Ness monster, 274
Loneliness, 140, 173, 253, 296, 321, 331, 338, 367, 378, 401
Lynn, 375-377
Lyons, Dora, 27-28, 29-31, 355
   memories of 38 Keele Street, 27-28
   memories of Gwen, 27-28
   memories of Gwen's father, 44
Lyons, Marion, 3, 27-28, 46, 87, 207
   husband encourages Gwen, 59-60
   memories of 38 Keele Street, 28-33
   memories of Gwen, 54
   memories of Gwen's father, 32, 44

M

McDermid, Anne (agent), 312
McEwen, Alick (father of Gwen), 2, 3
   alcoholism, 38-39, 44-45, 62, 72, 82-83
   Carol's memories of, 22, 24, 25-26, 44, 45
   death, 82-83
   dependent personality, 66
   effect of Elsie's problems on, 13-14
   Gwen's memories of him, 310, 331
   Gwen taken from him, 46
   letters to Gwen, 50-53, 62-63, 64-65, 68-70, 74
   Marion Lyons' memories of, 32
   as a photographer, 11, 14, 22, 36, 38, 310-311
   relationship with Gwen, 40, 44-45, 46, 53-54, 55, 72-73, 80, 83
   returns to Toronto, 55
   sales rep for Kodak, 36, 38
   separation from Elsie, 45-46
   writes stories, 69-70
   youth, 11
McEwen, Carol (sister of Gwen), 3, 33, 71, 83, 151, 188, 207, 355, 410
   birth and childhood, 12, 13, 14-15, 20-21, 22, 36-37, 38
   memories of Aunt Margaret, 24-25, 26
   memories of Bob Mallory, 163
   memories of father (Alick), 21, 22, 24-25, 44, 45
   memories of Gwen, 36, 40, 45, 46, 58, 255, 289
   memories of mother (Elsie), 20-22, 25, 26, 36-37, 38, 39
   memories of Uncle Charlie, 23-24, 32
   relationship with Gwen, 36, 39-41, 129, 231-232

relationship with mother, 311
separates from her family, 39, 46
McEwen, Elsie Mitchell (mother of Gwen), 3, 27, 49, 50, 82, 83, 84, 129
  appearance, 21-22
  birth and childhood, 8-9, 370
  birth of Gwen, 19
  Carol's memories of, 20, 21, 25, 26, 36-37, 38, 39
  death, 355, 356
  fears, 10
  "good times", 14, 15, 27, 32-33, 36
  Gwen's dreams of her, 257-258
  letters to Gwen, 63
  Marion Lyons' memories of, 31-33
  marriage, 12, 27
  mental problems, 7, 9-10, 12-19, 21, 25-26, 28, 33, 35, 36-37, 38, 39, 54, 174-176, 311, 354
  pride in Gwen's poetry, 123-124, 179
  reaction to marriage of Gwen and Milton, 129
  relationship with Gwen, 72, 175, 176-178, 183, 243, 291, 322-323, 354-355
  separates from Alick, 45
  violence of her illness, 37
MacEwen, Gwendolyn Margaret
  AWARDS AND HONOURS
    A.J.M. Smith Award for Poetry, 288
    appointed writer-in-residence at University of Toronto, 393-394, 402
    appointed writer-in-residence at University of Western Ontario, 378
    Canada Council grant (1965), 192
    Canada Council grant (1976), 299
    Canada Council grant (1984), 369
    Governor General's Award (1970), 268-270
    Queen's Silver Jubilee Medal (1978), 316
  FAMILY RELATIONSHIPS
    aunts in England, 369-370
    father's death, 83, 85, 140, 144, 156
    grandmother, 370, 371
    memories of her father, 310-311, 331
    nephews and nieces, 261-262, 290
    realizes violence of her mother's illness, 37
    relationship with Carol, 36, 39, 129, 231-232
    relationship with her father, 40, 44-46, 53, 55, 72-73, 80, 83, 177-178, 214, 259
    relationship with her mother, 72, 79, 82, 174-175, 176-177, 178, 183, 257-258, 291, 311-312, 322, 354-357
    searches family roots in England, 6, 369-370
    taken from her father, 45-46, 331
    see also LETTERS, *below*
  LETTERS
    correspondence with Aunt Maud, 312
    from her father, 50-53, 62-63, 64-66, 68, 69-70, 74
    from Judith Merril, 388-391
    from Margaret Atwood, 229, 246-247, 276-277
    from Milton Acorn, 128, 153-154, 195-196, 198, 269-270
    from Salah, 222-223
    to Al Purdy, 133, 167, 168, 169-170, 178-179, 193
    to Aviva Layton, 395-396
    to Charles Pachter, 318
    to David Mason, 182-183
    to her father, 56, 60-62, 66-67
    to Irving Layton, 95-98, 165-166, 172
    to Judith Merril, 378-380
    to Margaret Atwood, 109, 113, 192, 194, 196-197, 198, 201-203, 208-209, 219, 221-222, 226, 227, 228-229, 230, 231-233, 237, 241, 242, 244, 247, 248-249, 252, 262-263, 268, 273, 274, 275-276, 287-288, 321, 397
    to Milton Acorn, 118-122, 126-127, 149, 152-153, 155-158
    to Robert Weaver, 254, 268-269, 270
    to Samar Attar, 271, 278, 287, 294, 299-300, 302-305, 315-316, 320-321, 339, 342, 351
    to Tom Marshall, 241
  LIFE AND DEATH
    birth, 19, 311, 337

childhood fears and suffering, 1-2, 3, 28, 34-49
early sexual trauma?, 206-208, 251, 258, 337-338
early writings, 40, 56, 57-58, 59-60
fascination with magic and mysticism produces *Julian the Magician*, 72, 73, 74-76, 85, 89-101
finds cultural centre in Bohemian Embassy, 107-108, 112
first marriage (to Milton), 129-135
Israel (1962), 134, 135, 136-148, 149, 151-152, 338
leaves Milton, 152-158
living with Mallory, 152-165
meets and loves Salah, 188-190, 210-230
Nikos and Greece, 245-249, 253-255, 278-296
recognition as an outstanding poet, 268-270, 287-288, 316
torment of alcoholism *see* Alcoholism
writer dies young, xi-xii, 408-409

PERSONAL CHARACTERISTICS
appearance, ix, x, xvi, 243
bravery, 338, 411
clothes, 243, 263, 264-265
drawn to outsiders, 58-59, 72, 134, 143, 155, 173-175, 182, 328-329, 382, 400-401, 408
dreams *see* Dreams
"drive to life" vs. "drive towards death", 275, 406, 409-410, 246, 247, 308
exile, imaginative, 246, 247, 308
fears *see* Fears
humour, 265, 275, 310, 311, 366, 377, 380, 395-396
illnesses *see* Alcoholism; Asthma
language fluency, (Arabic and Egyptian hieroglyphics) 187-188, 191-193, 271; (Coptic) 220; (French) 190-191; (Hebrew) 73-74, 75, 138; (modern Greek), 242, 244, 246, 272, 294, 310
loneliness, 140, 253, 296, 321, 331, 338, 367, 378, 401
musical talent, 26, 40, 54, 56, 57, 82, 243-244, 331

mysticism, 72-76, 84-91, 100-101, 215-216, 220-221
political interests, 77-80, 82, 172-173, 320
psychic side, 169, 244, 275-276, 285-286
repression, 72, 219, 224-225, 282, 322-323
risk-taking, 46-47, 49, 165, 180
secretiveness *see* Secretiveness
self-doubt, 225, 226, 368, 370-371, 408
shyness, 197-198, 370, 385
"stage self" *see* Poetry readings

POETRY (CHARACTER, SOURCES)
alternate realities, 87-88
archetypes, 236, 239, 364
childhood suffering as source of gift, 41, 43-44, 258, 259
darkness of imagination, 259
discusses her motivations for poetry, 124
dreams *see* Dreams
ideas on art and the artist, 318
muse, 114, 246, 311-312, 352
myths *see* Myths
independence, 149-151, 187, 188
poetic vision, 385
reading, 40, 42-43, 72, 73, 89, 99-101, 187, 221-222, 396
what writing meant to her, 95-97, 165-166, 260

McEwen, Maud (aunt of Gwen), 10-11, 26, 27, 52, 53, 84, 129, 312, 339
McFadden, David, memories of Gwen, 399-401
MacFarlane, Myra, 396
Macmillan of Canada, 99, 178, 191, 232, 240, 241, 261
Macpherson, Jay, 106, 108, 112, 241
"Magic Cats" (MacEwen), 386
Magic and magicians, 41, 42, 72, 75, 88, 100, 159, 162, 163, 164, 167, 168, 169, 276-277
Mailer, Norman, 170
Major, Leon, 306, 307, 308
Mallory, Bob, 291
  author's meetings with, 162-164
  describes Salah, 188
  memories of Gwen, 162-164, 169
  others remember him from the 1960s, 160-162

paintings, 160, 161, 163, 164, 182
relationship with Gwen, 152, 154, 161-163, 164-165, 167-168, 170, 180, 181-183
Mandrake, Leon, 163
Manuscrits de Pauline Archange, Les (Blais), 244
Manzini, Mario, 84, 88, 89
Marinatos, Spiros, 293
Marshall, Joyce, 319, 378, 391, 392, 404, 409
memoir of Gwen, 392
Marshall, Tom, 235, 241, 291
Martin, Charles (uncle of Gwen), 3, 5-6, 27, 55, 83, 207
Carol's memories of, 23-24
Marion Lyons' memories of, 31-33
Martin, Margaret Mitchell (aunt of Gwen), 3, 4, 5, 6, 7, 10, 12, 13, 14, 19, 21, 22-24, 25, 35, 36, 37, 39, 44, 46, 54, 55, 70, 73, 83, 312
Carol's memories of, 24-25, 26
the Lyons sisters' memories of, 27-28, 29-33
Marvel Family (comic books), 42-43
Mason, David, 160, 161, 162, 181-183
memories of Gwen, 181-182
remembers Bob Mallory from the 1960s, 160-161
Maudsley Psychiatric Hospital (London), 9
"Meditations of a Seamstress" (MacEwen), 264-265
Melody Mill (jazz club), 102
"Memoirs of a Mad Cook" (MacEwen), 263-264, 296
Mermaids and Ikons (travelogue by MacEwen), 279, 285, 286-287, 300, 309, 316
Merril, Judith, 319-320, 321, 330, 367, 378, 388-391, 407, 408
Middle East *see* Arabs; Egypt; Israel; *T.E. Lawrence Poems*
Miller, Henry, 170
Miller, Peter, 99, 164
"Mirrored Gem" (MacEwen), 61
Misogyny of 1960s, 109-111, 270
Moment (magazine), 126
Money problems, 179, 190, 191, 263, 293, 295, 298-299, 312, 316, 319, 324, 333-334, 385-386, 399-400, 404

Monotheism, 233, 235
Montreal, cultural mecca in the 1950s, 106, 116
"Morning Laughter" (MacEwen), 176-177
"Morphing" (computer programme), 338
Morrison, Arthur, 4
"Mountain of Glory" (MacEwen), 60
Mulhallen, Karen, 333
Muse, 114, 246, 311-312
Mysticism, 72-76, 89-91, 100-101, 215-216, 220-221, 352
Mystras, Greece, 285-286
Mythology, 112-113
Myths, 168-169, 170-171, 187, 189, 214, 215, 217, 236-237, 246, 276, 284, 358

N

Names, 75, 162
Gwen changes, 40-41, 60
"Nefertiti" (poem by Gwen at age 16), 57-58
Newlove, John, 232
Nimchuk, Michael John, 84
"Nine Arcana of the Kings, The" (MacEwen), 240, 362
Niverville, Louis de, 34-35, 207
Noman (collection of stories by MacEwen), 168, 216-217, 251, 275-277, 288
Noman's Land (novel by MacEwen), 203-204, 312, 318, 320, 358-360, 368, 388, 389, 390
"November" (MacEwen), 368
Nowlan, Alden, 275
Now magazine, 386
Nynych, Stephanie, 296, 297, 299
Nyquist, Professor Mary, 394

O

"Oarsman and the Seamstress, The" (story by MacEwen), 216-217
October Crisis of 1970, 268
Old Angelo's, 103
Ondaatje, Michael, 151, 190, 288, 385
"One Arab Flute" (MacEwen), 148
On the Road (Kerouac), 110, 170

P

Pachter, Charles, 317-319
  memories of Gwen, 318
Palance, Jack, 395-396, 406-407
Papandreou, Andreas, 246, 292
Papa Stephanos, 269, 282, 285
"Parents, The" (MacEwen), 345
Paros (Greek island), 280
Patchen, Kenneth, 72
"Peace Conference, The" (MacEwen), 343
Persephone, 113
Physics, Gwen reads, 396
"Poem" (MacEwen), 239
Poetry in contemporary culture, 385-386
Poetry readings, 84, 126, 177, 179, 185, 190, 232, 244, 252, 262, 294, 312, 402
  at Allan Gardens, 134-135
  at the Bohemian Embassy, 107-108
  reading in Town Hall, St. Lawrence Centre (1972), 288
Polk, Jim, 220-221, 309-316
  memories of Gwen, 313-315, 316, 325-326, 357
Pollock, Jackson, 111
Polytheism, 235
Prism International, 188
Protestant Children's Home, 3, 6, 27, 31
Purdy, Al, 116, 117, 167, 168, 169, 172, 179, 193, 198, 397
  best man at marriage of Gwen and Milton, 129
  on Gwen and Milton, 131-132, 133, 152

Q

Queen's Silver Jubilee Medal, awarded to Gwen (1978), 316
Queen Street Mental Health Centre, 7, 9, 63, 82, 175-176, 243, 311, 331, 354, 355, 356
Queen Street West, 59, 82
Queen's University, 190

R

Rapoport, Janis, 406
Red River Flood (Winnipeg, 1950), 36
Reynolds, Mac, 159, 193, 290, 330, 335, 336, 339, 369, 370, 391
  memories of Gwen, 272, 317, 339, 355, 408
Rising Fire, The (MacEwen), 164
Ritchie, Charles, 370
Ritsos, Yannis, 246, 294, 300-301, 304
Rivas, Ricardo, 398-399
Rivera, Diego, 155, 366
Rochdale College, 232
Romantic love, 368
Rosenblatt, Joe, 135, 251, 367
Royal Ontario Museum, 193, 312
Rule, Jane, 193, 197, 261
Ryerson Press, 232

S

Safed, Israel, 145, 146
Sage, Joe, 116
St. Lawrence Centre, 320
Salah, 188-190, 191-194, 197, 199, 201, 210-219, 242
  author's visit to, 211-218
  ending of relationship with Gwen, 221-230
  Gwen devastated by ending of relationship, 224-230, 250
  Gwen's love poems to, 210-211, 240, 396
  Gwen visits his relations in Egypt, 201, 208
  letters to Gwen, 221-224
  life with Gwen in 1965, 191-192
  memories of Gwen, 211-216, 217, 411
Saturnalia (source of *Noman*), 168, 169, 170, 171, 275
Save the Children programme, 387
School friends, 56, 57, 58
Scissors-Grinder, The (MacEwen, unpublished play), 308
Secretiveness, xv, 188, 206-207, 214, 230, 274, 287, 293-294, 301-302, 323, 369, 382, 385, 399, 403

"Seeing Eye Dogs" (MacEwen), 383-384
Seferis, George, 280, 284
Selah (MacEwen), 123
Self-education, 87
Seven Pillars of Wisdom (Lawrence), 340-345
Sex
  terror for child, 31, 49
  and violence, 172-173
Sexual politics, 170
Sexual revolution, 170
Shadow-Maker, The (MacEwen), 233, 238-240, 241
"Shelley" (Gwen's friend), 82
"Skulls and Drums" (MacEwen), 158
Smith, Cedric, 117, 397-398
Smoking, 251, 312
"Snow" (story by MacEwen), 248
"Social protest" poems, 267
Sokolowsky, Jonah, 143
"Solar Wind" (MacEwen), 351-352
Souster, Raymond, 106, 123, 164
Star Wars, 364
Stein, Gertrude, 172
Steryannis, Thanasis, 246
"Stones and Angels" (MacEwen), 300-301
Sufi, 215
Suicide, Gwen writes about, 180-181
Susan (Gwen's cousin in Scotland), 374
Sward, Robert, 352, 353
Swimming, 282, 283, 336, 357, 358-359, 365, 383

T

"Tafas" (MacEwen), 350
Tamarack Review, The, 80, 123, 179, 396
"Tao of Physics, The" (MacEwen), 410
Tarot cards, 72, 169, 219, 221
Tean Dadóir (magazine), 124
T.E. Lawrence Poems (MacEwen), ix-x, 331, 338-353
Terror and Erebus (verse play by MacEwen, included in *Afterworlds*), 191, 296
Tesla (MacEwen), 191
Theodorakis, Mikis, 289, 292
"There Is No Place to Hide" (MacEwen), 341
Thirty-eight Keele Street, 2, 3, 6, 19, 20, 22, 23, 25, 26, 27, 28, 30, 395, 411
  darkroom in basement, 25, 26
  foster children, 24-25, 27, 28-33, 207
  Gwen and mother return to, 50
  Gwen's basement room, 55, 72
  in Gwen's dreams, 34, 257
  see also Lyons, Dora; Lyons, Marion
Tin Drum, The (Grass), 79
"To Mallory" (MacEwen), 164, 165
Toronto
  in the 1980s, 385-386
  "cultural revolution" in 1967, 232
  Noman's Land shows Gwen's knowledge of, 358
Toronto Dance Theatre, 363
Toronto Psychiatric Institute, 13
Toronto Star, The, 134-135
Toronto Symphony, 316
Town, Harold, 103, 104
Translation projects, 190-191, 233
  into Greek, 294
Travel
  first visit to Greece (1971), 278-287
  Gwen develops fear of fast travel, 252-253, 271
  second trip to Greece (1976), 287, 300-301
  stoned by Arab boys in Israel, 142
  suffers rape attempt in Israel, 138-139, 140, 207
  visit to Egypt (1966), 199-204
  visit to England (1984), 369-374
  visit to Israel (1962), 134, 135, 136-148, 149, 151, 338
Travel notebooks (England), 369-374; (Greece), *see Mermaids and Ikons*; (Israel), 140-141, 146
Trojan Horse café, 255, 289-293, 295, 298-299, 399
  becomes a centre for Greek culture, 293
  Gwen and Nikos open, 289-292
Trojan Women, The (Euripedes, translation by MacEwen), 246, 306-308, 320

Trudeau, Pierre, 230, 233, 244
Tsingos, Nikos, 245-249, 253-256, 258-259, 278-296, 310, 361, 367, 368
  dancer and musician, 253-255
  divorced from Gwen, 367, 375
  first meeting with Gwen, 246
  Gwen's dreams of him, 255-256, 257-259, 301-302, 305
  Gwen's jealousy, 254-255, 289
  happiness of love relationship for Gwen, 248-250, 382
  life with Gwen, 261, 269, 271-273
  memories of Gwen, 246-250, 251, 252-253, 262, 279-280, 283-284, 284-290, 294, 300, 301
  opens Trojan Horse with Gwen, 289-291
  personality, 255
  remarries, 381
  stays a friend after separation, 301, 312, 315, 320-321, 407
  wedding to Gwen, 278-287
Tyson, Ian, 103

U

Unconscious, 236, 237, 239, 313
"Universe And" (MacEwen), 144-145
University of Toronto, 327
  Gwen appointed writer-in-residence, 393-394, 402
  Gwen enters and quits programme in Middle Eastern studies, 193-194, 208-209
University of Toronto Quarterly, 123
University of Western Ontario, Gwen writer-in-residence at, 378

V

Van Dijk, Rudi, 316-317
Varma, D.P., 233
Vietnam, 173, 232-233
Village Book Store, 160, 165, 186
Violin, 26, 40, 54, 56, 57, 82, 243-244, 331
Vocal Magazine, 102

W

Wah Mai Café, 59, 72
Walker, Lawrence, 84, 129
War, 78-80, 172-173
Ward's Island, 130-131, 159-160, 168, 170, 172
War Measures Act invoked (1970), 268
Weaver, Robert, 80, 123, 179, 191, 260, 268, 270, 293, 324
Webb, Phyllis, 100, 106
Wedding with Nikos, 278-287
  honeymoon, 285-287
  wedding day, 285
Western Technical-Commercial School (Western Tech), 54, 55-56, 57, 58, 395
  Gwen leaves, 66-70
Whitby Psychiatric Hospital, 16-18, 19, 29, 35
White Goddess, The (Graves), 112-113, 302
"White Horse, The" (MacEwen), 283-284
Whiteson, Leon, 332, 365, 395
  memories of Gwen, 334
Wilentz, Eli, 98
Wilson, Carol. *See* McEwen, Carol (sister of Gwen)
Wilson, Edmund, 191
Wilson, Milton, 123
Winnipeg, 36-46
  Gwen revisits, 395
Winnipeg Children's Aid Society, 46
Winola Court Apartments, 81
"Wombs" (MacEwen), 171
Women
  misogyny of 1960s, 109-114
  position of women writers in 1960s, 170
  The Trojan Women, 306-308
Women's liberation, 110
Wonder Woman (comic book), 40-42
World of Neshiah, The (radio drama by MacEwen), 260, 320
Writer's Quarterly, 307
Writing community in Toronto of early 1960s, 109

Y

"Yellow House, The" (MacEwen), 380
Yoga, 336-357
Yorkville, 184

Z

Zellermeyer, Ruben, 328-331, 369, 372, 374, 402, 403, 409
   memories of Gwen, 329, 330-331, 355, 356, 386-387, 388, 393, 395, 404, 406-407
Zembekiko (Greek dance), 253, 255, 272
Zohar, The, 72, 73, 217
Zorba's (tavern), 242, 245, 254